Languages *in* BRITAIN & IRELAND

Languages *in* BRITAIN & IRELAND

Edited by
GLANVILLE PRICE

Emeritus Professor of French
University of Wales Aberystwyth

BLACKWELL
Publishers

Copyright © Blackwell Publishers Ltd 2000. Editorial selection and introductions copyright © Glanville Price 2000.

First published 2000

2 4 6 8 10 9 7 5 3 1

Blackwell Publishers Ltd
108 Cowley Road
Oxford OX4 1JF
UK

Blackwell Publishers Inc.
350 Main Street
Malden, Massachusetts 02148
USA

British Library Cataloguing in Publication Data

A CIP catalogue record for this book is available from the British Library.

Library of Congress Cataloging-in-Publication Data is available for this book.

ISBN   0-631-21580-8
           0-631-21581-6 (pbk)

Typeset in 10½ on 12 pt Ehrhardt
by Best-set Typesetter Ltd., Hong Kong
Printed in Great Britain by TJ International, Padstow, Cornwall

This book is printed on acid-free paper

Contents

The Contributors

Michael P. Barnes, Professor of Scandinavian Philology, University College London.

Janet Davies, writer on the Welsh language.

Viv Edwards, Professor of Language in Education and Director of the Reading and Language Information Centre, University of Reading.

Kenneth MacKinnon, Visiting Professor and Emeritus Reader in the Sociology of Language at the University of Hertfordshire and Honorary Research Fellow in Celtic at the University of Edinburgh.

Cathair Ó Dochartaigh, Professor of Celtic, University of Glasgow.

Philip Payton, Reader in Cornish Studies and Director of the Institute of Cornish Studies, University of Exeter.

Glanville Price, Emeritus Professor of French, University of Wales Aberystwyth.

Jeremy J. Smith, Reader in English Language, University of Glasgow.

Robert L. Thomson, formerly Reader in Celtic, University of Leeds.

Lauran Toorians, independent scholar, former chairman of the A. G. van Hamel Society for Celtic Studies (Netherlands).

D. A. Trotter, Professor of French, University of Wales Aberystwyth.

Maps and Figures

Preface

This volume derives in part from my book *The Languages of Britain* (London, Edward Arnold, 1984), to the extent that some chapters are revisions of the corresponding chapters in that book. It differs from it substantially, however, in particular in the fact that over half of the chapters in the present volume are written by other scholars. The coverage is also wider, in that, this time, the principal chapter on Irish covers the whole of Ireland and not just Northern Ireland as in the 1984 book, and in the fact that a substantial chapter on Community Languages is now added.

Editor's Acknowledgements

Many more people than I could hope to name individually have helped with the writing of the chapters that I have myself contributed to this book, by answering queries, supplying information, or discussing points arising in connection with one chapter or another. To all of them I am grateful. Particular mention, however, must be made of Dr Katherine Forsyth, Dr Mari Jones, Professor Jonathan Powell, and my wife, Mrs Christine Price. They have saved me from many errors and omissions, but are in no way responsible for those that remain – particularly since on occasion I have not acted on suggestions they have made. My indebtedness to those colleagues who so readily agreed, and at rather less than a year's notice, to provide chapters for the volume is, of course, immeasurable. I am also most appreciative of the help provided by the staffs of the National Library of Wales and the Hugh Owen Library at the University of Wales Aberystwyth.

The editor and the relevant contributors also wish to express their thanks to the following for granting permission to reproduce or adapt maps: Dr W. T. R. Pryce (map 5), Professors John Aitchison and Harold Carter (map 6), the University of Wales Press (maps 5 and 6), Blackwell Publishers (map 7), Scottish National Dictionary Association and Mrs Millicent Gregg (map 8); and to Anne Haavaldsen for figure 2.

Note on References

The list of books, articles, etc., at the end of each chapter contains items referred to in the chapter. References in the body of the text follow the 'author–date' system: for example, 'Ekwall 1960' in the chapter on 'British' refers to E. Ekwall's 1960 book, *The Concise Oxford Dictionary of English Place-names*, listed at the end of that chapter, and 'Chadwick 1963, 146' in the same chapter to p. 146 of N. K. Chadwick's 1963 article.

Introduction

The subject of this book is the languages that are now spoken, or were spoken at some time in the past, in Britain, Ireland, the Isle of Man, or the Channel Islands.[1]

In general, the languages we are concerned with are each associated with a more or less clearly definable geographical area. The exceptions to this are, on the one hand, Latin and Anglo-Norman, each of which was probably an urban rather than a rural language, perhaps even the language of the ruling, educated and mercantile sections of the population, and, on the other hand, Romani, the traditional language of the nomadic Gypsies, and what are now widely known as 'community languages'.

What is known of the languages under discussion varies enormously. On the one hand, we have English, Welsh, Irish and Scottish Gaelic, which are still spoken and have lengthy literary traditions behind them. At the other extreme, there are languages like Cumbric and Pictish, known only from a few fragments and proper names. Between, we find a wide range of possibilities. The French dialects of the Channel Islands, though they have little by way of literature and have not been as thoroughly studied as they deserve, have (apart from Alderney French) not yet disappeared. Manx has little literature but survived until the age of the tape-recorder and so is relatively well known. Anglo-Norman is known from a substantial body of written texts and documents. The grammar of Cornish is well enough documented, in spite of a few gaps, but much of the vocabulary is irretrievably lost. British represents an earlier stage of Welsh and Cornish for which we have no direct evidence. Scots has its own literary tradition but is sometimes considered to be a dialect of English. Though evidence for Latin, Norse and Romani originating specifically from Britain is somewhat scanty, and in the case of Flemish virtually non-existent, the languages themselves are well known from other sources. And then we have the multiplicity of community languages which are those of relatively recently arrived populations who have brought with them languages that are still primarily associated with their original homelands.[2]

The book is arranged as follows:

I   *The prehistoric period.* Although nothing is known of the languages of the earliest inhabitants of these islands, there can be no doubt that they had the faculty of speech and so it seems justifiable to say something about them.

II *The Celtic languages.* These fall into two groups, the Goidelic or Gaelic languages (Irish, Scottish Gaelic, Manx) and the Brittonic or Brythonic languages (British, and its descendants Welsh, Cornish and Cumbric), together with the somewhat problematic Pictish.

III   *Latin.*
IV   *The Germanic languages*, i.e. English, Scots, Norse (and its descendant, Norn) and
      Flemish.
V   *French*, including both the French dialects of the Channel Islands and Anglo-
      Norman.
VI   *Romani.*
VII   *Community languages.*

Given the vast difference in what is known about the various languages discussed, there is no attempt to adopt a uniform approach. The plan of each chapter is dictated by what is known about the language in question and by what strikes the author as particularly important or interesting. The one thing that is common to all chapters is that they deal with the languages as social phenomena, that is, with such topics as the circumstances (where they are known) of their arrival in these islands, with their role as standard or literary languages (but not, except incidentally, with literary history), their interaction with other languages, with (in most cases) their decline, and, except for English, their disappearance or their present-day struggle for survival. We are not therefore concerned with the phonetic or grammatical structure of the languages.

Notes

1   The Isle of Man and the Channel Islands are possessions of the British Crown but are not
    part of the United Kingdom. Man, Jersey, and the Bailiwick of Guernsey (which includes,
    in addition to Guernsey itself, the islands of Alderney, Sark, Herm and Jethou) are each
    largely self-governing, though the Westminster Parliament (in which they are not repre-
    sented) may legislate for them but rarely does. The United Kingdom is also responsible for
    them in matters of defence and foreign relations.
2   Inevitably, a selection has to be made among these. As an indication of the impossibility of
    covering all of them, we may note that a survey of the home languages of pupils in its schools
    undertaken in the late 1980s by the Inner London Education Authority arrived at a total of
    172 different languages.

1 Prehistoric Britain

Glanville Price

Britain and Ireland have existed as such, i.e. as islands, for perhaps no more than 8,000 years. Before that, they formed part of the north-west European land mass. But traces of habitation by humans go back much further, and the first Stone Age humans may have visited these parts a quarter of a million years ago.

During the Palaeolithic (Old Stone Age) and Mesolithic (Middle Stone Age) periods, the population of the area that was to become the British Isles may well have been numbered in hundreds rather than in thousands. And, of course, nothing is known of their language or languages. Human society at this time was characterized by a subsistence economy based on hunting and fishing but, some five or six thousand years ago, communities characterized by a farming economy arrived from the Continent. We have now reached the Neolithic period or New Stone Age which, in these islands, probably lasted from about 3500 BC or a little earlier to a little after 2000 BC.

We know no more about the languages of the Neolithic people than about those of their predecessors. Two eminent Celtic scholars, John Morris-Jones and Julius Pokorny, argued vigorously (Jones 1900; Pokorny 1926–30) that Welsh and Irish respectively have many syntactical features that are not generally characteristic of the Indo-European languages[1] but which do have striking parallels in the Hamitic languages of North Africa, and in particular in ancient Egyptian and its descendant, Coptic, and in Berber.[2] They point out that anthropological evidence is consistent with the view that some pre-Celtic stratum in the population could have migrated to Britain from North Africa via Spain and France and are therefore led to the view that the features in question are derived from a pre-Celtic and probably Hamitic substratum. What this implies is that, when the incoming Celts interbred with the pre-Celtic population, a mixed language resulted which was basically Celtic but which contained syntactical features carried over into it from the other languages. This is at best an intriguing hypothesis that is likely to remain an unproven one.

The first Bronze Age people probably arrived from the Continent around the middle of the third millennium BC. In some parts of the world, evidence for the languages of Bronze Age populations survives, such as, for example, the language of the inscribed tablets (dating from *c.*1500–1100 BC) in the so-called 'Linear B' script of the Bronze Age civilization of Minos and Mycenae, which has been shown to be an early form of Greek. But nothing is known of the Bronze Age languages of these islands (or, indeed, of western Europe generally).[3]

If any pre-Celtic elements remain anywhere in the place-names of Britain, the most likely place to find them would be in names of rivers and streams which, generally speaking, seem more likely than hills or human settlements to retain their original names when an area is occupied by a community speaking a different language. But such elements are not easily identified. Ekwall (1928, lv), while not excluding the possibility that some unexplained English river-names *may* be pre-Celtic, regards this as a 'rather remote contingency' and comments that he cannot point to any definite name that strikes him as 'probably pre-Celtic'. On the other hand, William Nicolaisen argues persuasively (1976, 173–91) that various Scottish river-names (including *(Black)adder*, *Ale*, *Ayr*, *Farrar*, *Naver*, *Shiel*) are Indo-European but not Celtic, and so are presumably pre-Celtic. If so, then 'when the Celts first arrived in Scotland, there were already people present who, as immigrants from Europe centuries before them, had introduced an Indo-European language to the British Isles' (ibid., 191).

Who the earliest inhabitants of these islands were and what their languages were is, then, very much of a mystery. The earliest arrivals to have any kind of recognizable identity were Celtic-speakers. The Celtic languages can be divided into two main groups, known respectively as Goidelic (or Gaelic or Q-Celtic) and Brittonic (or Brythonic or P-Celtic). The terms Q-Celtic and P-Celtic are based on an important difference in the phonetic development of the two groups. Indo-European had a consonant that can be represented as [k^w]. In Goidelic (which survives as Irish, Scottish Gaelic and Manx) this at first remained, represented in the ogam script (see figure 1, p. 12) as *q*, but was later simplified to [k] (written as *c*), but in Brittonic (i.e., principally, Welsh, Cornish and Breton – but see also the chapters on British, Cumbric and Pictish below), it became [p].[4] The point is illustrated by such pairs as Irish *ceathair*, Welsh *pedwar* 'four', Irish *ceann*, Welsh *pen* 'head'.

It is far from clear when the first Celtic-speakers arrived, how many waves of them there were, or what were the ethnic and linguistic relationships between the various waves. Nor is there agreement among scholars as to whether the earliest Celts to reach Ireland passed through Britain or whether (as the most widely held view has it) they made their way there directly from the Continent. And did the distinction between Q-Celtic and P-Celtic arise before the Celts left the mainland of Europe, or after they had settled in these islands? 'The fact', says Patrick Sims-Williams (1998, 21), 'is that we simply do not know whether Celtic was brought over as late as the second half of the first millennium BC, as some distinguished Irish scholars have supposed, or whether it had gradually evolved *in situ* from late western Indo-European over many millennia, from 4500 BC, as argued by Colin Renfrew.'[5]

I shall not attempt to enter further into these questions where even specialists find it impossible to arrive at a consensus. What is certain is that, whatever may have been the factors that brought this about, before the beginning of the Christian era Ireland was mainly Goidelic-speaking and Britain predominantly Brittonic-speaking, but that there was much traffic in both directions.

Notes

1   The Indo-European languages include nearly all the languages now spoken in Europe, and a number of extinct and extant Asian languages, including Sanskrit, Persian, Hindi, and various other languages of the Indian sub-continent.

2 Some of the features quoted by Jones are quite striking – e.g. the fact that the verb takes a 3rd person singular form when the subject is a plural noun (e.g. Welsh *daeth* 'he came', *daethant* 'they came', *daeth y dynion* 'the men came'), but many are trivial, or easily paralleled elsewhere, or far-fetched.

3 Some scholars maintain that those who brought the Bronze Age to these islands were Celts. But, even if they were, no epigraphic evidence for their language or languages remains.

4 The explanation for this is that [kʷ] has two 'points of articulation': the tongue is raised until it touches the velum or soft palate (as for the *k*-sound in *calm*) but at the same time the lips are drawn together until they almost, but not quite, touch. In languages where this sound occurs, it frequently changes to a [p], i.e., instead of the flow of air being stopped at the velum, it is stopped at the other point of articulation, the lips – one can compare, for example, Greek *hippos* 'horse', where this has occurred, with Latin *equus*, where it has not.

5 *Archaeology and Language. The Puzzle of Indo-European Origins*, London, 1987, p. 242.

References

Ekwall, E. 1928. *English River-names*. Oxford.

Morris-Jones, J. 1900. Pre-Aryan syntax in insular Celtic. In Rhŷs, John and Brynmor-Jones, David (eds), *The Welsh People* (4th edn, London, 1906), 617–41.

Nicolaisen, W. F. H. 1976. *Scottish Place-names. Their Study and Significance*. London.

Pokorny, J. 1926–30. Das nicht indo-germanische Substrat im Irischen. *Zeitschrift für celtische Philologie*, 16 (1926–7):95–144, 231–66, 363–94; 17 (1927–8):373–88; 18 (1929–30):233–48.

Sims-Williams, P. 1998. Celtomania and Celtoscepticism. *Cambrian Medieval Celtic Studies*, 36:1–35.

2 Irish in Ireland

Cathair Ó Dochartaigh

The history of the Irish language involves a series of complex interactions over time between internal and external factors, with their results reflected in the grammar, including syntax, morphology and phonology, as well as in the lexicon. This chapter[1] surveys the external history of the language and summarizes those influences which have left their mark on its internal history, by drawing on the results of recent scholarship.[2] External influences of this sort are examples of cultures in contact where aspects of a non-indigenous culture are grafted on to another without overwriting all elements of the original. The resulting admixture, with adaptation of the influenced to accommodate aspects of the influencing, is a widely recognized fact of social life, and one not restricted to the domain of language. All societies are modified through interaction with others whether in the domains of religion, art, literature, or any of the myriad other spheres of human social activities. Given the range and dissemination of the internal linguistic effects of such influences over a time span of 1,500 years, it is difficult to deal in a strictly date-oriented manner with their results on the language, and references to dates should be taken as indicative rather than definitive, as transitions between linguistic periods usually span several centuries. Although all the factors discussed have left their mark on the language and are interrelated, the chapter deals separately with several central socio-linguistic topics in order to examine the results of the various influences, though the interpenetration of factors will be apparent from many remarks in the different sections.

Irish can be divided into a number of historical periods which are relatively well defined linguistically. The earliest is that of pre-Old Irish (or Proto-Irish), from around the fourth to the seventh centuries AD, as Irish emerges as a Q-Celtic (see p. 4) or Goidelic variety of Insular Celtic, the latter a descendant of Western Common Celtic on a par with Gaulish. Following the appearance of literacy, the sources become increasingly numerous, and the period from the late sixth to around the twelfth century is taken as Old and Middle Irish. Breatnach (1994, 221) reckons Old Irish as coming to an end around AD 900, with Middle Irish disappearing AD 1200–1250. The period from AD *c*.1200 to 1650 represents Early Modern Irish, followed by Modern Irish from around the mid-seventeenth century to the present; the term Late Modern Irish is sometimes used for the language of the late nineteenth and twentieth centuries.

Although these datings are based on internal criteria, they are also useful for considering the influence on Irish of a number of external socio-political factors. The first of these, with the transition from Proto-Irish to Old Irish, is the introduction of Christianity to Ireland in the fifth and sixth centuries, and the start of Middle Irish corresponds with the appearance of Norse settlements in the country in the tenth century. The emergence of Early Modern Irish can be correlated in general terms with the appearance of new forms of monasticism around AD 1200 and also with the first Anglo-Norman settlements in the country in the period following AD 1169. The last of the Ulster earls left in AD 1607, and their going prefaced the collapse of the socio-cultural matrix which supported the native society. The seventeenth century marks the emergence of Modern Irish as the individual dialects emerged into prominence following the collapse of the previous relatively standardized Classical Modern language. In the nineteenth and twentieth centuries the opposing political movements with a focus on Irish nationalism, which led to the establishment of the Irish Free State (later Republic of Ireland) and Northern Ireland in 1921, have been major influences on Irish, affecting the language both externally and internally.

The earliest counts of the population of Ireland were those of the late seventeenth century based on the state needs for taxation and availability of manpower for military service. Such counts are regarded as inaccurate until the early nineteenth century due to popular distrust of the government, and it was not until 1821 that, as Connell describes, 'relations between the Government and people were easier [. . .] and the Catholic clergy [. . .] encouraged members of their Church to give accurate information' (1950, 2). These early decennial census counts took no account of the numbers of Irish-speakers in the population, and estimates for this group first appear in reckonings by missionaries interested in furthering the spread of Protestantism. Associated with this, there was a developing interest in establishing an educational system for the country, and similar estimates were made for what had become a subset of the population. From these early surveys we have estimates for numbers of Irish-speakers of 2,400,000 in 1799 and 2,000,000 in 1812 and an estimate for educational purposes of 1,500,000 in 1835. These estimates distinguish between monoglot Irish-speakers and bilinguals, usually on the assumption that monoglots represent around one third of the total number of speakers. The figures lie between 19 and 33 per cent of the population of the country and demonstrate that by the first quarter of the nineteenth century Irish had become a minority language in a bilingual state with a majority of English-speakers, and that the majority of Irish-speakers had become bilingual.

It is difficult to investigate the period before the availability of enumerated figures due to difficulties of interpretation, but a useful study uses the figures for decennial age-groups in the nineteenth-century census reports down to the year 1881, and extrapolates these back to provide estimates for children born within several decade periods from 1771 onwards. Using these, Fitzgerald (1984, 123–6) conservatively estimates the minimum percentage of the first decennial age cohort (i.e. children aged up to ten years) which was Irish-speaking in the decade 1771–81 at 45 per cent of the total population. As Connell (1950, 25) has estimated the overall population in 1772 as 3,584,000, on the basis of Fitzgerald's figures for the youngest age-group, it is possible to suggest that well over 50 per cent of the population, or a figure of around 2,000,000, constituted an Irish-speaking majority at the beginning of the last quarter of the eighteenth century. Fitzgerald notes that the only areas where Irish formed a minority grouping were 'north-east Ulster [. . .], parts of south-east Leinster and the south midlands [i.e. roughly south Leinster]' (1984, 124). As Ó Murchú points out, over the next two generations until around the middle of the nineteenth century the 'population would con-

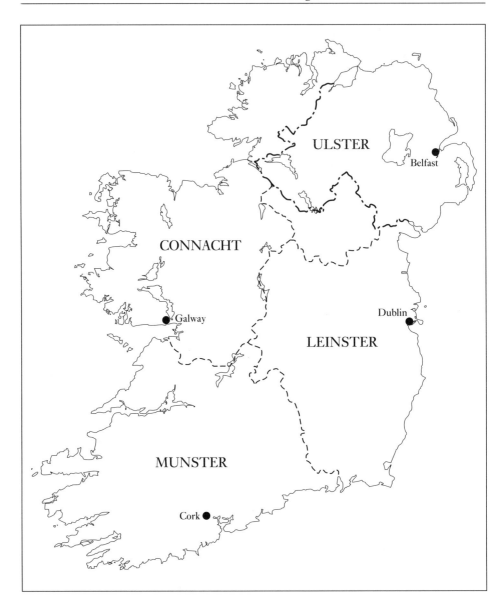

Map 1 *Ireland.*

tinue to grow rapidly for the first forty-five years' (1998, 341), leading to a figure of 8,175,124 in 1841, which declined in the aftermath of the Famine to 6,552,386 in 1851. This census showed Irish-speakers representing 23.3 per cent of the total, and the greatest change from the late eighteenth century was in that sector which had turned to English, presumably through Irish bilinguals changing to this as their language of preferred usage both in public and then within the family, thus creating English monoglots in the following generation following the normal socio-linguistic patterns for language replacement. The percentage of monoglot Irish-speakers as a proportion of total Irish-speakers in 1851 was 21 per cent, a figure which falls to 3 per cent by the 1901 census when it is assumed that most of the declared monoglot Irish speakers were young children.

A question on the use of Irish was included for the first time in the census of 1851, producing a figure of 1,524,286 speakers out of a total population of 6,552,386, and this question, with some variations of wording, was repeated in all following enumerations for Ireland until 1911. Fitzgerald discusses some of the problems associated with the use of language census figures, which were based on a standard printed form which for each census until 1871 included the question as a footnote that might easily have been overlooked, but which was replaced for the 1881 census by a separate column entry headed 'Irish language'. He notes that the general report for the 1881 census does recognize the possibility that 'the increase in the number returned as being able to speak Irish and English may [. . .] be attributed to [the] more precise method of seeking the information' (1984, 140).

The decline in the numbers of Irish-speakers in Ireland has been examined on the basis of both quantitative census figures and on qualitative reports collected for local statistical accounts in the early nineteenth century. Some of these analyses are broad spectrum works examining the whole of the country, such as those by Ravenstein (1879) in the nineteenth century and Ó Cuív (1951) in the twentieth, and can be supplemented by more recent descriptions for smaller districts such as that of Nic Craith (1993) who describes the decline of Irish in County Cork in the nineteenth century. For the twentieth century Ní Mhóráin (1997, 155–203) deals with the Iveragh peninsula in County Kerry, finishing with a discussion of 'seventy years of decay 1922–1996' as she examines the effects of language shift on the native Irish-speaking population of this district.

The reasons for this massive decline in numbers and percentages of Irish-speakers can be sought in the history of Ireland from the early sixteenth century onwards, when by around 1600 the chieftain rulers of Irish society had been removed by English state policy, military pressure and political interventions. Perhaps as a result of the loss of this stratum of society, the middle classes turned towards an acceptance of the British Stuart kings in 1603 and, as Ó Buachalla points out (1996, 2), their belief in these 'did not weaken or lessen' until the end of the century. This century accomplished the military defeat of this class, culminating in the Treaty of Limerick of 1692 at the end of the Williamite wars, with the subsequent departure of over 20,000 Irish soldiers to the Continent, where they and their successors continued their military opposition to England through to the war of the Austrian succession and beyond.[3] The eighteenth century brought an attack on the remainder of the native middle classes with the implementation of Penal Laws which were primarily articulated as anti-Catholic measures aimed at the ownership of wealth and property, but also maintained a downward pressure on the social status of Irish-speakers. During this century the idea of a relationship between language and the notion of statehood became a matter of increased understanding in Ireland. However, in a political environment where Irish statehood was no longer a viable option, it is apparent that the choice of the majority was to assert its shared sense of identity, not through the Irish language but through other markers of identity, particularly the religious culture of Roman Catholicism, as well as by using the linguistically neutral domains of political nationality[4] or of Irish music, for example.

The nineteenth century marks both a culmination of the officially inspired linguistic dismemberment of the Irish-speaking population, and is also notable for the beginning of a political reaction to the disappearance of the language. This reaction had its origins outside the population of native speakers, and did not become fully active until after the agriculturally impoverished Irish-speaking districts were affected disproportionally by the famine years of 1846–50 with their deaths and resulting voluntary emigration. This individual or family solution to the physical disaster can perhaps be paralleled by a notion of internal cultural emigration from Irish-speaking communities, through the mechanism of switching to English and allowing Irish to be replaced in its remaining heartlands. Ó Murchú summarizes this mid-century period in his comments that 'the socio-economic and political circumstances of the nineteenth century had finally deprived Irish speakers of the last vestiges of their autonomy as a speech community. They became an insecure linguistic minority within the English-speaking world and were subject to the same pressures to undergo a language shift as were the immigrant ethnic groups in the United States, and they did so over a comparable period of time' (1998, 348).

Over the second half of the century, figures show a decline in numbers of Irish-speakers, both numerically and in percentage terms, from 1,105,536 (19.1 per cent) in 1861 to 680,245 (14.5 per cent) in 1891. In addition, the overall population of Ireland declined from 5,798,967 to 4,704,740 over the same period, a loss accounted for by emigration to the English-speaking world. It was the popular perception of the need for an escape route from rural poverty which drove the social attitude of the Irish-speaking cohort towards ensuring that their children acquired English as quickly as possible, without a consideration of societal bilingualism as a viable socio-linguistic option. After the political division of Ireland into the Irish Free State and Northern Ireland in 1921, figures for Irish-speakers continued to be collected in the decennial census in the Republic only, and were included for the first time in the 1991 census of Northern Ireland. Figures from 1901 onwards have been influenced by the increasing political profile of the language, and in 1991 the counts were 1,095,830 (32.5 per cent) for the Republic, and 79,012 (5.3 per cent) in Northern Ireland.

All of these census figures are based on the mass collection of relatively simple propositions such as 'can speak Irish', and responses to such questions are subject to a range of socio-political interpretations and considerations by the interviewed population. For example, Hindley draws attention to the fact that 'the proportion of the population returned as Irish speakers was by 1981 almost a third of the total and despite massive emigration losses was in absolute numbers close to the totals recorded for 1861. [. . .] Unfortunately [. . .] the statistics represent very largely the replacement of dwindling numbers of native speakers by primary English speakers who in the large majority lack fluency in Irish and hardly ever have occasion to speak it' (1990, 21). In this comment he draws attention to the replacement of primary language acquisition of Irish with a new focus on second language learning, a concept which is quickly disseminating through the native Irish-speaking population. Ó Riagáin summarizes the current situation as one where 'the age-specific data in the census show that the national increase in the proportions of Irish-speakers was primarily caused by a continual improvement – since the 1920s – in the proportion of young adult cohorts able to speak Irish.

Although over time the proportion [. . .] in older adult cohorts also [. . .] continued to improve, the improvement is much smaller than the ratio of Irish-speakers in school-age cohorts would suggest' (1997, 166).

Ó Riagáin notes that native Irish-speakers 'had receded by the early twentieth century to a widely fragmented group of districts which were situated mostly in the western periphery' (1997, 17) and for these districts the term 'Gaeltacht' is used. Its current definition has gradually emerged from its use by Irish revivalists in the twentieth century for a native population which was identified as a focus for their wish to revive Irish. For official purposes it was defined by the Irish government as those areas with a majority[5] of Irish-speakers recorded in a census, a definition which ignores the fundamental socio-linguistic distinction between language ability (particularly self-reported as in a census enumeration) and language use. From a social geographer's perspective, Hindley would reserve the term Gaeltacht for those areas where Irish is 'the main language, i.e. the one habitually and normally used [. . .] and their language of "first resort"' (1990, 47), a term which he would reserve for those parts of the Gaeltacht where more than 90 per cent of the population is returned in a census as Irish-speaking.

Hindley reports that an 'attempt at revival by transplantation began when between 1935 and 1940 three "Gaeltacht colonies" were established [consisting of] 772 persons from [. . .] the fíor-Ghaeltacht'[6] (ibid., 131); these were located on around 3,000 acres in part of County Meath in Leinster, about fifty kilometres north of Dublin. However, the smallest group was soon absorbed socially by its anglophone neighbours and the second largest failed because 'it was badly planned linguistically, for it drew colonists from six different Gaeltacht districts with mutually "difficult" dialects for which English formed an easier lingua franca' (ibid., 131). The remaining families, which formed a linguistically coherent group, maintained their original language over one generation though with decreasing usage, and this Meath experiment has effectively failed in its avowed attempt to re-introduce Irish into the area, although its establishment did attract considerable support from language revivalists. Similar support has also focused on what Maguire calls 'an Urban Gaeltacht [. . .], Belfast's own Gaeltacht' (1991, 67), referring to a community of perhaps several hundred speakers[7] who have chosen to use Irish as much as possible in their daily lives, and whose children attend an Irish-medium primary and secondary school in West Belfast.

The economic basis of the Gaeltacht was recognized as exceptionally weak, and increasing state attention was paid to this aspect of life there, with the quango Údarás na Gaeltachta now given the primary task of social and economic regeneration of the area. As to the everyday use of Irish in these districts, there has been an increasing disparity between the official census figures and the reality of the socio-linguistic situation of the area. Hindley suggests (1990, 184–5) that there is 'now probably a Gaeltacht maximum of 20,000' native Irish-speakers, and Gearóid Ó Tuathaigh, the chairman of Údarás, is reported as saying that 'the linguistic basis for the Gaeltacht is fast eroding [. . .], parents [. . .] rely on schools to give Irish to their children', noting that neither the state nor language enthusiasts can 'stop this erosion [nor] put in place a strategy to renew the language' (*Irish Times*, 8 February 1998). Ó Riagáin sums up the situation by describing how state policy has moved towards 'the maintenance pole of the overall strategy [with] a consequent weakening of emphasis on the revival dimension' (1997, 25).

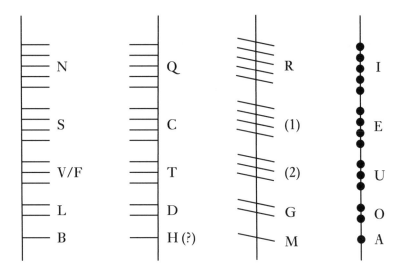

Figure 1 *The original ogam alphabet. Most reference works transcribe (1) as ⟨Z⟩ and (2) as ⟨Ng⟩ respectively, but Sims-Williams (1993) argues cogently that (1) represented [sw] or possibly a reflex, of uncertain phonetic value, of Indo-European [st], and that (2) represented [g^w].*

State support for the Gaeltacht as expressed through the allocation of additional resources towards it has also presented a focus for social envy on the part of those excluded from such support, either English monoglots living within the area or those living in contiguous districts whose socio-economic problems are shared with those of the Gaeltacht districts. One policy, of awarding a small annual financial grant to those families in the Gaeltacht which were defined as native Irish-speaking, has been particularly contentious for its effects. This was implemented by using reports from inspectors of education based on interviews with children in the first year of primary school. As inspectors are all assigned from the Department of Education in Dublin, this implementation of the policy suggested a perception of a disjunction between the notion of community language and that provided as part of the educational environment, a view which is increasingly being taken by the local inhabitants as reflected in Ó Tuathaigh's comments above. The immediate monetary value of this grant was very small, but it was also used to determine the right of families to receive state grants for house improvement and rebuilding, and was thus perceived locally as an important metric. The associated increase in social envy of the Gaeltacht on the part of anglophone neighbours suggests a reason for state strategy moving towards supporting communities on purely economic grounds, with less emphasis on the language used. It is also interesting to note that West Belfast English-speakers who are familiar with the Irish-language community there tend to have somewhat disparaging views of it, with comments expressed similar to those passed by rural anglophones living on the fringes of traditional Gaeltacht areas.

The earliest method of symbolizing the language is that of the ogam[8] alphabet (see figure 1) found on lapidary inscriptions, and consisting of a series of straight strokes placed at varying angles to a vertical stem line, with each stroke representing an alphabetic letter. This form of writing appears to be a scholarly adaptation of the orthography of the Latin alphabet designed for use on stones and perhaps also on wooden staves. However, instances of only short stone inscriptions have survived and we do not find examples of phrases or clauses with their verbal elements similar to those available from runic sources. The language which they represent is that of Proto-Irish and is similar to Latin of around the first centuries of our era, with a comprehensive system of nominal morphophonology. The main body of inscriptions has been dated from the fourth to the seventh centuries, and their chief value is for the linguistic information which they provide at a time when pre-Old Irish was undergoing a wide range of phonological changes; there was a more or less contemporary set of changes as the P-Celtic dialects (see p. 4) of Britain gave rise to Proto-Welsh. In rough parallel to the modifications from late Latin to the Romance languages, the main phonological changes for both Goidelic and Brythonic involved phonological modifications such as the loss of final syllables, and Goidelic differs from Brythonic in that in the former there was no loss of nominal case morphology, and a process of infection of consonants by their vocalic environment produced a major feature of Irish phonology.

The period of Irish epigraphy extends down to the twelfth century, with the post-ogam inscriptions appearing in alphabetic characters, where Byrne notes that 'the forms of the letters do not derive from classical Latin epigraphy, but are those of the early Irish majuscule or half-uncial book hand. [. . .] Palaeographers have detected elements of Italian, Spanish and North African scripts in the Irish or insular script which had fully evolved by the seventh century' (1984, xii). A similar script was used for the manuscript literature, including the display scripts of the great Irish gospel books of the seventh to the twelfth centuries with their Latin scriptures. In addition to the vellum-based materials where a goose-quill was the writing instrument with ink made from oak-galls, Byrne states that wax tablets inscribed with a metal stylus were in use for 'notes, memoranda, and the drafts of texts' (ibid., xiii).

The introduction of Christianity over the fifth and sixth centuries brought with it the regular use of writing to Irish society. These new elements arrived in tandem, as we know from an examination of the range of lexical borrowings into the language which include many words associated with the new religion and the practice of writing and literacy. These words were taken into Irish from Latin in the context of an oral contact, rather than a written one, and the pronunciation of Latin was originally that of monks whose mother tongue was early Welsh, itself undergoing a series of phonological modifications over this period. The phonological results of these borrowings have been used to provide relative dating evidence for the spread of the underpinning phonetic developments in both P-Celtic and Q-Celtic (see p. 4) over these two centuries. The phonetic realizations of the phonological shifts differ between the two groups of languages and led to the emergence of linguistically separate Goidelic and Brythonic branches of Insular Celtic in Ireland and Britain. McManus summarizes one aspect of the process by noting that 'the Latin loan-words in British and Primitive Irish were inflected in accordance with Celtic rather than Latin morphology' (1984, 152), suggesting that the absorption of Latin loan-words involved complete morphemic substitution rather than partial adaptations of the originals. Byrne notes that up until the twelfth century 'the Irish used the Old British pronunciation of Latin which they had learned from the fifth-century missionaries. [. . .] Thus they pronounced Latin as Old Irish' (1984, xv), demonstrating both the continuity of the native tradition, as well as its imperviousness to some Continental influences at this stage. It seems that the Irish accepted Latin only as a written language rather than one which could be understood as an archaic version of French, Spanish or Italian, as was the case in these countries with languages descended from Vulgar Latin.

One important linguistic feature of Goidelic consonantism which became phonologized at this period through the loss of syllables in various positions in the word is that of consonant quality deriving from the previous or new vocalic environment, and up to three degrees of quality are identifiable at this period, though not with all consonants. Another aspect of consonants is the feature of length which, following the historical development of phonological lenition of consonants in vocalic environments, emerges as a concept of consonantal 'strength', where this is variously realized phonetically, as simple length or in some other phonetic manifestation. These phonetic processes developed gradually (and interactively in the linguistic environment) over a period of several centuries, and a similar variation also marks the emergence of an orthographic representation of the phonological system, developments which McCone notes took place 'when, in all probability not long before the middle of the seventh century, [. . .] the Roman alphabet began to be used in monastic circles to write continuous Irish texts on vellum' (1996, 31). These orthographic adaptations from Latin are summarized by Byrne and include the use of the apex or acute accent to symbolize long vowels, the extension of the *punctum delens*[9] to indicate consonantal lenition, and the use of positional (within-word) variants between the letters *b, d, g* and *p, t, c*[10] (1984, xiv–xv). A major innovation is the extension of the use of vowel characters to indicate the secondary articulation of a preceding and/or following consonant or consonant group, in addition to carrying their normal phonetic values, in order to cater for the development of phonological consonant quality.

One of the important features of the transition from Middle to Early Modern Irish was the development of a standardized (or non-dialect-specific) form of Irish grammar and prosody, but Ahlqvist points out that this standardization did not extend to the orthography and that over the Early Modern period 'a new system comes into being but the two are mixed together in the manuscripts' (1994, 33), where he is here referring to the two systems, one primarily for poetic compositions, the other for the less formalized prose literature. He also draws attention to the continuity of the Irish literary tradition which means that we often find spellings copied from law texts of the Old Irish period into manuscripts of Early Modern provenance. This period also shows a gradual replacement of vellum by paper manuscripts, though the former were still in use in the fifteenth century.

As Ahlqvist has noted (1994, 41), the transition from Early Modern to Modern Irish was not reflected to any great extent in the orthography and the basics of the Classical system remained 'without many changes to it until the present century'. As far as the script was concerned, scribes were professionally trained and although they do display individual differences, these do not affect the basic shapes of the letters throughout this period. As O'Neill suggests, the last of the professional scribes disappeared in the seventeenth century and 'from the eighteenth century onwards a certain detached formality is evident in the Gaelic script of most non-professional scribes' (1984, 89). Such non-professional scribes carried on the manuscript tradition down to the mid-nineteenth century when they finally ceased working, and while there appear to be minor variations in their work which have some areal basis, suggesting a training in local

schools, the massive loss of Irish manuscript material from this period makes it difficult to trace the history of these developments.

Printed books overcame most of the problems associated with loss of individual
manuscripts, but, as Lynam points out, 'like most other inventions which had their
origin on the Continent, printing was introduced very late into [. . .] Ireland' and from
1571 to 1721 'practically every book in the Irish language [. . .] was for religious pro-
paganda' (1969, 1–2). The first example is a broadside religious poem printed in Dublin
in 1571, and between this year and 1652 there followed 'several books, some purely religious, some combining grammatical with religious instruction [. . .] from the Dublin
press' (ibid., 5). The fonts were based on the letter shapes of the manuscript tradition
and departed little from the orthographic norms used there, including the acute accent
for vowel length, and the use of the overdot to indicate consonantal lenition, as well as
the adoption of a number of manuscript suspensions or abbreviations. However, we also
find an early use of the letter *h* to indicate lenition, and the font complexities of cutting
various abbreviations were soon recognized and most were dropped from the sets.[11]
Printing, of course, changed the whole process of textual reproduction away from the
individuality of manuscript copying, although one final interface between the old and
the new is found in reproductions of three important early manuscripts which were
published by the Royal Irish Academy between 1870 and 1880. These were intended to
replicate the original manuscripts in an age before the full development of photogra-
phy, by using lithograph reproductions transcribed and engraved by the last member
of a well-known family of Munster scribes, Joseph O'Longan, with the engraving
emulating as closely as possible the script and layout of the originals, including the
occasional holes on imperfectly prepared vellum sheets.

The introduction of English-based typefaces, which retained the accented vowels of
Irish for both upper- and lower-case letters and replaced the lenition dot by *h*, could not
be long delayed in a country where the majority of native Irish-speakers were illiterate
in Irish. Lynam points out that the Roman Catholic presses of the early seventeenth
century 'began to print Irish books in Roman type. [. . .] From 1735 [. . .] the Roman type
has always been used for a certain number of Irish books' (1969, 3). The schooling system
of the nineteenth century exposed the mass of the population to material written in
English using the normal fonts for that language. One factor influencing the decision to
use Irish or Roman type in publications of the later part of the century was an interpretation by some cultural nationalists that the use of Irish or Roman typefaces represented
native and foreign influences respectively. In 1877 a new hybrid font was produced,
which, as Lynam says (ibid., 34), was 'intended to be a compromise between the Irish
and the Roman letter and to end the dispute between them'. Although this particular
experiment failed to gain general acceptance, variants of the Irish font continued to
appear in print sporadically until the late 1950s when it was finally superseded by the
Roman font, except for decorative use. More recently it has been given a new lease of life
with the introduction of computer technology, and Irish font characters, including over-
dotted consonants, have been assigned locations in the 16-bit standard character set
Unicode, with a number of laser printer fonts produced for it.

The first mention of the need to print Irish with a Roman font in official documentation of the Irish Free State appears in a memorandum from the Department of
Finance drawing attention to the additional costs imposed by the requirement to
have two typewriters in every office to service the need for bilingual materials. The

subsequent history of this question is copiously documented from state papers by Ó Riain who describes a process of planning which began with 'most writers strongly against the roman font' (1994, 64) in the years immediately after 1921, and which used the central powers of the Department of Education to implement a gradual change towards this font mainly through the schooling system, and extending over almost fifty years. There were many delays to the process as political views swung for and against it and state resource allocation varied from year to year, and it was not completed until the papers were set for the final secondary school examinations of 1972.

The associated matter of an orthography which had remained almost unchanged since the twelfth century finally emerged as a burning question for state language planning in Ireland after 1921. Again, as with the font changes, the implementing authority for the development of a new spelling system was a department of State, in this case the Translation Section of the Oireachtas, the Irish parliament, working closely with the Department of Education. The need to provide as far as possible for a perceived equality of treatment for the three main dialect areas of Munster, Connacht and Ulster meant that frequent committee meetings were required, with many arguments and minor points of spelling to be settled. A major figure in this work was Niall Ó Dónaill, a native speaker of Donegal Irish and a civil servant based in Dublin from the 1930s onwards. He worked as a collaborator with the editor Mc Cionnaith for the first state-supported English–Irish dictionary (published 1935), and de Bhaldraithe for the successor dictionary (published 1959), and finally as editor of an Irish–English dictionary, *Foclóir Gaeilge–Béarla*, which appeared in 1977.

It is clear that the major drive towards a change came from the personal intervention of Éamonn de Valera who became Taoiseach in 1932, and remained in power with a break of only three years until 1959, when he was elected President of Ireland and spent a total of fourteen years in this office. His intervention ranged from small meetings with one or two linguists when he authorized particular changes, to a continuing interest in the full process of implementation of the reforms extending through to the publication of the necessary language tools, two major bilingual dictionaries, English–Irish and Irish–English. In his introduction to the latter, Ó Dónaill acknowledges de Valera 'who began the work [. . .] and who urged it on zealously during his Presidency and afterwards' (1977, vi). Ó Riain describes a process beginning in the late 1920s and leading to a codification of new spelling reforms published in 1945 with a slightly amended version appearing two years later (1994, 68–75). The preparation of a new Irish–English dictionary lasted almost twenty years from the late 1950s and the work drew attention to previously unrecognized anomalies in the Official Standard; in these cases Ó Dónaill notes that further adjustments had to be made 'collaboratively between the Translation Section and the Dictionary Team' (1977, vii). The Department of Education has recently reprinted a number of books from the pre-standard period, having revised their orthography and now employing the Roman rather than the Irish font.

The history of Irish begins in a period when the society had not yet adopted literacy and from which sources are correspondingly scarce. The lithograph inscriptions in ogam and their alphabetic counterparts[12] are formulaic materials, usually consisting of Proper Name + 'son of' + Patronymic with the three nouns appearing in the genitive case, and their main use is as evidence for historical changes occurring over the Proto-

Irish period. During the fifth and sixth centuries with the introduction of Christianity it is clear that literacy emerges among the native scholars, in parallel to its use in a Christian context. However, as Ó Cathasaigh observes, 'unfortunately, we do not have firm historical evidence for the earlier, formative period' (1996, 59) of this developing literacy. From the several centuries following its appearance the surviving contemporary manuscripts contain only Latin texts with occasional Irish glosses or comments, and Byrne points out that 'the Book of Armagh is the oldest manuscript to contain examples of connected Irish prose narrative' (1984, xv). This book dates from AD 807 and contains mainly Latin religious or hagiographical texts, one at least having been copied from 'a volume which Patrick wrote with his own hand'. The Irish content of the Book of Armagh consists of several poems attributed to the saint as well as Irish prose notes on him, showing, as Hyde says, 'what the Irish language was, as written about the year 800' (1967, 152). Carey points out that the sources from this early period, with their evidence for a mingling of native and external influences, demonstrate 'the scope of its learning, [. . .] its positive evaluation [. . .] of the vernacular language. [. . .] The literary use of the native language reflects the [. . .] cultural self-confidence which [. . .] is so salient a trait in Irish tradition' (1998, 13). It is obvious that lay literati in this society were fully conversant with the materials being written down in the monastic scriptoria, and that they shared an interest in these.

Following this, there is a gap in the surviving manuscript record until the twelfth century, when we find the first books containing solely Irish literary materials, the first three dating from *c*.1106 (*Lebor na hUidre*, 'Book of the Dun Cow'), from *c*.1130 (Book of Glendalough) and from *c*.1150 (*Lebar na Núachongbála*, also known as the Book of Leinster). All three were written in monastic environments with their texts copied from earlier manuscripts, and Byrne describes them as 'compendious miscellanies, [. . .] in effect each a complete library bound as a single volume' (1984, xvi), containing prose tales, poems, histories, kingship lists, hagiographical texts, and similar material from the native tradition. A continuing scholarly debate exists over the saga tales of this period, in deciding whether they represent a writing down by the scribes of stories which had been preserved for centuries in an oral tradition (the 'nativist' view), perhaps even reflecting myths going back to Indo-European, or whether they are conscious literary reworkings of native themes by writers operating, as Ó Cathasaigh remarks, 'in a literate Christian community' (1996:60). Current research is tending to favour the latter interpretation of the relationship between the compositions of monks and those of the secular *filid*, 'commonly translated "poets" but more aptly described [. . .] as the official savants and littérateurs of Ireland' (ibid., 58).

The extension of literacy from the monastic environment to its widespread use by laymen is much better illustrated by the Early Modern Period, which, over four centuries with many extant manuscripts, provides an overview of a wide range of materials covering most uses of literacy. From the monastic scriptoria, we have religious materials of various types, both prose and poetry, as well as a number of monastic annals some of which are continued to the late sixteenth century. Moreover, as Byrne points out, 'prior to the fourteenth century all [. . .] extant manuscripts are the products of monastic scriptoria, even when they contain texts of secular origin' (1984, xv), demonstrating the close relationship between these institutions and the native tradition of scholarship and literary composition. This is also the period when we find many instances of literary ideas and themes adopted from Continental European sources, including translations of Homer, Lucan and Vergil, as well as of Maundeville and Marco Polo, and of Arthurian stories. One major theme taken from a general European context is that of love poetry in the *amour courtois* idiom, which as Mac Craith points out, produced 'a common European heritage' (1989, 7) as it spread from its original heartland in twelfth-century Provence. Another example of this external influence was the interest in ideas of European medicine as it had been taken over from the Arab world in the twelfth century, particularly with the founding of the first schools of medicine in Italy, and the main Irish medical manuscripts are translations from Latin exemplars which include Irish borrowings or adaptations of their technical terminology.

Internecine battles by local chieftains seeking to aggrandize themselves or their clan groups, through the pursuit of wealth, territory or political influence, are a hallmark of Irish social history from the earliest period, with regular reporting of such events in various annals. Although the Vikings have traditionally had a bad reputation and been blamed for destruction of native materials, recent scholarship has suggested a more favourable view of the two centuries of their influence in the country. Ó Cróinín notes that 'the larger-than-life Vikings of the popular imagination, barbarous, savage and heathen [. . .] are the stuff of medieval and modern legend' (1995, 262). The period following the Anglo-Norman incursions of the twelfth and thirteenth centuries was marked by an increase in fighting across the areas of their main settlements, mainly in Leinster, Munster and East Connacht. There was much more widespread warfare in Ireland over the course of the sixteenth and seventeenth centuries as English policy towards the country changed from a broad tolerance of dissent at the edges towards one of securing the western boundaries of an emerging British state. Coupled with this was the spread of the English Reformation into Ireland with the monasteries being singled out for attack.

Such constant warfare over the centuries, even when on a minor scale, created an environment where destruction of property was commonplace, with a concomitant effect on the chances for survival of individual manuscripts, as their locations were subject to random attack. It is possible that paper manuscripts might have suffered more than vellum materials, as the latter would have been extrinsically more valuable to their scribes and possessors because of the effort of treating and preparing the calf-skins and the labour of writing, and hence more likely to have been rescued – where possible – by their guardians from external destruction. Some modern scholars too have tended to view the contents of vellum codices as more valuable than those of paper manuscripts, although on occasion very early material is now available only in paper manuscripts.

All manuscripts were subject to the effects of entropy, whether naturally as ink faded and leaves became worn through use, or by other human causes such as random loss and the destruction associated with warfare. The other source of human-caused changes lay in the copying of manuscripts, a process which was clearly understood by scribes as a necessary link in the chain of preservation of their contents. Such a process is necessarily open to misreadings and miscopyings in the chain, with direct links extending in some cases for hundreds of years, through perhaps six generations of copies. This process was subject to the vagaries of historical changes in the language, as scribes became less familiar with earlier grammatical forms or obsolete words, and adjusted their exemplars in an effort to make them meaningful, as evidenced by the manuscript stemma which appear in scholarly editions of texts. The tradition of scribal copying continued down until the mid-nineteenth century, and comments in manuscripts and letters indicate that networks of scribes passed manuscripts around as part of the process. Scribes worked for individual patrons who were increasingly located in urban areas and valuable collections were built up, most of which eventually passed into public or institutional libraries.

A psychological collapse of the internal culture of Irish-speaking areas was one of the effects of the Famine, and this was coupled with the rapid disappearance of the language and an inability of new owners to understand the contents of inherited manuscripts. The possibility for capital accumulation was transferred out of the rural society through population movement to cities and towns in Ireland, or abroad with the diaspora of the late nineteenth century. Book dealers were able to treat manuscripts as commodities, by buying them around country areas and selling either to individuals of the urban middle classes or to members of the emigrant communities in the anglophone world, presumably as memorabilia. This process has led to an unquantifiable loss of literary material, as the majority of the new owners were unable even to read their acquisitions, let alone appreciate their possible intrinsic value. The results of these historical processes can be summed up in a comment by Mac Néill on a manuscript written in 1740–1 which he was cataloguing in a Belfast library early in the twentieth century, that 'all the Irish writing in this volume is remarkably clear and well formed, and spelling is good [. . .]. The whole MS, after a life of a century and a half in Dublin, Cork, Belfast, and perhaps many other places, is splendidly preserved. *O si sic omnes*' (1906, 4). It may be relevant to mention that this manuscript is now missing from the library in question.

From the late eighteenth century and throughout most of the first half of the nineteenth, we find the appearance of printed versions of Irish literary materials, chiefly of the Early Modern period, along with poetry from Modern Irish. In the beginning, these books were mainly published by and for members of the Anglo-Irish aristocracy who had developed an increasing interest in the early (that is, Gaelic) history of the country or in its more recent native poets, and Irish materials appear with facing English translations. Sometimes only translations appear, as, for example, Keating's *History of Ireland* which was supported, as O'Connor observes, 'by the nobility and gentry of the kingdom, who had the original in that esteem, that it thought it justly deserved a translation' (1865, xi). The movement of Irish revivalism of the second half of the nineteenth century brought with it a new era of Irish literacy, as published materials appeared to support the reading demands of the movement. For the most part such materials were aimed at the new learners of the language as well as the relatively few native speakers who had become literate in Irish, and their emphasis was on educationally oriented works such as edited versions of folk tales and folk poetry, normally with accompanying translations, but with editorial linguistic and literary notes and comments on the texts. In addition to books, periodicals appeared for the first time, presumably an influence from the publishing models of English, as well as the use of columns in local newspapers, mostly weekly or bi-weekly. Usually the contents of these more ephemeral sources were matters of immediate popular relevance to Irish aimed mainly at learners and the periodicals also included materials in English, though the latter were not normally translations of Irish articles. As Ó Háinle notes, at the end of the nineteenth century 'there were major obstacles [. . .] in the attempt to cultivate Irish as a literary medium [. . .] connected with the wretched state of the Irish people at this time' (1994, 746), and the history of the next century is of attempts to overcome these obstacles.

The twentieth century with its political changes in Ireland brought a new lease of life to Irish writing, with many more outlets for authors as publishers came forward to take up the opportunities offered by the new regime. Coupled with this were further developments from some of the mechanisms of the late nineteenth century, including several weekly newspapers entirely in Irish, and more recently a daily newspaper. A popular format has been the monthly magazine with several interest groups targeted, for example university students and graduates of Irish, children, and women. From the writers' viewpoint, the twentieth century has seen an expansion in the range of literary types produced: short stories, novels, biographies, autobiographies, plays and poetry, as well as a range of functional writing, including its use for various 'educational' purposes intended to allow for the delivery of a normal secondary school curriculum through the medium of Irish. Between the years 1850 and 1936 de Hae lists 979 major published items, including 31 periodicals containing mainly Irish, almost 600 original prose works, as well as around 150 plays (many translations from English) and a great deal of poetry; in addition he gives 122 titles of other periodicals (excluding newspapers) which contained some Irish, with a total of 24,386 pieces, both poetry and prose materials (1938–40, ix–xiii). The last half of the century has surpassed this in its range of materials and outlets.

Irish-language materials have never had more than a minority audience – apart from educational works where several mainstream publishers have felt able to publish these – and the state has provided various forms of subsidy to support their production. The main publishing body for the language has been the Publications Branch of the Department of Education, which has produced over 1,500 books in its general series, including prose, poetry and drama, books for children, and information books of various types, as well as over 350 titles in its textbook series. One significant part of its output has been translations mainly of English-language books with some relevance to Ireland. Between the years 1928 and 1948, for example, there are 351 translated books and 418 original titles in its general series, and in its textbook series translations dominate for the production of the required classroom materials, and over a period of seventy years constitute more than one half of the list of titles.

Two essential tools for any literary use of language are dictionaries and grammars, and examples of both were in use from the earliest period down to the present day. The earliest dictionaries were glossaries to texts, and Isidore of Seville (*c*.560–636) appears to have provided an impetus for native work on etymologizing, as exemplified in glossary collections such as that of Cormac, a ninth-/tenth-century Munster bishop and king. Further collections of glossaries appear over the period of Early Modern Irish, with some continuity of copying extending down to the nineteenth century. The first modern type of partially alphabetized dictionary is that of Risteard Pluincéad in a Latin–Irish manuscript dictionary completed in 1662. Printed dictionaries or technical glossaries are found from the eighteenth century, and the earliest for Irish–English was that of Edward Lhuyd published as an extended glossary to his *Archaeologia Britannica* in 1707. The first English–Irish dictionary dates from 1732 and the first Irish–English appeared in 1768, both published in Paris. As might be expected, the nineteenth and twentieth centuries have provided many more instances of both types, including a number of works aimed at the new audience of learners, and recently a computer-based index to words and phrases in *Foclóir Gaeilge–Béarla* has appeared.

Scholars from the Old Irish period onwards were aware of the importance of studying and codifying grammar, and one tract, *Auricept na nÉces* ('The scholars' primer'), is summarized by McManus as containing 'a basic purely native Irish doctrine of poetic learning [and later] grammarians drew heavily on it in matters of terminology' (1991, 148). Native scholarship had a strongly prescriptive view of the importance of grammar, and throughout the Early Modern period there is a continuing emphasis on the practical application of grammar in writing especially for poetic composition. Descriptive grammars from the modern period are based on the models of Latin grammar with its emphasis on morphophonology, and they use similar structures for nominal and verbal paradigms.

As with all languages, for most of its history the amount of spoken Irish has far outweighed all written expressions of the language. Equally, this is a facet of any language which we know least about, and it is only within the past hundred years, with the beginning of dialectal research, that the collection of limited first-hand data has been carried out. Some evidence for earlier pronunciations can be gained from the rhyme schemes of poetry and by examining the spelling variations found in manuscript copies of poems as scribes adjusted their exemplars to cope with their own different pronunciations, varying either synchronically or diachronically from their exemplars.

A standardized form of language was used within the tradition of the court poets composing in Classical Modern Irish, but it is obvious that the training of these poets did permit variations within the pronunciation of individual words for metrical purposes of rhyme. We have no knowledge of the phonetics of this form of Irish from any contemporary source, and assumptions about its pronunciation derive from a phonemic interpretation. This is based on the symbol–sound correspondences of the orthography, but it is also necessary to consider the various synchronic dialectal[13] realizations of these correspondences to derive phonetic interpretations.

Towards the end of the Classical period, notions of dialectal differences were based mainly on literary norms, with up to five divisions being recognized, including those of the common people, the poets, and the lawyers. Following the collapse of the Classical system, socio-geographical dialect distinctions emerged with a new acceptability in the seventeenth century, with their pronunciations taking on a patina of popular respectability, to form four recognized dialect groupings, of Ulster, Munster, Leinster and Connacht. This division is demonstrated in the saying 'phonetics without morphophonology in Ulster, morphophonology without phonetics for Munster, phonetics and morphophonology in Connacht, neither phonetics nor morphophonology in Leinster',[14] which draws attention to a feeling for correctness associated with both the phonetics and the morphophonology, though not necessarily for lexical correctness. As Ó Cuív points out, history has 'reduced the Irish-speaking districts and isolated them from one another. [. . .] The fact that the dialects are isolated makes us inclined to exaggerate the differences that exist between them and to forget that in former times these differences were diffused [. . .] over the intervening areas, with the result that one dialect blended into another' (1951, 48). His comment draws attention to the extreme difficulty of filling in these widening inter-dialectal spacings, and modern perceptions tend to overstress the differences, leading to a localization which borders on isolationism and an attitude of language-internal insularity.

Such views have been especially prevalent over the past century as the language has moved towards a degree of public acceptability in Ireland. Around the end of the nineteenth century a major controversy arose over the standards of correctness which ought to prevail, and although the arguments were ostensibly based on the idea of a written standard, at their root lay the question of acceptability of a set of norms deriving from dialectal sources, of Munster, Connacht or of Ulster, as Leinster Irish had effectively disappeared by this time. Most of the new users of the language were learners who had acquired their knowledge from native speakers of one dialect area and had usually developed a partisan view of the speech of their adopted districts. Essentially the discussion centred round the ideas of those 'classicists' who suggested a model based on the prose styles of the seventeenth century, versus the views of those who favoured *caint na ndaoine* 'speech of the people', where the norms would be those of the oral cultures of the Gaeltacht areas. One of the major protagonists of the latter approach was Peadar Ó Laoghaire, a native speaker of Munster Irish who published a number of creative literary works, adopting the style of the *seanchaí* ('oral tradition bearer') of his native area and modifying it for written material. Eventually his views prevailed, but at the expense of some public perception of Munster Irish as the sole legitimate norm, leading to suspicions on the part of Ulster Irish speakers in particular that their dialect was being undervalued in both its written and spoken forms.

The effort put into the teaching of Irish in the twentieth century, at first outside the state schooling system and within it from 1922 onwards, was based on deploying teachers using an identifiable dialect. The paucity of available teachers meant that it was not possible to match class teachers to the generally accepted dialect norms of the provinces in which they worked, nor was it possible to integrate the taught curriculum across the years of school attendance. The resulting class-to-class mixture from teachers of both spoken and written Irish led to confusion on the part of learners, and within Gaeltacht areas to a perception by native speakers that what was described as 'Dublin Irish' was being foisted upon them. One effect of this was the development of several areal koines, based on Donegal, South West Connacht, and several Munster dialects, as learners from outside the Gaeltacht accommodated their pronunciations towards norms representing a common core for each of the three Gaeltacht areas in which they had acquired their Irish, and few learners achieved a high level of native-like accuracy in any local dialect variety.

The exception to this polydialectal approach was the education system of Northern Ireland, where eventually[15] the Department of Education specified Donegal Irish as the norm. All teachers were expected to conform to this, both in their spoken forms and in their teaching of the morphophonology (or more accurately perhaps, morphographology) of this dialect area. This approach led to the production of a short learners' grammar as well as sets of course materials for Ulster Irish, an approach which served to intensify some of the perceptual differences between the Gaeltacht areas.

Following the introduction of a standard norm for the written language described above (pp. 20–1), the Department of Education of the Republic decided in 1979 to produce an equivalent set of norms for the spoken language. The work was carried out as part of the preparation of a new pocket dictionary (both Irish–English and

English–Irish) aimed at the schools and which was published in 1986. As its phonetic editor, Ó Baoill describes the new *lárchanúint* 'central dialect' as containing 'a common core between the three dialects [. . .] not containing any sound rules which are not in active use in at least one dialect of Irish' (1986, 7). The set of rules was developed by bringing together a group of linguists whose own speech was representative of that of the three main dialect areas. The suggested norms are aimed primarily at learners with the published dictionary containing around 15,000 Irish headwords (compared with approximately 50,000 in the standard *Foclóir Gaeilge–Béarla*), and it is too early to assess how successfully the proposed central norms can be put into practice through the schools.

Christianity was intimately associated with the introduction of literacy to Irish, and the Church and its monasteries acted as an early focus for learning and scholarship as witnessed by the Old Irish glosses on scriptural works. This relationship continued through to the end of the Middle Irish period with its influences on the literature as described above, and carried on through the Late Middle Ages. During these periods the connections of the Church with mainstream European society facilitated the transfer of new influences into Irish literary culture, and, as Lennon points out, 'the overlapping of ecclesiastical and lay scholarly families and personnel added stability to the conduct of relations between church and secular administration' (1994, 63). The scriptoria of established monasteries became centres of literacy and record-keeping, with local annals in Irish being kept in many of them, though not all the religious orders accepted a connection with Irish. As Carey emphasizes, 'the introduction of the continental religious orders, although not far removed in time from the arrival [. . .] of the first Anglo-Norman military force [. . .] was the result of native initiative' (1998, 17), and Byrne points out that, although 'sterner Anglo-Norman clerics frowned on any survival of Gaelic culture' (1984, xxiii), in general those houses in those parts of the country where Irish predominated continued their close connections with the language and culture.

The Reformation, particularly that version of it which took root in England and its associated countries under the aegis of the last four monarchs of the Tudor dynasty, had its effect on Irish, coming as it did at a time when government policy towards Ireland had become one of conquest and subjugation of the native population. As Lennon points out, the organizational structures of the Roman Catholic Church came under direct attack and confiscation from 1537 onwards with 'the exploitation of monastic resources for public or private gain' (1994, 140). While much of the materials associated with traditional learning and literacy contained in the manuscripts of these monastic houses would possibly have survived the destructive part of this process, their dispersal to the care of individuals and the loss of stable supporting structures for this learning had a deleterious effect. In the early seventeenth century, following the departure of the Irish chieftains, a native priest and several members of a religious order attempted to record some of the history of the country. Keating describes how he prepared his work 'gathered and collected from the chief books of the history of Ireland' (1902, 95) and Ó Cléirigh, the originator of the Annals of the Four Masters which was completed in 1636, writes of his difficult collection of materials 'from all the best and most copious books of annals' which he found throughout Ireland.

The Counter-Reformation strategy of the Roman Catholic Church appears to have had two strands which turned out to be mutually contradictory as far as Irish was concerned. One part of it was driven by members of the monastic orders, especially the Franciscans, and involved the production of printed Irish works in Continental religious houses as described above. In the same period these mendicant orders supplied Irish-speaking missionaries for Ireland, and also for the west of Scotland, where the Scottish Gaelic community (see chapter 4) was considered to be sufficiently similar linguistically to Irish to be open to preaching and conversion activities from this source.

Those members of the diocesan clergy who re-established the social dominance of the Roman Catholic Church in Ireland over the latter half of the eighteenth century after the relaxation of the Penal Laws seem to have taken a different view, that their strategy should be based on the re-conversion of members of the Church of England to the older faith. To this end, Ireland was seen as a source of English-language missionaries, and support for the Irish language would have detracted from this possibility. The main focus of the Roman Catholic Church over the nineteenth century was on rebuilding its socio-political influence in the country, an approach which was assisted by a change of British policy from the late eighteenth century. Any support for the Irish language offered by the Church in the course of this century with the growth in Irish nationalism was at the level of a few individual bishops and a number of priests. This attitude has prevailed down to the present as the institutional church has adjusted its priorities to those of the majority socio-political movements of the country, and it is summed up in the comment of Nic Craith that 'it is not the case that the Catholic clergy were working against Irish [but] they showed little active interest [. . .] in it' (1993, 34).

The Protestant establishment in Ireland had access to local printers in the seventeenth century and were able to produce Irish material, concentrating on its use in worship. It was a member of the Established Church of Ireland[16] who organized the printing of a catechism as the first Irish-language book in 1571, and Uilleam Ó Domhnaill translated and published the Old Testament in 1602, as well as the Book of Common Prayer in 1608. Archbishop Bedell carried out most of the translation work for the Old Testament published in 1685, and Williams draws attention to a number of Irish-language publications which continued until 1724, after which 'Irish Protestants did little for Irish' (1986, 129). In the eighteenth century, the interest of the Church in education led to an involvement with various societies operating in rural areas where the importance of the language was soon recognized and attempts made to cater for it, though, as Ó Snodaigh points out (1995, 35), on the whole its legislation was 'antipathetic', with active support coming only from occasional bishops or clergy. The Presbyterian Church, particularly in the North of Ireland, sent Irish-speaking missionaries into rural areas to work with the local population and members were concerned with the production of Irish-language educational materials, including a grammar, in nineteenth-century Belfast.

Weinreich identifies a notion of language contact when 'two or more languages [. . .] are used alternately by the same persons. The language-using individuals are thus the locus of contact', noting that such contact in the individual mind can generate interference when the speaker deviates 'from the norms of either language [. . .] as a result of [. . .] familiarity with more than one' (1968, 1). When instances of such interference are taken up by others in the surrounding community of speakers, most of whom may not be bilingual, these external interfering elements can be treated on a par with other examples of language variation arising out of purely internal factors. The effects of such variation can be observed in changes to the linguistic systems of the affected language and some of these are described here, concentrating on changes to the lexicon. We should take into account that dating the introduction of borrowed words by using the first indication of their appearance in the literary record masks the underpinning reality of their first use in the spoken language, through which most borrowings – though not all[17] – would have made their entry into the language. Where borrowed words have continued in use to recent times, they are quoted here in a modern Irish spelling.

As regards the pre-history of Irish in Ireland, O'Rahilly suggests that the island was inhabited by speakers of a P-Celtic dialect before the introduction of Irish from Gaul around the first century BC. His evidence is based on the identification of a number of Irish words as borrowings from a substratum P-Celtic language, and he lists words such as *pata* 'hare', *Gael* 'Irish' and *Gaeilge* 'Irish language', pointing out that 'the earliest name by which the Goidels are known to have called themselves was *Féni*' (1935, 326). The first evidence for external linguistic contacts is provided by the borrowings from Latin into Irish, a process which may have begun as early as the fourth century when it is possible that there were trading contacts between Ireland and Gaul, an example being *ór* 'gold'. However, the majority of Latin borrowings appear with the introduction of Christianity over the fifth and sixth centuries, a cultural change mediated by British monks who also introduced literacy in Irish. The borrowings associated with the new religion and literacy include *peaca* 'sin' from *peccatum* and *scríobh* '(to) write' from *scribo*. This first wave of borrowings is clearly identifiable linguistically as it happened over a period when both Old Irish and Old Welsh were undergoing a massive series of mainly phonological changes (see p. 13), so that it is possible to provide approximate dates (or a least a series of relative datings) for the borrowings. The continuing widespread familiarity with Latin on the part of the educated class over the course of the Middle Ages also provided a conduit for borrowings whose precise dates of introduction cannot be known.

The first identifiable source of linguistic borrowings into Irish taking place between two language groups settled in Ireland is that between the Irish and Viking communities of the ninth to the eleventh centuries, where the outsiders were relatively few and scattered in what appear to have been town-like settlements in the southern half of the country. Ó Cróinín states that 'the cultural and economic interaction which characterized Irish–Viking relations for three centuries and more after AD 800 is best seen in such areas as commerce and language. [. . .] The area of profoundest influence was that of shipbuilding and seafaring' (1995, 269). Irish, unlike Scottish Gaelic where Norse influence was of a longer duration and in a closer cultural contact (see pp. 44–5), was not affected phonologically by Norse, and lexical borrowings along with a few place-names are the main indications of the relationship between the two groups. In addition to seafaring terminology such as *accaire* 'anchor' (later replaced by the English borrowing *ancaire*), and *bád* 'boat', loans also include domestic elements, e.g. *sráid* 'cleared area around a house, street', *fuinneog* 'window' and *garraí* 'garden', and trading terms such as *margadh* 'market'.

Following the Anglo-Norman invasions of the twelfth century, Risk points out that their language[18] 'reached the common people through various channels, but its greatest influence would seem to have been felt in military, architectural and legal

affairs, areas in which contact between the two sections of the community was a necessity' (1968–71, 586). However, he notes that the influence from this particular source
of French, while 'strong in certain spheres [. . .] was also limited and not deeply rooted'
due to the relative size of this group and to their fairly rapid assimilation to the native
culture, although 'in law, justice and civic government French was employed until the
fifteenth century' (ibid., 589–90). This continuity of influence in the higher domains
of language over three centuries with their direct connections to France means that we
must allow for borrowings from French which do not derive from the mainstream
Anglo-Norman families of the twelfth century, and Risk's discussion includes such
words, which can usually be identified by their date of first recording.

Of a total of over 300 words, Risk notes that military terms constitute 12 per cent,
architectural words 13 per cent, mainly concerned with the building of military forti-
fications, with legal and administrative terminology accounting for 14 per cent (ibid.,
587). These words presumably belong to the early expansionist phase of Anglo-Norman
settlement; examples include *caiptín* 'captain', *pláta* 'plate, armour', *bárda* 'ward, garrison', *seomra* 'room', *gábla* 'gable', *coiléar* 'quarry', *cúirt* 'court (in both architectural
and administrative senses)', *giústís* 'magistrate', *barántas* 'warrant'. The remaining 60
per cent of French loan-words result from increasing cultural contacts over a longer
period and include elements from trade, religion, and general socio-cultural vocabulary.
They are represented by the words *bagún* 'bacon', *cóta* 'coat', *mála* 'bag', *garsún* 'boy',
paróiste 'parish', *buidéal* 'bottle', with the word *cóiste* 'coach', for example, being noted
by Risk in his listing as a 'late borrowing' (ibid., 76) whose first attestation in French
dates from 1545.

As might be expected, the penetration of Anglo-Norman linguistic influences was
greatest in those areas of densest settlement, mostly in Leinster, Munster and parts of
east Connacht, evidence for which is provided by the uptake of lexical loans into Irish
where a number of borrowed terms attested from southern dialects are not found in
Ulster or west Connacht; nor did many cross the North Channel to be assimilated into
local dialects of Scottish Gaelic.[19] However, such evidence is not definitive and
O'Rahilly comments that 'it is easy enough to say that a particular word is in use
to-day in a particular area; but to say that such and such a word is not in use in a
particular district may well be risky, in view of the fact that the vocabulary of most
districts has as yet been imperfectly explored' (1972, 244). The opportunities for
such exploration of the living dialects have faded rapidly since this comment was first
published in 1932, and have now effectively disappeared for most dialects. Although
O'Rahilly appeals to his notion that Scottish Gaelic is a different language from Irish
in order to explain a number of features of Northern Irish which he would identify as
of Scottish origin (1972, 161–91), I would prefer to treat his examples as instances of
internal variation within a single historical language.

Before examining the effects of English influence on Irish, it is worth noting that
Scots has made a small contribution to some dialects of Ulster Irish, arising from the
introduction of Scots settlers to parts of Ulster in the seventeenth century. These settlements had varying degrees of social contact with their Irish neighbourhoods, creating on the one hand a distinctive Ulster Scots (or perhaps colonial Scots) dialect, and
resulting in a number of lexical borrowings, both from Scots to Irish and vice versa.
However, as was the case with the French-language contacts of the Early Modern period

where the direct influence from French outlasted the specific Anglo–Norman effect, the close relationship between Scots and English and the dominating influence of English on both Scots and Modern Irish means that it is difficult to be certain in assigning a particular borrowing to English or Scots. In this respect sometimes what we might call micro-dialectal evidence can assist; however, such data do not usually appear in the literary record as opposed to that of the oral tradition, and evidence is slight. Ó Dochartaigh notes the words *craoipín* 'low stool' and perhaps *pigín* 'suckling pig', along with the words 'bumbee' and 'haunch' collected only from phonetic sources (1984, 166), as instances of such Scots borrowings which are not recognized by any Irish dictionary.[20]

The English element in Irish provides the most extensive evidence for two languages in contact, a contact extending from the introduction of English-speaking followers along with the Anglo–Norman leaders of the late twelfth-century incursions, to the present day. This influence has affected all aspects of Irish, from the level of phonetics to that of semantics, and includes modifications to the morphophonology, syntax and the lexicon, from straightforward single loan-words (and compound words adopted as single elements), to that of language in use, as shown by calques and translations of proverbial expressions. This loan traffic has not always been one-way, as shown by the adaptations of the language of these early settlers to what was a culturally dominant Irish adstratum. O'Rahilly points out that these settlers produced 'the dialect of English formerly spoken in the south-east of Co. Wexford [which] by the middle of the eighteenth century [. . .] was in process of rapid decay [. . .] supplanted by the ordinary type of Hiberno-English' (1972, 94), and which appears to share a number of word stress changes with south Leinster Irish.

The better known language Hiberno-English, which has its origins in the English settlements of the sixteenth and seventeenth centuries, also shows major linguistic adjustments deriving from the spoken Irish of its surroundings. A more recent instance of literary influence from Irish is that of the Anglo-Irish writers of the nineteenth and early twentieth centuries. Borrowings range from those of Synge whose familiarity with the Irish language allowed him to make use of the speech of local communities in his works, with a potency of English idiom derived, as Kiberd suggests (1993, xv), 'in great part from the reported death of Irish', to the highly sophisticated adaptation by Joyce in his short story 'The Dead' of parts of an early Irish saga which had appeared in English translation in the late nineteenth century. In a somewhat lower literary register, Bram Stoker quotes from a 'Gaelic verse' in a poorly lettered Irish font frontispiece to *The Mystery of the Sea*.

The counter-current, from English to Irish, has flowed with increasing strength over the past three centuries, with proliferating effects on all aspects of Irish. As Irish-speakers have become fully bilingual, with the last of the traditional Gaeltacht speakers being affected only within the past fifty years, we now find examples of language interference across the whole range outlined by Weinreich: phonetic, grammatical and in the lexicon. In his summary, the stimuli factors include for the phonetic level 'presence of distinction (only) in primary language', for the grammatical 'very different grammatical systems', and in the lexical domain 'structural weak points in recipient vocabulary, need to match differentiations in source language' (1968, 64–5), and instances of all these occur in Irish. In any discussion of this phenomenon, we must distinguish between the oral language and that of the written register, where the former shows all the features associated with language contact situations in a bilingual environment, with the latter – particularly in the more popular written registers such as journalism – now beginning to show increasing markers of borrowings, especially as calques. It is difficult to adduce evidence for the full range of cross-language borrowings into spoken Irish due to an unwillingness of Irish scholarship to accept, or at least describe, the fact that Gaeltacht speakers of Irish use in their bilingual environment all the language strategies described by Weinreich. Coupled with this may be a sensitization of native speakers towards a social requirement to speak 'proper' Irish in conversation with outsiders, in particular to refrain from code-switching to English as all do in conversations with other members of their communities.

It is in the lexicon and its associated contextualizations that we can find the greatest effects of English influence. Borrowings of nouns are most frequent and not only include the linguistically motivated and expected new loans to accommodate changes in the technological environment, but also involve replacement of native words with English translation equivalents. Nouns may be borrowed as simple single words which are monomorphemic in English, and some older speakers show instances of compound words, as Weinreich describes, 'transferred in unanalyzed form' (1968, 47), that is, treated as single morphs. The linguistic survey by Wagner conducted in the 1950s collected materials from around one hundred native-speaking informants from Gaeltacht and non-Gaeltacht areas, using a bilingual questionnaire requiring translations into Irish from single words or phrases presented orally by him in English. On the basis of his experience on field trips he comments that we are dealing with 'the ruins of a language', noting that 'as regards syntax and idiom, much of our collection may be corrupt, from the point of view of students of the older language, but most of these sentences may be heard in areas where Irish is spoken' (1959, x). From a generation later than Wagner's account, Lúcás, a native speaker of Donegal Irish, points out that 'Irish and English have been struggling for a long time [. . .], a situation which leaves a clear trace of English on the Irish, not only on the individual word, but on the structure of the sentence as well' (1986, i).[21]

Borrowings normally carry over the consonantal skeleton of the English original, usually with minor phonetic adaptations to the vowels to match the local accent of English or Scots, and they follow the stress pattern of the original, which may be on a syllable other than the first. Nouns usually adopt an Irish plural morpheme and the English plural /s/ is rarely used. Verbs borrowed from English monosyllables commonly add the native suffix *-(e)áil*, which has been extended from its previous relatively minor role in the system of verbal morphophonology.

As might be expected, borrowings from English are most extensive in the speech of those associated with the one urban district of Irish usage, effectively leading towards a creolized form of the language which we might call *Nua-Ghaeilge* 'new Irish'. For this Belfast community, Maguire describes in some detail the extent of linguistic adaptations of Irish, most apparently made under the influence of English, in the language of this group whose models of Irish correctness are no longer the Gaeltacht[22] speakers used by Irish learners from the Irish Republic (and formerly also by Northern Ireland learners) (1991, 186–228). She demonstrates a full range of modifications in a group of language learners developing their own community interlanguage, from simplification of the Irish target through loss of mutations and other phonetic adjustments, and over-generalization within the verbal paradigm by extending the use of the present tense suffix to the future of irregular verbs which use a suppletive root for this tense. In the lexical sphere she points out that a word may be borrowed from English without modification 'where the Irish cognate is unknown or temporarily forgotten' (ibid., 224) and examples abound in her quotations from members of this community.

Moving the focus from the individual speaker-hearer to the situation of language as community object allows us to observe the effects of bilingualism on various stages of Irish. Before the sixteenth century the level of bilingualism across the whole country was very low and concentrated on those areas of everyday contact between Irish-speakers and the external groups which affected them. The influences of these have been described above, and it is clear that no large-scale bilingual community developed until the sixteenth and seventeenth centuries once the contact with English had reached a critical mass of socio-linguistic importance to the community. From its introduction, this contact has spread bilingualism across the Irish social fabric over the past three centuries, until it finally reached speakers in the remaining heartlands of the Gaeltacht within the past fifty years. It has affected both languages as they underwent mutual adjustments in all aspects of their grammars, though Irish has undergone most change.

Proper names, whether personal or place-names, are one obvious area of bilingual adaptation where the new English forms have attempted to symbolize aspects of the Irish sound system through a non-native orthography. Such anglified forms represent caricatures of the original, in particular when phonetic distinctions not represented in English orthography are dispensed with in the transition. As Joyce outlines (1887, xiii–xiv), place-names can recall names of historical and legendary origin, events, or personages, refer to customs or measures of land, commemorate artificial structures, habitations, ecclesiastical edifices, or describe physical features such as mountains, lakes or rivers. Such namings carry with them cultural information, including that of history, and Irish literature recognized this in the importance attributed to topographical matters in the poetry and prose of *dindsheanchas* or 'lore of high places'. Proper names have a considerable presence in the public domain, in particular the legal system, and the new forms tend to become canonical and liable to spelling pronunciation, hyper-correction and semantic misinterpretation of their Irish antecedents. In particular, the transmogrification of place-names through spoken English has resulted in modifications to the originals, particularly as written forms become canonical and lead to spelling pronunciations based on the sound–symbol correspondences of English. This process has led to a high degree of opacity in the resulting forms and a break in the traditional understanding and interpretation of place-names which did form an integral part of an earlier cultural understanding. New English namings arising out of conquest also remove native elements, as for instance when Draperstown replaces Baile na Scríne ('townland of the shrine'), or in a current shibboleth from Northern Ireland, when Londonderry replaces Irish Doire.[23] Such rewritings of history and their associated memory loss are well illustrated in Act 2, Scene 1, of the play *Translations* by Brian Friel, and the playwright summarizes the results of the process of renaming: 'it can happen that a civilization can be imprisoned in a linguistic contour which no longer matches the landscape of [. . .] fact.' In this he subtly encapsulates the effects of historical loss of information on both the Irish and anglophone communities in Ireland.

Irish personal names also carry meaning, with the most common in speech being the use of a three- or two-name group of forenames, of the person, father (or mother), grandfather, where the latter two appear in the genitive case with initial lenition, as in Máirtín Dhónaill Fheidhlimidh. Sometimes an attributive adjective, such as *dubh* 'dark', *bán* 'fair', *mór* 'big', or *beag* 'small' can appear with one of these forenames as an epithet for a personal characteristic. Such forms are the norm in all Gaeltacht communities and their extension backwards in time, sometimes for five or six generations, is used to indicate family relationships of individuals. This structure shows the normal Irish grammatical marker of possession where the possessor noun in genitive case follows the possessed object. In those areas where English has taken over from Irish, the basic grammatical structure of the original is retained in forms such as Neal Charlie or Owen Hugh, with Anglicized name-equivalents without case-marking replacing the originals.

MacLysaght reports that 'Ireland was one of the earliest countries to evolve a system of hereditary surnames: they came into being fairly generally in the eleventh century, and indeed a few were formed before the year 1000' (1969, ix). The oldest forms were based on the pattern described above, with the addition of the word *mac* 'son' before a father's name, or *ó* before that of a grandfather or earlier ancestor. Sometimes these words were prefixed to an attributive adjective attached to a particular ancestor, with the original forename of that person dropped in favour of the characteristic epithet. In all cases the grammar requires the genitive forms of the word following the prefix, and it is these which underlie the anglified forms of surnames. All the normal patterns of interlanguage borrowings are represented in these modified surnames: translations (including misinterpretations), folk etymologies, abbreviations and phonetic adjustments, coupled with orthographic modifications, for example where the *-y* termination usually indicates the final syllable of an attributive adjective ending *-(a)igh*. A number of Anglo-Norman surnames were Gaelicized in the Early Modern period, demonstrating the assimilation of this group into the native culture. Because of the rural and essentially sedentary characteristics of the society, all surnames tended to have close associations with particular geographical, that is tribal, districts, and this is still generally true, though the urbanization of the country weakens these associations. In the course of the seventeenth and eighteenth centuries, in many cases the *Mac* and *Ó* prefixes were dropped from anglified forms, though the twentieth century has seen a reversal of this modification.

In general political terms, the two social forces which have had effects on Irish over the past two centuries are societal organizations and forms of state intervention. The former, which have existed since the late eighteenth century, are voluntary groups of like-minded individuals, and the latter has had a major impact only since the establishment of political independence after 1921. It is the voluntary associations which have had the greatest effect on driving state policies, and the latter usually appear in reaction to these external pressures so that no coherent overall policy for the support of even a bilingual society has been developed. In the 1920s there were suggestions for the development of a society in the Republic of Ireland in which all residents would be bilingual. It was soon realized that the achievement of such an outcome would require all the anglophone citizens (over 90 per cent of the population) to be taught Irish as practically all Irish-speakers were already bilingual, and faced with this political burden and its implications for state resource allocation, the government effectively lowered its sights and took shelter in a number of low-level reforms, accompanied by the rhetoric of external symbols. The only partially serious attempt was to use the school system as the weapon of change, a decision which appears to have been based on an analysis of the loss of Irish over the nineteenth century which attributed this solely to the imposition of English through the National School system. It is clear that this interpretation did not take into account the realities of the socio-economic situation of Irish-speakers over the previous two centuries, and it has proved to be impossible to reverse the process of change by using only the educational sphere.

The voluntary organizations had their origins in the urban middle classes of the late eighteenth century, when groups with an interest in education and Irish history and culture – which included aspects of the language – came into existence. The most famous of these is the Royal Irish Academy whose annual journal was established in 1786 and which continues to publish research on topics of mathematics, Irish archaeology and language and culture matters, including both Irish and English. Other groups formed in the nineteenth century included the Gaelic Society of Dublin, the Ulster Gaelic Society, and the Irish Archaeological and Celtic societies. As their names suggest, most of these were concerned with general cultural matters and not specifically with the Irish-speaking community or its language. It was not until the last quarter of the century that a group was established with an interest in this area. In 1876 the Society for the Preservation of the Irish Language was set up, with objectives which included encouraging the production of modern Irish literature as well as the family use of the language by parents who were native speakers. Out of this organization there eventually emerged Conradh na Gaeilge ('The Gaelic League') in 1893, a group which has continued to the present and which, along with its offshoots, has had the greatest influence on the history of the language over this period. Through its journal it encouraged the development of a modern literature, and this organ provided an opportunity for the discussion of many problems arising in connection with the support for Irish in the country. The League was particularly important for its creation of favourable public perceptions towards the language on the part of the anglophone citizens of Ireland. Like most other voluntary organizations which form part of the social fabric of any society, the League shared much overlap of membership with other groupings both cultural and political, and it became closely associated with the physical-force wing of the nationalist movement of the period, leading to some political fragmentation in support for the language.

After independence, the groundswell of practical support for the language, which had been developed particularly through the League's teaching Irish to adults in local classes, weakened and a large number of those who had supported this teaching programme effectively handed over responsibility for its implementation to the state. At this point, the voluntary organizations, of which there were by now several dozen each with a particular interest in some aspect of Irish culture, changed their previous focus of political pressure from the British government of Ireland to the native government of the new Irish state, and it has been the changing power balances between these two political groupings which has defined the external history of Irish down to the present.

All groups which form part of civil society show fissiparous tendencies, and one of the standard jokes in new Irish-language organizations has been the question, 'When do we have the split?' While such a process is natural, it is one which has led to perceived weaknesses on the part of the individual organizations in their approaches to state bodies, and this has tended to lessen their effectiveness. To counter this, an attempt was made to create a more effective group, and in 1943 Comhdháil Náisiúnta na Gaeilge ('National Congress for the Irish Language') was formed, though its establishment was fraught with political difficulties. Mac Aonghusa points out that it was the intention of de Valera 'to strike a mortal blow at the Gaelic League by developing another organisation which would put it off its stroke' (1993, 285), presumably because he had recognized that the continual infighting was not to the political advantage of the movement, and the new body was provided with state funding. Perhaps because of this, infighting and associated political weaknesses continued, and in 1978 the government established Bord na Gaeilge as a statutory body with annual funding. However, in addition to this quango, as Mac Aonghusa points out, Comhdháil Náisiúnta na Gaeilge was retained and expanded and 'each organisation is constantly looking for a definite rôle for itself' (ibid., 327), with a subsequent weakening of the political influence of the Irish language lobby.

As outlined above, the Irish state has provided a great deal of practical support for the language in a number of areas, particularly in the educational sphere, and it also established a small department for the Gaeltacht, though this did not have serious institutional support as it had no secretary-level appointment as head of department and it has now been remodelled as a department for Arts, Culture and the Gaeltacht. In the 1990s, the establishment of a National Lottery in Ireland increased state funding above that available through taxation revenue and this new money has been channelled into supporting a range of what may be defined as broadly cultural activities. Support for almost all activities associated with the Irish language now comes from this source, including the Publications Branch of the Department of Education which was previously a core section of the department and funded from the general budget.

Although the Irish constitution adopted in 1937 speaks of Irish as the first official language, no policies were devised to support this statement and it has taken on the iconization of an aspiration, with no relevance for the everyday life of the country. A good example of this was provided by the negotiations during the discussions to join the European Community, when Irish was accepted as an official language for the Community, but not as a working language, and hence not requiring the levels of cross-community support for translation and interpreter services provided for working languages. At present discussions are under way on the preparation of a language act to provide a legal framework for those aspects of the aspirations which can be easily articulated in such a document, as the government is required to accept some responsibility in the expanding Community for its treatment of minority language cultures within its territory. Current plans for funding a new English–Irish dictionary will be supported by equal funding from both the Republic of Ireland and the British Government if proposals for the resolution of the Northern Ireland conflict are successful.

One example of a political movement which developed from within the Gaeltacht is that of the late 1960s group Cearta Sibhialta na Gaeltachta ('Civil Rights of the Gaeltacht'), the focus of whose demand was for the extension of state support for the language culture of the area. This was fulfilled through the establishment of Raidió na Gaeltachta in the late 1970s as a service for the whole country. Previously Radio Éireann as the national channel had broadcast a short daily Irish news service, as well as a range of cultural programmes in Irish (music, sports, occasional plays, as well as children's material). Raidió na Gaeltachta was established as a service which maintained three studios, in Munster, Donegal and Connacht, with its headquarters in the latter. These studios broadcast in the dialects of their own areas, producing good local information and news but not being able to break the perception of listeners from other areas that they have little interest in the materials, which they consequently psychologically refuse to understand. More recently the state has required a new Irish-language television service to be broadly self-supporting, and current plans to move to a digital service will put an additional strain on the potential audience figures as the number of available English-language channels will increase by a factor of perhaps one hundred, so tending to further compartmentalize the audience. The future for Irish in these parts of the public domain appears to be one which will be based on cultural shrinkage, with music and song taking over the task of carrying a sense of national identity. For most of the past two hundred years, no one in Ireland would think of addressing a stranger in Irish and it is clear that in the private domain the spoken language will continue on the basis of social networks of those whose interests in Irish, which arise out of learning it, have brought them into contact with each other.

Notes

1　I am grateful to Dr Roibeard Ó Maolalaigh for a number of useful comments and suggestions.

2　A brief overview is found in Ó Dochartaigh 1992,11–34. A great deal of recent research has been published in Irish and quotations from such sources are silently translated.

3　O'Callaghan quotes from French sources that at the battle of Fontenoy in 1745 the Irish Brigade charged the Anglo–Dutch lines shouting 'in the old Celtic, or Gaelic tongue, "Remember Limerick" ' (1885, 358).

4　As Ó Murchú points out, 'Daniel O'Connell [. . .] addressed meetings in Irish. [. . .] Although he never thought to make a political issue of the Irish language, and pragmatically gave it little support, he was fully of the Irish-speaking community' (1998, 358).

5　The original state definition of the Gaeltacht also included the notion of *breac-Ghaeltacht* 'variegated-Gaeltacht' or partly Irish-speaking area where the percentage of speakers was less than a majority, and sometimes the term *fíor-Ghaeltacht* 'true-Gaeltacht' is used for the former districts. Such a distinction appears to have been an administrative method to enable the directing of state resources towards native speakers, but the difference between the two areas became less relevant as the percentages of native speakers have decreased within the traditional Gaeltacht populations, and the distinction is no longer made.

6　On this term, see note 5.

7　It is impossible to provide an accurate figure for this group, as it does not form a European-style nineteenth-century ghetto where there was usually a geographical coherence shared by a large group of families carrying on a daily round of life in an urban environment, and using their language in most situations of social intercourse.

8　The spelling 'ogam' is that of Old Irish, and is represented as 'ogham' in modern spelling, with a pronunciation of 'ogha' as a single long o-vowel.

9　A dot under a character indicating it is to be deleted. In Irish it is placed over the lenited character. Occasionally the *spiritus asper* of Greek orthography, where it is the equivalent of Latin *h*, was used for the same purpose over certain letters.

10   Byrne notes that it was not until the thirteenth century that the use of these two sets of symbols for the representation of the voiced and voiceless stop series respectively became more or less regularized (1984, xv).

11   With the exception of the abbreviation for *agus* 'and' which survived the later adoption of English fonts.

12   These usually begin with the word *Oróid* 'A prayer (for)', a formula not found in ogam materials.

13   Including evidence from Scottish Gaelic, which has a linguistic history in common with Irish.

14   In this rendering I take the word *blas* in the meaning 'pronunciation', and *ceart* as referring to correctness within the system of verbal and nominal morphophonology.

15   Against considerable political opposition, as described in Andrews 1997.

16   Disestablished in 1869.

17   Exceptions include high culture terms associated with religion and administration in the Early Modern period, as well as recent words coined for the purposes of terminology creation, a process which can lead to lexical enhancement as terms become accepted into the language.

18   Risk notes the difficulty of distinguishing 'between (a) words borrowed directly from Anglo-Norman and (b) those which came from Anglo-Norman through English' (1968–71, 591), thus drawing attention to a major problem in assessing language borrowings in a multi-ethnic contact situation.

19   Unlike the case of the earlier Latin religious and literary loans in Irish, which are found in spoken Scottish Gaelic, and thus draw attention to a gradual cultural – and hence linguistic – separation of these two languages over the period of the seventh to twelfth centuries.

20   Though some Scots borrowings do appear in an Irish orthographical dress in both editions of Dinneen's dictionary due to the Gaelicizing enthusiasm of one of the informants who supplied this lexicographer with lists of Irish words.

21   Lúcás uses Irish orthography in his word-list for these loans in order to symbolize the English pronunciation (which is that of the local Donegal English accent), and sometimes creates chimerical spellings which depart from the normal sound–symbol correspondences for Irish.

22   The punning epithet *Gaoltacht* or *Jailtacht* is used to refer to the new norm of this group, due to its origins among Republicans held in the prisons of Northern Ireland since the 1970s.

23   An interesting reversal of this process is the use of Éire rather than Republic of Ireland for the name of the state, as the preferred option in English discourse by members of the Unionist community in Northern Ireland.

References

Ahlqvist, A. 1994. Litriú na Gaeilge. In McCone, Kim et al. (eds), *Stair na Gaeilge*, Maynooth, 23–59.

Andrews, L. 1997. *The Very Dogs in Belfast will Bark in Irish*: The Unionist Government and the Irish language 1921–43. In Mac Póilin, Aodán (ed.), *The Irish Language in Northern Ireland*, Belfast, 49–94.

Breatnach, L. 1994. An Mheán-Ghaeilge. In McCone, Kim et al. (eds), *Stair na Gaeilge*, Maynooth, 221–333.

Byrne, F. J. 1984. Introduction. In O'Neill, Timothy, *The Irish Hand*, Portlaoise, xi–xxvii.

Carey, John 1998. *King of Mysteries*. Dublin.

Connell, K. H. 1950. *The Population of Ireland 1750–1845*. Oxford.

de Hae, Risteárd 1938–40. *Clár Litridheacht na nua-Ghaedhilge* (3 vols). Dublin.

Fitzgerald, G. 1984. Estimates for Baronies of minimum level of Irish-speaking amongst successive decennial cohorts: 1771–1781 to 1861–1871. *Proceedings of the Royal Irish Academy*, 84c:117–55.

Hindley, Reg 1990. *The Death of the Irish Language*. London.

Hyde, Douglas 1967. *A Literary History of Ireland*. London.

Joyce, Patrick W. 1887. *The Origin and History of Irish Names of Places* (vol. 1). Dublin.

Keating, Geoffrey 1902. *The History of Ireland*. London.

Kiberd, Declan 1993. *Synge and the Irish Language*. Dublin.

Lennon, Colm 1994. *Sixteenth-Century Ireland: The Incomplete Conquest*. Dublin.

Lúcás, Leaslaoi U. 1986. *Cnuasach Focal as Ros Goill*. Dublin.

Lynam, Edward W. 1969. *The Irish Character in Print 1571–1923*. Shannon.

Mac Aonghusa, Proinsias 1993. *Ar son na Gaeilge*. Dublin.

McCone, K. 1996. Prehistoric, Old and Middle Irish. In McCone, Kim and Simms, Katharine (eds), *Progress in Medieval Irish Studies*, Maynooth, 7–53.

Mac Craith, Mícheál 1989. *Lorg na hIasachta ar na Dánta Grá*. Dublin.

MacLysaght, Edward 1969. *The Surnames of Ireland*. Dublin.

McManus, Damian 1984. On final syllables in the Latin loan-words in Early Irish. *Ériu*, 35:137–62.

——1991. *A Guide to Ogam*. Maynooth.

Mac Néill, E. 1906. The Laverty Manuscripts. *Irisleabhar na Gaedhilge*, 16 (12):1–3, 16 (13):1–4, 16 (14):1–5.

Maguire, Gabrielle 1991. *Our Own Language: An Irish Initiative*. Clevedon.

Nic Craith, Máiréad 1993. *Malartú Teanga: An Ghaeilge i gCorcaigh sa Naoú hAois Déag*. Bremen.

Ní Mhóráin, Brighid 1997. *Thiar sa Mhainistir atá an Ghaolainn bhreá*. Dingle.

Ó Baoill, Dónall P. 1986. *Lárchanúint don Ghaeilge*. Dublin.

Ó Buachalla, Breandán 1996. *Aisling ghéar*. Dublin.

O'Callaghan, John Cornelius 1885. *History of the Irish Brigades*. Glasgow.

Ó Cathasaigh, T. 1996. Early Irish narrative literature. In McCone, Kim and Simms, Katharine (eds), *Progress in Medieval Irish Studies*, Maynooth, 55–64.

O'Connor, Dermod 1865. *Keating's General History of Ireland*. Dublin.

Ó Cróinín, Dáibhí 1995. *Early Medieval Ireland*. London.

Ó Cuív, Brian 1951. *Irish Dialects and Irish-Speaking Districts*. Dublin.

——1973. *The Linguistic Training of the Irish Bardic Poet*. Dublin.

Ó Dochartaigh, C. 1984. Some influences on Ulster Irish. *Éigse*, 20:164–70.

——1992. The Irish language. In MacAulay, Donald (ed.), *The Celtic Languages*, Cambridge, 11–99.

Ó Dónaill, Niall (ed.) 1977. *Foclóir Gaeilge–Béarla*. Dublin.

Ó Háinle, C. 1994. Ó chaint na ndaoine go dtí an Caighdeán Oifigiúil. In McCone, Kim et al. (eds), *Stair na Gaeilge*, Maynooth, 745–93.

Ó Murchú, M. 1998. Language and society in nineteenth-century Ireland. In Jenkins, Geraint H. (ed.), *Language and Community in the Nineteenth Century*, Cardiff, 341–68.

O'Neill, Timothy 1984. *The Irish Hand*. Portlaoise.

O'Rahilly, Thomas F. 1935. The Goidels and their predecessors. *Proceedings of the British Academy*, 21:323–72.

——1972. *Irish Dialects Past and Present*. Dublin.

Ó Riagáin, Pádraig 1997. *Language Policy and Social Reproduction*. Oxford.

Ó Riain, Seán 1994. *Pleanáil Teanga in Éirinn*. Dublin.

Ó Snodaigh, Pádraig 1995. *Hidden Ulster*. Belfast.

Ravenstein, E. G. 1879. On the Celtic languages in the British Isles. *Journal of the Royal Statistical Society*, 42:579–636.

Risk, H. 1968–71. French loan-words in Irish. *Études celtiques*, 12:585–655, 13:67–97.

Sims-Williams, P. 1993. Some problems in deciphering the early Irish ogam alphabet. *Transactions of the Philological Society*, 91:133-80.

Wagner, Heinrich 1959. *A Linguistic Atlas and Survey of Irish Dialects* (vol. 1). Dublin.

Weinreich, Uriel 1968. *Languages in Contact*. The Hague.

Williams, Nicholas 1986. *I bprionta i leabhar*. Dublin.

3 Irish in Early Britain

Glanville Price

There is firm evidence that some western parts of Wales and England were at some stage occupied by Irish-speaking communities. Some scholars[1] once held that these were the remnants of the earliest waves of Celtic-speaking immigrants who, in their view, first occupied Britain and only later crossed to Ireland. This view is now generally regarded as untenable.

There are a number of Irish words in Welsh that must have entered the language during the Dark Age period (see below), but these do not in themselves prove that there were Irish-speaking communities on Welsh soil. The strongest evidence for the existence of such communities is provided by the Irish inscriptions in the so-called 'ogam' script found in Wales and other western parts of this island. Ogam is a method of representing characters of the Latin alphabet by means of notches and grooves cut on stone slabs. The vowels are represented by notches in one edge of the slab, and the consonants by grooves cut on one side or the other of the edge or obliquely across it (figure 1, p. 12). Although these combinations of notches and grooves look nothing like the usual characters of the Latin alphabet, they do stand for Latin letters and do not constitute a different alphabet. The point will perhaps be clear if one thinks of the Morse code in which different sequences of dots and dashes, whether expressed visually by means of flashing lights or audibly as 'buzzes', correspond specifically to letters of the Latin (and not, say, the Greek or Russian or Arabic) alphabet.

The great majority of the ogam inscriptions are to be found in Ireland itself, where about 300 of them survive, mainly in the south-west. There are also a few in Scotland and the Isle of Man. Most of them probably date from the fifth and sixth centuries, though some could be earlier and some are certainly later (seventh or perhaps even eighth century).

Our immediate concern, however, is with the substantial number of Irish ogam inscriptions outside these areas. Of these, forty are in Wales (mainly in the south-west) (map 2), eight in Cornwall and Devon, and one in Hampshire. One important distinction is that, whereas in Ireland the inscription is only in Irish, the great majority of the ogam stones found outside Ireland also bear an inscription in Latin (which in all but two cases, both in Wales, is the almost exact equivalent of the ogam inscription in Irish) or, at the very least, a Celtic name in normal Latin letters. Although it is far from easy to date the Latin inscriptions, they do provide some help, and Kenneth Jackson suggests (1950, 205) that some twenty-seven or twenty-eight of the thirty bilingual

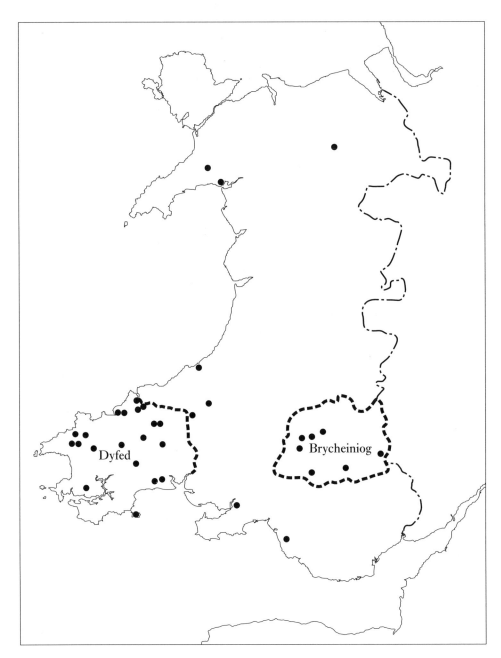

Map 2 *The distribution of stones with Irish ogam inscriptions in Wales.*

Dyfed

Brycheiniog

inscriptions belong to the period between about 450 and 600, the remaining two or three being from the early seventh century.

The inscriptions are in general very brief, and what Nash-Williams (1950, 6) says of the ogam stones in Wales is also true of the others: 'The language of the Ogam inscriptions is purely funerary, and is limited in the main to the use of the personal name, either simply or in various combinations.' Where the inscription consists of only one word, a personal name, this is in the genitive case and so must be interpreted as meaning something like 'the stone (or memorial) of . . .'. A stone from Jordanston (Pembrokeshire), for example, has, in ogam, only DOVAGNI, i.e. '(The stone of) Dovagnus' (though in this case, as in some others, the Latin version is a little fuller, viz. TIGERNACI DOBAGNI, i.e. '(The stone of) Tigernacus Dobagnus'). Among the longer inscriptions are:

(i)   (from Eglwys Cymyn, Carmarthenshire) (Nash-Williams 1950, 109):
      Irish: INIGENA CUNIGNI AUITTORIGES
      Latin: AVITORIA FILIA CUNIGNI
      i.e. 'Avitoria the daughter of Cunignus'

(ii) (from St Dogmaels, Pembrokeshire) (Nash-Williams 1950, 213):
      Irish: SAGRAGNI MAQI CUNATAMI
      Latin: SAGRANI FILI CVNOTAM1
      i.e. '(The stone of) Sagra(g)nus son of Cunotamus'

The amount of linguistic information to be culled from the ogam inscriptions is limited, but not negligible. As far as grammar goes, the inscriptions give us examples of the nominative and genitive cases but little else. The vocabulary, apart from the proper names, is restricted to such words (in the genitive) as MAQI 'son' (a number of instances), one example (quoted above) of INIGENA 'daughter', AV(V)I 'grandson' or 'descendant', together with MOSAC, 'a common-noun of unknown meaning rendered in the Latin [. . .] as PVVERI [i.e. "of the boy"]' (Jackson 1953, 171). Jackson makes shrewd use of these and other linguistic features of the inscriptions to argue convincingly that Irish remained as a spoken language in western Britain at least until the sixth or even the seventh century.

We now turn to the problem of identifying, at least approximately, the areas of southern Britain where the Irish in fact settled.

The earliest serious Irish raids seem to have been on south-west Wales, probably around AD 270–5. These incursions soon developed into something much more than raids, since there is evidence that, perhaps as early as the late third century, settlers from the Déisi tribe of Co. Waterford established a dynasty of Irish kings in south-west Wales, where they continued to rule until the tenth century. This does not of course necessarily imply either that the British population was driven out of the area or that British ceased to be spoken there.

From Dyfed, the Irish seem to have thrust further east, where they founded the tiny kingdom of Brycheiniog, whose name remains in that of the former county of Brecknock (in Welsh, Brycheiniog) (now forming the southern part of the county of Powys), and, in English only, in the name of its county town, Brecon (in Welsh, Aberhonddu). The ruling dynasty of Brycheiniog, claiming descent from an Irish prince, Broccán (or in Welsh, Brychan), and a Welsh princess, Marchell, lasted from the fifth to the tenth century. It is noteworthy that this area has a greater number of Irish inscriptions than any other part of Wales except the south-west (map 2).

Further south, although little is known from historical sources, it is generally agreed that Irish colonies were established in Cornwall and Devon. The existence of six ogam inscriptions in Cornwall and two in Devon, and the evidence provided by archaeological field-work, led Professor Charles Thomas to suggest (1973–4, 6) that Irish-speaking settlers reached the area in two waves, one affecting north-east Cornwall and part of west Devon from the late fifth century AD, and the other reaching west Cornwall and the Isles of Scilly in the following century.

That the Irish settled in North as well as in South Wales, though apparently much less densely, is indicated not only by the presence in that area of three Irish inscriptions but also by place-names that either make reference to the Irish or are of Irish origin:

> The peninsula of Caernarvonshire, and also Anglesey and West Merioneth, were settled by Irish about the same time as Dyfed, and the Irish language was spoken all over the area [. . .] and is deeply embedded in place-names. At the head of Afon Lledr in Caernarvonshire is *Llyn Iwerddon*, 'Lake of Ireland'. Lower down, near the falls of the Conway River is a hill or place called *Iwerddon* 'Ireland', and half-way between is *Dolwyddelan*, 'Gwyddelan's meadow', Gwyddelan being derived from *Gwyddel*, 'a Gael', an Irishman. [. . .] The Irish of Caernarvonshire, however, came apparently from further north than those of Dyfed, for the northern peninsula was known, and is still known today, by the name of *Lleyn*, from Irish *Laigin*, 'the Leinstermen', while the little village on Nevin Bay still bears the name *Porth Dinllaen*, 'the harbour of the fort of the Leinstermen'. (Dillon and Chadwick 1972, 40)

Specific reference to the presence of Irish settlers in north-west Wales is found in the ninth-century *Historia Brittonum* ('History of the Britons') by Nennius (who perhaps drew on seventh-century sources). According to Nennius, a force of Britons led by Cunedag (or, to give him the modern Welsh form of his name, Cunedda) moved from an area in south-east Scotland to north-west Wales to combat the Irish settlers in that area, and, according to Nennius (whose account may or may not be accurate), he succeeded in expelling them. It is not certain precisely when this migration took place, though a date around AD 400 seems probable.

That there was much contact of many kinds, peaceful (religious and commercial, for example) as well as hostile, between the various populations making up what has been called 'the Irish Sea province' is beyond all doubt, and its linguistic effects are to be found both in the numerous words of Welsh origin in Irish and in the Irish loan-words in Welsh. The latter include *brechdan* 'bread-and-butter, sandwich' (Old Irish *brechtán* 'bread-and-butter', now *breachtán*), *cerbyd* 'vehicle' (O. Ir. *carpat* 'war chariot', now *carbad*), *codwm* 'a fall' (Ir. *cutaim* 'a fall'), *cogor* 'to chatter' (O. Ir. *cocur* 'whisper', now *cogar*), *croesan* 'buffoon, jester' (O. Ir. *crossán* 'buffoon, jester'), *dengyn* 'grim, stubborn, inflexible' (O. Ir. *dangen* 'strong, firm', now *dáingean*), *dichell* 'trick, stratagem' (Mid. Ir. *dichell* 'concealment'), *tolc* 'dent' (Ir. *tolc* 'tear') (Lewis 1946, 82–4). A few Welsh place-names are also probably of Irish origin, including in particular a number of names of rivers and streams ending in *-ach* or *-an* (see R. J. Thomas 1938), such as *Clarach* (Ir. *claragh* 'level place') or *Desach* (which may perhaps include the name of the invading tribe of the Déisi).

How long did Irish remain as a spoken language in those western parts of this island where it is known to have been introduced? As far as North Wales is concerned, one cannot accept at its face value Nennius's statement that the Irish were totally expelled by Cunedda and his followers, which would have been about the year AD 400, since their inscriptions show that the Irish were still there, and still using Irish, as late as the sixth century. There are, however, only three such inscriptions in North Wales, and Charles Thomas may well be right in arguing (1972, 260) that this indicates not only that Irish settlements must have been 'far less intensive' and 'more localised' in that area than elsewhere but that they were 'more swiftly assimilated'. Jackson (1953, 171) regards it as certain, on the basis of the ogam inscriptions in Dyfed and of features of the spelling of various Irish names in the corresponding Latin inscriptions, that Irish was still spoken in south-west Wales in the second half of the sixth century and probably even in the seventh century. Similarly, the forms of Irish names occurring in Latin inscriptions in Devon and Cornwall suggest that, there too, Irish survived into the sixth and perhaps as late as the seventh century (ibid., 172). Charles Thomas's conclusion (1973–4, 6) is not much different:

> On the reasonable assumption that an inscription with an Irish name (in Ogam, or Roman letters) marks the grave of an Irish-speaker, and that where all inscriptions in a district are in Ogam this implies at least the adoption there of an Irish mode of commemoration, then we can state that there were Irish-speakers in north-east Cornwall and west Devon c. AD 500, and for some time afterwards.

There was presumably a period – perhaps a lengthy one – of bilingualism before Irish died out in the areas in question and the population of Irish or mixed Irish and British descent became absorbed into the British-speaking population.

What of Irish further north and, to begin with, in the north-west of England? The presence of Irish raiders was certainly felt there, perhaps as early as Roman times. But were there any Irish settlements? No Irish inscriptions are known in that area, but this in itself does not constitute proof that there were no such settlements. The existence of Irish place-names (though admittedly only a handful) in Cumberland – e.g. *Greysouthern* ('Suthan's cliff', from an Irish personal name and *craicc* 'crag, rock, cliff') and *Ravenglass* ('Glas's share', from the personal name *Glas* and Irish *rann* 'part, share') (Ekwall 1960, xxiii, 205, 381) – may perhaps suggest that Irish influence in that area could have amounted to something more lasting than coastal raids. But it would be dangerous to build too much on these, as it is not certain that these names can be attributed to Irish of the period we are at the moment interested in. An alternative explanation is that they are due to the influence of Scandinavians who crossed from Ireland to Cumberland in the tenth century. These Viking communities had become so far Celticized during their stay in Ireland that 'they had adopted the Irish method of forming compounds by placing the defining element last' (Reaney 1960, 69) as in such Cumberland names as *Dalemain* 'Máni's valley', *Gillcamban* 'Camban's ravine'. They also introduced at least one place-name element that they had themselves borrowed from Irish, viz. Old Norse *erg* 'shieling, hill pasture', from Irish *airghe*, which occurs in numerous place-names in north-west England, including the first syllables of *Arrowe*, *Argam*, *Arkholme*, and the final syllable of *Torva*, *Berrier*, and *Mozergh* (ibid., 98). So it is a not unreasonable assumption that 'what Gaelic influence there is on [English] place-names is due almost entirely to the immigration of Irish-Norwegian vikings into the north-west in the tenth century' (ibid.).

There remain to be mentioned the Isle of Man and Scotland.

The presence of six ogam inscriptions in Man is sufficient to indicate that Gaels arrived in the island not later than the fifth century and perhaps earlier. They found there a British-speaking population. However, whereas in Wales and south-western England the Irish-speaking community was eventually absorbed into the British-speaking population, here the reverse was the case. In Man, it was British that died out, and Gaelic that survived.

It was probably in the second half of the fifth century that the Gaels of Dálriada (in Antrim) crossed to Argyll where a new Dálriada in due course came into being. The Gaels of Scotland maintained close links and a community of language with their ancestral homeland in the north of Ireland and one can properly use the term 'Common Gaelic', or indeed 'Irish', with reference to the Gaelic speech of Ireland, Scotland and Man for a period of several centuries after the initial invasion. Jackson's conclusion (1951, 91–2) is that 'there is absolutely nothing to suggest that the Gaelic of Ireland, Scotland, and Man differed in any respect before the tenth century; and on the contrary, there is a body of decisive positive evidence tending to show that so far as we can tell they were identical', and that, though some difference between Western Gaelic (i.e. Irish) and Eastern Gaelic (i.e. Scottish and Manx Gaelic) began to appear in the tenth century, they 'continued to be one language, sharing many new developments in common, from the tenth until the thirteenth century'. And even after the separation from Irish in the thirteenth century, Scottish Gaelic and Manx continued for the most part to develop as one language until, probably, the fifteenth century.

The fortunes of the two branches of Eastern Gaelic are traced in the following chapters, devoted to Scottish Gaelic and Manx respectively.

Note

1   For a brief account of their views, see Thomas 1972, 253–4.

References

Chadwick, Nora K. 1964. *Celtic Britain*, 2nd impression, revised. London.
Dillon, Myles and Chadwick, Nora K. 1972. *The Celtic Realms*, 2nd edn. London.
Ekwall, E. 1960. *The Concise Oxford Dictionary of English Place-names*, 4th edn. Oxford.
Jackson, Kenneth 1950. Notes on the Ogam inscriptions of southern Britain. In Fox, Cyril and Dickins, Bruce (eds), *The Early Cultures of North-West Europe*, Cambridge, 199–213.
—— 1951. Common Gaelic. *Proceedings of the British Academy*, 37:71–97.
—— 1953. *Language and History in Early Britain. A Chronological Survey of the Brittonic Languages, 1st to 12th c. AD*. Edinburgh.
Lewis, Henry 1946. *Datblygiad yr Iaith Gymraeg* ('The Development of the Welsh Language'), 2nd edn. Cardiff.
Nash-Williams, V. E. 1950. *The Early Christian Monuments of Wales*. Cardiff.
Reaney, P. H. 1960. *The Origin of English Place Names*. London.

Thomas, C. 1972. The Irish settlements in post-Roman western Britain: a survey of the evidence. *Journal of the Royal Institution of Cornwall*, 6:251–75.

—— 1973–4. Irish colonists in south-west Britain. *World Archaeology*, 5:5–13.

Thomas, R. J. 1938. *Enwau Afonydd a Nentydd Cymru* ('Names of Rivers and Streams in Wales'). Cardiff.

4 Scottish Gaelic

Kenneth MacKinnon

Scottish Gaelic[1] is a Celtic language closely related to Irish (see chapter 2) and to Manx (see chapter 5). During the so-called 'Dark Ages', there was no substantial divergence between Old Irish and Early Scottish Gaelic, and throughout the Middle Ages, the two languages shared a common literary standard, sustained by hereditary literary orders and travelling bardic schools (Jackson 1951, Thomson 1968). Scottish Gaelic thus shares with Irish a rich and extensive ancient literature and strong common cultural roots. Modern Scottish Gaelic has developed a vigorous and distinctive poetic literature of its own, and by the late twentieth century has developed a small prose literature of some quality.

Scotland's linguistic history is complex. Its original inhabitants spoke a form of British (see chapter 6) – but the language of the Northern Picts is conjectural (see chapter 10). The Gaelic language originally came to Scotland c. AD 500 with the expansion of the northern Irish kingdom of Dàl Riata into the western Highlands and Islands of Scotland, as detailed by Bannerman (1974). The expansion of this settlement and the subsequent absorption of the Pictish kingdom in Northern Scotland, the British kingdom of Strathclyde in south-western Scotland and part of Anglian Northumbria in the south-east, established a largely Gaelic-speaking Scottish kingdom, largely coterminous with present-day Scotland, by the eleventh century. Celtic Christianity gained influence throughout this area with the coming of Columba from Derry to Iona in 563, and this missionizing Celtic Church first brought literacy and learning not only to the Gaelic Scots and their near neighbours but to most of England also (Green 1911, 43–8).

From the reign of Malcolm III 'Ceannmor' (1054–96), Gaelic lost its pre-eminence first at court, then amongst the aristocracy, to Norman French influences, and subsequently in the Lowlands through the establishment of English-speaking burghs in eastern and central Scotland, to Scots (see chapter 13). Displacing the British of Strathclyde and the Gaelic spoken further north, Scots became the language of state administration in late medieval and reformation Scotland, and of a vigorous renaissance culture (MacKinnon 1974, 19–29). In the Northern Highlands and Islands, Norse settlement brought about the development of the Norn language in Caithness and the Northern Isles (see chapter 14). By the eighteenth century Norn became extinct as a distinctive vernacular, but has strongly influenced both literary Scots and especially its northern dialects (Geipel 1971, 74–5). Gaelic continues as one of Scotland's living indigenous languages and, as a Celtic language, has been better able than has Scots to resist English influences in its speech forms.

There are of course many loan-words from English in Gaelic borrowed during the long period of contact between the two languages. Examples include *ad* 'hat', *barant(as)* 'warrant', *breacaist* 'breakfast', *brot* 'broth', *comhfhurtail* 'comfortable', *geata* 'gate', *mionaid* 'minute (of time)', *paidhir* 'pair', *rathad* 'road', *sràid* 'street', *targaid* 'target'. Some of these were originally Latin or Middle French words that entered Gaelic via English. Direct borrowings from Latin (or from Greek via Latin) include *airgiod* (from Latin *argentum*) 'silver, money', *crois* (Latin *crux*) 'cross', *Ifrinn* (Latin *infernum*) 'Hell', *feasgair* (Latin *vesper*) 'evening', and, from Greek via Latin, *aingeal* (Latin *angelus* from Greek *angelos*) 'angel', *eaglais* (Latin *ecclesia* from Greek *ekklesia*) 'church', *manach* (Latin *monachus* from Greek *monakhos*) 'monk'; the influence of the religious domain in giving rise to these is obvious. Substantial contact with Norse (see chapter 14) also led to a considerable number of borrowings, including *cuidh* (from Norse *kví*) 'enclosure', *faodhail* (Norse *vaðill*) 'ford, crossing', *sgalag* (Norse *skalkr*) 'lackey', *sgioba* (Norse *skip*) 'crew', *uinneag* (Norse *vindauga*) 'window'.

By the seventeenth century Gaelic had retreated to the Highlands and Hebrides, which still retained much of their political independence, Celtic culture and social structure. These differences came to be seen as inimical to the interests of the Scottish and the subsequent British state, and from the late fifteenth century into the eighteenth a number of acts of the Scottish and British Parliaments aimed at promoting English-language education first amongst the aristocracy and subsequently amongst the general population, at outlawing the native learned orders, and finally on disarming and breaking the clans and outlawing Highland dress and music.

In the nineteenth century, contemporaneously with the enforced migration of the crofting population in the notorious Highland Clearances, a popular and successful voluntary Gaelic Schools system came into being. This was superseded after legislation in 1872 by a national English-medium school system in which Gaelic had little if any place. The crofting community gained some security by legislation in 1886. Despite all adult males gaining the vote in 1867, and the development of local government in the 1880s and 1890s, recognition of Gaelic was very slow in coming.

The neglect of Gaelic in the education system after 1872 resulted in the language surviving as an oral rather than a literary medium for many of its speakers. The purpose of school was to promote English literacy. Thus traditional Gaelic literacy was associated with a religious culture which emphasized Bible reading, home worship and the singing of the Metrical Psalms. Calvinism has promoted Gaelic literacy, and in the strongholds of the Free Church and Free Presbyterian Church, adult Gaelic reading ability compares well with English reading ability. Where Protestantism, supportive education policies and high incidence of Gaelic-speakers combine, Gaelic literacy can be compared with English literacy levels, as in northern Skye, rural Lewis, Harris and North Uist. Gaelic literacy is lower in Catholic South Uist and Barra, as the religious culture has not emphasized the Gaelic scriptures as has Calvinism. This effect can also be shown as between Gaelic-speakers in mainland Catholic and Protestant areas (MacKinnon 1978, 65–7).

The recent development of Gaelic in education is further described below. Suffice it to say here that the twentieth-century history of Scottish Gaelic has been one of steady decline in numbers with few upturns. At the end of the nineteenth century there were over a quarter of a million speakers: 254,415 enumerated in the 1891 census. This had declined to 65,978 a century later in the 1991 census. In 1891, 88.5 per cent of all

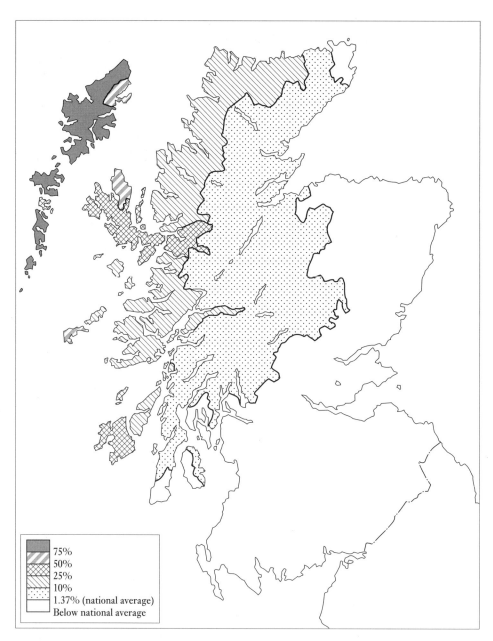

Map 3 *Scottish Gaelic in 1991. Map based on data provided by the General Register Office for Scotland's 1991 census of population. Percentages relate to the proportion of the usually resident population aged 3 and over recorded as Gaelic-speaking. The shaded areas are those that had a higher proportion of Gaelic-speakers than that for Scotland as a whole (i.e. 1.37%).*

Gaelic-speakers resided in the Highlands and Islands, a century later only 59.7 per cent. Migration has affected distribution patterns. Two world wars have greatly speeded the process. In the First World War there was great loss of life amongst the menfolk of the Highlands and Islands, and in the 1920s considerable emigration from the Hebrides. Since the mid-1970s there have been increasingly vigorous efforts to improve the position of Gaelic in education, the media, official and public life. At the same time the use of Gaelic is collapsing in its traditional domains: the family, neighbourhood life and the church. The problem now facing the language and its speakers is how to strengthen Gaelic in the family now that fewer than one Gaelic-speaker in three lives in a family where both parents or both of a married couple are Gaelic-speakers, or in local neighbourhoods where Gaelic is the majority language.

At the 1991 census the Scottish Gaelic speech community totalled 65,978. The Western Isles Islands Area was home to 19,546 of this total, Highland Region 14,713, and Argyll & Bute District 4,583. These areas, approximating to the traditional Gaidhealtachd, or Gaelic-speaking area, thus contained 38,842 – or about 59 per cent – of Scotland's Gaelic-speakers. Local native Gaelic-speakers, chiefly of the older generation, were still to be found in the western coastal areas of Highland Region and the western coasts and islands of Argyll & Bute District. There were also still some vestiges of native Gaelic in most parts of the mainland Highlands, even in highland Perthshire.

At the 1991 Census, 11,418 (17.3%) of all Gaelic-speakers lived in local neighbourhoods (census enumeration districts) which were 75% or more Gaelic-speaking; 17,943 (27.2%) in areas over 50%; 24,963 (37.8%) in areas over 25%; and 42,310 (64.4%) in areas above the national rate (1.37%). There is thus today an important and growing proportion of Gaelic-speakers resident in Lowland and urban areas. In 1991, 41% of Scotland's Gaelic-speakers lived within Lowland Scotland, 10,881 of them in the Central Clydeside conurbation in and around Glasgow. These trends are undoubtedly continuing and accelerating, through the 1990s. This implies that the concept of providing educational and cultural support for Gaelic only in the traditional 'Gaelic-speaking areas' has been well overtaken by events. Demands amongst young articulate city Gaels for Gaelic-medium education for their children were difficult to resist under the Conservative government's 'Parents' Charter', which was supposed to give parents some choice over their children's schooling. In 1985 two Gaelic-medium primary units commenced in Glasgow and Inverness. By 1999–2000 the number had grown to 59 throughout Scotland, with 1,831 pupils, and Gaelic-medium streams have proceeded to the secondary stage. By 1993 there were four such schools with pupils taking part of the curriculum through Gaelic, and by 1999 there were 13 schools with 232 Gaelic-stream pupils. These advances developed from a successful Gaelic playgroup movement, commencing in 1982 (Scammell 1985), and growing to 141 playgroups with over 2,500 children, within fifteen years.

All parts of the traditional Gaidhealtachd still had a proportion of Gaelic-speakers greater than the national average in 1981. But it could no longer be said, as it still sometimes is, that Scotland's Gaelic-speakers are to be found mainly in the Hebrides and north-west coastal fringes. Today, the majority are in fact to be found elsewhere in Scotland, resident in areas which could not be described in any sense as Gaelic in either present-day or recent historic character. This provides an acute problem for the future of the language. Contacts within the Gaelic speech community are particularly difficult. Within the islands, small populations are separated by the sea, and on the Highland mainland which is mountainous and deeply indented by the sea, communities are very much isolated from one another. The roles of the communications media and of local administration are thus particularly important in overcoming these difficulties.

The Western Isles council, now Comhairle nan Eilean Siar, has been a unitary local government authority since its inception in 1975. It has developed a bilingual administrative policy, conducting its affairs and deliberations in both languages, introducing Gaelic on to its public signs and notices, and greatly enhancing its position in education. Four other local authorities formulated bilingual policies and set up Gaelic committees between 1975 and 1996. These were Highland Region, Skye & Lochalsh District, Ross & Cromarty District, and Argyll & Bute District. Strathclyde Regional Council designated a councillor with responsibility for Gaelic. With the reformulation of Scottish local government into 32 unitary authorities in 1996 the position is now no longer clear and has already posed a threat to Gaelic-medium education.

The Gaelic speech community is on the whole an ageing sector of the population – but there have been some recent small ostensible increases in Gaelic-speaking abilities. Between the 1961 and 1971 censuses the number of persons speaking Gaelic increased by 10 per cent (from 80,978 to 88,892) – but this increase occurred entirely within Lowland Scotland. Between 1971 and 1981, numbers of Gaelic-speakers again declined (to 79,307) – but for the first time there were proportional and numerical increases of Gaelic-speakers in the Western Isles and parts of Skye (together with some other areas attracting oil-related industry, and suburban fringes of the larger cities) (MacKinnon 1991a, 122). In the Gaelic areas these general increases were the result of specific age-related increases amongst older children and young adults, producing a 'bulge' in the population profile. This was a feature not only of the most strongly Gaelic areas such as the Western Isles, but more generally of all areas with primary Gaelic teaching schemes. The population profile of Gaelic-speakers in the Lowland area, and of Highland areas where Gaelic had not featured in education, was greatly attenuated in the age-ranges of childhood and youth (MacKinnon 1987b; 1991b, 527–9).

In the 1991 census these encouraging developments received a setback. Numbers of Gaelic-speakers again declined overall, to 65,978, and the upturn amongst school-aged children and young people was checked. Although within areas such as Highland Region (which had pursued supportive Gaelic-medium primary provision) this trend had continued, in the Western Isles (which was the principal stronghold of the language) there was a considerable reduction in numbers of Gaelic-speaking children. In terms of usual resident population, the proportions of pre-school and school-aged children (3–15 years) speaking Gaelic in Highland Region increased from 4.2% (1,593 speakers) in 1971 to 4.8% (1,810 speakers) in 1981 and to 5.6% (1,988 speakers) in 1991. In the Western Isles the corresponding proportions were: 67.6% (4,396 speakers), 67.8% (4,385 speakers) and 49.5% (2,571 speakers) (General Register Office 1971, 1981, 1991, Census Small Area Statistics). The Gaelic language-loss amongst Western Isles children in the decade 1981–91 (from just over two-thirds to just under one-half of the total age-group) was the principal factor in reversing the trend of increase of speakers in this age-group nationally.

In 1981 there were within the Gaelic-speaking areas local neighbourhoods in which the proportion of young people (aged 5–24) speaking Gaelic matched or exceeded the proportion in the older age-ranges. These areas were thus potentially viable Gaelic communities, and comprised 30 of the 140 enumeration districts in the Western Isles (chiefly in western Lewis, southern Harris, the Uists and Barra) and nine of the 50 enumeration districts in Skye (chiefly in its northern and southern extremities) (Registrar General (Scotland) n.d.). Comparison with 1991 is not possible as the basis of local areas has changed, but the impression is clearly one of substantial contraction of areas where Gaelic is successfully maintained.

There is some evidence that in the most strongly Gaelic communities, supportive attitudes and usage of the language are less well represented amongst the younger women, as compared with other age and gender groups. There is also a definite differential migration of younger women as compared with younger men from the most strongly Gaelic areas (MacKinnon 1977, 1985, 1986, 1987a). Other research suggests that within the occupational continuum of Gaelic communities, Gaelic is best conserved within the semi-skilled agricultural group, which comprises the crofting 'core' of these communities. Supportive attitudes and Gaelic-speaking partners may be sought, but often it will be a non-Gaelic-speaking bride who is brought home. As the young women remaining within the community tend to be marginally less supportive of Gaelic, the prospects for intergenerational transmission of Gaelic are diminished.

The social distribution of Gaelic-speaking abilities also seems to be patterned by migration. The prospects for employment in professional, managerial, skilled non-manual and skilled manual occupations are limited within the Gaelic-speaking areas. Community leadership roles, which tend socially to be associated with these occupational categories, are in a sense exported to urban Lowland Scotland and elsewhere, and thus tend to diminish in the Gaelic home areas. The skilled occupational categories – especially the non-manual group – tend to be less supportive of Gaelic in usage and loyalty terms (MacKinnon 1985, 1988), but where new industry has attracted young, skilled and semi-skilled Gaelic-speakers back to the home areas to work, this has increased both the incidence of Gaelic (MacKinnon 1987a, 1991a) and its profile in the community (Prattis 1980).

Virtually all Gaelic-speakers are today functionally bilingual. Gaelic monolingualism is restricted to a handful of the most socially isolated old people and to pre-school infants. Code-switching and calquing are thus common – and often even engaged in for effect (MacAulay 1982). One of the chief influences of English upon Gaelic is in new terminology. (For example, English *satellite* has been rendered in Gaelic as *saideal* and *seat-belt* as *crios-sabhailte*.) In 1987 a database project was established at Sabhal Mor Ostaig, the Gaelic college in Skye. Such a development was long overdue as academic Celtic departments had tended to concentrate upon historical rather than contemporary lexicography. The Gaelic Department of the BBC has, however, always played a key and conscious role in this respect – and today many Gaelic neologisms in common use were first introduced in broadcasting.

Broadcasting is also a butt for controversies regarding Gaelic dialects and speech varieties. Mainland dialects are today moribund – especially the eastern dialects. Probably the largest dialect in numbers of speakers is that of Lewis, which has a somewhat 'sing-song' character often and easily parodied by speakers of other dialects (MacAulay 1978, Gleasure 1983). Listeners often state they resent dialects other than their own. Paradoxically, survey informants frequently claim that 'the proper Gaelic' is not spoken in their home area. Such reactions result from lack of exposure to alternative speech-varieties and perhaps to some image of 'pulpit Gaelic' or 'newsreaders' Gaelic' as in some way providing a standard variety. Both reactions probably result from deficiencies of the education system in insufficiently developing people's linguistic repertoire and awareness in Gaelic as compared with English.

Gaelic usage is typically diglossic, and its character has been studied in a number of Gaelic communities. In East Sutherland and Mull, where Gaelic is now almost extinct, Dorian (1981a, 112; 1981b) reported Gaelic being used in high domains (such as the church), and English in low domains (doubtless the family). In a study of a rapidly weakening Gaelic community in Mull, although not focusing on diglossia itself, Dorian also reported on the unfavourable reactions of non-Gaelic-speakers when Gaelic was used in mixed company to exclude non-speakers from a conversational exchange – and of its continuing value to Gaelic-speakers (Dorian 1981b, 171–2, 179–80).

Gaelic–English diglossia was studied in Harris in the early 1970s (MacKinnon 1977, 143–57), in Barra and Harris in the late 1970s (MacKinnon and MacDonald 1980, 91–100; MacKinnon 1985, 73), and in Skye and the Western Isles in the late 1980s (MacKinnon 1988). The general pattern emerging from these various studies seems to indicate that community usage of Gaelic may often stand up better than family usage – especially where children's schoolwork, peer-group and sibling exchanges are concerned. The religious domain is weakening and may not function much longer as the bulwark for the language that it once was. In strongly Gaelic communities Gaelic predominates in most work domains – especially crofting – and exchanges with older relations. Local post offices and shops can be pivotal domains for community usage, and where these have been taken over by non-Gaelic-speaking incomers (as in southern Skye) Gaelic may rapidly retreat to within the family.

Gaelic has a long-established literary tradition.[2] The remnants of the Irish bardic tradition survived until the mid-eighteenth century despite the attempts to ban the professional travelling bards through the Statutes of Iona in 1609. This was essentially an oral tradition, a highly formalized type of verse which tended towards elegy and eulogy of the chieftains who patronized these learned orders, poets and sometimes 'poetic dynasties', such as the MacMhuirich bardic family. The written literary tradition was until the fifteenth century or so common to Ireland and Scotland and used Common Classical Gaelic. From about this time there are signs of a Scottish vernacular coming into use, as evidenced particularly in the Book of the Dean of Lismore (1512–26), a manuscript anthology of verse from the fourteenth, fifteenth and sixteenth centuries containing bardic praise poetry, satire and Fenian ballads. Apart from verse there are various manuscripts from this period containing prose tales and clan-based historical accounts of events, and some legal documentation. As well as a move towards a Scottish vernacular Gaelic at this time, there is evidence that the bardic tradition was breaking down as different metres were used in songs and verse, and the poetic provenance is not so exclusive as non-professional bards began to come into prominence.

During the seventeenth century bards did not occupy the niche that they had previously, as the old order began to fragment. Poets such as Iain Lom (*c*.1625–1707 or later) and Mairi nighean Alasdair Ruaidh (*c*.1614–1707), and composers such as An Clarsair Dall (Ruairidh Mac Mhuirich) (*c*.1646–*c*.1725), however, still had a semi-official status within chieftains' houses. The range of subject matter incorporated traditional themes of praise, clan history and clan life as well as a wider commentary on national political events, particularly the Civil War.

The eighteenth century saw a burgeoning of Gaelic verse as poets described the inroads made into the 'way of life' in the Highlands and had more contact with English cultural mores which expanded their repertoires of form. The first printed book of secular poetry in Gaelic was published in 1751 by Alasdair mac Mhaighstir Alasdair (*c*.1695–*c*.1770).

It was during this century that the Gaelic literary world was brought on to a European stage with the publication in the 1760s of Macpherson's *Ossian*. This purported to be a translation of ancient manuscripts containing the Fenian tales. In fact it was a retelling, in Macpherson's own words, of various tales and songs imbibed from the oral tradition. Nevertheless it was a source of great interest to European writers and learned men, and despite its doubtful provenance was an instrumental source of the 'Celtic Twilight' movement which has so influenced perceptions towards Gaelic to the present day.

In the nineteenth century the preoccupation of many Gaelic poets concerned political events, particularly the Clearances. Donnchadh Bàn Macintyre (1724–1812), Mary MacPherson (Màiri Mhór nan Òran, 1821–98) and John Smith (Iain Mac a' Ghobhainn, 1848–81) composed verse describing the depopulation of their land, and many of their songs are still sung today. In fact the song and verse traditions are closely entwined in the Gaelic world. Until recently, there still existed a strong oral tradition through which tales and songs were passed from generation to generation. Remnants of Fenian lays and praise poetry from the sixteenth century have been recorded from singers in the 1950s in the Uists, singers who had heard the songs from their forebears.

The song tradition incorporated a wide repertoire from the formal bardic verse, including praise elegy and eulogies, as mentioned above, down to the more homespun comic and bawdy varieties celebrating village heroes and village events. Gaelic culture has had its fair share of women poets: the waulking song was essentially a work song with a strong choral refrain, used by women at work, for example, whilst waulking the cloth. Mouth music or *puirt-à-beul* was generally based upon melodies or dance tunes. In tandem with this are the incredibly complex and beautiful *pìobaireachd* 'the great tune', laments and other celebratory music, generally played on the bagpipe, and the haunting evocative psalms sung with the aid of a precentor in church. In the nineteenth century many 'homeland' songs were composed by those emigrating from Scotland. The oral tradition also incorporated historical events and genealogy, and many Gaelic-speakers living in the islands today know about local clearances and evictions through word of mouth. Until recently, some could trace their forebears back for eight or nine generations and knew kinship relations between themselves and other local people which stretched as far as sixth cousins.

There have been interesting developments in twentieth-century Gaelic poetry. Within the Gaidhealtachd there are still village bards who make verse and song out of local events and local people. The oral tradition as such has all but broken down today, but until the Second World War most villages had a *taigh céilidh* – a specific house in which people would gather to talk and sing. On a national dimension one of the foremost poets of contemporary Britain is Gaelic – Sorley MacLean (1911–96) – and he is read widely in translation even by non-Gaelic-speakers. The subject matter of his poetry has encompassed European events, particularly the Second World War and the Spanish Civil War, and such areas as urban poverty and decay as well as the traditional Gaelic themes of love, landscape, loss and homeland. Other notable poets who write in Gaelic now live outwith these areas, for example Donald MacAulay (1930–) and Derrick Thomson (1921–). Iain Crichton Smith (1928–98) wrote bilingually in English and Gaelic, as does Aonghas MacNeacail (1942–). Incorporating elements of traditional Gaelic subject matter as well as that from outside the Gaelic world, this poetry has been influenced in terms of rhyme and metre by developments in form and structure within poetry written in English. A number of poets writing in Gaelic are learners of the language, such as George Campbell Hay (1915–84), Meg Bateman (1959–), Rody Gorman (1960–) and Christopher Whyte (1952–).

A number of Gaelic periodicals were started – mainly by expatriate Gaels living in the Lowlands. Much of the writing of the late nineteenth and early twentieth centuries is associated with these Gaels, many of whom had settled in Glasgow and Clydeside and founded the various Highland and Island associations which exist there to this day. In 1891, An Comunn Gaidhealach ('The Highland Association'), an organization dedicated to the promotion of Gaelic, was formed. Since 1892, An Comunn has been responsible for organizing the annual National Mod, a festival of competitions for Gaelic singing, instrumental music, prose reading and drama. It has also been active in educational, publishing and cultural fields. With the appointment of a professional director in 1966, it involved itself in socio-economic issues and much more active political pressure on both central and local government. In the mid-1980s these roles in public life and education, together with youth work and the media, were taken up by a new organization, Comunn na Gaidhlig (CNAG), funded by the Highlands and Islands Development Board (HIDB), a governmental development agency (and now by its successor Highlands and Islands Enterprise and the Scottish Office). This left An Comunn with a purely cultural remit. In 1987 the Scottish Arts Council funded a National Gaelic Arts Project, which continues. In 1982 the HIDB both assisted the newly established Gaelic playgroups organization, Comhairle nan Sgoiltean Araich (CNSA), and helped to establish a Gaelic learners' organization, Comann an Luchd-Ionnsachaidh (CLÌ).

Since 1963 a government-assisted Gaelic Books Council has considerably stimulated Gaelic publishing. The first all-Gaelic magazine, *Gairm*, has appeared regularly since 1952, and has developed a publishing business. This was followed by a number of other ventures in Gaelic publishing, for example *Sruth*, a bilingual fortnightly paper in the late 1960s, a book club in the early 1970s (both now defunct), and most recently the Acair publishing house at Stornoway formed by a consortium chiefly for educational material, and chiefly in Gaelic. There are Gaelic features in local newspapers such as the *Oban Times*, *Inverness Courier*, *West Highland Free Press* and *Stornoway Gazette*, and in *The Scotsman*, a national daily.

The Conservative government produced official statements concerning Gaelic in 1985 and 1987 which went little beyond unspecific general support. However, the Scottish Office did provide an annual television fund for Gaelic of £9.5 million annually from 1992–3, and commenced a specific grants fund for Gaelic in education from 1986. The Labour government on taking office in May 1997 appointed a Minister of State with responsibility for Gaelic and announced new policies for the language later in the year. There are already some examples of central governmental official usage of Gaelic.

These developments must be understood in the context of Gaelic literacy. In 1991, 58.9 per cent of Scotland's 65,978 Gaelic-speakers claimed to read Gaelic, and 44.6 per cent to write it. The practice of writing Gaelic – even for personal letters – is very rarely undertaken, and amongst older Gaelic-speakers, and in areas where the language is not taught in the schools, writing ability is weak. Baker (1985, 22–40) has observed that in Wales higher levels of Welsh literacy associate significantly with language retention. There was census evidence in 1981 that this was also true for Gaelic; reading and writing levels correlated significantly with language maintenance in Skye and Western Isles enumeration districts (MacKinnon 1991a).

There is once again, after a considerable gap, a professional Gaelic theatre company, Tosg. Amateur Gaelic drama is vigorous and popular. With aid from the National Gaelic Arts Project, a children's theatre group, Ordag is Sgealbag ('Thumb and Forefinger'), commenced in the early 1990s. A Gaelic community film unit, Suil ('Eye'), in the 1970s developed into the Celtic Film Festival with headquarters now in Glasgow. In 1987 a professional Gaelic film and video unit was established in Lewis, Fradharc Ùr ('New Vision'), and is training young Gaels in film and video production. With the advent of the Gaelic television fund, a further 200 hours annually of Gaelic programming on ITV (in addition to the 100 hours on BBC) has stimulated new Gaelic television production companies.

The present pattern of BBC Gaelic radio, broadcasting on VHF under the banner Radio nan Gaidheal nationally, also provides services of a more local kind: in the outer islands and on the Highland mainland during the day, and nationally in the early evening. By the late 1990s Gaelic sound radio totalled 42 hours per week inclusive of schools' broadcasting.

The more vigorous local branches of An Comunn and self-help learners' groups provide Gaelic-medium social events in various places, such as Edinburgh and Dingwall where Gaelic cultural centres have been established.

Since 1882 it has been possible to take Gaelic as part of a university degree in Celtic, and the 1918 Education Act provided for Gaelic to be taught 'in Gaelic-speaking areas' – although these were not defined. The act was similarly unspecific as to whether instruction was to be through the medium of Gaelic, or merely of Gaelic as a specific subject.

Although there is no general provision for Gaelic in Scottish education, as there is for Welsh in Wales, by the mid-century some provision for Gaelic had been made by the Highland county education authorities, and from 1958 Gaelic was used as an initial teaching medium in the early primary stages in Gaelic-speaking areas, and it could be studied as an examination subject in parity with other languages at the secondary stage. Gaelic in education has undergone very rapid development since the late 1950s (MacKinnon 1987b, 1988, 1992). By the mid-1970s schemes for provision of Gaelic as a second language had been introduced in many Highland primary schools, and in the highland area of Tayside. With the establishment of the Western Isles Islands Area in 1975, an early development was the primary Bilingual Education Project (Mitchell et al. 1987). Highland Region implemented a similar policy in Skye a few years later. In 1985 the first Gaelic-medium primary units commenced in Glasgow and Inverness following parental pressure (MacIllechiar 1985), growing to 59 such units by 1999–2000. The development of Gaelic-medium secondary education was hindered first by the reluctance of Western Isles to extend its bilingual project in 1979, and by Her Majesty's Inspectors' report in 1994 declaring Gaelic-medium secondary education to be 'neither desirable nor feasible' (Scottish Office 1994, 3). Since 1982 there had been a very rapidly developing playgroups movement (Scammell 1985, MacKinnon 1992), growing to 144 groups by 1997 with over 2,500 children. In 1988 Highland Region established two

Gaelic-medium nursery schools, and by 1999–2000 the total number of education authority Gaelic nurseries had increased to 33, with 2,276 pupils.

Gaelic has thus featured in the school system in three distinct ways. In the Western Isles and Skye (and in some measure, Tiree) primary education is bilingual. Since 1958 Inverness-shire and Ross-shire had developed the use of Gaelic as an initial teaching medium in the early primary stage in the Gaelic areas. From 1975 the new Western Isles authority developed a pilot bilingual teaching project in 34 of its then 59 primary schools, which after 1981 was extended to almost every school as its general policy. A similar scheme has been adopted by Highland Region first for northern Skye, and subsequently extended to the whole island, covering all 20 primary schools.

Gaelic is also taught as a second language elsewhere. In all these cases, Gaelic primary teaching schemes (whether bilingual or second-language) seemed in the 1981 census to have had some stabilizing effect upon the speech community and to have enhanced the local profile of the language (MacKinnon 1984b, 1987b). Gaelic is also taught as a second language in about 40 secondary schools in these areas, and in three others in Lowland areas.

The third type of schooling is Gaelic-medium education, as noted above. Teacher supply is a problem. In 1994 a report by Her Majesty's Inspectors of Schools for the Scottish Office observed that 'availability of teachers of quality [. . .] will be a continuing obstacle' (Scottish Office 1994, 1.12, p. 3). The demands for Gaelic-medium education, and the willingness of education authorities to provide it, have been hampered by shortage of qualified teachers. There is still officially no proper concept of qualification to teach other subjects through Gaelic. By the late 1990s this was still unmet and unresolved by either the Central Committee on the Curriculum or the General Teachers' Council. Thus with developing demand for Gaelic education, a crisis of supply of teachers of Gaelic and teachers trained to use Gaelic as a medium is already upon us, and impedes development.

The increasing demands for Gaelic in education have already been noted – together with the incipient threat of a crisis in teacher supply. Education has proved to be a most fruitful field for language conservation and enhancement. Gaelic education today certainly clearly calls for the creation of system, and some degree of co-ordination has come through the establishment of an Inter-Authority Special Grants co-ordinating committee (IASG). Career development, movement around the system, initial and in-service training are agenda priorities. Curriculum development has received attention and a national resource centre has been established in Lewis. At Sabhal Mor Ostaig, a Gaelic Affairs Research Unit, Lèirsinn, was established in 1992.

There are five terrestrial and over twenty satellite television channels currently broadcasting in Scotland. However, Gaelic programming totalled only 475 hours in 1996–7. BBC radio has five channels plus Radio Scotland – and although broadcasting time for Gaelic has greatly improved we are still far away from a dedicated all-day Gaelic radio channel. This was half-promised in 1985, and is now long overdue. The advent of digital broadcasting presents a challenge and an opportunity for Gaelic.

These demands in education and the media are reminders that there is as yet no coherent national policy for language in general – nor for Gaelic in particular. If a 'national curriculum' is to be developed for Scottish education there is a danger that Gaelic will be marginalized along with much else into the minority time available for 'other studies' rather than be included in the curricular 'core', as has been conceded for

Welsh in Wales. The chance to formulate a national language policy involving English, 'modern', indigenous and 'indigenizing' minority languages in the curricular core has been missed.

The most urgent need for the future of the language may, however, lie in the domains of family and community life. The demographic processes which have weakened the language in these fields have been illustrated in recent research surveys. Between 1985 and 1988 the Economic and Social Research Council funded a 'Language Maintenance and Viability Survey' in Skye and the Western Isles (MacKinnon and Macaulay, ESRC: GOO 23 23 28)[3] which drew attention to intergenerational decline of use of Gaelic in the home (MacKinnon 1988, 1991a, 1994). Almost a decade later in 1994–5 the Euromosaic Project funded the first national sample survey of Gaelic usage throughout Scotland. With very similar methodology and questions, its findings suggested that the continued weakness of Gaelic usage intergenerationally was gathering momentum. Compared to use of Gaelic to and between grandparents and parents in previous generations, the use of Gaelic 'always' or 'mainly' by parents to children and between children themselves was minimal. In the community, use of Gaelic, whilst standing up to some extent amongst neighbours and in pubs, was declining drastically in shopping and at church. The problem for Gaelic and its language-planners is how to supplement and reverse these declines. Unless tackled promptly and effectively, the prospect of Gaelic continuing as a family and a community language is likely to cease with the present generation.

Although the political climate is one of economy, there is now a vitality about Gaelic issues and Gaelic culture in Scotland. Great strides have been made in creating infrastructure for the language in education, the media and the arts. Gaeldom has successfully seized and pressed its opportunities. Analysis of recent censuses has indicated for Gaelic that even at its 'eleventh hour' there still exists the possibility of a future for the Gaelic speech community. At the most recent census there were still 'green shoots' wherever successful educational and cultural policies had been pursued. The opportunity is still there – but it requires some vision and courage to exploit it. Without them we may have fine vestments for the language but clothing an invisible body of speakers.

Notes

1   Thanks are due to Hatfield Polytechnic (now University of Hertfordshire), and to Euromosaic Project (at the University of Wales, Bangor) for support on the projects referred to. Likewise grants from SSRC (HR 4039/1, 1976–8) and the ESRC (GOO 23 23 28, 1985–8) are acknowledged with thanks. I also wish to thank personally research colleagues working on these projects, especially Morag MacDonald (now MacNeil) and Cathlin Macaulay (see also note 2 below), and the many part-time workers and respondents.

  Permission to use census material and small area statistics (RSAS 1971, SAS 1981, LBS 1991) supplied by General Register Office (Scotland) is acknowledged with thanks.

2   I am particularly grateful to Cathlin Macaulay who has supplied the following survey of Gaelic literature.

3   This was an Economic and Social Research Council research project undertaken by Kenneth MacKinnon and Cathlin Macaulay and reported on in MacKinnon 1988.

References

Baker, Colin 1985. *Aspects of Bilingualism in Wales*. Clevedon.

Bannerman, John 1974. *Studies in the History of Dalriada*. Edinburgh.

Dorian, Nancy C. 1981a. *Language Death. The Life Cycle of a Scottish Gaelic Dialect*. Philadelphia.

——1981b. The valuation of Gaelic by different mother tongue groups resident in the Highlands. *Scottish Gaelic Studies*, 13:169–82.

Geipel, John 1971. *The Viking Legacy: The Scandinavian Influence on the English and Gaelic Languages*. Newton Abbot.

General Register Office 1971. *Census 1971 Scotland. Reformatted Small Area Statistics* (Table 40, p. 9). Edinburgh.

——1981. *Census 1981 Scotland. Small Area Statistics* (Table 40, p. 9). Edinburgh.

——1991. *Census 1991 Scotland. Local Base Statistics* (Table L67S). Edinburgh.

Gleasure, J. W. 1983. Gaelic: dialects, principal divisions. In Thomson, Derick S. (ed.), *The Companion to Gaelic Scotland*, Oxford, 91–5.

Green, Alice Stopford 1911. *Irish Nationality*. London.

Hulbert, John (ed.) 1985. *Gaelic: Looking to the Future*. Longforgan, Dundee.

Jackson, K. H. 1951. Common Gaelic. *Proceedings of the British Academy*, 37:71–97.

MacAulay, D. 1978. Intra-dialectal variation as an area of Gaelic linguistic research. *Scottish Gaelic Studies*, 13:81–97.

——1982. Borrow, calque and switch: the law of the English frontier. In Anderson, John (ed.), *Language Form and Linguistic Variation*, Amsterdam, 203–37.

MacIllechiar, I. 1985. Gaelic-medium schools – why? and when? In Hulbert 1985, 28–33.

MacKinnon, Kenneth 1974. *The Lion's Tongue*. Inverness.

——1977. *Language, Education and Social Processes in a Gaelic Community*. London.

——1978. *Gaelic in Scotland 1971: Some Sociological and Demographic Considerations of the Census Report for Gaelic*. Hatfield.

——1984a. *Gaelic in Highland Region – the 1981 Census*. Inverness.

——1984b. *Gaelic Language Regeneration amongst Young People in Scotland 1971–1981 from Census Data*. Hatfield.

——1985. The Scottish Gaelic speech-community – some social perspectives. *Scottish Language*, 5:65–84.

——1986. Gender, occupational and educational factors in Gaelic language-shift and regeneration. In Mac Eoin, Gearóid, Ahlqvist, Anders and Ó hAodha, Donncha (eds), *Third International Conference on Minority Languages: Celtic Papers*, Clevedon, 47–71.

——1987a. *Occupation, Migration and Language-Maintenance in Gaelic Communities* (paper to Ninth International Seminar on Marginal Regions, Skye, 5–11 June 1987). Hatfield.

——1987b. *The Present Position of Gaelic in Scottish Primary Education*. Leeuwarden.

——1988. *Language-Maintenance and Viability in the Scottish Gaelic Speech-Community* (Report to Economic and Social Research Council). Hatfield.

——1991a. Language retreat and regeneration in the present-day Scottish Gaidhealtachd. In Williams, Colin H. (ed.), *Linguistic Minorities, Society and Territory*, Clevedon, 121–49.

——1991b. Language-maintenance and viability in contemporary Gaelic communities: Skye and the Western Isles today. In Ureland, P. Sture and Broderick, G. (eds), *Language Contact in the British Isles*, Tübingen, 496–534.

——1992. *An Aghaidh nan Creag: Despite Adversity – Gaeldom's Twentieth Century Survival and Potential*. Inverness.

——1994. Gaelic language-use in the Western Isles. In Fenton, A. and MacDonald, D. A. (eds), *Studies in Scots and Gaelic: Proceedings of the Third International Conference on the Languages of Scotland*, Edinburgh, 123–37.

——and MacDonald, M. 1980. *Ethnic Communities: The Transmission of Language and Culture in Harris and Barra* (Report to the Social Science Research Council). Hatfield.

Mitchell, R., McIntyre, D., MacDonald, M. and McLennan, S. 1987. *Report of an Independent Evaluation of the Western Isles Bilingual Education Project*. Stirling.

Prattis, J. I. 1980. Industrialisation and minority-language loyalty: the example of Lewis. In Haugen, E., McClure, J. D. and Thomson, D. S. (eds), *Minority Languages Today*, Edinburgh, 21–31.

Registrar General (Scotland) 1983. *Census 1981 Scotland, Gaelic Report*. Edinburgh.

——(n.d.) Additional tables for Scotland. Table 40: Gaelic language. In *Census 1981. Small Area Statistics*, *SASPAC*, p. 22.

Scammell, K. 1985. Pre-school playgroups. In Hulbert 1985, 21–7.

Scottish Office 1994. *Provision for Gaelic Education in Scotland*. Edinburgh.

Thomson, D. S. 1968. Gaelic learned orders and literati in medieval Scotland. *Scottish Studies*, 12:57–78.

5 Manx

Robert L. Thomson

The Manx language, the Celtic language of the Isle of Man, situated in the middle of the north Irish Sea (once more appropriately known as *muir Manann* 'the sea of Man'), is one of the languages which surfaced as a by-product of the Renaissance and the Reformation.

Before this, the silence is so complete that there is disagreement even over the language's affiliation, whether to the Brythonic or the Goidelic branch of the Celtic group. During this dark age, extending from at least the beginning of the Christian era to the early sixteenth century, the evidence is so slight or so uncertain that it is perhaps safer to speak of the 'languages of Man', without presuming to decide whether there was one or more than one at any given date, and if so which, and on what terms they co-existed.

It is a reasonable guess based on the situation of the island, surrounded as it was in the first centuries of the Christian era on three sides by the Brythonic-speakers of south-west Scotland, of Cumbria, and of north Wales, that Man was first settled (as far as the Celts were concerned, and we know nothing of the languages of earlier peoples) from one or more of these areas. The evidence is slight, consisting of an inscription at Knock-y-Doonee, dated *c*.500, commemorating in Latin letters one Ambicatus son of Rocatus. The names are Celtic but the inscription is intended to be Latin, for 'son' is *filius*, and the use of Latin points to Christianity from Britain having reached Man. The same conclusion may be drawn from the slightly later commemoration of Avitus in Latin at Santan. The Knock-y-Doonee inscription, however, is a bilingual one bearing the same information in Goidelic Celtic written in ogam, *Imbicatōs maqi Rocatōs* '(the stone) of Imbicatus son of Rocatus', the same names in their pre-Irish form.

Jackson concluded (1950, 210): 'The existence of the two forms here implies a bilingual population, speaking both Irish and British, able to give the two equivalents of a name, the British giving evidence that the language was a spoken one in process of evolution. This is a valuable linguistic proof of the existence of a British-speaking population in the Isle of Man in the Dark Ages.' In his 'Common Gaelic' lecture, Jackson adds (1951, 78): 'I think it likely that this language [i.e. Gaelic] had been brought to Man in or about the fourth century from Ireland, exactly as it was brought, about the same time, to Scotland and to parts of Wales and Cornwall.'

Later indications, with varying degrees of authority, point (but less clearly) in the same direction, that Brythonic was the first Celtic language to reach Man. One such is the ninth-century inscription CRUX GURIAT to which Jackson draws attention (1950, 210, n. 1); Gwriad and others of his family were indeed connected with Man as well as

North Wales, but even Welsh suzerainty would not necessarily mean the inhabitants of Man were Welsh-speaking. Bede (see Plummer 1896, II.9), a century earlier and writing of an expedition of the Northumbrian King Edwin early in the seventh century to assert his overlordship of Anglesey and Man, links them together as 'Mevanian' or perhaps better 'Menavian' Isles and describes them as 'islands of the Britons'. As regards Man, this may be a political rather than a linguistic comment, and Bede is not likely to have had any information from his Anglian sources about language.

Another indication occurs in a story relating to the time of St Patrick (fifth century) preserved in the information about the life of the saint collected by Muirchú (*c.*700) (Bieler 1979, 102–7). A northern Irish brigand named Maccuill (who is apparently to be identified with St Maughold, though there are phonological difficulties) was condemned for his offences against Patrick to be set adrift in a boat without oars or food. He landed in Man, and found there two bishops who had come to the island to convert the inhabitants. He assisted them and eventually succeeded them in office. Their names are given as Conindrus and Romulus. The first of these appears to be a Latinization of the Welsh name Cynidr (and there is a Llangynidr in Powys), while the second is a good Latin name such as is to be found among British Christians (as was the case of Patrick himself, his father Calpurnius, and his grandfather Potitus). The two bishops seem likely to have come from Britain, and the implication *may* be that Man offered them a promising field for evangelism, free from linguistic barriers because it was Brythonic in speech. (On the other hand, of course, Maccuill may have been of assistance to them precisely because the island was wholly or partially Gaelic in speech.)

In favour of an early Gaelic settlement and possibly a consequential predominance of Goidelic speech in Man, we may cite first the historian Orosius (early fifth century) who says that, like Ireland, Man was inhabited by the Scotti, i.e. the people later known as the Irish, who, as noticed earlier, expanded into Britain and most successfully into Scotland, to which their name has been transplanted. If Orosius is correct, he confirms the conclusion drawn from the Knock-y-Doonee inscription, but the date of his information is unknown and so does not enable us to decide whether the Brythonic or the Goidelic form of Celtic was established in Man first.

Only a few years later than Edwin's expedition to Man and Anglesey a story is told about a visit to Man by Senchán Torpéist, chief poet of Ireland, whose death is recorded in 647. The account is preserved in *Cormac's Glossary* in the ninth century, and the incident is paralleled by one in the late Middle Irish saga *Tromdámh Guaire*. The visitors were challenged on landing in Man, and had to prove the truth of their claim to be poets by extemporizing verses to match those of the challenger. The story takes it for granted that the population of Man was Gaelic-speaking, though this is not a proof that it was so in the seventh century (when Bede tells us that the two islands belonged to the Britons), or even in the ninth when Cormac was writing.

A new linguistic element is introduced by the advent of Norse raiders into the Irish Sea area about the end of the eighth century and their settlement in Man a century later. The date of their first appearance in the British Isles is recorded by the annals as the arrival of three vessels from Norway in the time of King Beorhtric of Wessex (*Anglo-Saxon Chronicle*, 787) who died in 800. The *Annals of Ulster* are more precise, recording a general devastation of all the islands of Britain in 794, but Man is not mentioned by name at this period, though it can scarcely have escaped the notice of the Norsemen.

The Norse political connection in Man lasted from the ninth century to the early thirteenth. It is unlikely, however, that Norse ever became the only language used in Man. The Norsemen had reached the Irish Sea by a gradual movement southward via Orkney and Shetland, where their language did establish itself, through the Hebrides where they encountered the northern fringe of the Gaelic world, and where they also settled and intermarried and became bilingual. As a consequence, when they reached the Irish Sea and founded trading stations around the Irish coast and penetrated the north-west of England to join up with the Norse kingdom of York, some already had some acquaintance with the language of Man and with the language of Ireland, while the Anglian dialects of English were similar enough to their Norse speech to make communication possible and gave rise eventually to a linguistic compromise between the two.

For the period from 1016 to 1316, the *Chronicle of the Kings of Man and the Isles* (Broderick 1996), probably written at Rushen Abbey which was founded in 1134, gives some account of Manx affairs, though not of the language for the chronicle was kept in Latin according to the custom of the time. The other source of information for the Norse period is the collection of stone crosses with inscriptions in the runic script and the Norse language associated with it (see figure 2 in chapter 14).

The *Chronicle* provides two kinds of information, indirectly, about the language(s) of the island. We find confirmation for the assumption of a bilingual society in the fact that, though the Norse rulers remained loyal to the language of their ancestors, it was not unknown for them also to have Gaelic by-names. Godred I (1079–95) is referred to as Godred Crovan 'the white-handed', and a later Godred, who was slain in Lewis in 1231, was known as Godred Don 'the brown-haired', while Olaf II (died 1237) is called in an English official document Olaf Duf 'the black-haired'.

That they were not ignorant of the Irish language or incapable of appreciating its literary forms is suggested by the existence of an anonymous Irish poem of *c*.1200, in praise of Reginald I (Gaelic Raghnall) who died in 1229. The poet would hardly have gone to the trouble of paying a visit to Man unless he had good reason to expect a welcome for his praise and an appropriate reward.

A similar conclusion may be drawn from the Manx surnames, which are of the patronymic type (Kneen 1937, 289, 290–1). By the time we have lists of (male) names of members of the legislature and tenants of the Lord of Man (in the fifteenth century), the range of forenames is severely restricted but the variety of forenames of the ancestors which appears in the patronymics is very wide indeed, mainly Gaelic but including a number of Norse personal names. In both languages, most if not all of these forenames survive only in the formation of patronymic surnames.

Secondly, the *Chronicle* contains as an appendix of uncertain date a list of place-names, the boundaries of the lands of Rushen Abbey, which may be extracted from the original foundation charter of 1134, though the writing has been dated to *c*.1280. The place-names recorded in the boundaries of the monastic properties are sometimes difficult to analyse but there is usually an element which can be recognized as Gaelic or Norse (Broderick 1996, f.53r–54v). A few were sufficiently transparent for the notary to turn them into Latin so that we cannot be quite sure what they were called in the vernacular, since we do not know whether he was a Norse- or a Gaelic-speaker. Others show the vocabulary of one language but the syntax of another, the so-called 'inversion compounds', with Norse elements in Gaelic word-order, implying the co-existence and mutual influence of the two languages. Because of the absence of certainty about a number of the names it is difficult to calculate the proportion belonging to each language, and in any case the figure would seem to vary from one estate to another, but there is at least a certainty that both languages are represented, with at least a probability that the Gaelic elements are as old as, if not older than, the Norse.

A peculiarity of the transmission of these Norse place-names to modern times is that they appear for the most part to be quite unaffected by any Gaelic pronunciation, differing in this respect very markedly from the Norse place-names of Gaelic Scotland. The explanation appears to be the influence of 'the language of record'. The Stanleys from the beginning of the fifteenth century, and possibly other feudal lords before them, drew their soldiers, servants and administrators from the north of England where Norse had also left its mark on the language, and place-names of Norse origin were already familiar to them. Keeping their records in English, it would be natural for them to prefer the familiar to the Gaelicized versions of names, and to use them and by using them perpetuate them as the 'official' versions, as opposed to the pronunciation of the natives. An example to the contrary is the mountain name Barrule, which appears in the monastic bounds as *Worzefel*, later *Warthfel*, and would probably have ended as **Wardfell*. The Gaelicized name treats the initial *w* as the lenition of *b*, which is therefore 'restored', turns *f* into its voiced equivalent *v*, vocalizes it to produce from *fell* a syllable [u:l], which being long attracts the stress and so produces the surviving form, Barrule or Barooyl. Snaefell, on the other hand, produced a Gaelicized form *Shniaul* by a similar treatment of the *-fell* element but this was not taken into official use and the name was even further Anglicized at one time to *Snowfield*.

The belief that Man was predominantly or wholly Norse-speaking down to the end of the thirteenth century is difficult to maintain against the evidence that Gaelic flourished during this period, and perhaps least of all sustainable in view of the very small deposit of Norse loan-words in the general vocabulary of the Manx language.

As regards the epigraphic evidence during the Norse period, the language is Norse but the same inscription may contain both Norse and Gaelic personal names. This may be taken in either of two ways: either it confirms the co-existence of two linguistic communities with proof of their intermarriage, or it witnesses to the Norse having earlier intermarried in Gaelic-speaking territory, possibly before they reached Man, and having adopted Gaelic names (perhaps along with Christianity) from the mothers' families. And, of course, both alternatives may be true.

A third source of information from this period proves a disappointment in the form in which it has survived (Cheney 1984). Bishops of Man promulgated groups of synodal statutes in 1229, 1291 and 1350, and on the second and third of these occasions provision is made for instructing the laity in the form of emergency baptism and for teaching the Apostles' Creed, in each case in the mother tongue. Unfortunately, the vernacular is named in neither place, nor is any vernacular version given. No doubt both would have seemed superfluous at the time, but an opportunity was missed of extending the written existence of Manx by two centuries at least. It can scarcely be doubted, however, that by 1350, if not by 1291, the vernacular was Gaelic.

The Norse period, i.e. the period during which Man was part of a Norse 'empire', came to an end after the battle of Largs (1263), and by the Treaty of Perth (1266) Man and all the islands of the Hebrides were ceded to Alexander III of Scotland. The end of the Norse period is overlapped by the acquisition of the lordship of Ireland by Henry II of England with the agreement of Popes Adrian IV (an Englishman) and Alexander

III on the pretext of reforming the Irish church and civilizing the people. Henry visited Ireland in 1171 and introduced the feudal system, a concept hitherto unknown to the Irish, and gave grants of land to Norman adventurers who had learned the art of war in Wales, leaving it to the grantees to make good their title by force of arms. While this change of suzerainty was not aimed at Man, it affected the island in two ways: it marked the beginning of the introduction of French and particularly Norman French words into Irish and Gaelic generally, as it was already doing into Welsh, and secondly it created some political ties between Man and the Normans who acquired lands in the north-east of Ireland. These were not slow to form alliances with the Viking settlers in Ireland and Man to assist them in fighting the Irish. The *Chronicle* records in 1176 that John de Courcy subjugated Ulster (in fact only a small part of the province), but under King John he was driven out and took refuge in Man with Reginald I, his father-in-law, with whose assistance he attempted the following year to recover his lands, but was defeated and never returned to Ireland. It is, of course, unlikely that Norman French elements came directly into Manx at this early date; more probably we should think of their being acquired gradually as they began to circulate in the Gaelic area as a whole. It is also to be remembered that relatively few of them show specifically Norman characteristics, and therefore some at least of the rest may have found their way into Manx from English which absorbed a very large French element, both Norman and Central French, in the medieval period.

The Scottish sovereignty of Man was not of long duration, hardly extending beyond the reign of Alexander III who left no obvious male heir. The choice of successor among his remoter kindred was referred to Edward I of England, who finally chose John Baliol as King of Scots in 1292. After Baliol's abdication in 1296, the island was occupied by Edward I and held from the English crown (1298–1310) by Antony Bek, Bishop of Durham, who had been the king's agent for Scottish and Norwegian affairs, and by others of less note, on various terms, during the remainder of the fourteenth century, with a brief reversion to Scottish possession between 1313 and 1333, inaugurated by Robert the Bruce, King of Scots, landing at Ramsey and taking Castle Rushen, the seat of government.

The fact that there is no record of Manx from its beginning till the sixteenth century means that we have no contemporary materials for tracing its development through the stages comparable with Old, Middle and Early Modern Irish at the level of morphology by seeing the changes in the forms of words taking place period by period. The same may be said of Scottish Gaelic in the main, since literary composition in Gaelic in Scotland, primarily in verse, adhered to traditional forms as current in contemporary Irish. To judge from the morphology of Manx when it appears in 1610, it was already less conservative than Irish. With regard to pronunciation, it stood at a considerable distance from both Irish and Scottish Gaelic, though this, of course, is harder to quantify or even to describe with certainty, especially as Manx came to be written in a different orthography from the traditional Gaelic one. Its syntax is probably somewhat less varied and, to give a particular example, the tendency to a decline in the variety of the forms of the copula and in the frequency of their use is greater than in Irish, and had probably set in quite early.

In his 'Common Gaelic' lecture (1951), Jackson deduced from the written record of the members of the Gaelic family of languages that there had been no observable major changes that were not common to all the members of the family before the thirteenth century. After this point he detected a split between East and West Gaelic, i.e. between Scottish Gaelic and Manx on the one hand and Irish on the other. Subsequently, while remaining substantially closer to each other than either of them was to Irish, Scottish Gaelic and Manx went on to develop further lesser differences between themselves. To quote the concluding summary of the lecture (1951, 91–2):

> There is absolutely nothing to suggest that the Gaelic of Ireland, Scotland, and Man differed in any respect before the tenth century. [. . .] Eastern and Western Gaelic continued to be one language, sharing many new developments in common, from the tenth until the thirteenth century. [. . .] The final break between East and West in the spoken tongue came in the thirteenth century, after which neither shared new creations with the other except by independent coincidence. In the thirteenth and fourteenth centuries and possibly later, Scottish Gaelic and Manx continued for the most part to grow as one single language; but probably by the fifteenth century and demonstrably by the sixteenth they had at last become separated.

(We may note the coincidence in 'by the fifteenth century' and the series of Anglo-Norman feudal lords culminating in the Stanleys in 1405.)

Manx retains the special features common to the Celtic languages, though sometimes in an attenuated form. These include the mutation of initial consonants, the combination of prepositions with personal pronouns in a single word, and a preference for the word-order Verb + Subject (+ Object). It shares with Scottish Gaelic (and with Welsh, a feature which has given rise to the suggestion that this is the product of a Brythonic substratum in East Gaelic) the shift of the present tense into future meaning, with the concomitant creation of a periphrastic present with the auxiliary 'to be'. Manx, however, goes further than Scottish Gaelic in this remodelling of the verb, and also creates a periphrastic form with the auxiliary 'to do', in parallel with the inflected future, conditional and preterite tenses and the imperative. In the Manx of the last generation or so of native speakers, this periphrasis with 'do' had almost entirely ousted the inflected tenses.

As regards vocabulary, the least stable part of language, the external influences already noted, together with the Latin in which Christianity was introduced, left their mark on the language. A few illustrations, in chronological order, will illustrate the result:

From Latin: *agglish* 'church', *annym* 'soul', *aspick* 'bishop', *bannaght* 'blessing', *cainle* 'candle', *credjal* '(to) believe', *doonagh(t)* 'Sunday', *feailley* 'festival', *gloyr* 'glory', *jouyl* 'devil', *keeill* 'cell, chapel', *lhaih* '(to) read', *lioar* 'book', *mollaght* 'curse', *mwylin* 'mill', *obbyr* 'work', *padjer* 'prayer', *peccah* 'sin', *pobble* 'people', *saggyrt* 'priest', *screeu* '(to) write', *side* 'arrow', *soalt* 'barn', *soost* 'flail', *Trinaid* 'Trinity'.

From Norse (omitting those that may have come through northern English): *aker* 'anchor', *baatey* 'boat', *baie* 'bay', *beck* 'bench', *brod* 'goad', *clet* 'standing rock at sea', *garey* 'enclosure, garden', *giau* 'ravine in cliffs', *leigh* 'law', *margey* 'market, fair', *naboo* 'neighbour', *ping* 'penny', *ronsaghey* '(to) search', *sker* 'reef', *uinnag* 'window'.

From French (Norman or other): *ashoon* 'nation', *barrant* 'trust', *cashtal* 'castle', *conaant* 'condition, covenant', *corneil* 'corner', *danjeyr* 'danger', *daunsin* '(to) dance', *eirey* 'heir', *foayr* 'favour', *greeishyn* 'stairs', *jinnair* 'dinner', *livrey* '(to) deliver', *ooill* 'oil', *paitchey* 'child', *resoon* 'reason', *sauail* '(to) save', *shamyr* 'room', *sharvaant* 'servant', *shirveish* 'service', *spooilley* '(to) despoil', *streeu* 'strife', *stroie* '(to) destroy', *surranse* '(to) suffer', *tooilleil* '(to) toil', *troailt* 'travel, travail', *vondeish* 'advantage'.

From English, of various origins and periods: *ansoor* 'answer', *boayrd* 'table', *coau* 'chaff', *crout* 'craft', *cront* 'knot (in timber)', *farling* 'farthing', *gamman* 'game', *giat* 'gate', *gioot* 'gift', *kiarail* 'care', *laccal* '(to) want', *lhiettal* '(to) prevent', *mayle* 'rent', *naim* 'uncle', *oaseir* 'overseer', *pabyr* 'paper', *pohlldal* '(to) uphold', *pollal* '(to) prune', *pundail* '(to) impound', *punt* 'pound', *saaue* 'saw', *shickyr* 'sure', *sneg* 'latch', *stampey* '(to) tread', *stowal* '(to) bestow', *voalley* 'wall'.

In one respect, and that the most obvious, namely orthography, Manx shows that it has parted company with its sister languages. The ordinary Gaelic system is a development of that devised for writing Old Irish in the roman alphabet, conditioned by the fact that Gaelic had a greater range of consonants than Latin and that the pronunciation of the Latin consonants was subject to considerable changes in the various spoken languages of Europe. Furthermore, in Gaelic the consonants varied in quality according to the vowels (now lost in final position) which originally followed them, and the quality was a marker of distinctions such as case in nouns and adjectives which it was necessary to indicate in writing.

Those who devised the spelling of Manx were, as a result of their isolation from the rest of the Gaelic world, not acquainted with this system and they made use of the orthography they were familiar with, that of Middle English, and in this they wrote such words and names as they had occasion to write, with results very similar to those of the sixteenth- and seventeenth-century English administrators in Ireland when faced with Irish personal names and place-names.

Such a method runs the risk of neglecting phonetic features of the language if they do not exist or are not significant in English, or, if an attempt is made to record them, then the result cannot be interpreted within the conventions of English orthography. The contrast between non-palatal and palatal versions of a consonant, in earlier usage termed 'broad' and 'slender', is such a phonetic feature. In writing such palatal consonants in English orthography in Scotland and Ireland, palatal *t* and *d* are written as such, whereas in Manx, either because they were more fully assibilated than in the other types of Gaelic or because English usage presented a ready approximation, they are represented by *ch* and *j* respectively, while palatal *k* and *g* appear as *ki* and *gi*. In final position the traditional Gaelic expedient of placing the *i* before the final consonant is adopted: thus *ain*, *awin*, *dowin* are all monosyllables. In the palatal group *st* where both consonants are palatal, i.e. *sh* + *ch*, the convention has been to mark the palatalization in only one, latterly in the first (as *sht*) but in Phillips's translation of the Prayer Book (see below) in the second (as *sch*). It will be seen that Manx spelling has its own conventions and that its being based on English does not make it immediately transparent to the English reader.

The first Manx book, the manuscript of the translation of the Book of Common Prayer by Bishop John Phillips, a Welshman, agrees with this Manx orthography as regards the consonants, except perhaps in one or two details, but appears to depart from it as regards the vowels as we know from the contemporary criticism that 'it is spelled with vowels wherewith none of them [i.e. the Manx clergy] is acquainted'. Phillips uses *a*, *æ*, *e*, *i*, *o*, *u*, *w* and *y* as vowels, and the probability is that he was using the Welsh values as his standard (as Lhuyd was to do a century later). The translation survives in a fair copy of about 1630 but was not printed until 1893 (Moore and Rhŷs 1893–4).

In the next book, a Manx–English bilingual catechism (Wilson 1707), the first book to be printed in Manx, the local system is restored, though with a defensive comment in the preface, which may be a reference to the spelling: 'They that have had the Trouble of Translating it, are very Sensible that the Liberty which every Man takes *of Writing after his own Way*, will expose them to some censure: But [. . .] this would have been the Case, whoever should have undertaken it.' The most obvious changes are *ee* for Phillips's *ii* and *oo* for his *w*. The spelling in print was very largely stabilized by the translation of the Bible (1770–5) with only occasional minor variations, but in manuscripts such as collections of carvals (see below) a good deal of unconventional spelling is found. One feature of this system is that words that one would expect to be homophones or very nearly so are regularly spelt so as to distinguish them to the eye if not to the ear. The rest of the Gaelic world regards Manx spelling as something between an inconvenience and a deplorable aberration.

The social conditions in Man did not encourage written literature in Manx, and as early as the sixteenth and seventeenth centuries outside observers were commenting on the degree of Anglicization of the wealthier landowners and the gentry. Those who would have benefited most from books in Manx were too poor to afford them, and the consequence was that only such works as attracted subsidy or were distributed free, for example by the Society for the Promotion of Christian Knowledge or tract societies, were likely to be produced.

There are, however, survivals of popular verse transmitted orally, such as the *Traditionary* (or *Manannan*) *Ballad*, a summary account of the island's history down to the early sixteenth century (Thomson 1960–3). Although it exists only in eighteenth-century copies, the language and vocabulary are as old as Phillips at least. A presumably contemporary ballad on the execution of Illiam Dhone in 1662 was revived in the following century for political purposes and printed; and an Ossianic ballad, perhaps only a fragment, was noted later in the same century. Other pieces about notable events date, on paper at least, to the late eighteenth and early nineteenth centuries.

More substantial in the aggregate, and even individually, are the *carvals*, religious poems in hymn metres of a narrative or didactic nature, and late in the eighteenth century a considerable number of hymns were translated, but very few original compositions were produced: all the originality seems to have gone into carvals.

The most ambitious piece is the 4,000-line abridgement of Milton's *Paradise Lost* by the Rev. Thomas Christian, vicar of Marown, perhaps the grandfather rather than the grandson of that name to judge from the language and spelling, printed only in 1794 but circulating earlier in manuscript and orally (Thomson 1995). Apart from this, the tendency is to attempt translations of contemporary English verse, of which the most successful is a version of Parnell's *Hermit*.

In prose, the largest single work is the translation of the Bible, including part of the Old Testament apocrypha, from 1748 (Matthew) to 1773 (Job to Ecclesiasticus), with, in between, Gospels and Acts (1763), Epistles and Revelation (1767), and Genesis to Esther (1771), all rendered into Manx by the parochial clergy. The Book of Common Prayer first appeared in 1765, with the Psalms preserving a great deal of Phillips's version, which was then transferred unaltered into the translation of the Bible. A selection of metrical psalms, authorized in 1761, was later added. In addition to the Bible translation, Bishop Hildesley arranged for a substantial tract of 1685, *The Christian Monitor* or *Fer-raauee Creestee*, to be translated into Manx by the Rev. Paul Crebbin, vicar of Santan; this appeared in 1763 and is one of the best pieces of writing in Manx (Thomson 1998). The translator died shortly afterwards and must have been born about the beginning of the century, and so had a better grasp of the language than his successors. The first of a succession of translated catechisms appeared in 1769, and its language contrasts markedly with that of the *Monitor*. Among the tracts, six of the sermons from the first *Book of Homilies* were translated, *c.*1820 (Thomson 1997).

Two other works by Bishop Wilson, in addition to that of 1707, were translated into Manx, *A Short and Plain Introduction* for communicants in 1777, and a selection from his English sermons in 1783. A large body of Manx sermons is extant in manuscript.

Not a great deal of interest in the language has been taken by people unconnected with the island, but some work has been done of which the following are the most significant. Edward Lhuyd, 'the father of Celtic philology', cites a few words in his *Archaeologia Britannica* (1707), and the remains of a collection parallel to the Scottish and Irish ones and in Lhuyd's 'phonetic alphabet' has come to light in the National Library of Wales at Aberystwyth (Ifans and Thomson 1979–80). The spelling is that of Lhuyd's collection from Scotland, quite independent of any Manx orthography. It therefore sheds some light on the pronunciation as perceived by an observer without preconceptions and provides, for example, the first clear evidence of the fronting of Gaelic *á* (see Thomson 1999; and 1996, 369–75).

John Rhŷs, professor of Celtic at Oxford, made several visits to the island in the 1870s and recorded material from a variety of speakers in a system of his own, and subsequently wrote a description of the phonetics of Manx that was printed with the second volume of the edition of Phillips's prayer-book (Moore and Rhŷs 1893–4).

Carl Marstrander, professor of Celtic at Oslo, whose principal interest in this connection was Manx place-names and their historical significance, contributed a study of this material with some linguistic matter to the *Norsk Tidsskrift*, vol. 6 (1932), and left to the Manx Museum a large body of notes and transcriptions of the speech of native Manx-speakers with some phonograph recordings on wax cylinders made *c.*1930.

Native scholarship produced a grammar and a dictionary by John Kelly. The former was published in 1804 and dealt almost entirely with morphology. The latter, the end-product of a scheme started in connection with the Bible translation, remained in manuscript until it was published in the old Manx Society series in a heavily edited form as the Manx–English part of a dictionary in 1866. The Manx part of Kelly's Triglott of the Gaelic languages was completed but not published and provided the (also edited) English–Manx part of the same dictionary. A second, rather better, dictionary by Archibald Cregeen, with a slight grammatical sketch prefixed, appeared in 1835 (Thomson 1969, 177–210). No grammar of Manx as a whole has yet been written. For the language in its last stages, George Broderick's *Handbook of Late Spoken Manx* (Tübingen 1984–6) provides a comprehensive account. An English–Manx dictionary based on de Bhaldraithe's English–Irish dictionary (1959) was produced by Douglas Fargher in 1979, containing a large number of neologisms unfortunately not distinguished in any way from genuine Manx. A similar dependence on Irish is found in

J. J. Kneen's Manx grammar (1931), slavishly based on the Christian Brothers' Irish grammar and therefore quite unreliable as a description of Manx at any time known to us.

The decline of the Manx language has been fully documented by George Broderick (Broderick 1999) and there is space here for only the barest outline. English was making headway in the towns of the island in the later eighteenth century with increasing trade and a greater number of foreign residents, and the tendency would gain strength throughout the nineteenth, especially in the second half of the century. Manx was thereby made more emphatically the badge of rusticity and poverty, with the concomitant stigma of ignorance and backwardness. This was felt by those who were themselves Manx-speaking, and gave rise to a determination that their children should not suffer the same disadvantages. Provided they were themselves to any extent bilingual, they made sure that their children were taught English and themselves used it with them, reserving Manx for keeping secrets, in the same way as servants had done with their masters in earlier times, and discouraging their own parents from teaching the language to their grandchildren. Before the end of the century, this tendency had been so effective that Rhŷs noted specially his meeting with a Manx-speaking child, the only one he could remember encountering. Marstrander noted that young people did not use or even know the language, and commented in his diary in the same way as Rhŷs on meeting a youngish man (in his forties) in Castletown who had a little Manx, which he had acquired from his grandfather.

On the basis of his own observation of the ages of the current speakers of Manx, Marstrander estimated that the language would be extinct (as far as native speakers were concerned) in about ten years, i.e. about 1940. That its life was prolonged for thirty years beyond this is partly due to instances of exceptional longevity, partly to remote places of residence, and partly to family circumstances favouring a close connection in childhood with an older generation, like the man in Castletown referred to by Marstrander, but to a higher degree, such as being brought up entirely by grandparents.

A question about the language was first asked in the census of 1871, when there were 190 people speaking Manx only and 12,340 speaking both Manx and English, out of a total population of 54,042, i.e. 22.8 per cent, which was not a desperate situation provided the bilinguals made use of the language and passed it on to the next generation. This they were probably not doing. Moreover, the introduction in 1872 of the English education system, which had no place for teaching local languages other than English or using them as a medium of instruction, meant that there was no counterweight to parental apathy, and probably no public opinion in favour of teaching Manx. By the next time the question was asked at the decennial census, in 1901, the monoglots were down to 59 and the bilinguals to 4,598, or 8.5 per cent of the population; by 1911 it was 4.6 per cent, and the cause was clearly lost. Ned Maddrell, the last native speaker of Manx, died on 27 December 1974, at the age of 97.

In the meantime, however, some interest in the Manx language had been aroused, and the notion of reviving or restoring its use had achieved some currency. Henry Jenner's survey of 1874, conducted on a parochial basis, confirmed the census results with local detail, and reinforced the impression that the language was on the way to extinction. There was general interest in matters Celtic in the latter part of the nineteenth century, emanating largely from Ireland where the Gaelic language was in a similar state to Manx. The first significant move was the foundation of Yn Cheshaght Ghailckagh (The Manx Language Society) in 1899 to preserve Manx as the national language of Man, to study and publish Manx Gaelic literature and cultivate a modern literature in Manx, to seek to have Manx taught in the schools, to promote Manx music and songs, and to collect oral literature. The promotion of the language by establishing classes and encouraging its use has continued, as has the publishing of Manx texts and teaching materials, but the fostering of modern literature in the language has been very much less successful, and the teaching of the language as an (optional) part of the school curriculum made no headway until 1992, though Manx was intermittently studied as a voluntary or hobby subject in various places.

In the decade before the foundation of Yn Cheshaght Ghailckagh, A. W. Moore had produced a book on Manx folklore, a venture into the dangerous field of personal names and place-names, a collection of carvals (previously printed in the newspaper *Mona's Herald*), his *Manx Ballads* (a collection of verse in Manx from manuscript and oral sources), a history of the diocese of Sodor and Man, as well as the edition of the Phillips Book of Common Prayer, and a substantial two-volume history of the island (1900). An important contribution (among others) to the teaching of the language was made in 1901 by the publication of *First Lessons in Manx* by Edmund Goodwin who had the benefit of an extensive knowledge of languages; the work remains in use in a slightly revised form. The English dialect of the island was not neglected and in 1924 Moore, Goodwin, and Sophia Morrison published *A Vocabulary of the Anglo-Manx Dialect*. J. J. Kneen produced the six parts of his *Place-names of the Isle of Man* between 1925 and 1928, his *Personal Names of the Isle of Man* in 1937, and an *English–Manx Pronouncing Dictionary* in 1938.

The Second World War interrupted these activities, but shortly afterwards those students of the language who had learnt their Manx from the last generation of native speakers began to make tape recordings of the speakers and to seek out any who were unknown. Enquiries in 1946 produced a list of twenty. Recordings were made by the Irish Folklore Commission, the Manx Museum, Yn Cheshaght Ghailckagh and others so that the pronunciation at least might be preserved, though in many other respects the language of the last speakers was defective through long disuse.

Yn Cheshaght Ghailckagh continued its activities of teaching, and with the assistance of loans from the Manx Arts Council and the Manx Heritage Foundation the publishing programme increased in volume, mostly with reprints of out-of-print books though one completely new book, a sequel to Goodwin's *First Lessons*, was commissioned. With the co-operation of the Northern Universities' Joint Matriculation Board an O-level examination in Manx was created in 1982, and successfully taken by a number of adult learners, some with long experience of the language.

The census of 1991 bore witness to the effectiveness of this activity. The respondents were asked whether they spoke, wrote, and/or read Manx: out of a total of 741 who claimed a knowledge of Manx, 643 spoke, 343 wrote, 479 read. The bulk of these were adults, in the 25–74 age-group, 35 per cent of them between 25 and 44, reflecting the increase in activity since 1945.

In 1985 a Manx Language Council (Cooinceil ny Gaelgey) was appointed to give advice to government, local authorities, and the public on the appropriate expression in Manx of various kinds of titles and notices, such as street names, government departments, commemorative plaques, and the like. The Council has recently been re-formed and has undertaken the additional task of creating and standardizing neologisms, so necessary in a language that ceased growing naturally a century or two ago.

A poll on the quality of life in Man in 1991 surprised the Government by showing that 36 per cent of the respondents were in favour of Manx as an optional subject in schools, and the following year a Manx-language officer was appointed in the Department of Education to organize teaching and devise a syllabus, first for junior schools and then for a two-year course for the seniors on the model of GCSE courses in modern languages. The intention is to provide an A-level in the subject in due course. As Broderick remarks (1999, 182): 'It remains to be seen what the future holds for the maintenance and promotion of Manx Gaelic.'

References

Bieler, L. 1979. *The Patrician Texts in the Book of Armagh*. Dublin.

Broderick, G. 1996. *Chronicle of the Kings of Man and the Isles*. Douglas.

——1999. *Language Death in the Isle of Man*. Tübingen.

Cheney, C. R. 1984. Manx Synodal Statutes, 1230(?)–1351. *Cambridge Medieval Celtic Studies*, 7:63–89.

Ifans, D. and Thomson, R. L. 1979–80. Edward Lhuyd's *Geirieu Manaweg. Studia Celtica*, 14–15:129–67.

Jackson, K. H. 1950. Notes on the Ogam inscriptions of southern Britain. In Fox, Sir Cyril and Dickins, Bruce (eds), *The Early Cultures of North-West Europe*, Cambridge, 199–213.

——1951. Common Gaelic: the evolution of the Goidelic languages. *Proceedings of the British Academy*, 37:71–97.

Kneen, J. J. 1937. *The Personal Names of the Isle of Man*. Oxford.

Moore, A. W. and Rhŷs, J. 1893–4. *The Book of Common Prayer in Manx Gaelic* (2 vols). Douglas.

Plummer, C. 1896. *Venerabilis Baedae Opera Historica*. Oxford.

Thomson, R. L. 1960–3. The Manx traditionary ballad. *Études celtiques*, 9 (1960–1):521–48, 10 (1962–3):60–87.

——1969. The study of Manx Gaelic. *Proceedings of the British Academy*, 55:177–210.

——1995. *Pargys Caillit [. . .] with [. . .] The Hermit*. Douglas.

——1996. Edward Lhuyd's *Geirieu Manaweg*, III. *Scottish Gaelic Studies*, 17:369–75.

——1997. *Sharmaneyn oikoil Agglish Hostyn*. Douglas.

——1998. *Yn Fer-raauee Creestee (1763)*. Douglas.

——1999. Edward Lhuyd's *Geirieu Manaweg*, II. *Celtica*, 23:390–407.

Wilson, T. 1707. *The Principles and Duties of Christianity*. London.

6 British

Glanville Price

We saw in chapter 1 that, some time before the Christian era, various waves of Celtic-speaking peoples had settled in Britain, namely the Goidels or Gaels on the one hand, and, on the other, the peoples known collectively as Britons. The language spoken by the Britons in the early period is variously known as Brittonic, Brythonic or British. In this book, the term 'Brittonic' or 'Brythonic' is used as a general classifier for the languages descended from that branch of Celtic, viz. Cumbric, Welsh, Cornish and Breton, and 'British' as a name for the language of the pre-literary period, which is the subject of this chapter.

An important geographical distinction can conveniently be introduced here. The island of Britain falls fairly clearly into two geographical zones, a Lowland zone, consisting more or less of England (other than the south-west) south of the Pennines, and a Highland zone, consisting approximately of Scotland, the north of England, Wales, and Devon and Cornwall (see map 4).

It cannot reasonably be doubted that, by the time of the Roman invasion of AD 43, most or all of Britain south of the Forth–Clyde valley was occupied by British-speaking tribes. The names of many of these tribes are known to us from Roman sources, among them the Damnonii, the Votadini, the Novantae and the Selgovae in Scotland, the powerful tribes of the Brigantes occupying much of northern England, the Parisi in eastern Yorkshire, the Deceangli and the Ordovices in North Wales, the Demetae (whose name remains in that of the former county of Dyfed) and the Silures in South Wales, the Cornovii and the Coritani and south of them the Dobunni and the Catuvellauni in the English Midlands, the Iceni (Boudicca's tribe) in East Anglia and, to the south of them, the Trinovantes, and, in the south of England, from west to east, the Dumnonii, the Durotriges, the Belgae, the Atrebates, the Regnenses and the Cantii (whose name remains in that of the county of Kent).

Of the British language of this early period, very little is known. No written texts of any kind, not even the briefest of inscriptions, are known to have existed. Certainly none have survived. At most, we have, as contemporary material evidence, a few names, in the Latin alphabet and often in abbreviated form, on coins struck for British chieftains. The names of Tasciovanus, king of the Catuvellauni, who died about AD 15, and his son Cunobelinus, for example, are found on their coins in the abridged forms *Tascio* and *Cuno*. Otherwise, such direct knowledge as we have of the British language of the Roman period derives entirely from the names of places, peoples and individuals quoted in Latin or, occasionally, Greek texts of one kind or another (and often preserved in a manifestly corrupt form).[1] Tacitus's *Life of Agricola*, published in AD 98, mentions,

Map 4 *(a) The Highland and Lowland zones of Britain; (b) the northern British kingdoms from* c. *the sixth century* AD.

among others, such names as *Boudicca, Clota* (the Clyde), *Cogidumnus* (a British king), *Mona* (Anglesey – modern Welsh *Môn*), *Orcades* (Orkney), and the tribes of the *Brigantes*, the *Ordovices* and the *Silures*. The Greek writer Ptolemy (second century AD, but much of his material derives from earlier Latin sources) gives very many names including *Dounion* (Maiden Castle, in Dorset), *Eborakon* (York), *Katouraktonion* (Catterick), *Londinion* (London), *Maridounon* (which should be *Moridounon*) (Carmarthen), *Otadinoi* (the tribe of the Votadini in Southern Scotland), *Ouirokonion* (Wroxeter), *Rigodounon* (an unidentified place in the north of England) and *Vectis* (Isle of Wight). The 'Antonine Itinerary', a gazetteer dating perhaps from about AD 300, of Roman roads throughout the empire, listing the main towns and the distances between them, gives us, for example, the forms *Calleva* (Silchester), *Danum* (Doncaster), *Duroverno* (Canterbury), *Letoceto* and *Pennocrucio* which survive in the names of Lich(field) and Penkridge (Staffs) respectively, *Mamucio* (Manchester), *Sorbiodunum* (Salisbury) and *Viroconium* (Wroxeter). The *Notitia Dignitatum*, a collection of lists, possibly dating from the late fourth or the fifth century, of military and civil administrative posts in various parts of the empire, gives a number of British place-names, among them *Bremetennacum* (Ribchester), *Derventio* (Malton, Yorks), *Braboniacum* (Kirkby Thore), the names of forts on Hadrian's Wall, including *Axelodunum* (which, as we know from other sources, is an error for *Uxelodunum*) (Castlesteads), *Borcovicium* (Housesteads), *Cilurnum* (Chesters), *Vindobala* (Rudchester) and *Vindolan(d)a* (Chesterholm), and, in the south-east, the names of forts along the 'Saxon shore', including *Branodunum* (Brancaster), *Othona* (Bradwell-juxta-Mare), *Regulbium* (Reculver), *Dubrae* (Dover) and *Lemannae* (Lympne).

Many of the elements contained in these names are readily identifiable, and have corresponding forms in modern Welsh. The widely distributed element *-dunum, -dounon* 'fort' is cognate with Welsh *din(as)* 'fort' (now 'city'); the *mori-* and *rigo-* of *Moridounon* and *Rigodounon* are connected with Welsh *môr* 'sea' and (obsolete) *rhi* 'king' respectively, so the names mean 'sea fort' and 'royal fort'; *Durovernum* probably contains an element *duro-*, also meaning 'fort', and *verno-* (Welsh *gwern*) 'swamp' or 'alder trees'; *Derventio* has to do with oak trees (Welsh *derwen* 'oak'); the two elements of *Letoceto* correspond to Welsh *llwyd* 'grey' and *coed* 'wood', and those of *Pennocrucio* to Welsh *pen* 'head, top, end' and *crug* 'hillock, heap, mound'; *Dubrae* and *Lemannae* can be shown to contain the same Celtic roots as Welsh *dwfr*, *dŵr* 'water' and *llwyfen* 'elm'; and *Uxelo-* survives in Welsh *uchel* 'high'.

From the time of the Roman invasion of AD 43 until Roman domination came to an end early in the fifth century, British was in competition with Latin, at least in the towns and probably to some extent in the low-lying rural parts of central and south-east England. But even before the Romans left, the earliest manifestations of what was later to become a new and major threat had appeared, with the coming of the first of the Anglo-Saxons. Little is certain about this period, but it appears that, some time before they left, the Romans had installed Anglo-Saxon mercenaries or *foederati* in parts of the south-east of England, in what was to become known as the *Litus Saxonicum* or 'Saxon shore', stretching roughly from the Wash to Portsmouth. There had also been sporadic raids by Germanic tribes on the east and south coasts of the island from the third century AD onwards. The first Anglo-Saxon invasions and settlements however, which marked the beginning of the process by which the island was to become in due course almost wholly English-speaking, date from the middle of the fifth century. According to the British chronicler, Gildas, writing in the sixth century, the Britons scored a great victory over the Saxons in or about the year 500 at the battle of Mons Badonis, a so-far unidentified site that must have been somewhere in the south of England. This seems to have halted the advance of the invaders for about forty years. However that may be, the various tribes of Germanic invaders – traditionally, the Angles, Saxons and Jutes – gradually worked their way westwards and northwards and in due course split the territory still held by the Britons in the west and north of the island into three geographically separate areas. In AD 577, the Saxons of Wessex made a new thrust forward, defeating the Britons at the Battle of Dyrham (near Bath). By their subsequent occupation of territory in the Cotswolds and up to the lower Severn valley, by about AD 600 they had divided the Britons of the south-west from those of what is now Wales. The later story of the British tongue in those areas is the subject of our chapters on Cornish and Welsh respectively.

It is by no means clear when the Welsh were likewise cut off by land from the Britons of the north as a result of the expansion into Cheshire and south Lancashire of the Angles of Mercia, who had probably first entered England via the Humber estuary. Traditionally, a significance similar to that of the Battle of Dyrham has been assigned to the defeat of the Britons at the battle of Chester in AD 616 or thereabouts, but it is far from certain that this led to permanent occupation of the area. However, there seems little doubt that a substantial wedge had been driven between the Welsh and their northern kinsmen by the middle of the seventh century or not much later. The language of these northern Britons, or 'Cumbric' as it has come to be known, is almost entirely lost, but enough is known about it to justify our devoting a brief chapter to it.

Although there could in any case have been no good reason, even in the absence of any positive evidence, to doubt that the whole of the areas now known as England and Wales together with southern Scotland was largely and perhaps entirely British-speaking in the period before the Romans came and, to some extent (perhaps even to a considerable extent in the case of the Highland zone), throughout the three and a half centuries of the Roman occupation, we are not in fact totally deprived of supporting evidence. We have already seen that names of undoubted British origin are attested in Greek and Latin texts and that they are widely distributed over the whole island. There are in fact many more names of natural features (hills, rivers) and human settlements (towns, villages) in England whose British origin has been clearly demonstrated (see Ekwall, 1928, 1960; Reaney, 1964; Nicolaisen, Gelling and Richards 1970; in what follows, I shall not make specific reference to these works, on which I have drawn extensively, except when quoting directly from them).

It is hardly surprising that names of Brittonic origin should survive in those parts of England that were not Anglicized until the Middle Ages or later, such as Devon, western parts of Herefordshire (where some Welsh survived up to the eighteenth century) and of Shropshire (where some Welsh is still spoken in one or two villages just across the border from Wales), and Cumbria. What is much more significant is the fact that there is at least a sprinkling of names of Brittonic origin over the whole of England, and that they occur even in areas like Essex, Surrey and Kent.

Names of undisputed or generally accepted British origin are so numerous and, though less thick on the ground in the east than in the west, so widely distributed, that one must conclude that most or all of the Lowland zone must at one time have been British-speaking. Forms cognate with Welsh *mynydd* 'mountain', for example, occur not only in *Myndtown*, *Minton* and *Longmynd* (all in Shropshire) and *The Mynde* and *Meend's Wood* (Herefordshire), but much further east, as in *Mendip* (Somerset; the second element is perhaps Old English *hop* 'valley') and *Mindrum* (Northumberland), whose second element corresponds to Welsh *trum* 'ridge'. As we have seen, the first syllable of *Lichfield* comes from *Letoceto* 'grey wood' (Welsh *llwyd* + *coed*), and the same form gives *Lytchett* (Dorset). Welsh *moel* 'bare' is akin to the first syllable of *Malvern* ('bare hill' = Welsh *Moelfryn*), *Mellor* (Derbyshire, Lancashire) (also 'bare hill' = Welsh *Moelfre*), and possibly *Melchet* (Hampshire), of which the second element is again *cet-* 'wood'. British *cet-* also turns up as the first element of *Cheetham* (Lancs), *Chicklade* and *Chitterne* (both in Wiltshire), *Chetwode* (Bucks) and *Chatham* (Kent), all of which have an English second element, and of *Kesteven* (Lincs), whose second element is Scandinavian, and also in *Penge* (Surrey), a much reduced derivative of the roots *penn-* 'top' and *cet-* (it occurs in 1067 in the form *Penceat*). *Liscard* (Cheshire) is cognate with Welsh *llys* 'court' + *carreg* 'rock' (so perhaps 'hall on the rock'), *Wenlock* (eastern Shropshire) with Welsh *(g)wyn* 'white' and (obsolete) *llog* 'monastery', *Berk(shire)* with (obsolete) Welsh *bar* 'top, summit, crest', *Pant* (Hampshire) with Welsh *pant* 'valley, depression', *Crewe* with Welsh *cryw* 'weir, stepping-stones', and *Ross* (Herefordshire, Northumberland), *Roose* (Lancashire) and *Roos* (Yorkshire) with Welsh *rhos* 'moor'. The root *cruco-* (Welsh *crug* 'hillock, heap, mound'), which we saw in the 'Antonine Itinerary' in the name *Pennocrucio* (Penkridge), also survives in *Creech* (Dorset, Somerset), *Crutch* (Worcester) and *Crich* (Derbyshire). *Chevening* (Kent) and *Chevin* (Yorkshire) probably correspond to Welsh *cefn* 'back, ridge' (indeed, *Chevin* appears in Old English as *Scefinc*, in which the initial *S-* may well correspond to Welsh *is* 'below', so the whole name, like Welsh *is y cefn*, would mean 'below the ridge'). The name of the *Andred* forest (Kent and Sussex) contains a British prefix of uncertain meaning and the root *ritu-* (Welsh *rhyd*) 'ford'.

The various rivers *Avon* (six of them in all) preserve the British word *abona* 'river' that survives with the same meaning in Welsh *afon*, while the word for water, *dubro-* (Welsh *dwfr*, *dŵr*), occurs in the names of the river *Dour* (and the town of *Dover*, which stands on it), *Doverdale* (Worcestershire), *Doverburn* (Warwickshire), *Dover Beck* (Notts), *Dovercourt* (Essex), and as the second element of the names (now of towns but originally of streams) *Andover* and *Micheldever* (both in Hampshire) (the first element in each case is obscure), *Candover* (Hampshire) (first element = Welsh *cain* 'fair, beautiful'), *Wendover* (Bucks) (first element = Welsh *gwyn* 'white'), and of the various streams in Lancashire and Yorkshire called *Calder* (Welsh *caled* 'hard' and *dwfr*, *dŵr*, so the meaning is perhaps 'turbulent stream'), and probably, in the same area, in the name of the *Hodder*, whose first element may correspond to Welsh *hawdd* 'pleasant' (now 'easy'). *Winford* (Somerset) takes its name from that of a stream, and corresponds to Welsh *Gwenffrwd* 'white stream'. The names of the numerous rivers *Derwent*, the *Darwen* (Lancs), the *Darent* (Kent), and the *Dart* (Devon), all go back to a British *Derventio* (which is attested in the 'Antonine Itinerary' for the Yorkshire Derwent) which includes the root *derva (Welsh *derw(en)*) 'oak'. Among very many other river-names of British origin, *Cole* and *Leam* (both in Warwickshire) are related to Welsh *coll(en)* 'hazel' and *llwyf* (British **lem-*) 'elm' respectively, *Laughern* Brook (Worcestershire) to Welsh *llywarn* (obsolete) 'fox', *Laver* (Yorkshire) to Welsh *llafar* 'speech' (probably here in the sense of 'chattering'), and *Leadon* (Gloucestershire) to Welsh *llydan* (British **litano-*) 'broad', and Yarrow (Lancashire) is probably connected with

Welsh *garw* 'rough'. The name of the various rivers *Dove* (two in Yorkshire, one each in the Midlands and Suffolk) contains reflexes of a root *dubo-* 'black' (Welsh *du*). This also occurs with an element connected with an obsolete Welsh word *glais* 'stream' in a number of river-names (some of them now also the names of towns or villages), including *Dalch* and *Dawlish* (Devon), *Dowlish* (Somerset), *Dowles* (Worcestershire), *Douglas* (Lancashire) and *Devil's Water* (Northumberland).

The very fact of the survival of a substantial number of British names in those parts of England that were occupied relatively early by the Anglo-Saxons raises the question of the relations that may have existed between the Britons and the invaders and, in particular, that of the fate of the Britons.

It is likely that no serious scholar would now contend that all or even the great majority of the Britons who had formerly inhabited the Lowland zone were massacred or put to flight, though such a view was fashionable at one time. Not only does it seem on general grounds more likely that very many of them remained and survived, but Nora Chadwick, after a wide-ranging and penetrating survey of the linguistic, historical and archaeological evidence, found that it led her to the conclusion that the Anglo-Saxon occupation of England was 'a gradual process which involved no change of population on any large scale' (Chadwick 1963, 146). On the contrary, 'everything points to a *modus vivendi,* with the incoming Saxons as heirs to the Roman arms for defending the south-east, and the unchronicled Britons quietly carrying on their former way of life' (ibid., 142).

To suggest that the Britons carried on under Anglo-Saxon domination with their way of life virtually unchanged strains belief somewhat. However, one can accept that, with or without significant interruption to their habits and customs, they – or at any rate large numbers of them – probably did remain in their former haunts. It is indeed possible, likely even, that here and there, particularly in the more inaccessible or economically less desirable areas, areas of moorland, swamp, or forest for example, enclaves of unassimilated Britons and their language remained for some considerable time after the areas around them had come under the sway of the English. This is suggested, though admittedly not proved, by the fact that the element *Wal-* in some English place-names is connected with the words *Wales* and *Welsh*.[2] It is generally accepted, for example, that forms of Old English *W(e)alh,* plural *W(e)alas,* 'Briton(s)', are at the origin of such names as *Walden* (Herts), *(Saffron) Walden* (Essex) 'valley of the Britons', *Walpole* (Suffolk) 'pool of the Britons' (but the Norfolk *Walpole* means 'pool by the wall'), *Walmer* (Kent) 'mere of the Welsh'. In the north-west, *Wallasey* appears in 1086 as *Walea* (with *ea* from *ēg* – which later became *ey* – 'island') 'island of the Britons'.

One area that almost certainly remained British for some time was the kingdom of Elmet (the name corresponds to that of Elfed in Wales) in south-west Yorkshire (the name survives in that of the villages of Barwick in Elmet and Sherburn in Elmet), which preserved its independence until the beginning of the reign of Edwin of Northumbria (617–32). J. N. L. Myres argued (Collingwood and Myres 1937, 454) that, to the north of the Yorkshire wolds, among the moors of Hambleton and Cleveland, there may well have been another British enclave.

There is even some reason for thinking, though the evidence is not conclusive, that there were also British enclaves in the south of England. In particular, the *Anglo-Saxon Chronicle* records a victory won over the Britons by a Saxon chieftain, Cuthwulf, in 571 at a place named Bedcanford (perhaps Bedford), which was followed by the occupation of the towns of Aylesbury, Limbury, Bensington and Eynsham. This suggests that a substantial number of Britons survived at least until that date in an area just north of the Thames (see Collingwood and Myres 1937, 406, 408). Other enclaves may have persisted in the heath and forest country of West Suffolk and Essex (see Collingwood and Myres 1937, 446 and 453; Jackson 1953, 236), and in the Fens, where, Jackson suggests (ibid.), British-speaking natives were perhaps still to be found as late as the beginning of the eighth century. Jackson is of the view that, further west, British was still spoken in Somerset and Dorset at the end of the seventh century. In support of this, he draws attention to a reference in an Anglo-Saxon charter of the year 682 to a place in Somerset having distinct British and English names, *Britannica lingua Cructan, apud nos Crycbeorh* ('in the British language "Cructan" but we call it "Crycbeorh"') which proves 'not only that the [British] language was still alive here at the time but also that the English were adapting British place-names and that the two forms could exist side by side' (ibid., 239). Whether British lasted into the eighth century in Somerset and Dorset he regards as uncertain.

Our discussion so far has been largely confined to the fate of British in the Lowland zone. This is because there is not a great deal to be said about its role in the Highland zone except that there – or, more precisely, in most of the Highland zone south of the Forth and the Clyde – British emerged in due course as two closely related but distinct languages, viz. Welsh and Cornish, and remained for some centuries further north in yet another form, Cumbric (see chapter 9).

Leaving aside for the moment the problem of Cumbric, one might ask: at what period had the language of the south-west and the language of Wales diverged to such an extent that one has to consider them as separate languages rather than as dialects, or regional varieties, of one and the same language?

The evidence on which any such conclusion can be based is strictly limited since there are no written texts of any kind in British, not even the briefest of inscriptions on stone. There are, however, a few Latin inscriptions (mainly on tombstones) from the relevant period that contain Latinized versions of a number of British names and so constitute direct evidence for British. Among the British names that occur, usually in the Latin genitive case, are VOTEPORIGIS, MAGLOCVNI (which was later to become *Maelgwn*), CVNIGNI, CVNOTAMI, CVNOCENNI. These fifth- or early sixth-century forms are to be regarded as British (rather than Welsh or Cornish) in a Latin garb. In the seventh century, one finds occasional British names occurring in Latin inscriptions in Wales without any case endings, e.g. VIRNIN, CUURIS, CINI, and these forms are considered by Jackson to be already Primitive Welsh.

In brief, Jackson concludes that the phonetic changes that transformed British into Welsh, Cornish and Breton belong mainly to the period between the middle of the fifth and the end of the sixth century and that, therefore, 'from the middle of the sixth century we can begin to speak of these [i.e. Welsh, Cornish and Breton] as separating languages, and from the end of the century as separate' (1953, 5).

All this raises the question of the survival, perhaps until the eleventh or twelfth century, of a Brittonic language in the north-west of England and the south-west of Scotland. Are we to be content to continue to call it merely 'British', and discuss it in the present chapter, or could it be considered under the heading of Welsh, or is it to be looked upon as a separate language? Having defined 'British' as the British speech common to the whole of the island south of the Forth–Clyde valley, and having accepted that the term is no longer applicable, with reference to the period from about AD 600 onwards, to the south-western and western varieties which are thereafter to be referred to as 'Cornish' and 'Welsh' respectively, we cannot, to be consistent, regard any variety of Brittonic speech that continues in use well beyond the seventh century as merely 'British'. And since, from about the seventh century, this north-western speech-area was as completely divided from Wales as was the Cornish-speaking area, and since it can reasonably be supposed (even in the almost total absence of supporting evidence) that the language of the north-west continued to change and diverge from that of Wales, there is no justification for referring to it as 'Welsh'. Consequently, bizarre though it may seem to devote a chapter to a language of which only three words have survived (though much more can be learned, as we shall see, from other sources), that is the only logical solution.

Notes

1   For a comprehensive and authoritative survey and discussion of the British and other names attested in Roman Britain, see Rivet and Smith 1979.
2   See, for example, Faull 1977, 12–13. This is not, however, the origin of all English place-names in *Wal-*. In many such names it represents Old English *weald* 'forest', *weall* 'wall', or *waelle* 'well, spring'. Furthermore, in some names *w(e)alh* perhaps meant 'serf' rather than 'Welshman' (see Gelling 1978, 93–5). On other place-names in northern England that also suggest a continuing British presence in Anglo-Saxon times, see Faull 1977, 13–20.

References

Chadwick, N. K. 1963. 'The British or Celtic part in the population of England'. In *Angles and Britons* (six O'Donnell Lectures by various scholars), Cardiff, 111–47.
Collingwood, R. G. and Myres, J. N. L. 1937. *Roman Britain and the English Settlement*, 2nd edn. Oxford. (1st edn, 1936.)
Ekwall, Eilert 1928. *English River-names*. Oxford.
——1960. *The Concise Oxford Dictionary of English Place-names*, 4th edn. Oxford. (1st edn, 1936).
Faull, M. L. 1977. British survival in Anglo-Saxon Northumbria. In Laing, Lloyd (ed.), *Studies in Celtic Survival* (British Archaeological Reports, 37), 1–55.
Gelling, Margaret 1978. *Signposts to the Past. Place-names and the History of England*. London.
Jackson, Kenneth 1953. *Language and History in Early Britain. A Chronological Survey of the Brittonic Languages, 1st to 12th c. AD*. Edinburgh.
Nicolaisen, W. F. H., Gelling, Margaret and Richards, Melville 1970. *The Names of Towns and Cities in Britain*. London.
Reaney, P. H. 1964. *The Origin of English Place-names*, 3rd impression (with corrections and bibliographical additions). London. (1st impression, 1960.)
Rivet, A. L. F. and Smith, Colin 1979. *The Place-names of Roman Britain*. London.

7 Welsh

Janet Davies

Of all the languages spoken in Britain today, Welsh has by far the oldest roots. Wales is the only part of Britain in which a version of Brittonic has been spoken uninterruptedly down to the present day, the transition from Brittonic to Welsh having taken place, probably, somewhere between AD 400 and 700.

Traces of Early Welsh, the period which lasted until about 850, are sparse, consisting of only a few inscriptions and glosses. One such is to be found in the parish church of Tywyn, on the west coast of Gwynedd, where an inscription carved on a memorial around the year 810 records CINGEN CELEN TRICET NITANAM ('the body of Cingen dwells beneath'), words related to the modern forms *celain* ('corpse'), *trigo* ('to dwell') and *dan* ('beneath'). Evidences of Old Welsh, the next stage in the language's history which extends from 850 to 1100, are also slight: marginal notes, a few brief texts and poems. The *Surrexit* memorandum offers an account of the settlement of a land dispute in the margin of an eighth-century gospel book. Two poems of about 880 are preserved as marginal notes on the Juvencus manuscript. The Computus Fragment of about 920 discusses methods of recording the courses of the moon.

But despite the paucity of literary manuscripts dating from the period before 1100, the date considered to mark the transition from Old to Middle Welsh, a substantial body of literature was almost certainly composed in Old Welsh. The thirteenth-century Book of Aneirin records the attack made, probably about 595, by the men of the Gododdin (the Votadini, who lived around the Firth of Forth) on Catraeth (Catterick). The *Historia Brittonum*, a collection of material put together about 830, mentions both Aneirin and Taliesin, the reputed author of the Book of Taliesin. Taliesin celebrated the deeds of Urien, who ruled in Rheged (Dumfries and Cumbria) about 580. Although the poems of Aneirin and Taliesin, the earliest of the Cynfeirdd (the early poets), which have come down to us are not in Old Welsh, but in the Welsh of several centuries later, it is generally accepted that the nucleus of the work was composed about 600, and that oral repetition over the centuries led to its modification. The Red Book of Hergest, dating from about 1400, contains the ninth-century poems associated with Llywarch Hen, and also the Heledd cycle, which commemorates the defeat of the royal house of Powys at the hands of the English. *Armes Prydein*, written probably about 930, calls on the Welsh to rise up and drive the English out and is a powerful example of the vaticinatory verse which was an important element in medieval Welsh literature.

The codification of the Law of Wales associated with the name of Hywel Dda (d. 950) survives in forty-two texts, six of them in Latin, written down between 1230 and 1500, but they contain, together with later material, passages which have a distinctly early flavour. Welsh was the language of the law and the rich legal vocabulary of the Lawbooks, together with their form and style, makes them works of literature as well as of law. The collection of stories known collectively as the Mabinogi represents an even more impressive literary achievement, being described by Gwyn Jones and Thomas Jones as being 'among the finest flowerings of the Celtic genius' (1949, ix). Probably written down some time between 1050 and 1170, they provide links with the remote Celtic past and are a distinctive contribution to the prose literature of the Middle Ages.

By 1100, the beginning of the period of Middle Welsh, the Normans had made their presence felt in Wales and some native Welsh princes and noblemen acquired a knowledge of French. In 1108, a colony of Flemings was established in what was to become south Pembrokeshire (see chapter 15), while extensive English settlement took place in Gower, the Vale of Glamorgan and parts of Gwent and the north-east. The towns planted by the Normans were also centres of French and English influence, and there was a further wave of English immigration following the collapse of Llywelyn ap Gruffudd's principality in 1282–3. Despite these incursions, Wales remained overwhelmingly Welsh-speaking throughout the Middle Ages. The greater part of the population of marcher lordships like Brecon and Abergavenny was monoglot Welsh and considerable numbers of Welsh-speakers were to be found over the border in parts of present-day Herefordshire and Shropshire.

Spoken Welsh contained a variety of dialects, such as Gwyndodeg (the speech of Gwynedd) or Gwenhwyseg (the speech of Gwent). Gerald of Wales (d. 1223) commented that 'it is thought that the Welsh language is richer, more carefully pronounced and preferable in all respects in North Wales, for that area has far fewer foreigners', while 'others maintain that the speech of Cardiganshire in South Wales is better articulated and more to be admired, since it is in the middle and the heartland of Wales'.[1] There was, however, only one literary language, a language which was an effective medium for religious literature and for legal texts and which was used in works on medicine, heraldry and husbandry, as well as in a wealth of prose sagas and romances. Above all, it was used in poetry. The poets who sang to the Welsh princes between 1100 and 1300 – the Gogynfeirdd or 'fairly early poets' – reached their apogee with Gruffudd ab yr Ynad Coch's resplendent elegy for Llywelyn ap Gruffudd. In the years between 1300 and 1600 their successors, Beirdd yr Uchelwyr ('the poets of the gentry'), praised their patron, his house and his hospitality in *awdl*, *englyn* and *cywydd*, using an intricate system of sound chiming known as *cynghanedd* (harmony). The *cywydd* was their favourite metrical form, and its greatest exponent Dafydd ap Gwilym (*fl.* 1320–70).

Among the patrons of Beirdd yr Uchelwyr were gentry families of English origin who had been assimilated to Welsh-language culture. The Vale of Glamorgan became increasingly Welsh-speaking during the later Middle Ages, as did the towns, although the linguistic boundary, or Landsker, in Pembrokeshire remained remarkably stable. At the same time, however, English law was gradually replacing Welsh law and the framing of official documents was falling more and more into the hands of professional scribes. As a result of these developments, English was increasingly becoming the medium of legal transactions and the Welsh gentry, even in the remoter parts of Wales, came to feel the need to be fluent in English. By the time the Tudor dynasty, with its roots in Penmynydd, Anglesey, established itself on the throne of England, English had already acquired a dominant role in the official life of Wales.

The so-called 'Act of Union' of 1536 incorporated Wales into England and laid down that English should be the language of the courts of Wales and that only those able to speak English should hold public office. Designed to provide administrative uniformity, the Act created a Welsh ruling class for whom proficiency in English was essential. The gentry became justices of the peace and members of parliament, sent their sons to school in England and intermarried with English families. Although the acquiring of English did not necessarily mean the abandonment of Welsh, over the next 250 years the gentry did cease to be Welsh-speaking. Welsh culture, previously maintained by aristocratic patronage, fell into the hands of 'the middling sort of people' – craftsmen, artisans and the lower clergy – while the standardized Welsh which the poets had zealously defended was in danger of breaking up into an assortment of mutually unintelligible dialects.

The danger in which the Welsh language stood was averted by the Protestant Reformation, with its emphasis on the use of the vernacular as the language of worship. The use of English in services of course excluded the largely monoglot Welsh, a source of concern to those who held that the Welsh people should be granted the opportunity to gain an understanding of the new religion. One such was Sir John Price of Brecon, who in 1547 published the first printed book in Welsh, known (after its opening words) as *Yn y lhyvyr hwnn* ('In this book') and containing the Lord's Prayer, the Creed, the Ten Commandments and instructions on reading Welsh. His example was followed in 1551 by William Salesbury, who published a translation of the Epistles and Gospels of the first Book of Common Prayer, *Kynniver Llith a Bann*. Confronted with the spectacle of a continent torn by religious dissension, the government concluded that religious conformity was to be prized above conformity of language. An Act of 1563 ordered the bishops of Wales and Hereford to ensure that a Welsh translation of the Bible and the Prayer Book should be available by 1567, and that 'divine service shall be said throughout all the dioceses where the Welsh tongue is commonly used in the said Welsh tongue'. The Welsh Bibles were to be accompanied in every parish church by English versions, so that the congregation might 'by comparing both tongues together the sooner attain to a knowledge of the English tongue'. A Welsh translation of the New Testament and the Prayer Book, largely the work of William Salesbury, was published in 1567. The task of producing the entire Bible in Welsh was undertaken by William Morgan and it was published in 1588. Couched in the lofty and archaic diction of the medieval poets, the language of the Bible differed considerably from the spoken Welsh of the time, a difference made still more marked by the increased archaism of the revised version of 1620 and by the evolution of the spoken language over the centuries. It provided, nevertheless, a model of correct and exalted Welsh, whose solemn cadences rang in the ears of generations of Welsh people. Welsh was the only non-state language in Europe into which the Bible was translated less than a century after the Reformation, a fact of profound and crucial significance for the future history of the language.

The scholarship and commitment which made the translation of the Bible and the Prayer Book practicable came from a remarkable group of lexicographers and grammarians deeply influenced by the ideas of the Renaissance. This group of humanists included William Salesbury, who in addition to translating most of the New Testament also published a collection of Welsh proverbs, a Welsh–English dictionary and a guide to Welsh pronunciation; Gruffydd Robert, a Catholic exile who published a Welsh grammar in Milan; and John Davies of Mallwyd, the most distinguished scholar of his day, who produced the revised version of the Bible in 1620 as well as compiling a Welsh grammar written in Latin and a Latin–Welsh dictionary. The humanists aimed to demonstrate the richness of Welsh vocabulary and idiom and to prove that the language had, from its inception, been a vehicle for learning and religion.

But by the seventeenth century Welsh was no longer a language of high culture. Some literary works of distinction continued to be written, notably those of Morgan Llwyd (1619–59), and a few enthusiasts continued to transcribe and collect the productions of earlier periods. The mass of the population, however, required literature of a humbler sort. Free-metre poems produced by poets of humble origin replaced the strict-metre poetry of the bards. The new poets, as Geraint Jenkins points out (1987, 227), although 'pale shadows of their illustrious professional forebears [. . .] fulfilled a much wider social function. Welsh poetry became an open rather than a closed shop.' Eisteddfodau, meetings in which poets competed against one another and the victor was chaired and toasted, were held from 1700 onwards and had by the 1730s become fairly numerous. The poetic and musical contest held by Rhys ap Gruffudd at Cardigan in 1176 is generally considered the first recorded eisteddfod and others were held in Carmarthen about 1451 and in Caerwys, Flintshire, in 1523 and 1567. In the early eighteenth century they were less exalted and frequently rumbustious affairs.

Folk literature began to be published in the eighteenth century and the productions of Thomas Jones, the almanacker, proved that literacy was no longer the exclusive province of the wealthy and the leisured. The first book to be published on a permanent printing press in Wales – a ballad called *Cân o Senn i'w Hen Feistr Tobacco* ('A Song of Rebuke to his Old Master Tobacco') – was published by Isaac Carter at Atpar, near Newcastle Emlyn, in 1718. Carter soon moved to Carmarthen, the first town in Wales to become the centre of a lively Welsh-language printing venture. Devotional literature accounted for a large proportion of books published in Welsh. In 1674 Thomas Gouge, a London Dissenter, set up the Welsh Trust with a view to establishing schools in which children should learn English and become capable of reading English devotional works. Gouge was persuaded by Stephen Hughes, the 'Apostle of Congregationalism' in Carmarthenshire, that the children's salvation should not have to wait until they had acquired English, and that part of the Trust's funds should be devoted to publishing and distributing Welsh books. The Welsh Trust's work was continued by the Society for the Promotion of Christian Knowledge (SPCK), founded in 1699, and between 1660 and 1730, 554 Welsh books were published, five times the number published between 1540 and 1660. The publications included eleven editions of the Bible, four editions of *Pilgrim's Progress*, and fourteen editions of *Cannwyll y Cymru* ('The Welshman's Candle'), a collection of edifying verses by Rhys Prichard of Llandovery. The period's finest literary work, Ellis Wynne's *Gweledigaetheu y Bardd Cwsc* ('The Visions of the Sleeping Bard'), made its appearance in 1703. By the early years of the eighteenth century, these publications in Welsh had done much to sow the seeds of a religious and educational awakening.

Various grandiloquent but unfounded theories of the origins of the Welsh and their language had been in vogue over the centuries, and in 1716 Theophilus Evans, the vicar of Llangamarch in Breconshire, published *Drych y Prif Oesoedd* ('The Mirror of Past

Ages'), which portrayed the history of the Welsh as a glorious epic. The book was com-
pellingly written and extremely popular; it was also totally unconcerned to distinguish
between myth and historicity. However, the origins of the Welsh and their language had,
by 1716, already been the subject of a rigorous and scholarly investigation. Edward
Lhuyd, the Keeper of the Ashmolean Museum at Oxford, had, in the course of four
years of travel, accumulated a vast amount of material on the Celtic countries and
became, by virtue of his analysis of it, the founder of Celtic philology. Despite Lhuyd's
work, bizarre linguistic notions continued to win wide acceptance, although he did have
emulators, one of whom, William Gambold, published in 1727 the first English book
to be printed in Wales, *A Grammar of the Welsh Language.* Lewis Morris of Anglesey
(1701–65) also considered himself a follower of Lhuyd and the correspondence between
him and his brothers gives a fascinating and wide-ranging view of cultural life in mid
eighteenth-century Wales. The Honourable Society of Cymmrodorion was established
by Lewis's brother Richard in 1751 in the hope that it would transform Welsh culture.
The hope was not realized, but the Morrises and their circle did succeed in stimulating
interest in the language and literature of Wales. Perhaps their greatest achievement was
the publication in 1764 by Evan Evans of *Some Specimens of the Poetry of the Antient
Welsh Bards*, the first serious study of early Welsh poetry.

Much more momentous for the Welsh language were the activities of Griffith Jones,
the rector of Llanddowror in Carmarthenshire. In 1731 he began establishing schools
to teach both children and adults to read the Bible and to learn the Anglican Catechism.
In the Welsh-speaking areas, these schools were conducted in Welsh. They were held
in the winter, when work on the land was less pressing, and when the pupils had grasped
the essentials of reading the teacher moved on to another parish. Cheap, flexible and
efficient, the schools were supplied with materials by the SPCK while the teachers were
paid by affluent well-wishers. Griffith Jones established 3,325 schools in almost sixteen
hundred different locations between 1731 and his death thirty years later. The schools
were attended by possibly as many as 250,000 pupils, a huge proportion in a country
with a population of perhaps 480,000. Welsh acquired a new prestige, stimulating
publication; more than 2,500 books in Welsh were published in the eighteenth century.
This very remarkable initiative, one of the most successful of its kind in Europe, was
undoubtedly the most important happening in the history of the Welsh language
between the translation of the Bible and the Industrial Revolution.

The Methodist Revival also gave an impetus to the spread of literacy, since
Methodist Sunday schools were, like Griffith Jones's schools, attended by children and
adults alike. The Methodists in Wales became a separate denomination in 1811.
Although not especially concerned to foster Welsh, the fact that those they sought to
convert were monoglot Welsh-speakers obliged them to cultivate it, which they did with
great effect, using the language with a greater directness and simplicity than those who
strove consciously to promote it. The sermons of Methodists such as Daniel Rowland
created a tradition of powerful preaching in Welsh; the itinerant preachers who travelled to all parts of Wales created a standard spoken Welsh which was understood everywhere, and the hymns produced by writers such as William Williams and Ann Griffiths
became the new folk-songs of the nation. The structured and centralized form of government which characterized the new denomination operated through the medium of
Welsh at every level, giving ministers and laymen the opportunity to make public use
of their mother tongue.

One of the factors which facilitated the advance of Methodism and which also encouraged a growth in the numbers of the older dissenting denominations was the perception that the Anglican Church, which since the days of William Salesbury and William Morgan had made an impressive contribution to Welsh-language culture, had turned its back on that culture and become Anglicized. No native Welshman was appointed to a see in Wales between 1714 and 1870, while Welsh-speaking clerics, regarded as rustics by their superiors, were rarely elevated beyond the rank of parish clergymen. The scholar Evan Evans, who remained a curate all his life, heaped execration on the *Esgob Eingl* (English bishops) who were driving the people into the arms of the Methodists. The notorious appointment of the Englishman Thomas Bowles as rector of two parishes in Anglesey where only five of the 500 parishioners spoke English led to an attempt to oust him from his living. His attorney argued in defence of the appointment that 'Wales is a conquered country' and that 'it is the duty of the bishops to promote the English in order to introduce the language', but although Bowles kept the living, the judge declared that in future no clergyman unable to speak Welsh should be appointed to a parish where the majority of the parishioners spoke nothing else.

The vast majority of parish clergymen in Wales were, in fact, Welsh-speaking. Details of the language of services held in parish churches bear this out and at the same time provide information on the distribution of the Welsh language around 1750. Some western towns were centres of Anglicization, there was a bilingual zone along the eastern border and the southern coast, and some districts, notably south Pembrokeshire and Radnorshire, were almost completely Anglicized, but the only language used in over 80 per cent of church services was Welsh.

In 1750 Wales, with a population of less than 500,000 and almost completely rural in character, stood on the brink of revolutionary economic and demographic change; by 1851, the population was to number 1,163,000 inhabitants, less than a third of whom would be engaged in agriculture. Most notable was the transformation taking place in the south Wales coalfield, where mass communities were developing in areas which, a hundred years earlier, had been virtually uninhabited. Such changes inevitably had a profound effect on the Welsh language. The vast majority of incomers to the burgeoning industrial districts were from rural areas which were, for the most part, Welsh-speaking. In the process of colonizing their own country the Welsh brought their language from the countryside to the towns, and not merely to the new industrial districts; in the 1830s the language was spoken widely in Newport and there is some evidence that more than half the inhabitants of Cardiff had a knowledge of it. Welsh is the only one of the Celtic languages which has succeeded, to a considerable degree, in becoming an urban tongue.

The number of Welsh-speakers rose. Official statistics are not available until 1891, but it likely that they numbered about 470,000 in 1801, rising to about 800,000 by 1851. Living in mass urban communities, these Welsh-speakers used their language in a range of cultural activities; eisteddfodau multiplied and publishing flourished. Between 1800 and 1850, some 3,000 books were published in Welsh and dozens of periodicals were established. But although the numbers of Welsh-speakers increased, there was a decline in proportionate terms from 80 to 67 per cent. The assimilation of non-Welsh-speaking newcomers, possible when the percentage involved was relatively low, became impracticable in places like Pontypool, where in the 1840s

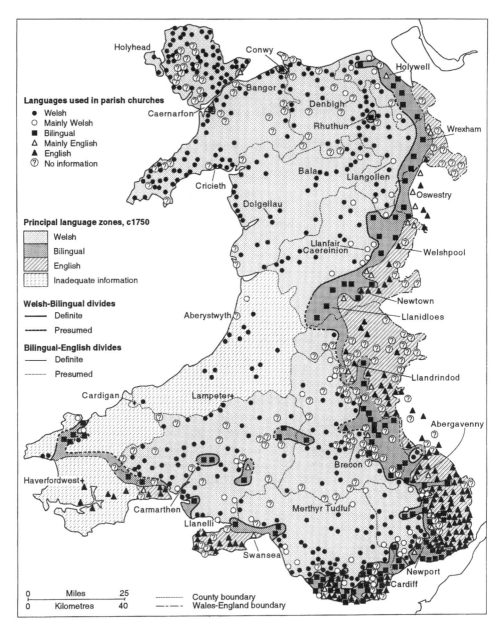

Map 5 *Language zones in Wales in the mid-eighteenth century. Map copyright Dr W. T. R. Pryce, Cardiff; published by permission of Dr Pryce (corrected and revised version of the map 'Principal language zones in Wales, c.1750' in Janet Davies,* The Welsh Language *(Cardiff, University of Wales Press, 1993)).*

44 per cent of the population had been born outside Wales. The bilingual zone was also becoming wider in north-east Wales, a fact reflected in the work of the novelist Daniel Owen. The quarrying communities in the north-west, however, remained solidly monolingual.

While the Industrial Revolution transformed the Welsh economy, a parallel trans-formation of the Welsh language was undertaken by scholars and enthusiasts. Dictio-naries were compiled which contained new words designed to meet the demands of a new age. John Walters's English–Welsh dictionary appeared between 1770 and 1794, and William Owen Pughe's in 1803. Some of the words coined, particularly by Pughe, did not win acceptance, but large numbers did make their way into common parlance, greatly enriching the vocabulary of Welsh. William Owen Pughe also published two grammars, in which he gave free rein to his belief that the function of the grammarian is to describe a language as it should be, not as it is. His work had a detrimental effect on Welsh writing in the nineteenth century.

Although Pughe was also involved in the publication of the *Myvyrian Archaiology* (1801–7), three volumes which made available a range of medieval Welsh poetry and prose, the most notable figure associated with the venture was Edward Williams, better known as Iolo Morganwg. Iolo threw himself with fervour into the invention of tradi-tion characteristic of the period, writing much of the *Archaiology* himself. An enthusi-ast for his native county of Glamorgan, he claimed that there alone was to be found a knowledge of the druidic lore which had subsequently descended to the bardic order. The druidic ceremonies were revealed by Iolo on Primrose Hill in London in 1792, and the Welsh literati were persuaded to join the Gorsedd (congress) of the Bards of the Isle of Britain, the supposed antiquity of which gave an added lustre to the Welsh lan-guage. In 1819, at Carmarthen, Iolo succeeded in linking the Gorsedd with the eisteddfod, a connection which still survives. The first modern eisteddfod was held at Corwen in 1789 and by the 1820s and 1830s the meetings were organized on a provin-cial basis, chiefly through the efforts of a group of Anglican clergymen. One of these, Thomas Price (Carnhuanawc), was prominent in the eisteddfodau held at Abergavenny, gatherings which attracted Celtophiles from all over the world and which produced such scholarly works as *The Literature of the Kymry*, a volume submitted to the 1848 eisteddfod by the Merthyr chemist, Thomas Stephens.

The early years of the nineteenth century witnessed the growth of the Welsh provin-cial press. Denominational periodicals were initially the most successful, but more overtly political publications subsequently made their appearance and in 1843 the first Welsh newspaper, *Yr Amserau* ('The Times'), was established in Liverpool. In 1859 it merged with the Denbigh-based *Baner Cymru* ('Banner of Wales') published by Thomas Gee, and by the late nineteenth century the twice-weekly *Baner ac Amserau Cymru* ('Banner and Times of Wales') claimed over 50,000 readers. In 1859 Gee launched *Y Traethodydd* ('The Essayist'), a quarterly modelled on the successful English publications of the day.

The Welsh-language press was written for, and by, the middle and lower classes, the upper classes having abandoned the language. English was associated with a superior social status. In 1847, a government report (see below) remarked of the Welsh working man, 'his language keeps him under the hatches [. . .], he is left to live in an under-world of his own and the march of society [. . .] goes completely over his head'. English-medium schools were considered to be the answer to this problem, but the impact in Welsh-speaking Wales during the first half of the nineteenth century of the schools run by the National Society, an organization concerned to teach the principles of the Church of England, was probably not great. In 1846, 30,000 pupils attended English-medium day schools in the counties of Carmarthen, Pembrokeshire and

Glamorgan, compared with 80,000 who attended the mainly Welsh-medium Sunday schools.

In 1846 a commission was set up to investigate the state of education in Wales and on 1 April 1847 the three commissioners, all of whom were English and Anglican, issued their report, under the title *Reports of the Commissioners of Inquiry into the State of Education in Wales* (3 vols). The picture of Welsh society which emerged was dark, insisting as it did on the gulf between classes, the deficiencies of the educational system and, above all, the pernicious influence of the Welsh language, to which it chiefly attributed the moral and material degradation of the Welsh. The report, published in the usual 'blue book' format of such official reports and popularly known as *Brad y Llyfrau Gleision* ('The Treachery of the Blue Books'), provoked a furore, and many of the complicated and contradictory forces at work in Wales during the second half of the nineteenth century sprang from it. For some, English contempt for the Welsh and their language was a goad spurring them on to give voice to a new linguistic nationalism, but some of the loudest voices from within Welsh-speaking Wales accepted, or even welcomed, the prospect of an end to Welsh distinctiveness. Other factors seemed to facilitate the demise of Welshness: the railways, which opened up the country to English influences; Darwin's theory of evolution, which seemed to give scientific validity to the disappearance of the weaker language; the growth among the middle classes of Utilitarianism, with its emphasis on what is useful and fosters progress. Yet there were also factors which told in favour of Welsh: it had a standard literary form which the majority of the population could read; it had a recognized and dignified role within the Nonconformist denominations; it was spoken by a people who had, on the whole, sufficient material means to sustain it. Even the coming of the railways had its positive aspect, facilitating the distribution of periodicals and allowing people to travel to eisteddfodau and other gatherings, thereby making possible the concept of a wider Welsh allegiance, an allegiance which gave rise to a demand for specifically Welsh institutions. A University College was established at Aberystwyth in 1872, others at Cardiff and Bangor in 1883 and 1884 respectively, and in 1893 the three were federated as the University of Wales. In 1907 charters were secured for a National Museum and, a matter of particular significance for the language, a National Library to house the manuscripts which bore witness to the richness and longevity of the Welsh literary tradition.

It was a tradition which continued to flourish in the latter half of the nineteenth century. Poetry enjoyed great popularity, the volumes of Ceiriog (John Ceiriog Hughes) selling over 200,000 copies. This was the golden age of the Welsh periodical press, and it was estimated that the five quarterlies, twenty-five monthlies and eight weeklies published in Welsh attained a combined circulation of 120,000. Thomas Gee began publishing his *Gwyddoniadur* ('Encyclopaedia') in 1854, and the ten-volume venture was completed in 1871, a second edition being published between 1889 and 1896.

These publications catered for a people the majority of whom spoke and read only Welsh. Apart from in Radnorshire, south Pembrokeshire, Gower, parts of the Vale of Glamorgan and the eastern parts of the counties of Flint, Montgomery, Brecon and Monmouth, Welsh held its ground as the chief and often the only language of the inhabitants. George Borrow, walking through the country in 1854, noted that English greetings frequently brought the response 'Dim Saesneg' ('No English'). Welsh-language culture was not confined to Wales. In 1865 a Welsh colony was established in the Chubut valley in Patagonia, and this self-governing community conducted its affairs entirely through the medium of Welsh. Welsh-speakers are still to be found in Patagonia. More significant in numerical terms was migration to North America. By 1872, 384 Welsh-language chapels had been established in the United States and communities which were largely Welsh-speaking existed in industrial Pennsylvania and rural Wisconsin. The most extensive emigration was, however, to England, which by the late nineteenth century contained almost a quarter of a million people who had been born in Wales. The largest diasporic community was established on Merseyside, and Liverpool, with over fifty chapels, may be considered to have produced the only nineteenth-century example of a Welsh-speaking urban elite.

In the later nineteenth century, Welsh-language culture, both within Wales and without, was dominated by Nonconformity. The chapels became the focus of Welsh-language activity, and the social as well as the religious life of communities became centred upon them. The situation, although it generated a vigorous and productive culture, had its negative aspects. As Professor Ieuan Gwynedd Jones has commented, Welsh 'entered into an alliance with the chapel on the terms of the chapel' (1980, 65), and 'English [. . .] became the language for what [Welsh] scorned or feared to express' (ibid., 65–6). Because Welsh-language culture was so thoroughly permeated by the Nonconformist ethos, it tended to alienate those whose sympathies were modernistic, libertarian or hedonistic. Furthermore the Nonconformists, aware of their numerical superiority to the Anglicans, tended to portray the Established Church as an alien force in Wales. The Anglicans, who had for many years sustained the Welsh cultural activities which the Nonconformists, particularly the Calvinistic Methodists, had often spurned, were driven to rely on their links with England for support and the resultant denominational divide created a rift in what could have been a consciously shared heritage.

It was a divide which was to bedevil the establishment in Wales of a network of elementary schools, a development which disputes over the nature of religious education delayed until the 1870s. However, the number of elementary schools increased during the 1850s, as did the state's involvement in financing them, and in 1861 the 'Revised Code' instituted capitation grants of twelve shillings per child, two-thirds of which could be withheld if the pupil failed to satisfy the examiners in arithmetic and the reading and writing of English. The teaching of Welsh was not prohibited, but as the livelihood of teachers depended on their pupils' proficiency in English, there was no incentive to teach Welsh, and pupils in some areas were punished for speaking it.

In 1870 the Elementary Education Act opened the way to the establishment of a network of elementary schools and in 1880 attendance became compulsory. The payment-by-results system was retained and the education provided was almost entirely in English. The 1870 Act is widely considered to have had a devastating effect on the Welsh language. Its impact has, however, been much exaggerated, English having been used as a teaching medium in schools in Welsh-speaking areas since the seventeenth century. In areas where Welsh was already weak, the Act probably struck the final blow, but it was only one of many factors, not the sole determinant of linguistic change.

Welsh did make one significant advance in the field of education at this time. The practice of teaching Welsh-speaking children through the medium of English gave rise to concern among educationists, one of whom, Dan Isaac Davies, an inspector of schools in Glamorgan, established in 1885 the Society for the Utilization of Welsh in Education, more generally known as the Welsh Language Society or Cymdeithas yr Iaith Gymraeg (of the first creation). In the same year Davies published a collection of his articles, *Tair Miliwn o Gymry Dwy-ieithawg* ('Three Million Bilingual Welsh People'), in which he argued that an enlightened educational policy would produce three million bilingual citizens by 1985. The memorandum on the use of Welsh submitted to the Royal Commission on Elementary Education was also largely his work, and he gave evidence to the commission shortly before his death in 1886.

The commission recommended that capitation grants should be given to schools which taught Welsh, and the use of bilingual books was authorized and the teaching of Welsh history and geography encouraged. These were meagre concessions, grafted as they were on to a basically English curriculum; no school was obliged to teach Welsh. Nevertheless, they represented a development of great significance, since all subsequent advances made by the Welsh language in the field of education stemmed from this first toe-hold in the system. Further progress was made in the twentieth century under the auspices of Owen M. Edwards, the Welsh Board of Education's chief inspector of schools between 1907 and 1920 and an indefatigable producer of children's books. The situation was less favourable at the secondary level. Of the secondary schools established under the provisions of the Welsh Intermediate Education Act of 1889, less than half offered Welsh lessons, and although the subject gradually won recognition, the ethos of the schools remained almost entirely English, even in the Welsh-speaking areas.

Despite its rather tenuous hold on a place in secondary education, Welsh was gaining acceptance as a subject of academic study. With the publication of Kaspar Zeuss's *Grammatica Celtica* in 1871, Celtic philology was at last placed on a sound foundation. A chair of Celtic was established at Oxford in 1871 on the urging of Matthew Arnold, who somewhat oddly combined a desire for the demise of the Celtic languages with an ardent advocacy of their study. *Lectures on Welsh Philology*, the work of John Rhŷs, the first holder of the Oxford chair, showed that scholars were at last following in the footsteps of Edward Lhuyd. Celtic studies also found a place in the new Welsh university colleges, and chairs were created at Aberystwyth (1875), Cardiff (1884), Bangor (1895) and Swansea (1920). Although most departments taught in English until the 1920s and were hindered in their work by the absence of linguistic studies and published texts, this was a development of crucial significance; the work of university teachers transformed Welsh scholarship. In particular, John Morris-Jones, who taught at Bangor from 1889 until 1929, established the orthography of Welsh, described its grammar and analysed the system of strict metres used in traditional poetry. Students of and graduates in Welsh figured with increasing prominence in the life of Wales and the prestige of the language rose.

Increased prestige was not, however, accompanied by any official status and Welsh made little impact in the fields of law, administration and commerce. Some small rural businesses conducted their affairs in Welsh and use was very occasionally made of the language in official notices. Agitation against monoglot English judges was only fitfully pursued and the fact that courts and official meetings had to make extensive use of translation – 34 per cent of the witnesses who appeared before the Royal Commission on Land in Wales in the 1890s gave their evidence through a translator – did not give rise to any widespread demand that official bodies should transact their business in Welsh. One who did advocate the use of Welsh in public life was Michael D. Jones, the architect of the Patagonia venture. The issue came to the fore following the creation of county councils in 1889. The first meeting of the Meirionnydd County Council was attended by six English monoglots, three Welsh monoglots and fifty-seven members whose fluency in Welsh far surpassed their command of English. Michael D. Jones suggested that, in these circumstances, business should be conducted in Welsh and the issue was referred to the Attorney-General, who decided in favour of English. Michael D. Jones subsequently distanced himself from the proceedings and the members of the council were left to carry out their duties through the medium of an unfamiliar tongue. The indefatigable journalist and pamphleteer Emrys ap Iwan (Robert Ambrose Jones) also argued passionately for the increased use of Welsh, deploring the establishment by his denomination, the Calvinistic Methodists, of English-medium chapels and urging the formation of a group of 'covenanters' prepared to defend the Welsh language.

In the 1890s official statistics relating to the distribution of Welsh and English in Wales became available for the first time. The census of 1891 was the first to concern itself with the linguistic situation in Wales; forms were distributed asking the country's inhabitants to specify whether they spoke English only, Welsh only or both languages. The census showed that 54.4% (910,289) of the population of Wales over the age of two spoke Welsh, the percentage varying from 95% in Cardiganshire to 6% in Radnorshire. No record was made of the tens of thousands of Welsh-speakers living elsewhere in the United Kingdom; had they been included, together with Welsh-speakers in the colonies and dominions, in the United States and in Patagonia, the total number in 1891 would undoubtedly have exceeded a million. Of those resident in Wales, 56% (508,036) were returned as speaking Welsh only, a figure which is very close to the 508,098 Welsh-speakers recorded one hundred years later. It is likely that many of those returned as bilingual in the censuses of the early twentieth century had only a very minimal knowledge of English; on the other hand, the drastic drop in Welsh monolingualism between 1891 and 1901 – from 32.1% to 7.3% in Merthyr, for example – indicates that the way the question was posed in 1891 led large numbers who spoke Welsh habitually, but who had some knowledge of English, to return 'Welsh' rather than 'Both'. This confusion is reflected in the fact that the returns were sometimes altered by the enumerator; in Clydach Dingle, near Brynmawr in Breconshire, for example, 'Welsh' was frequently crossed out and 'Both' substituted.

According to the 1891 figures, 54.4% of the inhabitants of Wales claimed to be able to speak Welsh, while 69.7% claimed a knowledge of English. A significant shift had occurred since 1801, when the population had probably been 70% monoglot Welsh, 20% monoglot English and 10% bilingual. In that ninety-year period, 1801–91, the population of Wales trebled, the number of Welsh monoglots rose by 25% and the number of English monoglots multiplied by seven; twice as many of Wales's inhabitants had a knowledge of Welsh in 1891, while the number with a knowledge of English had increased seventy-fold. Nevertheless, Welsh was much more widely spoken and there remained areas into which English had hardly penetrated at all. It may cause little surprise that all the inhabitants of the parish of Blaenpennal spoke Welsh and that 96% of them had no knowledge of English, for Blaenpennal lies in the heart of

Cardiganshire. But the situation was very similar in Llangadwaladr in Denbighshire, a parish only three miles from the English border, where 99.5% of the inhabitants spoke Welsh and 88% knew no English.

Between 1881 and 1901, 160,000 people migrated from such districts as Blaenpennal and Llangadwaladr; this exodus, caused by the depressed state of agriculture, was to have a profound effect upon the fortunes of the Welsh language. During that same period, 130,000 people flooded into the industrial areas of south-east Wales, the bulk of them from the largely Welsh-speaking rural counties of Wales. The census of 1891 shows that almost half those claiming to speak Welsh lived in the industrial belt which extended from Llanelli in the east to Pontypool in the west. The southern coalfield became a linguistic mosaic. In the Rhondda, of the first seven households in Dumfries Street, Treorci, one was monoglot English, two were bilingual and four were monoglot Welsh. Many English-speaking migrants had been assimilated, the collieries of the Rhondda being, it was claimed, the best linguistic schools in Wales. There was little intergenerational language loss, at least in the upper Rhondda, the children of Welsh-speaking parents almost invariably having a knowledge of the language. The pattern was rather different further east. In Brynmawr, which had a high incidence of marriages between monoglot English-speakers and bilinguals, the children were almost always monoglot English; English monolingualism in children was also common when both parents were bilingual. In some families, the elder children had a knowledge of Welsh and the younger ones did not, and there were also three-generation households with monoglot Welsh grandparents, bilingual parents and monoglot English children. Yet examples of English incomers learning Welsh are to be found even on the eastern fringes of the coalfield. A number of servants from England were employed at Sir Joseph Bailey's mansion in the parish of Llangatwg, Breconshire, which, like many gentry houses, was a centre of Anglicization; nevertheless, his gamekeeper, a native of Bermondsey, is recorded as speaking Welsh.

In the twenty years between 1891 and 1911, the population of Wales rose from 1,771,451 to 2,420,921, a dramatic change caused not only by natural increase – the coalfield was a most prolific area – but also by in-migration on a scale which placed Wales, in the first decade of the twentieth century, second only to the United States in its ability to attract in-migrants. In that decade, more than 100,000 people moved from England to the industrial areas of Wales. The results of this huge influx of population are reflected in the censuses of 1901 and 1911. Based on somewhat different criteria from those used in 1891, and as yet available only as published reports, the returns show an increase in the number of Welsh-speakers, to 929,824 in 1901 and to 977,366 in 1911. There was, however, a decline in the percentage claiming a knowledge of Welsh, to 49.9% in 1901 and to 43.5% in 1911. The number of monoglots declined to 208,905 in 1901 and to 190,292 in 1911, which suggests that they were either overestimated in 1891 or underestimated subsequently. The percentage returned as English-speaking rose to 84.9% in 1901 and to 91.5% in 1911. By the beginning of the twentieth century, therefore, less than half the population of Wales was recorded as being able to speak Welsh. This was a change of profound significance, for the Welsh could no longer be defined as a people who were predominantly Welsh-speaking. Subsequent attempts at a viable definition were to lead to controversy. Welsh-speakers continued to describe themselves as *Cymry*, while referring to English speakers as *Saeson*; this usage, when translated as 'Welsh people' and 'English people' – a translation which implied that

English monoglots were not a part of the Welsh nation – gave rise to resentment and bitterness.

Industrialization and the developments that came in its wake had hugely important implications for the Welsh language; to it can be attributed the sharp decline in the proportion of Welsh-speakers. Nevertheless, it has been argued, notably by the economist Brinley Thomas, that industrialization was the saviour, not the destroyer, of the language, leading as it did to the establishment in Wales of a population sufficiently large to support a wide range of cultural activities and institutions. But if industrialization had a positive role to play in the fortunes of the Welsh language, it also had its negative aspects. The sheer scale of in-migration in the early years of the twentieth century made the linguistic assimilation of incomers increasingly difficult in all areas and virtually impossible in some. Industrialization also introduced new ideas and allegiances, and the Welsh language, identified as it was with Liberalism and Nonconformity, could appear anachronistic and divisive in a society increasingly dominated by Labour politics and secular philosophy.

By 1921, Welsh-speakers accounted for 37.1 per cent (922,092) of the inhabitants of Wales. As many as 20,000 young, Welsh-speaking men may have died during the First World War, the best remembered of this lost generation being the shepherd poet Hedd Wyn (Ellis Humphrey Evans), killed twenty-seven days before he should have been chaired at the National Eisteddfod of 1917. After the war, Wales had to contend with new social and economic factors. Agricultural depression led to rural depopulation; in the later 1920s and throughout the 1930s, deaths outnumbered births in Anglesey, Caernarfon, Meirionnydd and Cardigan, counties in which Welsh-speakers were the overwhelming majority. But bad as the situation was in the countryside, the impact of the depression on the industrial areas was more dramatic. Migration into the coalfield ceased. By August 1932, unemployment among insured males had reached 42.8 per cent. Emigration seemed the only option, and between 1925 and 1939, 390,000 people moved out of Wales. With emigration to England appearing to be the only course open to the younger generation, there seemed little point in passing the Welsh language on to them. In some coalfield communities in the 1930s, three-quarters of those aged over 65 claimed a knowledge of Welsh, while less than a quarter of those aged under 11 did so.

The penury created by the depression curtailed the ability of chapel-goers to sustain the range of chapel-based activities which had been central to the Welsh-language culture of the coalfield. It was also widely held that scientific socialism held the only answer to the problems of the depression and to social injustice in general; those holding such views tended to be contemptuous of religion and of the Welsh language which was so closely associated with it. During the 1920s, popular daily newspapers indulged in a brisk circulation war; the sale of London daily papers soared and the numbers taking Welsh periodicals fell sharply. The cinema became increasingly popular and from 1927 the talkies introduced English (or American) throughout Wales. The BBC began broadcasting in 1923 and Cardiff became the headquarters of the West Region, which served the West of England as well as Wales; the service was overwhelmingly English. Buses, charabancs, cars and motorcycles brought tourists to all parts of Wales; remote villages, where Welsh alone had been heard for fifteen hundred years, now reverberated every summer to the sound of English voices.

But there were also more positive developments during the inter-war years. Urdd Gobaith Cymru (the Welsh League of Youth) was established in 1922, with the aim of attracting the young to the Welsh language by means of games, athletics and camps, as well as through cultural activities. By 1934 it had some 50,000 members, and the rapidity of its growth testifies to the strong appeal of Welshness. The year 1925 saw the formation of Plaid Genedlaethol Cymru (the National Party of Wales). Initially, the new party concentrated its attention upon the defence of the Welsh language, functioning entirely through the medium of Welsh and based in almost entirely Welsh-speaking areas. It attracted little support, but its introduction of the concept of the sovereignty of Welsh brought a new element into discussions about the language.

Welsh literature also reached new heights during the inter-war years; poets like T. Gwynn Jones, T. H. Parry-Williams and R. Williams Parry introduced a more naturalistic style of poetry, while prose was represented by the short stories of Kate Roberts, the essays of R. T. Jenkins and the writings of Saunders Lewis. Another important development was the publication in 1927 of *Welsh in Education and Life*, the report of a committee appointed by the President of the Board of Education to examine the position of Welsh in the educational system and to make recommendations as to how the study of the language could be promoted. Differing greatly in tone from the Blue Books published eighty years earlier, the report noted that, although Welsh had made great advances, there were serious deficiencies to be addressed. It outlined policies for the different linguistic areas of Wales and advocated the allocation of adequate resources to teacher training and the preparation of educational materials. The report's authors were particularly concerned about the education of the children of Welsh-speaking families living in the larger towns. Interestingly, in view of later developments, they did not recommend the establishment in such towns of designated Welsh schools, fearing that such a development would involve the children in too much travelling and might also lead other schools in the area to abandon the teaching of Welsh.

The report's authors were also concerned about the impact of broadcasting on the Welsh language, and pressure for a broadcasting station serving Wales alone finally brought about the establishment, in 1937, of the Welsh Region. Producers based at Cardiff were expected to deal with programmes in both Welsh and English; this situation led to large-scale recruitment from the Welsh-speaking community and gave rise to the belief that Welsh-speakers had a virtual monopoly of the BBC in Wales. In fact, the BBC became a significant patron of both Welsh and Anglo-Welsh literature. It was also a highly significant development in the history of the Welsh language, taking over the function, formerly performed by the chapels, of supplying a standard spoken Welsh and thereby doing much to unite a language in which dialect differences were considerable.

The improvement in the position of Welsh in the fields of education and broadcasting was not mirrored in the courts of law. In 1936 Saunders Lewis and two others set fire to an RAF bombing school in Llŷn, in protest against the fact that the government had bowed to opposition to such schemes in England while refusing even to receive a deputation from Wales, and out of concern for the effect the bombing school would have on a place steeped in the language and culture of Wales. During the subsequent trial at the Caernarfon assizes, the judge refused to allow the defendants to address the court in Welsh, a contemptuous attitude which threw into stark relief the subordinate status of the Welsh language. At the 1938 National Eisteddfod, a petition was launched demanding the repeal of the language clauses of the Act of Union and the granting to Welsh of equal status with English. Signed by more than a quarter of a million people and by thirty of the thirty-six Welsh MPs, the petition resulted in the Welsh Courts Act of 1942, which laid down that Welsh might be used in court should the person using it feel that he or she would otherwise be at a disadvantage. It was also stated that the court should bear the cost of the translation. The Act was a meagre concession, falling far short of what the petition had demanded.

There were many in Wales who feared that the Second World War would destroy the country's distinctiveness, and Pwyllgor Amddiffyn Diwylliant Cymru (the Committee for the Defence of the Culture of Wales), formed in December 1939, reflected that concern. Such fears proved exaggerated. Casualties were one-third of those suffered in the First World War; adult evacuees, on the whole, made only a short stay in Wales and child evacuees in Welsh-speaking areas were easily assimilated. Most of the land commandeered by the War Office – with the exception of Mynydd Epynt in Breconshire, where a community of 400 Welsh-speakers was permanently dispersed – had been restored by 1945.

Because of the war, no census was held in 1941. A comparison of the returns for 1931, when 36.8% (909,261) of the inhabitants of Wales spoke Welsh, and those for 1951, when 28.9% (714,686) did so, reveals the changes which had taken place over a twenty-year period. Most western rural counties recorded a decline of some 8%, but in the depression-ravaged county of Glamorgan the figure was 33%. Almost all the areas with a high proportion of Welsh-speakers were rural, the exceptions being an area to the north of Swansea and Llanelli and a group of quarrying parishes in the north-west. The 1951 census also strikingly reveals the disappearance of a solidly Welsh-speaking bloc extending unbroken over vast tracts of land; instead, a series of islands rose up in the midst of an increasingly Anglicized sea.

The three subsequent censuses mirrored the trends which had become apparent in 1951. The percentage of the inhabitants of Wales able to speak Welsh fell to 26% (656,002) in 1961, to 20.9% (542,425) in 1971 and to 18.7% (503,520) in 1981. The most dramatic drop, that recorded in the 1960s, is to be attributed in part to changes introduced in the census of 1971; from that year onwards, questions were asked not only about the ability to speak Welsh, but also about the ability to read and write it. Many Welsh-speakers, reluctant to admit that they were illiterate in the language, stated that they spoke English only. Literacy levels varied considerably from region to region. In 1981, 89.76% of the Welsh-speakers of Dwyfor (the Llŷn peninsula) were literate in the language; in Port Talbot, the figure was 54.83%. Areas which contained designated Welsh-medium schools or a high proportion of middle-class Welsh-speakers also recorded high percentages: 72.14% in Cardiff, for example, and 76.4% in Taff-Ely (the southern part of the present borough of Rhondda Cynon Taf). The census of 1981 was the last to concern itself with the ability to speak English. Monolingualism in Welsh among very young children was considerable; among adults, it probably disappeared in the 1960s, although some bilinguals chose to declare themselves monoglot Welsh. By 1981, only 0.8% (21,283) of the population was recorded as speaking Welsh only.

Throughout the twentieth century, those areas which recorded a very high proportion of Welsh-speakers continued to contract. In 1961, 36.8% of the surface area of Wales consisted of 279 communities, more than 80% of whose inhabitants claimed a knowledge of Welsh. In 1981, 9.7% of the surface area – sixty-six communities – contained a proportion of Welsh-speakers in excess of 80%. By 1991, in only thirty-two of the 912 wards into which Wales was by then divided did Welsh-speakers account for more than 80% of the population. The islands in an Anglicized sea, visible since 1951, had contracted to form five core areas: central Anglesey; the old quarrying areas of Gwynedd and the Llŷn peninsula; an area centred upon Penllyn in eastern Meirionnydd but extending into Conwy, Denbighshire and Montgomeryshire; a group of scattered nuclei in the upland south-west; and the westerly valleys of the South Wales coalfield.

The second half of the twentieth century witnessed the contraction of the industries which sustained those communities that formed the core of the Welsh-speaking areas of Wales. The quarries of Gwynedd, which had employed 20,000 men in the 1890s, provided work for fewer than 500 by the 1980s. The coalmines and tinplate works of east Carmarthenshire and West Glamorgan – an area which accounted for roughly a quarter of the Welsh-speakers of Wales – declined rapidly. Carmarthenshire, which had contained 14,644 coalminers in 1921, was home to only a few hundred in 1991. The decline of agriculture had an even greater impact. In Anglesey, Caernarfonshire, Meirionnydd, Cardiganshire and Carmarthenshire – the only ancient counties to have substantial Welsh-speaking majorities – the 40,000 families engaged in farming in 1921 had dwindled to barely one-third of that number by 1991. As the traditional industries declined, the rich Welsh vocabularies associated with them fell into disuse. Tens of thousands of Welsh-speakers found employment in new industries in which the use of Welsh was minimal, or moved away altogether, leaving behind them an ageing population. Between 1921 and 1971, the population of the quarrying parish of Llanddeiniolen in Caernarfonshire fell by 20%, that of the industrial parish of Llan-giwg in West Glamorgan by 25%, that of the Rural District of Tregaron by 38% and that of the Rural District of Penllyn by a staggering 43%.

The contraction in agriculture created surplus housing stock in the countryside, and many of these houses were bought as holiday or retirement homes. For some incomers, the motivation was provided by the self-sufficiency movement and the comparative cheapness of land in Wales. Tourist resorts, which had long been centres of Anglicization, became increasingly popular, while military bases, expanding centres of higher education and attempts to industrialize parts of rural Wales all contributed to the influx of population. In some parishes in rural west Wales, the proportion of the inhabitants born outside Wales rose to almost 50%, and they were in the majority in Colwyn Bay, Abergele, Prestatyn and even in such remote districts as Llanfair Mathafarn Eithaf in Anglesey. This demographic revolution had obvious implications for the Welsh language. Not all the incomers were hostile or indifferent to it – by 1991, indeed, 10% of the Welsh-speakers of Wales had been born outside the country – but nevertheless the inhabitants of the traditional heartland areas came to feel that the influx might squeeze them out of existence.

The demographic change caused by in-migration to the traditionally Welsh-speaking areas had far-reaching implications. In 1961, 57% of the surface area of Wales had recorded a Welsh-speaking majority; by 1991, the figure was 33.9%, and the Welsh-speakers of that 33.9% represented 41.6% of the total number of Welsh-speakers in Wales. By the late twentieth century, therefore, the majority of Welsh-speakers did not live in areas in which Welsh was the majority language, and over the greater part of the country it became the language of networks within the community rather than of the community as a whole. In the most westerly region of the South Wales coalfield and in

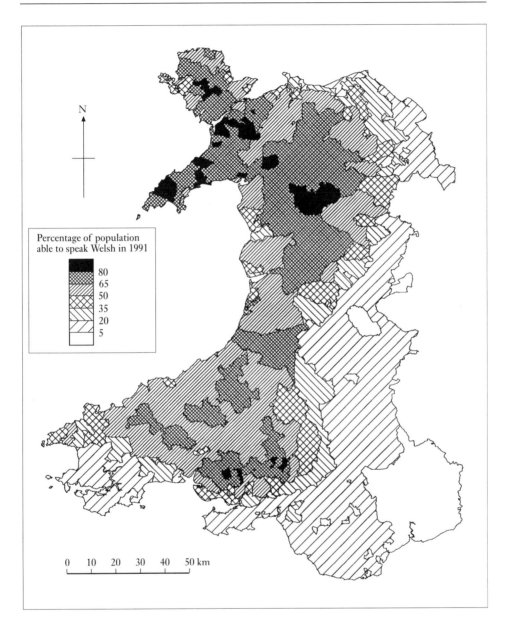

Map 6 *The Welsh language in 1991. Map based on data provided by the 1991 census of population. From John Aitchison and Harold Carter,* A Geography of the Welsh Language 1961–1991 *(Cardiff, University of Wales Press, 1994).*

the quarrying districts of the north, Welsh-speakers still lived in a largely Welsh-speaking environment; elsewhere, they formed a substantial presence in the resorts of the North Wales coast, in the districts around Cardiff, Swansea, Llanelli and Wrexham and in parts of Mid Glamorgan, all areas in which English was the language of the majority.

The areas which contained substantial numbers of Welsh-speakers can be divided into two categories. In one category are those districts which had contained a Welsh-speaking majority in the recent past. In such areas, intergenerational language loss had been substantial, with the result that knowledge of the language had become concentrated among the older age-groups. For example, the 1971 census for Merthyr Tydfil records that 41% of the borough's Welsh-speakers were to be found among the 15% of the population aged over 65. Slippage between generations is largely accountable for the fact that the number of Welsh-speakers declined by 206,479 between 1951 and 1981. The other category of areas with high numbers of Welsh-speakers presents a sharp contrast. These were areas of high employment which attracted a substantial number of in-migrants from the traditionally Welsh-speaking areas: towns like Newtown, Mold, Llandrindod and – above all – the city of Cardiff.

Between 1951 and 1991 the number of Welsh-speakers in Cardiff rose from 9,623 to 17,236, an increase of 79%, while in a wide belt surrounding the city the percentages speaking Welsh doubled and trebled (admittedly from low bases). In 1951, 5% of all Welsh-speakers lived within twenty-five kilometres of Cardiff; forty years later, 10% did so. The percentage is still low, and the ability of such a dispersed linguistic community to create viable networks has been questioned. By 1991, however, several wards of the city contained more than 350 Welsh-speakers per square kilometre and the evidence suggests that the number is continuing to rise. Most of the Welsh-speaking incomers to Cardiff are employed in education, administration and the media and live in the more affluent areas of the city. (It remains to be seen whether or not the establishment of the National Assembly in Cardiff in 1999 will lead them to colonize what have hitherto been less prosperous districts.) The association of Welsh with the middle classes has raised the social status of the language, low since the Anglicization of the gentry, a new development apparent not only in Cardiff but in other areas as well.

The transformation of the position of the Welsh language in Cardiff and other Anglicized urban areas was not the only new development revealed by the 1991 census. One hundred years after the first language census, the steady decline in the number of Welsh-speakers appeared at last to have been halted. The 1991 figures, because of changes in the enumeration system, are not strictly comparable with those for previous censuses, but they do offer grounds for optimism about the future of Welsh. According to the returns, 18.6% (508,098) of the inhabitants of Wales over the age of 3 claimed to have a knowledge of Welsh. The percentage figure represents a very slight decline from the 18.7% recorded in 1981; the actual number represents an equally slight increase on the 503,520 recorded in that year.

A significant feature of the 1991 returns is the marked increase which was recorded in the number of children claiming to speak Welsh, from 18% of those aged between 3 and 15 in 1981 to 22% in 1991. For the first time in a hundred years, knowledge of Welsh was more widespread among the young than among the old. In Gwynedd, 61% of the total population was recorded as speaking Welsh, compared with a figure of 77.6% for those between 3 and 15; in the Llŷn peninsula, the respective percentages were 75.4 and 94.1. The really striking differentials, however, were to be found in the Anglicized areas: 9.6% of the total as compared with 27.2% in the age-group 3–15 in the north-eastern district of Alyn and Deeside; 8.3% and 27.6% in Radnorshire.

This increase in the number of young people claiming a knowledge of Welsh can be attributed very largely to changes which took place during the second half of the twentieth century in the field of education. In the 1940s, Welsh was the main medium of education in nursery and primary schools in those areas in which it was also the language of the vast majority. Elsewhere, the amount of Welsh teaching given to monoglot English children varied according to the policy of the local education authority, and little specific provision was made for children from Welsh-speaking homes. In 1947, the Carmarthenshire Education Authority took the innovative step of designating one of its Llanelli schools a Welsh-medium school. Another dozen such schools were established during the next four years and a private Welsh-medium school at Aberystwyth was taken over by the local education authority. Originally intended to provide education in their mother tongue for Welsh-speaking children, by the late 1950s Welsh-medium schools drew the majority of their pupils from English-speaking homes. By 1974, sixty-one designated Welsh schools had been established and were attended by 8,500 pupils. Welsh nursery education developed in close association with the primary schools. Mudiad Ysgolion Meithrin (the nursery schools movement) was established in 1971, by which time there were already sixty-eight nursery schools attended by 950 pupils; by 1998, there were 577 schools and 9,338 pupils, as well as 393 mother-and-child groups attended by 4,525 children.

The secondary sector also experienced an expansion of Welsh-medium education. In the 1940s, in schools in the English-speaking areas, Welsh was taught in the same manner as French, a practice which put pupils at a disadvantage when they were subsequently confronted by examination papers intended for those for whom Welsh was the mother tongue. In the Welsh-speaking areas, Welsh was virtually the only subject taught through the medium of Welsh until the early 1950s, when some schools began to use it to teach such subjects as Welsh history and religious instruction. The first mainly Welsh-medium secondary school, Ysgol Glan Clwyd, was established by Flintshire County Council in 1956. Other such schools followed, mainly in the English-speaking north-east and south-east, though some, like those at Aberystwyth, Bangor and Carmarthen, drew upon Welsh-speaking catchment areas. Most of these schools were bilingual rather than exclusively Welsh-medium, and science subjects were frequently taught through the medium of English, while non-designated schools, particularly in Gwynedd and Dyfed, offered an increased number of subjects through the medium of Welsh.

The effects of the growth in Welsh-medium education on the numbers of young people claiming a knowledge of Welsh became apparent throughout the Anglicized areas. For example, 2,190 of Cardiff's Welsh-speakers were under the age of 15 in 1971; by 1991, the figure was 5,208, and the ability to speak Welsh in this age-group was 153% higher than it was among those over 65. An equally marked contrast was to be found in such neighbouring areas as Llantrisant, Pontypridd and Caerffili, and in Mold in the north-east. Striking as these figures are, it should be borne in mind that those attending Welsh-medium schools constitute a very small percentage of the pupils of Wales. The degree to which Welsh is taught as a second language in English-medium schools varies considerably, though the situation, largely unsatisfactory in the 1940s, altered for the better in the 1950s and 1960s with the introduction of improved teaching methods and attractive teaching materials. The existence of Welsh-medium schools may arouse indifference or even hostility towards the Welsh language among the pupils of English-medium schools, although hearing their friends and neighbours speaking Welsh may equally well encourage those attending English-medium schools to learn it. Pupils attending Welsh-medium schools in the Anglicized areas live in an environment in which the English language is dominant. In 1988, a report suggested that Cardiff pupils made little use of Welsh outside school, but more recent research in the Bridgend area indicates that the language is increasingly used in adult life by those who acquired it at school.

Originally, the designated Welsh schools were established in the Anglicized areas, it being assumed that, in the traditionally Welsh-speaking areas, Welsh would be the principal medium of primary education. However, as pressures, caused largely by in-migration, began to pose a threat to Welsh-medium teaching in rural schools, demands for the establishment of designated Welsh schools in the Welsh-speaking areas were made by those who feared that Welsh would be squeezed out of schools in which it had hitherto been the dominant language. At the same time, many of the incomers were pressing for English-medium education for their children, and were supported by a minority of Welsh-speaking parents. In the areas in which designated Welsh schools had originally been established, an English-medium alternative could be found close at hand; in the rural areas, this option was not usually available. Opposition to the teaching of Welsh became more vocal in the 1970s, and the eight new counties established in 1974 set about the business of evolving language policies. The policy adopted varied from county to county, the most far-reaching being that of Gwynedd, which offered facilities designed to assist pupils who did not speak Welsh to obtain rapid fluency in the language. A further reorganization in local government took place in 1996, and Welsh-medium primary schools are to be found within all the twenty-two new unitary county authorities. The degree to which Welsh is taught as a second language in primary schools varies from county to county but, in accordance with the provisions of the National Curriculum as laid down by the Education Act of 1988, all pupils receive some Welsh lessons. The National Curriculum also requires that all secondary schools offer Welsh as a second language to pupils up to 16 years of age.

Although no use was initially made of Welsh as a medium of instruction in the colleges of the University of Wales, the Department of Welsh in Cardiff began lecturing in Welsh in the 1920s and by the 1940s all Welsh departments throughout the university operated almost exclusively through the medium of Welsh. A proposal that one college of the university should offer a full range of subjects through Welsh met with no acceptance, but in 1955 the university authorities agreed to expand the use of the language in order to meet the needs of students who had received their secondary education through the medium of Welsh. Some two dozen lecturers were accordingly appointed, most of them in Arts departments. An external degree scheme was launched by the University College of Wales, Aberystwyth, in 1980, and the number of students following a degree course through the medium of Welsh proved a stimulus to the production of works of scholarship in the language. Welsh-medium courses became increasingly available in colleges of education, though provision was scantier in technical and further education colleges.

During the second half of the twentieth century classes for adult learners of Welsh proliferated. One of the most ardent advocates of teaching Welsh to adults was R. M. Jones, the first 'learner' to be appointed to a chair of Welsh and – under the name Bobi

Jones – a distinguished Welsh-language poet. The publication of his *Cymraeg i Oedolion* ('Welsh for Adults', 1965–6) was an important step in the provision of material for teachers and learners of Welsh. The increased use of Welsh by public bodies and the desire of parents whose children attended Welsh-medium schools to keep up with and assist their offspring in the study of the language fuelled a demand for courses for adults. These were organized by the university colleges and other bodies, language lessons on radio and television attracted considerable audiences, and Cyngor y Dysgwyr (CYD – the Learners' Council, founded in 1984) enjoyed wide support. Inspired by the renaissance of Hebrew in Israel, enthusiasts of the adult learning movement adopted the Hebrew word *ulpan* (rendered in Welsh as *wlpan*) to describe their intensive Welsh courses, the outstanding example of which was the eight-week course held yearly at Lampeter. Another venture has been the refurbishment of the dramatically sited and formerly deserted village of Nant Gwrtheyrn (on the north coast of the Llŷn peninsula, south-west of Caernarfon) as a year-round centre for language learning.

In the twentieth century, the declining circulation of old-established periodicals, such as *Baner ac Amserau Cymru*, bore witness to the increasingly precarious state of Welsh-language publishing. It was still capable of producing new initiatives; new newspapers and periodicals – the illustrated weekly *Y Cymro* among them – appeared even during the depressed 1930s, and the 1950s saw the launching of a host of new periodicals which included the monthly magazine *Barn*, the literary journal *Taliesin* and the scientific periodical *Y Gwyddonydd*. Yet most periodicals faced the kind of financial problems which finally overcame *Y Faner* (formerly *Baner ac Amserau Cymru*) in 1992. Costs were rising and potential readership was limited, and the case for public subsidy was persuasively argued. The Welsh Committee of the Arts Council had assisted Welsh publishers since its inception, and following the establishment of the autonomous Welsh Arts Council in 1967 most Welsh-language periodicals came, like the general interest weekly *Golwg*, to rely to some extent upon public funding. The publication of *papurau bro*, or neighbourhood newspapers was, however, an initiative which, initially at least, owed nothing to public subsidy. The first of them, *Y Dinesydd*, was launched in Cardiff in 1973 and by 1998 there were fifty-six, with a joint circulation of some 52,000, a far greater readership than that of nation-wide publications like *Golwg* and *Y Cymro*. Some substantial, some more modest and almost all published monthly, the *papurau bro* are produced by unpaid volunteers; some of them have diversified their activities, organizing drama festivals and publishing books of local interest.

Publishing Welsh-language books has been an uncertain business ever since the first printed book, *Yn y lhyvyr hwnn*, made its appearance in 1547. The nineteenth century was a flourishing period, with the number of Welsh books published annually trebling between the 1820s and the 1880s, but by the middle of the twentieth century the number had fallen almost to the early nineteenth-century level. As in the case of periodicals, public subsidy began to play a part. Cardiganshire County Council began subsidizing books for children in 1950, an example followed by other counties. The Welsh Joint Education Committee gave grants towards the production of school books in Welsh from 1954 onwards, and in 1956 the government launched a scheme to assist publications for adults. Following the establishment of the Welsh Books Council in 1961, virtually every book published in Welsh received some degree of state aid. A network of

Welsh-language bookshops was set up and long-established publishers, such as Gwasg Gomer (1892) and the University of Wales Press (1922), were joined by a range of newer ventures.

A third of all books published in Welsh are either children's books or school books, while poetry accounts for a third of books for adults. The mid-twentieth century produced major poets in D. Gwenallt Jones, whose roots were in both industrial Glamorgan and rural Carmarthenshire; Waldo Williams, who wrote of the unity of nature and of universal brotherhood; and Gwyn Thomas, a poet inspired by modernity rather than by the longing for a lost utopia which characterized much Welsh poetry. The work of Dic Jones of Blaenporth in Ceredigion testified to the fact that the erosion of the Welsh-speaking communities had not led to the extinction of the *beirdd gwlad* (country poets), while by the 1970s there was a marked revival of interest in *cynghanedd* (see p. 79 above). The period from the 1980s onwards saw the emergence of a new generation of younger poets, writing in a wide range of genres and styles.

Welsh prose writing also flourished, with the novel, neglected since the days of Daniel Owen, replacing the short story and the essay as the most popular prose form. T. Rowland Hughes published five novels in the 1940s; Islwyn Ffowc Elis's *Cysgod y Cryman* ('The Shadow of the Sickle', 1956) attracted a new, younger readership; and in 1961 Caradog Prichard produced his finest novel, the semi-autobiographical *Un Nos Ola Leuad* ('One Moonlit Night'). Publications included historical novels, particularly those of Marion Eames, family sagas such as T. Glynne Davies's *Marged*, Rhydwen Williams's cycle of novels set in the Rhondda, and books with more contemporary themes, like those of John Rowlands, the first Welsh-language author to include in his works explicitly sexual scenes. The geographical redistribution of the Welsh language has given rise to novels with an urban setting, like those of Harri Pritchard Jones and Siôn Eirian. Wiliam O. Roberts's remarkable post-modern work, the picaresque novel *Y Pla* (translated into English as *The Pestilence*), was published in 1990 and Robin Llywelyn and Mihangel Morgan exploit other aspects of post-modernism in their writing. The period was also a productive one for Welsh-language drama, with Saunders Lewis, John Gwilym Jones, Huw Lloyd Edwards and Gwenlyn Parry producing plays of distinction, although younger dramatists have tended to turn their attention to the more ephemeral, though profitable, business of writing for television.

The tradition of Welsh linguistic scholarship first associated with Edward Lhuyd produced, in the twentieth century, a range of distinguished works: D. Simon Evans's *Gramadeg Cymraeg Canol* ('Grammar of Middle Welsh', 1951); T. J. Morgan's *Y Treigliadau a'u Cystrawen* ('The Mutations and their Syntax', 1952); Stephen J. Williams's *Elfennau Gramadeg Cymraeg* (1959; English version, *A Welsh Grammar*, 1980); David A. Thorne's *A Comprehensive Welsh Grammar* (1993); Peter Wynn Thomas's *Gramadeg y Gymraeg* ('Grammar of Welsh', 1996); and the writings of D. Ellis Evans on Continental Celtic and Brittonic. International interest in this field is considerable, and it has attracted scholars from the United States, Japan and Continental Europe. The vital role in the evolution of the Welsh language played by the Bible was acknowledged when in 1988 a revised version was published to mark the four-hundredth anniversary of William Morgan's great achievement. There has been considerable study of dialect and, to a lesser extent, of place-names, while the statistical material which has become available has given impetus to the establishment of an academic study of Welsh sociolinguistics. In 1992, the Centre for Advanced Welsh and Celtic Studies initiated an exhaustive study of the social history of the Welsh language, and four volumes have already been published: *The Welsh Language before the Industrial Revolution* (1997) and *Language and Community in the Nineteenth Century* (1998), both edited by Geraint H. Jenkins, Dot Jones's *Statistical Evidence Relating to the Welsh Language* (1988), and *The Welsh Language and the 1891 Census* (1999), by Mari A. Williams and Gwenfair Parry.

Established in 1985, the first project undertaken by the Centre for Advanced Welsh and Celtic Studies was an exhaustive survey of the work of the Gogynfeirdd, the poets of the princes. The study of the Cynfeirdd – the earliest poets – had been the work of Ifor Williams, Professor of Welsh at Bangor, who made, over a period of half a century, an outstanding contribution to Welsh literary and linguistic studies. The Welsh literary tradition up to the end of the nineteenth century was examined by Thomas Parry in his volume *Hanes Llenyddiaeth Gymraeg* (1945), H. Idris Bell's English translation of which, *A History of Welsh Literature*, was published in 1955. Parry also established the definitive canon of Dafydd ap Gwilym's work and edited the *Oxford Book of Welsh Verse* (1962). The very extensive manuscript collections of Welsh medieval poetry are now available (at least in typescript). Welsh medieval prose has been the subject of scholarly studies, as has the work of the Renaissance writers, the early Puritans, the Methodists and the eisteddfod competitors and novelists of the nineteenth century. Twentieth-century literature has also been extensively surveyed; its political and social context was analysed by Ned Thomas in his *Welsh Extremist* (1971; new edition 1992), and the relationship between the two literatures of Wales has been examined in the distinguished studies of M. Wynn Thomas.

The expansion of the use of Welsh in universities, though slight, was sufficient to give an impetus to the production of scholarly works in the language in fields other than Welsh literary and linguistic studies. Works of education and philosophy made their appearance, and there was a positive flowering of publications in the field of history, notable among them J. Beverley Smith's study of Llywelyn ap Gruffudd (1986; English version 1998), *Cof Cenedl* ('A Nation's Memory'), a collection of essays published annually and edited by Geraint H. Jenkins, and John Davies's comprehensive survey, *Hanes Cymru* (1990; English version, *A History of Wales*, 1993).

New words have been coined to meet the demands of modern society. *Cyfrifiadur* ('computer'), *meddalwedd* ('software'), *disg hyblyg* ('floppy disk') and *safle wê* ('website') made their appearance, as did *darllediad* ('broadcast'), *tonfedd* ('wavelength') and *oriau brig* ('peak hours'). Sports commentaries gave rise to a whole range of neologisms, those coined by Eic Davies for rugby being especially apt and pithy. Two vast and ambitious lexicographical projects have undertaken the bringing together of words old and new. *Geiriadur Prifysgol Cymru* (the University of Wales Welsh dictionary) has been appearing in parts since 1947 and the third of its projected four volumes was completed in 1998. *Geiriadur yr Academi* (*The Welsh Academy English–Welsh Dictionary*), edited by Bruce Griffiths and Dafydd Glyn Jones, was published in 1995 and contains in its 1,710 pages a complete range of Welsh equivalents for English words and idioms.

By the second half of the twentieth century, the broadcast word was becoming increasingly influential and in the 1940s and 1950s sound broadcasting flourished. BBC radio producers, among whom were to be found prominent Welsh writers, offered their listeners such distinguished fare as Welsh translations of the world's greatest dramatists and talks on literary subjects but were obliged also, in order to attract sub-stantial audiences, to supply children's serials – *Galw Gari Tryfan*, which featured a detective, was particularly popular in the 1950s – and variety shows. In 1953, in accor-dance with the recommendations of the Beveridge Report on Broadcasting, Wales was given its own Broadcasting Council, some members of which urged that the number of hours devoted to broadcasting in Welsh should be increased. Any such expansion inevitably resulted in opposition from those listeners to the Welsh Home Service – the great majority – who did not understand Welsh. The development of VHF in the 1970s offered a solution and in 1977 a choice was given in Wales's opt-out from Radio Four, with English available on medium wave and Welsh on VHF. This division became complete with the establishment of Radio Wales and Radio Cymru in 1978. By the late 1990s Radio Cymru was offering an unbroken Welsh-language service from 6 a.m. to 12 p.m., but was subject to attacks which alleged that its increasingly populist approach had led to a lowering of programme standards, the use of slovenly Welsh and a propen-sity to broadcast English-language pop songs. Local radio stations such as Swansea Sound and Radio Ceredigion also broadcast Welsh programmes.

When the BBC's television transmitting station was opened at Wenvoe in 1952, it seemed natural that television should follow in the footsteps of sound broadcasting and provide a Welsh-language service. Both the BBC and the commercial station Television Wales and West (TWW), whose station at St Hilary began transmitting in 1958, offered Welsh programmes from the outset, and they were also broadcast from the BBC's trans-mitters at Sutton Coldfield and Holme Moss and, for a short period, by Granada of Manchester. BBC Wales, which was established in 1964 in the wake of the Pilkington Report, had the obligation of initiating twelve hours of programmes, half of them in Welsh, every week. An attempt in 1961 to set up a commercial station serving north and west Wales and providing a substantial number of Welsh-language programmes was unsuccessful and the company was taken over by TWW, who undertook to broadcast five and a half hours of Welsh programmes weekly, an obligation inherited by Harlech Television (HTV) in 1968.

By the early 1960s, therefore, the transition from sound to visual broadcasting had been successfully carried through, and the BBC and HTV between them were broad-casting some eleven and a half hours of Welsh-language programmes weekly. Since they were not understood by the majority of viewers, these programmes were confined to off-peak hours, a measure which did not prevent those living in areas where an alternative English-language service was available – the densely populated areas of the north-east and the south-east, for example – from aligning their aerials so as to receive exclusively English programmes. So extensive was this practice that only 70,000 copies of the Wales edition of *Radio Times* were sold in 1969, compared with 96,000 copies (in Wales) of other editions. Television programmes in Welsh were, in fact, causing many viewers in Wales to turn their back, not only on the Welsh programmes but also on the English-language programmes emanating from Wales, while those viewers who did not have such an alternative available were becoming increasingly vocal in their demand that Welsh programmes should cease to be broadcast. Yet Welsh programmes represented less than 10 per cent of the total output, and an English programme was invariably available on one channel when there was a Welsh one on the other. With English-language programmes taking up 90 per cent of total broadcasting time and almost all the peak-hour slots, those who wanted to watch Welsh programmes were also becoming increasingly restive. By the late 1960s, television had become an extremely divisive issue in Wales, and by the early 1970s both sides in the argument – monoglot English-speakers who wanted uninterrupted English-language viewing and Welsh-speakers who wanted more convenient scheduling for Welsh programmes – were arguing in favour of a separate channel for Welsh-language television broadcasts.

Not everyone concerned was convinced of the desirability of a separate channel. On the English-language side, it was argued that, since the number of monoglot Welsh-speakers was infinitesimal, there was no need to screen any Welsh programmes at all. On the Welsh-language side, fears were expressed that viewers who watched Welsh-language programmes shown on their favourite channel would cease to do so if those programmes were moved to a separate channel. There was also another group, not very prominent in the 1970s but increasingly vocal as the years passed, which held that there should also be separate provision for English-language programmes directly relating to Wales.

In 1973, a national conference convened by the Lord Mayor of Cardiff endorsed the proposal that the fourth channel, when it was brought into service, should in Wales be used primarily to give provide prime-time scheduling for Welsh-language programmes. Enthusiastically supported by Charles Curran, the Director-General of the BBC, the proposal also found favour with those who were concerned that the existing situation was leading to a dangerous degree of polarization. Originally envisaged as a channel to be shared by the BBC and ITV, opinion swung in favour of a separate authority, an arrangement which would allow independent producers to have a role. In 1974 the Labour government accepted the Crawford Committee's recommendation that a Welsh fourth channel be established.

In May 1979 the Conservatives, who in their general election manifesto had committed themselves to the provision of a Welsh fourth channel, were returned to power. In September of the same year the Home Secretary, William Whitelaw, announced that the government would not proceed with the separate channel, but would concentrate instead on improving existing provision. His statement was received with anger, by Cymdeithas yr Iaith Gymraeg (the Welsh Language Society), some of whose members had suffered imprisonment in the cause of the Welsh fourth channel, and by Plaid Cymru, 2,000 of whose members resolved not to pay the television licence fee. Raids on transmitters were carried out by well-known and influential figures and then, in May 1980, Gwynfor Evans, the president of Plaid Cymru, announced that he would undertake to fast to death unless the government honoured its election pledge. During the late summer he addressed a number of mass rallies, at which the atmosphere was such that the government feared that a significant section of the Welsh population might well become intransigent. On 17 September 1980, the government yielded.

Sianel Pedwar Cymru (S4C – the Welsh Fourth Channel) went on air for the first time on 1 November 1982 and Welsh became a fully-fledged 'television language'. Its viewing figures are low by British standards, although the popular soap opera *Pobol y Cwm* attracts up to 250,000 viewers, 50 per cent of the 508,098 Welsh-speakers recorded in the 1991 census. *Pobol y Cwm*, however – for which, as for most of S4C's programmes, subtitles are available – is also popular among those who do not understand Welsh. No viewing figures are available for the channel's numerous viewers in England

and Ireland. Of S4C's weekly output of 154 hours, between thirty-five and forty are in Welsh, while the rest consist of a selection from the British Fourth Channel. In November 1998, a new digital channel broadcasting in Welsh for twelve hours a day was launched. S4C is a commissioning, not a producing channel; the BBC supplies twelve hours weekly, the rest being bought from HTV and from the independent production companies which mushroomed in the 1980s around Cardiff and also in strongly Welsh-speaking areas, such as the Caernarfon area and parts of Carmarthenshire.

Although by the mid-twentieth century Welsh had achieved a certain foothold in education and in sound broadcasting, it still had virtually no status in public life. Welsh-speakers had no absolute right to use it in courts of law, it almost never appeared on official forms, it was excluded from use in the postal and telephone services and – Welsh chapels apart – it hardly ever appeared on public buildings. Road signs routinely carried awkwardly Anglicized versions of Welsh place-names, although in the 1950s some counties erected bilingual notices on their boundaries. In the same period, a few local authorities began to issue bilingual rate demands, but a request for such a demand, made in 1952 by Eileen and Trefor Beasley to Llanelli Rural District Council, was met by a peremptory refusal, and the battle, during which the Beasleys' property was seized for non-payment of rates, was only concluded when the council yielded in 1960.

It was against this background that Saunders Lewis, invited to give the annual lecture of the BBC in Wales, delivered on 13 February 1962 his lecture *Tynged yr Iaith* ('The Fate of the Language'). Lewis declared that only a revolution could save the Welsh language, and that the way to bring about that revolution was to make it impossible to transact government business in Wales solely through the medium of English. The lecture inspired a group of young nationalists to found, in the summer of 1962, Cymdeithas yr Iaith Gymraeg (the Welsh Language Society), a title chosen out of respect for the nineteenth-century society of the same name. Beginning with a day of organized law-breaking in Aberystwyth on 2 February 1963, the society campaigned for the use of Welsh in court summonses, in the post office, on car licences and on road signs. Members of the society were involved in a host of court cases and were frequently imprisoned. Although the activists were almost all young people, they were regarded with tacit approval by many older Welsh-speakers, and in 1970 a group of magistrates, urged on by the editor of the magazine *Barn*, Alwyn D. Rees, arranged for the payment of an imprisoned protester's fine.

The 1960s also witnessed the granting to Wales of a considerable degree of administrative autonomy. In 1964, a new context was created for the discussion of the role of the Welsh language in public life by the creation of a Welsh Office and a Secretary of State for Wales. These arrangements also coincided with an upsurge in political nationalism. In 1966 Gwynfor Evans was returned for Carmarthen, a seat which he subsequently lost, gained and lost again. Caernarfon and Meirionnydd, however, won by Plaid Cymru in February 1974, have come to be regarded as safe seats for the party, which later won Anglesey and Ceredigion & Pembroke North (now Ceredigion). These victories, suggesting as they did that Wales had a future as a national community, increased the confidence of Welsh-language activists, who also became increasingly aware, following Britain's entry into the European Community in 1972, of the existence of other minority linguistic communities in Europe with whom it would be possible co-operate.

During the 1970s, the members of Cymdeithas yr Iaith Gymraeg, though principally concerned with the campaign for a Welsh television channel, also challenged forces which they considered were undermining the viability of Welsh-speaking communities, protesting against holiday homes, demonstrating against estate agents and becoming involved in discussions over planning policy. Their activities, together with a greater awareness of the value of Welsh, enhanced the language's status, a process which became particularly apparent following the reorganization of local government in 1974. Gwynedd County Council adopted a bilingual policy and installed instantaneous translation facilities in its council chamber, while Dwyfor District Council, going one step further, made Welsh the principal language for all its activities. Other local authorities followed suit to a greater or lesser extent, though in some cases their efforts amounted to little more than tokenism. Other public bodies – the main utilities, the health service, social security offices and the University of Wales – also adopted varying degrees of bilingualism, and there have been some advances in the commercial field.

The legal status of Welsh had remained unchanged since the passing, in 1942, of the Welsh Courts Act, and in 1961 the ambiguity of the language's legal standing was highlighted when a returning officer at Ammanford refused to accept the nomination papers of an election candidate because the papers had been completed in Welsh. In 1965 a government committee, established in 1963 to look into the situation, recommended that anything done in Welsh should be as valid in the eyes of the law as if it had been done in English. It also urged that more forms and official documents should be available in Welsh and that anyone wishing to do so should have an absolute right to use Welsh in a court of law. A diluted version of these recommendations was incorporated in the Welsh Language Act of 1967, though the Act adhered to the fundamental principle of the Act of Union in retaining English as the language of record in the courts.

The 1970s and 1980s witnessed a growing demand for a new Welsh Language Act which would clarify and strengthen the provisions of the Act of 1967, and in 1993 an Act was passed which stated that Welsh and English should be treated on a basis of equality in the conduct of public business and in the administration of justice. It also gave statutory recognition to the Welsh Language Board (previously a non-statutory body), which was given the duty of advising central government and all bodies providing public services as to how the principle of equality for Welsh and English should be implemented; it was also charged with investigating complaints. The new Welsh Language Act fell short of declaring Welsh to be an official language, while the Welsh Language Board was given no mandatory powers to enforce its recommendations, and Cymdeithas yr Iaith began to campaign for stronger legislation. Despite these drawbacks the Board, under the chairmanship of Lord Elis-Thomas, has shown considerable energy and enterprise.

In September 1997 a referendum produced a majority in favour of the establishment of a Welsh Assembly which would take over the powers of the Secretary of State and have the right to pass secondary legislation. At the National Eisteddfod held at Bridgend in 1998, a historic meeting took place between the architect of the referendum victory, the Secretary of State, Ron Davies, and representatives of Cymdeithas yr Iaith Gymraeg. In that meeting Davies pledged that both languages would be equal in the Assembly. In the elections to the Assembly held in May 1999, Plaid Cymru, which had emerged from the general election of 1997 as the party for which a large proportion – possibly a majority – of the electors of the most intensely Welsh-speaking areas voted, made substantial and significant gains in the English-speaking industrial areas and established itself as the second largest party in the Assembly. The implications of these events for the Welsh language are not yet clear. It has been estimated that only some 10 per cent of Assembly business is transacted in Welsh, and there are those who wonder whether a body most of whose members are returned by Wales's English-speaking majority will prove less sympathetic and less open to the manipulation of a committed minority than was the Westminster government. On the other hand, decisions made by an all-Wales Assembly will bestow on future linguistic arrangements a validity and an endorsement which such arrangements previously lacked.

At the end of the twentieth century, the position of the Welsh language seems to justify a degree of optimism, though there are certainly no grounds for complacency. The steady decrease in the number of Welsh-speakers appears to have been checked and the language has a much higher profile in the fields of education, broadcasting and public life. This change is reflected in the vitality of the Welsh-language scene and in the proliferation of organizations which conduct their activities through the medium of Welsh. Once restricted largely to chapel-based activities, Welsh is now the language of licensed clubs. Nor is it any longer excluded from business and professional life; there are associations for Welsh-speaking doctors and scientists, for public relations experts and for commercial consultants. Business organizations have been established to encourage economic development in Welsh-speaking areas, and there are housing associations which operate through the medium of Welsh.

Welsh is extensively used in the field of the arts. Leading Welsh-language writers are members of Yr Academi Gymreig (the Welsh Academy), founded in 1959, an organization which since 1968 has also had an English-language section. Welsh authors are represented by Undeb Awduron Cymru (Union of Welsh Authors) and Welsh publishers and booksellers by Undeb Cyhoeddwyr a Llyfrwerthwyr Cymru (Union of Welsh Publishers and Booksellers). Bibliophiles and book collectors have their own association, Cymdeithas Bob Owen, which also publishes a magazine, *Y Casglwr*. There is a society, Gweled, for Welsh-speakers involved in the visual arts, and although Cwmni Theatr Cymru (and its counterpart, the Welsh Theatre Company) succumbed to financial difficulties in 1968, other companies continue to flourish and to perform in all parts of Wales and, in the case of the innovative Brith Gof, in other countries also.

Developments in the field of music have been particularly striking. There are now over a hundred Welsh-language groups, Y Tystion, Big Leaves and Topper prominent among them. A highly convivial folk festival, Gwyl Werin y Cnapan, is held annually at Ffostrasol in Ceredigion and attracts many visitors, especially from other Celtic countries. *Cerdd dant* (literally, string music), a melody sung counter to a tune played on the harp, represents a different aspect of Welsh folk music which has experienced a renaissance in recent years. A society, Cymdeithas Cerdd Dant, was founded in 1934, and there is a well-attended annual festival.

The wide and varied range of Welsh-language institutions includes Merched y Wawr, founded in 1967 as a reaction to the refusal of the National Federation of Women's Institutes to permit the use of Welsh at an official level. There is Cymdeithas Mynydda Cymru for mountaineers, Cymdeithas Edward Lhuyd for naturalists, Cefn, which is concerned to promote and safeguard the use of Welsh in the public domain, and Pont, which fosters an interest in the language among recent in-migrants. Urdd Gobaith Cymru, which will celebrate its eightieth birthday in 2002, continues its work among young people and its annual eisteddfod has been described as the largest youth festival in Europe. Undeb Athrawon Cymru (the Union of Teachers in Wales) conducts its business almost entirely in Welsh and other trade unions have made increasing use of the language. Rhieni dros Addysg Gymraeg (Parents for Welsh-language Education) has been an effective pressure group in the field of education. Independent television producers are represented by TAC (Teledwyr Annibynnol Cymru) and there are also Welsh-language facilities companies, such as Barcud of Caernarfon. The demand for translation services has grown side by side with the increased use of Welsh; there is a professional association, Cymdeithas Cyfieithwyr Cymru (Society of Welsh Translators), as well as a number of commercial translation companies.

All these groups and many others are represented at that apogee of Welshness, the National Eisteddfod. Held annually (except for the crisis years of 1914 and 1940) since 1881, the Eisteddfod alternates between north and south Wales, attracting an attendance of some 150,000. The Welsh language had always played a prominent part at the National Eisteddfod, and in 1952 its position was placed beyond doubt when a new constitution declared it to be the sole language of all the Eisteddfod's activities. This ruling was not accepted without controversy; it was argued that the rule would necessarily exclude and alienate the non-Welsh-speaking majority. However, the eisteddfodau held at Newport in 1988 and at Bridgend in 1998 were outstandingly successful, although only a very small percentage of Welsh-speakers was to be found in either of these towns.

The ritual of the Gorsedd – introduced into eisteddfodau by Iolo Morganwg – is the most widely known aspect of the National Eisteddfod, and the officers of the Gorsedd are responsible for the ceremonies which acclaim the winners of the principal prizes. But although the ceremonies and competitions form the core of the Eisteddfod's activities, the festival's cultural aspect is by now perhaps eclipsed by its importance as a social event. Many of its most ardent devotees find that the *maes* (the field) has far more to offer than the pavilion which houses the ceremonies and competitions. Whether the *eisteddfodwr* is interested in music, drama, literature, arts and crafts, politics, religion, history, natural history, linguistics, politics or a score of other subjects, there will be something to satisfy that interest among the hundreds of stands to be found on the *maes*, for the Eisteddfod encapsulates the organizational vitality of Welsh-speaking Wales.

Above all, the Eisteddfod is the place to meet those who are convinced of the value of the Welsh language and concerned to ensure that it has a future. Of all the factors which will influence that future, none is more important than the necessity of convincing the people of Wales that the loss of the Welsh language would impoverish the variety which is the main adornment of the cultural pattern of mankind.

Note

1   Here quoted in Lewis Thorpe's translation, Gerald of Wales, *The Journey through Wales and The Description of Wales*, London, 1978, p. 231.

References

Jenkins, Geraint H. 1987. *The Foundations of Modern Wales 1642–1780*. Oxford.
Jones, Gwyn and Jones, Thomas (transl.) 1949. *The Mabinogion*. London.
Jones, I. G. 1980. Language and community in nineteenth century Wales. In Smith, David (ed.), *A People and a Proletariat. Essays in the History of Wales, 1780–1980*, London, 47–71.

8 Cornish

Philip Payton

Cornish is a member of the Celtic family of Indo-European languages, descended from a hypothetical 'common Celtic', and one of the three modern Brythonic tongues (see p. 4). Of the other two, Breton is more closely related to Cornish than is Welsh. Cornish is more distantly related to the Goidelic group of modern Celtic languages, Irish, Manx and Scottish Gaelic.

Although no longer spoken as a 'natural' tongue, Cornish as a spoken vernacular survived until at least the end of the eighteenth century, with elements (including perhaps individual speakers) lingering into the nineteenth. In the twentieth century, echoes of the language are found in place-names, surnames and in some Celtic loan-words in the Cornish dialect(s) of English, while a vigorous revivalist movement has established a small but persistent body of Revived Cornish speakers. The great majority of these speakers have learnt Revived Cornish from textbooks or at evening classes but there is a now tiny minority whose speakers have learnt the language as infants, having been taught it deliberately by their parents in an effort to create a new generation of 'native speakers'.

In this way, Cornish can be said to have survived into the twenty-first century as one of the minority languages of the United Kingdom and western Europe. It has (unlike Welsh) no official status within the United Kingdom but it is recognized by the European Bureau for Lesser Used Languages and may yet attract British government support as a result of European Union and Council of Europe initiatives in respect of minority languages and cultures. The concern to accommodate both Irish and Ulster Scots in the context of the so-called 'Good Friday Agreement' of 1998 in Northern Ireland may herald a more proactive linguistic plurality within these islands, now that the British–Irish Council of the Isles has been created. This may well prove beneficial to Revived Cornish since Cornish too demands attention as one of the languages of the British Isles, not only because of its historical existence but as a result of the place of Revived Cornish in the cultural politics of contemporary Britain.

Cornish as a recognizably distinct language emerged in the early medieval period although, until the Reformation and beyond, Cornish and Breton remained mutually intelligible – a result of the Armorican emigration in the Dark Ages when many people left south-west Britain (prompted, perhaps, by the Saxon advance or Irish colonization) to settle in what is now Brittany. Although Anglo-Saxon traders or settlers had brought the English language into the far north-eastern tip of Cornwall by as early as the seventh century AD, place-name evidence shows us that, by 1200, Cornish was still spoken over the greater part of Cornwall (about 93 per cent of the landmass) by maybe as many as

30,000 people. Although the linguistic border had probably slipped further west by 1300 (with the language spoken in some 73 per cent of the territory of Cornwall), the numbers of speakers had swollen to perhaps some 38,000 as a result of general population growth. Some scholars, notably Nicholas Williams (1995), believe that the numbers may have been even greater than this, the language having enjoyed a resurgence under Norman and Breton patronage and at the expense of English after the Norman Conquest of 1066, and that in places it may still have been spoken up to the River Tamar (Cornwall's eastern frontier) until the early sixteenth century. However, most agree that by 1500 Cornish was probably spoken in a little over half the territory of Cornwall (i.e. west of the River Camel–River Fowey line in mid-Cornwall) by perhaps some 33,000 people or 48 per cent of the population.

In fact, Cornish in this early period is divided into two phases, Old Cornish and Middle Cornish. Old Cornish, the form of the language spoken from the ninth to the thirteenth centuries, survives in the form of glosses – scribbled marginal notes on Latin texts. The first nineteen are written on the text of *Smaragdus's Commentary on Donatus*, while three later glosses appear on the manuscript *Oxoniensis Posterior*. More significant are the *Bodmin Gospels*, in which are recorded in Old Cornish the names and details of slaves freed in Bodmin (then the principal town of Cornwall, an important religious centre) between the mid-tenth and mid-eleventh centuries. There is also an *Old Cornish Vocabulary*, an English–Latin vocabulary of *c.* AD 1000 to which was added (about a century later) a Cornish translation. Some 961 Cornish words are recorded, ranging from celestial bodies, through Church and craft occupations, to plants and animals. A final Old Cornish survival dates from 1265 and is a single sentence in an account of the founding of the church of St Thomas at Glasney, Penryn. The story explains that St Thomas had appeared in a dream to the Bishop of Exeter, telling him to establish a church at Polsethow in Penryn. Thus was fulfilled the ancient prophecy, 'In Polsethow ywhylyr anethow': *anethow* has two meanings, 'dwellings' and 'marvels', and so here we have a nice pun: 'In Polsethow shall be seen dwellings (*or* marvels).'

In fact, the sympathetic attitude of the pre-Reformation Church towards Cornish has assisted modern scholars in gauging the extent to which the language was spoken in medieval Cornwall. When Bishop John de Grandisson preached in the far-western parish of St Buryan in 1328 or 1329, his sermon had to be translated by an interpreter for the benefit of the monoglot Cornish. And although it is reasonable to assume that English was by that time already making inroads in east and north Cornwall, it is interesting to note that in 1339 a certain J. Polmarke was appointed to preach in the Cornish language at St Merryn, near Padstow. In 1354–5 Grandisson appointed two penitentiaries for Cornwall – one in Truro for those who spoke Cornish only, and one at Bodmin for those who spoke Cornish and English. As late as 1538 the Bishop of Exeter decreed that the Epistle or Gospel of the day should be read in Cornish in those parishes where English was not understood, and even in 1560 it was directed by the Bishop that those who had no English might be taught the Catechism in Cornish.

This 'Middle Cornish era' stretched from the thirteenth to the mid-sixteenth centuries, the period from which survives the extensive literature of the 'miracle plays' (plays based on the Bible or accounts of the lives of saints). The so-called *Charter Fragment*, dated *c.*1400, some forty-one lines of verse scribbled on the back of a charter relating to the parish of St Stephen-in-Brannel, may or may not be the fragment of one such play. Our earliest surviving miracle play, however, is the *Ordinalia*, written towards the end of the fourteenth century – probably at Glasney College, Penryn, a collegiate church which was the focus of Cornish-language scholarship in the medieval period. Designed, like other miracle plays, to be performed outdoors in a *plain-an-gwarry* or 'playing place' (such as those which survive today near Perranporth and at St Just-in-Penwith), the *Ordinalia* was a lengthy religious cycle tracing the Fall and Redemption of Man. It was arranged in three distinct parts or plays (*Origo Mundi* 'The Origin of the World', *Passio Christi* 'The Passion of Christ', and *Resurrectio Domini* 'The Resurrection of the Lord') and took three full days to perform. The first play begins with the creation of the world and the placing within it by God of Adam. However, Adam falls and it is not until the conclusion of the third play that, through the passion and triumph of Christ, Adam is at last restored to Heaven:

arluth ker bynyges os
a syv ioy gynef gothfos
an denses the thos th'en nef
an tas dev dre'n spyrys sans
th'en beys danvonas sylwyans
a huhon map dev a seyf

Dear Lord, ever blessed be,
joy it brings to us to see
man brought to heaven again,
The Father and Holy Ghost
redeemed a world that was lost
On high the Son will remain.
(Murdoch 1993, 73)

Aspects of the *Ordinalia* are echoed in the shorter *Pascon Agan Arluth* ('Passion of Our Lord', often referred to as the 'Passion Poem'), written at about the same time, where some twenty-three lines have apparently been borrowed from the larger work. There is also evidence of borrowing from *Origo Mundi* in a later play, *Gwreans an Bys* (*The Creacion* [*sic*] *of the World*). Although the surviving version of this play is a copy made by William Jordan of Helston in 1611, it is pre-Reformation in style and is thought to date from *c.*1530–40.

Also from the late medieval period is *Beunans Meriasek* ('The Life of St Meriasek'), the only saint's play to have survived in Britain. Celebrating a Breton saint with a Cornish dedication (at Camborne), the play is also religious in content but dwells on the theme of tyranny and shows the good Duke of Cornwall defeating the evil interloper Teuder – a fascinating echo, perhaps, of the events of the Cornish rebellion against the English king Henry Tudor in 1497. Thus although, as Brian Murdoch (1993) has argued, *Beunans Meriasek* should be seen as a standard late *vita*, composed in the wider tradition of European miracle drama and asserting the fundamental tenets of medieval Catholic Christendom, it may also, as Lynette Olson has suggested (1997), have a very Cornish context, not least because it is thought to have been written *c.* 1504 in the immediate aftermath of the rebellion. In that sense, *Beunans Meriasek* had become a subversive play, written in a language that the English could not understand but with a topical political message that its Cornish audience would have recognized and enjoyed.

The rebellious Cornish also rose in protest against the Reformation, in 1549 resisting the latest Tudor intrusion into Cornish affairs and refusing the new English-language Prayer Book. They insisted (correctly, no doubt) that many in Cornwall could not understand English, declaring in a petition to the king that the new Service was:

> like a Christmas game [. . .]. We will have our old service Mattins, Mass, Evensong and Procession in Latin as it was before. And so we the Cornish men (whereof certain of us understand no English) utterly refuse this new English. (cited in Cornwall 1975, 57)

Cranmer retorted that few Cornish people could understand Latin, the language of the Mass, but he was missing the point, for Latin was at least familiar (if not understood) across Cornwall, whereas English was not. Retribution was swift (a Cornish army was defeated near Exeter and executions were carried out the length and breadth of Cornwall), and amongst the casualties was the Cornish language itself. Although the Prayer Book and Bible were translated into Welsh, no such provision was made for Cornish, and at the end of the sixteenth century the chronicler John Norden (whose *Description of Cornwall* was eventually published in 1728) wrote that the language was now confined to the far west of Cornwall. He added that few could not understand English and predicted that the Cornish language would be abandoned in a few generations. In fact, pockets of Cornish-speakers survived in mid-Cornwall until at least the late sixteenth century (we know that there were monoglot Cornish-speakers at Gorran Haven in 1587 and bilingual Cornish/English speakers at neighbouring St Ewe in 1595). Moreover, John Tregear's translations into Cornish (the so-called 'Tregear Homilies') of Bishop Edmund Bonner's homilies (written 1553–8) indicate that the language enjoyed some literary and ecclesiastical significance in the brief return to Catholicism during Mary Tudor's reign. However, the closure of Glasney College (part of Henry VIII's dissolution of the monasteries) had deprived Cornish of an important source of status and learning.

Additionally, the Reformation had also weakened Cornwall's ties with Brittany, depriving Cornwall of an important source of cultural exchange and linguistic contact. Cornish pilgrims had visited holy sites in Brittany, and there had been constant two-way traffic for religious purposes and for trade. Bretons had come to Cornwall as sailors and fishermen but many had actually settled there, reinforcing the sense of a shared cultural-linguistic community. Many of these Breton settlers had been found in the western districts where the Cornish language was strongest – St Ives, Towednack, Zennor, Lelant, and Constantine (in which parish as late as 1558 there were still nine Breton families resident) – but they were also numerous in the east of Cornwall: at the southern ports of Fowey, Polruan and East Looe, and more generally in the Hundreds of Trigg and West Wivel where some 79 Bretons were registered in 1552–4. At North Petherwin, on the border with Devon, Bretons were employed as carpenters in the parish church in 1523–4, as they were at Bodmin in 1529–30. The decline of this intimacy by the late sixteenth century meant the dwindling of an important cultural resource and made the Cornish language increasingly isolated.

Indeed, Norden's pessimistic assessment of the future prospects for Cornish was echoed by Richard Carew, a member of the Cornish gentry who in 1602 wrote in his *Survey of Cornwall* that the language was by now 'driven into the utmost skirts of the shire' (Halliday 1953, 127). Carew, a champion of the 'superiority' of the English language, welcomed the supplantation of Cornish by English, a view no doubt shared by other Cornish gentry, and saw Cornish as the language of the poor and the illiterate. His own grasp of the language was slight but he did recognize that it was on occasions a vehicle for Cornish sentiment, noting that inquisitive visitors from across the Tamar border might be rebuffed with the phrase *Meea navidna cowzasawzneck* ('I will not speak English') (ibid., 127).

The overtly Catholic nature of miracle plays such as *Beunans Meriasek* meant that their performance rarely survived the Reformation, and where they did endure they had lost their meaning and status, by now chaotic parodies for the entertainment of simple country folk. For Carew, 'The gwary miracle, in English, a miracle play, is a kind of interlude, compiled in Cornish out of some scripture history, with the grossness that accompanied the Romans' *vetus comedia*', an extravaganza which attracted country people from many miles around but often ended in farce as the actors deliberately sabotaged their scripts and fluffed their lines: 'yet [they] defrauded not the beholders, but dismissed them with a great deal more sport and laughter than twenty such gwaries could have afforded' (ibid., 144–5).

The Civil War of the mid-seventeenth century was the cause of much upheaval, with Cornwall emerging as an important focus of support for the Royalist cause. Consequently, Cornwall became a battleground for the rival armies, and the resultant dislocation put further pressure on the Cornish language, as did the economic expansion of the second half of the century which led to increased contact with English-speaking merchants from outside Cornwall. During the Civil War, Cornish soldiers tended to serve together in Cornish regiments, led by Cornish officers, and Cornish-speakers were used by the Royalists (as the contemporary scholar William Scawen noted) as scouts and spies, able to communicate with impunity in a language the enemy could not understand. And yet Richard Symonds, a Royalist officer who served in Cornwall in 1644, noted that Cornish was now restricted to the area west of Truro, and in 1662 – after the Restoration of the monarchy in 1660 – the naturalist John Ray toured Cornwall and wrote that, even in the far west, 'we met none here but what could speak English; few of the children could speak Cornish, so that the language is like, in a short time, to be quite lost' (Pool 1975, 8). In fact, according to Ken George's analysis (1986a), the number of Cornish-speakers had fallen from an estimated 22,000 in 1600 to about 14,000 in 1650, with a core of some 5,000 left in 1700. By 1750 very few speakers remained, and half a century later Cornish had all but disappeared as a vernacular.

However, this period of rapid decline also witnessed an eleventh-hour attempt by a small band of enthusiasts to popularize and preserve the language. Foremost amongst these enthusiasts was Nicholas Boson of Newlyn who in the late seventeenth century wrote his *Nebbaz Gerriau dro tho Carnoack* ('A Few Words about Cornish') in which he indicated those parts of West Cornwall in which the language – now in its so-called Late Cornish stage – was still alive. It was, he said, 'spoken from the Lands-End to the [St Michael's] Mount & towards St Ives and Redruth, and again from the Lizard to

Helston'. But even in these remote districts, 'scarce any but both understand and speak English [. . .]. We find the young Men to speak it [Cornish] less and less, and worse & worse, and so it is like to decay from Time to Time' (Padel 1975, 24–5). This decline was mirrored and mourned in the epitaph written for James Jenkins, another of this group of scholars, by John Boson, Nicholas's kinsman (ibid., 48):

> Lebn duath Tavaz coth ny en Kernow
> Pag kar ny Jenkins gelles durt an Pow
> Vor hanow taz ny en Eue tha Canow.

> Cornwall now Mourne thy Tongue just lost and gone
> Jenkins, our Cornish Bard is fled among
> The Saints to sing his Everlasting Song.

Nicholas Boson's account of the state of the Cornish language was complemented by William Scawen in his analysis of the language's decline. Scawen lived at Molenick in the parish of St Germans in East Cornwall, many miles from the Cornish-speaking areas, but had served in the Cornish army during the Civil War where he no doubt encountered the language on the lips of many soldiers. Inspired by his new-found enthusiasm for the language, Scawen drew attention to the reasons for the decay of Cornish, including the loss of contact with Brittany, the demise of the miracle plays, a general antipathy towards the language, the dismissive attitude of the gentry (echoes of Carew), the proximity to Devon (no doubt felt keenly at St Germans), increased contact with outsiders (especially clergymen and traders in fish and tin), the lack of a Cornish Prayer Book, and the failure of people to correspond in Cornish or to preserve Cornish manuscripts.

Other activists concerned for the future of the language included William Gwavas (1676–1741) and Thomas Tonkin (1678–1742) who engaged in correspondence in Cornish and who composed and collected folk-songs. The latter wrote a song in Cornish praising William of Orange, and collected from Edward Chirgwin in about 1698 a Cornish-language version of the well-known folk-song, 'Whither are you going pretty fair maid, said he, With your white face and your yellow hair?':

> Pela era why moaz, moz, fettow, teag,
> Gen agaz bedgeth gwin, ha agaz blew mellyn?
> (Pryce 1790, 224)

All this activity caught the attention of Edward Lhuyd, the Oxford scholar who embarked on an exhaustive comparative study of the Celtic languages (and in so doing became a founder of the modern academic discipline of Celtic Studies). Lhuyd visited Cornwall in about 1700, painstakingly recording all he could of the Cornish language (including its sounds), and discovering that it was yet spoken in a string of some twenty-five parishes from the Lizard to Land's End. Although he saw little future for Cornish other than as an antiquarian curio for gentlemen (he compared it unfavourably with Welsh and Breton which were still spoken widely by all classes in their respective countries), he was sensitive enough to appreciate and record a rhyme given to him in 1700 by the parish clerk of St Just-in-Penwith (ibid., 229):

An lavar koth yw lavar gwir,
Na boz nevra doz vaz an tavaz re hir;
Bez den heb davaz a gollaz i dir.

The old saying is a true saying,
A tongue too long never did good:
But the man with no tongue lost his land.

But despite this activity, the decline of Cornish continued apace, and indeed the dying embers might have gone almost unnoticed if it had not been for the interest of a minor English antiquary, Daines Barrington (1727–1800), who in 1768 made a tour of West Cornwall in search of Cornish-speakers. At Mousehole, near Penzance, he was introduced to an old fishwife, Dolly Pentreath, who insisted that she spoke no English until the age of twenty and was now the last speaker of the Cornish language. However, although Dolly Pentreath (who died in 1777) has indeed gone down in history as 'the last Cornish-speaker', she was certainly survived by others with a knowledge of the tongue – notably William Bodinar who died in 1789 and left a short autobiographical note (written in both Cornish and English) explaining how he had learnt Cornish when at sea with fishermen. Bodinar conceded that 'Cornish is all forgot with young people' (Pool 1975, 27) but almost a hundred years later it could still be claimed that John Davey of Zennor, who died in 1891, was able to converse in Cornish on a few simple subjects. Indeed, in 1859 Mathias Wallis of St Buryan had certified that his grandmother, Ann Wallis, who had died in her ninetieth year some fifteen years beforehand, had spoken Cornish, as had one Jane Barnicoate who had been dead but two years. Thereafter, odd snippets of the language endured, not only as individual words in the Cornish dialect(s) of English but in fishermen's counting rituals which survived perhaps even into the 1920s and 1930s.

The Cornish economy was one of the first to industrialize, the growth of deep hardrock mining and associated steam engineering in the nineteenth century earning Cornwall an early place in the forefront of technological advance. Cornish industrial society was self-confident and expansive, and part of the ideology of Cornish industrial prowess was the belief that the demise of the Cornish language was all to the good – English was the language of modernity, and Cornish would have been an impediment in an English-speaking, industrializing world. However, an antiquarian interest in the language – both inside and without Cornwall – developed during the nineteenth century, keeping alive a knowledge of the literary heritage of Cornish and placing its consideration within the emerging discipline of Celtic Studies. When, in the latter half of the nineteenth century, Cornwall experienced rapid de-industrialization (with the collapse of copper- and tin-mining), the Cornish language was actually well-placed to assist in the 're-invention' of a post-industrial Cornish identity. Looking back over the debris of the industrial period to the 'golden age' of medieval Celtic-Catholic Cornwall, and taking its cue from Celtic revivalists in Ireland and Brittany, a new group of 'Cornish revivalists' emerged to try to rebuild Cornish culture anew. Foremost amongst these early revivalists was Henry Jenner, who in 1904 published his *Handbook of the Cornish Language* and in the same year secured Cornwall's membership of the Celtic Congress, asserting Cornwall's status as a Celtic nation.

Although the First World War interrupted the work of the Cornish revivalists, after 1918 their efforts to revive Cornish as a written and spoken language began to bear fruit. Although Jenner had at first advocated that Revived Cornish be based upon the language in its Late phase, in the form in which it had most recently been spoken in Cornwall, others preferred to locate the revival more securely in the medieval period – looking to the extensive body of Middle Cornish extant in the miracle plays for their raw material for reconstruction. This was the approach adopted by Robert Morton Nance, the architect of what became known as Unified Cornish, a form of Revived Cornish based on Middle Cornish but with a standardized orthography devised by Nance, drawing on Welsh and Breton when necessary to fill in the gaps. Thus constituted, Unified Cornish became the vehicle for language revival in the inter-war period. English–Cornish and Cornish–English dictionaries appeared, as did guides to learning the language. In 1928 a Gorseth Kernow (Cornish Gorsedd, an association of bards based on the Welsh model) was set up, modelled on the Welsh and Breton Gorseddau, and from the first it used Unified Cornish in its annual ceremonies.

After the Second World War, the revivalists resumed their work. A Cornish Language Board was set up in 1967 to administer the revival, bringing it to a wider public and organizing classes, publications and examinations, while an increasing 'Cornish consciousness' (linked to the emergence of 'anti-metropolitan' political sentiment) stimulated greater popular interest in the language. However, this apparent progress disguised a number of tensions and anxieties, not least the increasing criticism that Unified Cornish received at the hands of academic Celticists who attacked Nance's eclectic and 'unscientific' methodology. In particular, there was growing criticism of the apparent mismatch inherent in Unified Cornish, the wedding of an unashamedly medieval orthography to a system of pronunciation that Nance considered to be the 'authentic' survival of the sounds of Late Cornish, still to be heard in the speech of the older generation in places such as Newlyn and St Ives. Indeed, some critics not only acknowledged the incongruity of this mismatch but added that the speech of the far west was in any case not the remnant of Late Cornish; it was the result of the rapid replacement of Cornish by Standard English.

To this was added growing impatience in the revival movement itself, a concern that despite more than half a century of sustained activity the generation of fluent speakers (in 1981 thought to number only forty) was painfully slow. Later, others began to criticize the medievalist, Celtic-Catholic project of the early revivalists, arguing that this had bequeathed an ideological straitjacket from which it was difficult for the language movement (and its literature) to escape. At the practical level, one response to criticism was to further popularize the language, to bring it closer to everyday life and to encourage its use in an increasing number of social domains. To this end *Cowethas an Yeth Kernewek* ('The Cornish Language Society') was formed, and informal *Yeth an Weryn* ('Language of the People') meetings were held in public houses and other social settings across Cornwall.

At the academic level, however, the criticisms of the professional Celticists were taken seriously by Cornish revivalists, encouraging them to look again at their assumptions, aspirations and methodologies. One result of this process was the so-called phonemic revision, an approach based on the research of Ken George. George argued (1984, 1986b, 1995) that Revived Cornish should continue to be based on the Middle Cornish period (*c.*1500) but he insisted that it was important to discover how Cornish had actually been pronounced in that era. He criticized the mismatch inherent in Nance's view that Revived Cornish based on the language of about 1500 might safely be pronounced with what Nance had assumed to be a Late Cornish accent, and went further to agree with other critics that Nance's estimation of the survival of 'Late Cornish' pronunciation in the far west was also wrong. Moreover, George developed a complex computer program to enable him to analyse the structure of the Middle Cornish texts, allowing him to derive (to his satisfaction at least) the sounds of medieval Cornish. To this hypothetical sound-system George added a hypothetical spelling, devising a phonemic orthography which – George argued – accurately reflected the new-found pronunciation. The resultant system was known as *Kernewek Kemmyn* ('Common Cornish'), and was adopted by an enthusiastic Cornish Language Board in 1987. However, not all revivalists accepted George's proposals, and, from being the umbrella body charged with the welfare of the language movement as a whole, the Cornish Language Board found itself recast as a pressure group advocating one particular form of Revived Cornish.

Other revivalists in the 1980s had been drawn to the possibility, suggested initially by Henry Jenner (1904), that Revived Cornish should after all be based on the survivals of the Late Cornish period. At first, the idea was that Unified Cornish might be made more attractive by co-opting 'traditional' or colloquial uses from the Late period, but soon Richard Gendall was arguing (1991, 1995, 1998) that Unified Cornish should be abandoned altogether, to be replaced by a Modern Cornish (or *Kernuack*) based on the Late period. Gendall and his supporters founded a Cornish Language Council and organized classes and publications to promote Modern Cornish. Moreover, Gendall argued that the contemporary pronunciation of English in the far west of Cornwall was, after all, a guide to the sounds of Late Cornish because – he argued – these sounds agreed on almost every detail with those recorded from Cornish speakers by Edward Lhuyd about 1700.

Be that as it may, Gendall was successful in winning the sympathetic attention of at least part of the academic community, at a time when George's phonemic revision was being treated with increasing caution by many professional linguists and Celticists (see Payton 1999). At the same moment, however, Unified Cornish found an eleventh-hour academic champion in the form of N. J. A. Williams who argued (1995, 1996, 1997), in contrast to both George and Gendall, that Unified remained the best base from which the language revival might be taken forward. However, Williams added that there was considerable room for improvement in the Unified system, not least because the important 'Tregear Homilies' (see p. 112 above), which were not recognized until as late as 1949, had been unavailable to Nance during his reconstruction of the language in the inter-war period.

In effect, Williams was arguing for the development of Unified in a manner that would shift it from its medieval origins, orienting it towards the Late Cornish period but without losing its foundation in the later Middle Cornish texts. *Agan Tavas* ('Our Language'), a group dedicated to fostering Unified Cornish in the face of the phonemic revision, responded enthusiastically to Williams's intervention, and one interesting consequence was a new rapprochement of sorts between the Modern Cornish and Unified groups – supporters of both these forms of Revived Cornish embracing an apparent need for mutual understanding and co-operation. Although the Cornish

Language Board, in its unswerving commitment to the phonemic revision, was less ready to compromise or to accommodate alternative revivalist strategies, the uncomfortable fact of a still small community of competent Cornish speakers (in the year 2000 probably no more than two hundred), not to mention a Cornish public bemused by the apparent in-fighting of the rival groups, suggested that sooner or later there would have to be a more general recognition of the plurality that now existed in the language movement. In fact, the diplomatic intervention of the United Kingdom Committee of the European Bureau for Lesser Used Languages led to the establishment of a Cornish subcommittee, drawing together representatives of the rival revivalist groups and other interested parties to work together on various projects (such as the production in 1997 of bilingual road signs in the Penwith district of West Cornwall).

Although there is not yet a coherent policy for the teaching of Revived Cornish in schools, some schools have initiated Cornish-language classes, while Cornwall County Council is itself moving slowly towards the adoption of a Cornish language policy. Within the framework of the European Union, there is increasing recognition of the importance of 'pride of place' in economic regeneration, and of the significant relationship between culture and economic development, and it may be that it is within this context that the revivalist movement will be able to attract the attention and command the resources to take the Cornish language into the third millennium. Despite the aspirations of the revivalists, Revived Cornish is extremely unlikely to become a widely spoken second language but its symbolic importance as an icon of Cornwall as 'a land apart' should not be underestimated.

References

Carew, Richard 1602. *Survey of Cornwall* (see Halliday 1953).
Cornwall, Julian 1975. *Revolt of the Peasantry, 1549.* London.
Gendall, Richard 1991. *A Student's Grammar of Modern Cornish.* Menheniot.
——1995. *A Concise Dictionary of Modern Cornish.* Menheniot.
——1998. *A New Practical Dictionary of Modern Cornish, Part Two: English–Cornish.* Menheniot.
George, Ken 1984. Phonological history of Cornish. Unpublished *thèse de troisième cycle*, Université de Bretagne Occidentale.
——1986a. How many people spoke Cornish traditionally? *Cornish Studies*, 14:67–70.
——1986b. *The Pronunciation and Spelling of Revived Cornish.* Torpoint.
——1995. Which base for revived Cornish? *Cornish Studies*, 2nd series, 3:104–24.
Halliday, F. E. (ed.) 1953. *Richard Carew of Antony. The Survey of Cornwall, &c.* London.
Jenner, Henry 1904. *A Handbook of the Cornish Language.* London.
Murdoch, Brian 1993. *Cornish Literature.* Cambridge.
Norden, John 1728. *Description of Cornwall.* London.
Olson, Lynette 1997. Tyranny in *Beunans Meriasek. Cornish Studies*, 2nd series, 5:52–9.
Padel, Oliver J. 1975. *The Cornish Writings of the Boson Family.* Redruth.
Payton, Philip 1999. The ideology of language revival in modern Cornwall. In Black, Ronald, Gillies, William and Ó Maolalaigh, Roibeard (eds), *Celtic Connections: Proceedings of the Tenth International Congress of Celtic Studies*, vol. 1, Edinburgh, 395–424.
Pool, P. A. S. 1975. *The Death of Cornish.* Penzance.
Pryce, William 1790. *Archaeologia Cornu-Britannica.* Redruth.

Williams, N. J. A. 1995. *Cornish Today. An Examination of the Revived Language.* Sutton Coldfield.

—— 1996. Linguistically sound principles: the case against Kernewek Kemmyn. *Cornish Studies,* 2nd series, 4:64–87.

—— 1997. *Clappya Kernowek.* Portreath.

9 Cumbric

Glanville Price

Before the Roman invasion, most or all of Britain south of the Forth and the Clyde was settled by British-speaking tribes whose language survived in the Highland zone (see p. 70 and map 4) of Britain (and probably very extensively in the Lowland zone as well) throughout the period of the Roman occupation. In the fifth century, however, the Anglo-Saxon occupation of the Lowland zone began in earnest and British speech once again found itself in competition with that of invaders.

Within perhaps a couple of centuries, the various Germanic dialects of the Anglo-Saxons had ousted British from all of the Lowland zone with the exception of a few enclaves here and there (see pp. 75–6), and British was henceforward confined to the Highland zone. Even here, the onward thrust of the Saxons in the south-west and the Angles in the north-west divided the British-speaking territory into three geographically separated areas, which broadly speaking correspond respectively to Devon and Cornwall, Wales, and an area in north-west England and south-west Scotland that we shall refer to as Cumbria. Although the term 'Cumbria' now generally applies solely to the English part of the area in question, there is ample historical justification for using it in this wider sense.

In the late sixth century, much of the north of England and of Scotland south of the Clyde and Forth was still British territory, consisting principally of the three kingdoms of Gododdin, Strathclyde and Rheged (see map 4). Gododdin – the name derives from that of the pre-Roman tribe of the Votadini – took in the area between the Forth and the Tyne and had its capital at Din Eidyn, i.e. Edinburgh. To the west of Gododdin, occupying much of south-west Scotland, was Strathclyde, 'with its capital at Dumbarton [i.e. "the fort of the Britons"], its religious centre at Glasgow, and its heartland the valley of the Clyde, but reaching probably from Upper Loch Lomond and Cunningham to Peebles and the source of the Tweed' (Jackson 1969, 64). The area covered by Rheged is even less certain, but 'it seems fairly clear that it included the Solway basin (and perhaps Galloway), and the Eden valley up to the crest of the Pennines and possibly across them into Swaledale. The capital may have been Carlisle' (Jackson 1963, 68).

Some time in the seventh century the Angles of Mercia spread into the Cheshire plain and the area between the Mersey and the Ribble, and there is no evidence for the survival of the British-speaking population in that area thereafter. Meanwhile, the Northumbrian Angles were pressing forward along the east coast, taking over Gododdin from the Britons and capturing Edinburgh in or about 638. They had probably occupied the whole of south-east Scotland by the middle of the seventh century.

The two western kingdoms survived somewhat longer. It is not certain when the Northumbrians moved into Rheged, but it may have been during the reign of Oswy who was king of Northumbria from 642 to 671. However, the Cumbric language probably did not entirely die out at that time in the lands taken by the English.

Events were to take a different turn when the Northumbrians came under pressure from the Vikings, both in the east, when they lost Yorkshire to the Danes in 867, and some time later in the west when much of Galloway and, later still, in the early tenth century, the whole of north-western England were occupied by incomers from Ireland of mixed Viking and Gaelic origin. One important effect of this breaking of the Northumbrian grip on the former territory of Rheged was that the Britons of Strathclyde reoccupied south-west Scotland and north-west England as far south as the Derwent and Penrith. They held these areas until the early eleventh century when their kingdom was finally absorbed into Scotland.

Our knowledge of the course of events during the last period of the kingdom of Strathclyde is both fragmentary and uncertain. It appears that a tradition developed whereby the heir apparent to the Scottish kingdom was given British territory to govern. When, in 1015, Owen the Bald, king of Strathclyde, died, apparently without direct heir, the reigning king of Scots, Malcolm II, granted Strathclyde (which extended as far south as the Derwent) to his grandson and heir, Duncan, who in 1034 succeeded him as king of Scots. Strathclyde was now definitively incorporated in the kingdom of Scotland. The boundary between England and Scotland was pushed north from the Derwent to its present line when William Rufus annexed the southern part of the area in question in 1092.

Jackson argues (1963, 72–3) that Cumbric 'must have been reintroduced into Dumfriesshire and Cumberland, or at any rate greatly strengthened there if it had not previously quite died out, by the reoccupation from Strathclyde in the tenth century', but that it 'faded away throughout Cumbria in the course of the eleventh century, perhaps to disappear finally in the early twelfth'. More recently, Phythian-Adams argues (1996) that, rather than being reintroduced from Strathclyde, Celtic speech survived the Anglian occupation in at least parts of the area now known as Cumbria and may have lasted as late as the twelfth century.

We have virtually no written records of Cumbric. Our only direct knowledge of the language from more or less contemporary documents (but late ones, which could even date from a period after Cumbric had ceased to be a spoken language) is limited to three words and a few personal names. The three words occur in a Latin legal text, probably dating from the eleventh century, namely the *Leges inter Brettos et Scottos* 'Laws between the Britons and the Scots' (see Jackson 1953, 9–10, and 1955, 88). They are *galnes* or *galnys*, which corresponds to Middle Welsh *galanas* 'blood-fine', and *mercheta* and *kelchyn*, connected with Welsh *merch* 'daughter' and *cylch* 'circuit' respectively. The second of these Jackson interprets (1955, 88) as denoting 'a tax paid by a father to his lord on the marriage of his daughter', while the third refers to some sort of fine 'but perhaps originally a contribution paid when the king went on royal progress through his lands'. These legal terms were perhaps incorporated in a Latin text because they stood for concepts that had no precise equivalent in Scots law or in the Latin language.

Cumbric names figure in the Latin *Life of St Kentigern* which survives only in a twelfth-century version but draws on earlier sources. One such name is that of a king of Strathclyde, *Rederech*, which corresponds to Old Welsh *Riderch* and modern Welsh *Rhydderch*.

It is, however, the place-names that tell us most about Cumbric. They fall broadly speaking into three groups. The first group comprises names of British origin – that in many cases still survive – from the old kingdom of Gododdin, that fell to the Angles in the first third of the seventh century. Some of these names are based on roots corresponding to Welsh *coed* 'wood', *moel* 'bare', *rhos* 'moor', *pen* 'head, summit, end', *tre (f)* 'township'. The British root *cet-* 'wood' (= Welsh *coed*) provides the second element of *Bathgate* and *Dalkeith* (the first elements correspond respectively to Welsh *baedd* 'boar' and, probably, *dol* 'meadow'). *Melrose* corresponds to Welsh *moel + rhos*. *Pen* occurs in *Penicuik* (= Welsh *Pen y gog* 'cuckoo's summit') and *Pencaitland* (cf. Welsh *coedlan* 'copse'), and cognates of *tre (f)* occur in *Tranent* (found in the twelfth century in the form *Treuernent* = Welsh *tref + yr* 'the' + *neint*, an archaic plural of *nant* 'valley, stream'), *Traprain* (Welsh *pren* 'tree') and *Trabrown* (Welsh *bryn* 'hill'), and, preceded by an element meaning 'new', in *Niddry*, *Niddrie* and *Longniddry* in the Lothians. Towns in the area that also have Cumbric names include *Linlithgow* (= Welsh *llyn* 'lake' + *llaith* 'damp' + *cau* 'hollow', so the name means something like 'the lake in the damp hollow') and *Lanark* (= Welsh *llannerch* 'glade'). Forms (nowadays usually much mangled) corresponding to Welsh *pren* 'tree' occur in the names of two localities called *Pirn*, with an unidentified suffix in *Pirnie* and *Pirny*, with colour adjectives in *Prinlaws* (Welsh *(g)las* 'blue, green') and *Primside* (earlier *Prenwensete*, in which *wen* is 'white' and *sete* is English *seat*), and in a variety of other names including *Primrose* and *Barnbougle* (whose second elements correspond respectively to Welsh *rhos* 'moor' and *bugail* 'shepherd') (see Nicolaisen 1964, 146–8).

In south-west Scotland we have other Cumbric names from the kingdoms of Strathclyde and Rheged (see Jackson 1955, 1963, and Nicolaisen 1964). The root *tre* 'township' turns up again in *Trerregles* (= Welsh *tre'r eglwys* 'church town'), *Trostrie* (corresponding to the Welsh place-name *Trostre*, whose first element derives from *traws* 'across, athwart') and *Ochiltree* (Welsh *uchel* 'high'), while forms equivalent to Welsh *caer* 'fort' (but perhaps here having taken on the meaning 'hamlet', cf. Breton *kêr* 'town') occur in *Caerlanrig* (Welsh *llannerch* 'glade' – we have already seen this element in the name of *Lanark*), *Carfrae* (Welsh *fre* from *bre* 'hill'), and *Cathcart* and *Cramond* (found in the twelfth century as *Kerkert* and *Karramunt* respectively) 'the fort or hamlet on the river Cart/Almond'. *Pennersax* (Dumfriesshire) would in Welsh be *Pen y Sais* 'Englishman's summit', and *Leswalt* in Galloway corresponds to Welsh *llys* 'court' + *(g)wellt* 'grass', so the meaning is presumably 'grassy courtyard'. The Latin words *pontem* 'bridge' and *ecclesia* 'church' (originally a Greek word) have come down into modern Welsh as *pont* and *eglwys*, and are also found in the names of *Penpont* 'bridge-end' and *Ecclefechan* (Welsh *eglwys fechan*) 'little church'.

In the English part of Cumbria, there is a particularly high proportion of Brittonic names both of natural features such as rivers and hills, which are often taken over by an incoming community from those who were there before them, and of villages and other settlements which, in general, survive less frequently. Jackson shows (1963, 74) that, out of some 210 village names in the former county of Cumberland, about sixty are of Brittonic origin, and that over fifty of these 'occur in the area north of the Derwent, that is to say in the part of Cumberland reoccupied by Strathclyde in the tenth century, and that there is a particularly close concentration in the north, east and north of Carlisle'. It seems more than likely, therefore, that many of these names date from the time of the reoccupation rather than from the pre-Northumbrian period.

Among the Cumbric names of north-west England are many that contain elements we have already come across. The roots that have given Welsh *tre(f)* 'township', *pen* 'head, top, end', *coed* 'wood' and *blaen* 'summit', appear again in *Triermain* 'village by the rock' (Welsh *tre'r maen*), *Penrith* 'end of the ford' (Welsh *rhyd* 'ford'), *Culgaith* 'backwood' (Welsh *cil* 'recess, corner') (cf. *Culcheth* in Lancashire), *Blencarn* 'summit with a cairn' (Welsh *carn*), *Blaencogo* 'summit of the cuckoos' (Welsh *cog* 'cuckoo', plural *cogau*). Roots we found in *Lanark* and *Caerlanrig* (Welsh *llannerch* 'glade, clearing' and *caer* 'fort') occur again in *Lanercost* (with an uncertain second element) and *Cardew* (Welsh *du* 'black'). *Lamplugh* (found as *Lamplou, Lanplo* in the twelfth century) corresponds to Welsh *llan* 'church' and *plwy(f)* 'parish' and so means 'parish church'. *Carrock* (Fell) is Welsh *carreg* 'rock', and *Calder, Cumrew* and *Glendhu* correspond respectively to Welsh *Calettwr* (*caled* 'hard' + *dwr* 'water'), *cwm* 'valley' + *rhiw* 'slope', and *glyn* 'valley' + *du* 'black'. *Tallentire* 'end of the land' (probably a headland in ploughing, Jackson suggests) corresponds to Welsh *tâl* 'brow, front' and *tir* 'land'.

The fact that many of the names in question reflect words used in combination opens up the possibility that they may tell us something about pronunciation and grammar. For example, a feature of the Celtic languages is that, in certain constructions, initial consonants may change or, in the case of Welsh and Cornish *g*, disappear – so, Welsh *gwen* (feminine of *gwyn* 'white') and *glas* 'blue, green' become *wen, las* after a feminine noun. The word *pren* 'tree' in Welsh is masculine, so one has *pren gwyn, pren glas*, but the medieval names *Prenwen(sete)* (Roxburghshire) (now *Primside)* and *Prinlaws* (Fife) lead us to suppose that the original forms were something like *pren wen* and *pren las*, and therefore that in Cumbric the word *pren* was feminine (see Nicolaisen 1964, 146).

There is one possible remnant of Cumbric that we have not yet mentioned, and that is the set of numerals up to twenty, the so-called 'Cumbric Score', characterized by Jackson (1955, 88) as 'the old Cumbric numerals [which] have survived very extraordinarily to modern times among the Pennine shepherds of Cumberland and the West Riding, for the purpose of counting sheep'. These, he accepts, are none other than 'a garbled version of something which must have been identical with the numerals in Welsh'. A. J. Ellis who, over a century ago, published fifty-three versions of them (some of them incomplete), tells us that, although the use of the Score for counting sheep already seemed to have become obsolete, it was apparently still used by old women to count their stitches in knitting and by school-children for purposes of 'counting out' (like 'eeny, meeny, miny, mo') (Ellis 1877–9, 321).

Much more recently, the Score has been subjected to thorough scrutiny by Michael Barry, who published (1969) some seventy versions (many of them incomplete) reported to hail mainly from Cumbria, Yorkshire and other parts of the north of England, with a few from south-west Scotland and elsewhere. The various versions often differ considerably, but the following specimens (from Barry's article) will give an idea of how closely or otherwise some fairly representative sets approximate to Welsh:

	Welsh	Borrowdale (Cumb.)	Kirkby Stephen (Westmorland)	High Furness (Lancs)	Nidderdale (W. Yorks)
1	un	yan	yan	yan	yain
2	dau	tyan	tahn	taen	tain
3	tri	tethera	teddera	tedderte	eddero
4	pedwar	methera	meddera	medderte	peddero
5	pump	pimp	pimp	pimp	pitts
6	chwech	sethera	settera	haata	tayter
7	saith	ethera	littera	slaata	layter
8	wyth	hevera	hovera	owra	overo
9	naw	devera	dovera	dowra	covero
10	deg	dick	dick	dick	dix
15	pymtheg	bumfit	bumfit	mimph	bumfit
20	ugain	giggot	jiggot	gigget	jiggit

If anything at all is certain about these numerals, it is that no-one seems to have come across them in actual use, whether for counting sheep or for any other purpose. It is noteworthy that sixteen of the sets recorded from the north of England were reported to be used either for 'counting-out', or in children's games, or in nursery rhymes. This of course explains the fact that, apart from 'five' and 'ten', the numerals usually fall into rhyming pairs (*yan/tyan*, *teddera/meddera*, *haata/slaata*, *overo/covero*, etc.). Nevertheless, that they are in some way connected with the Welsh numerals cannot reasonably be doubted. This is particularly true of those forms that have not been affected by the tendency to group the numbers in rhyming or alliterative pairs, namely 'five', 'ten', 'fifteen' and perhaps 'twenty': *pimp* is exactly the Welsh *pump* (-*u*- being pronounced 'i'), and *dick* and *bumfit* are too close to Welsh *deg* and *pymtheg* (the first syllable of which is pronounced 'pum') for the resemblance to be purely fortuitous. There is also the fact that 'eleven' and 'sixteen' in the Cumbric Score are most frequently formed on the pattern of Welsh *un-ar-ddeg* (lit. 'one on ten') and *un-ar-bymtheg* ('one on fifteen'), e.g. Borrowdale *yan-a-dick*, *yan-a-bumfit*.

But is the Score really a relic (albeit a very corrupt one) of the Cumbric speech of the area, which has survived for some seven or eight centuries after the death of the language itself? The answer seems to be 'possibly, but not necessarily', and, if so, it cannot be proved.

The other possibility is that the numerals were imported to Cumberland and neighbouring areas at a relatively late date. They could have been imported from southern Scotland – but in that case the numerals would still be Cumbric: this is just the 'survival hypothesis' in a slightly different form. The only real 'importation hypothesis' is that the numerals were imported from Wales during the Middle Ages or later, but, as Barry points out (1969, 84), no substantial evidence in favour of this view has ever been presented. Other versions of the hypothesis suggest that the numerals may have been imported in medieval times or later through the agency either of Cistercian monks who had houses in Wales and the north country and an interest in sheep-rearing (a feature of both areas), or of natives of the Welsh lead-mining areas employed in the lead-mines of Cumbria.

The most one can say with any certainty is that the numerals must be of Brittonic origin but that there is no hard evidence to show where they came from.

While not one single complete phrase of Cumbric has come down to us, there is evidence to suggest that the language had a strong literary tradition, probably oral, and that some of this very early material is known to us in a Welsh version.

The earliest Welsh literary texts, traditionally ascribed to two sixth-century poets, Taliesin and Aneirin, have Cumbrian associations. The fifty-seven Taliesin poems, singing the praises of kings and princes of Rheged, are preserved in only one manuscript, dating from the thirteenth century, and the majority of them are certainly of relatively late composition. Sir Ifor Williams, however, argues (1960) that about a dozen of them could well have been, in their original form, the authentic work of Taliesin. Aneirin's long poem, the *Gododdin*, consists of a series of elegies on a band of three hundred warriors sent south from Eidyn (Edinburgh), capital of the kingdom of Gododdin, on a disastrous expedition against the Angles of Bernicia and Deira (later to be joined as Northumbria). A battle took place at Catraeth (almost certainly Catterick in northern Yorkshire) in which the force from Gododdin was wiped out almost to the last man. This must have taken place between 586 and 605, and perhaps in the period 588–90 (see Jackson 1969, 12), and Jackson states (ibid., 63) his 'firm conviction' that the *Gododdin* in its original form was composed 'quite soon after the battle'. Sir Ifor Williams (1938) had also argued that the earliest version of the poem was composed in the sixth century. On the other hand, there are those[1] who argue that a dating as late as the ninth century cannot be excluded.

If one accepts the early dating, then, to be consistent, one must also accept that Taliesin and Aneirin composed their poems in the kingdoms of the northern Britons (Rheged in the case of Taliesin, Gododdin in the case of Aneirin), and that the language they wrote in was Cumbric. What we now have, of course, is indisputably in Welsh, but this presents no real problem. These poems were composed not to be read but to be recited publicly or declaimed by bards, and they were transmitted orally from one generation of bards to another for some hundreds of years. In the course of time, the language would be to some extent modernized and, if necessary, adapted to Welsh rather than Cumbric conventions, and the text itself would be much modified, not only by the substitution here and there of one word or phrase for another but by the omission of some passages and the interpolation of others.

The most we can say, then, is that some of the poetry attributed to Taliesin and Aneirin *may* have been composed in the sixth century, and in Cumbric. Be that as it may, there is a certain irony in the possibility that the two earliest known literary works emanating from Britain were composed in one of the least-known languages to have been spoken in this island in historical times.

Note

1   See in particular D. Greene, 'Linguistic considerations in the dating of early Welsh verse', *Studia Celtica*, 6 (1971):1–11, and Proinsias Mac Cana's review of Jackson 1969, *Celtica*, 9 (1971):316–29.

References

Barry, M. 1969. Traditional enumeration in the North Country. *Folk Life*, 7:75–91 (+ tables).

Ellis, A. J. 1877–9. The Anglo-Cumbric Score. *Transactions of the Philological Society*, 316–72.

Jackson, Kenneth 1953. *Language and History in Early Britain*. Edinburgh.

——1955. The Britons in southern Scotland. *Antiquity*, 29:77–88.

——1963. Angles and Britons in Northumbria and Cumbria. In *Angles and Britons* (six O'Donnell Lectures by various scholars), Cardiff, 60–84.

——1969. *The Gododdin. The Oldest Scottish Poem*. Edinburgh.

Nicolaisen, W. F. H. 1964. Celts and Anglo-Saxons in the Scottish border counties. *Scottish Studies*, 8:141–71.

Phythian-Adams, C. 1996. Britons: survival or revival? In Id., *Land of the Cumbrians. A Study in British Provincial Origins, AD 400–1120*, Aldershot, 77–87.

Williams, Ifor (ed.) 1938. *Canu Aneirin*. Cardiff.

——(ed.) 1960. *Canu Taliesin*. Cardiff.

10 Pictish

Glanville Price

In 1955, F. T. Wainwright edited a volume of studies by various scholars under the title *The Problem of the Picts* (see References). The only criticism one might make of this title is that it suggests that there is only one problem associated with the Picts, whereas in reality there are several.[1]

The most intriguing problem, perhaps, but one that is beyond the scope of this book, is that of the truly enigmatic symbols that are found carved on stone monuments of the fifth to the ninth centuries (and very occasionally on pieces of silverware and other artefacts) over a vast area of the north of Scotland.[2]

The very name of the Picts, too, is problematic. Is the word *Picti*, which occurs in Latin as a name for them, merely the Latin *picti* 'the painted ones', and if so, precisely what does it mean? Does it refer to their practice, mentioned by various Latin writers, of painting and tattooing themselves? Or is it some quite unrelated word? We do not know what term they applied to themselves. There are philological grounds for thinking that, in the pre-Roman period, the terms *Pritani* (in southern Britain) or *Priteni* (in northern Britain) were applied, by others if not necessarily by themselves (there is insufficient evidence to judge), to the Celts of the island of Britain (see Jackson 1955, 158–60). On this basis, Jackson (who, as we shall see, thought that two languages were in use among the Picts, one Celtic and one non-Celtic) suggested (ibid., 160) that it would be convenient to use the term *Priteni* for the Celtic-speaking Picts and *Pritenic* for their language. These terms have also been adopted by some later scholars though they have not passed into general use.

Where did the Picts come from, and what in the end became of them? Here we have more mystery. There is, as Isabel Henderson says (1971, 52), 'no trace of the Picti having arrived at some point in time to settle in North Britain in the way that the Scots arrived in Argyll and the Anglo-Saxon peoples arrived in the south'. They are first referred to as *Picti* in a Latin poem of AD 297 but there can be no reasonable doubt that they had been dwelling in much of Scotland north of the Forth for some considerable time before that. Indeed, it is highly probable that the Caledonii, the Venicones, the Vacomagi, and the Taezali, mentioned by Ptolemy in the second century, and other peoples named by later writers, were in fact Pictish tribes. There are various references to the Picts over the next few centuries. We have (in medieval manuscripts, none of them dating from earlier than the fourteenth century but certainly deriving from much earlier sources) lists of the names of Pictish kings stretching beyond the historical horizon into the legendary past. From the sixth century, references in Gaelic, British and Anglo-Saxon sources reflect peaceful contacts, of an ecclesiastical and cultural nature, as well as political enmity and warfare. Contemporary sources cease to refer to Pictavia (the name occurs in the king-lists) in or about the year 900, with the creation of the new Gaelic-speaking kingdom of Alba by the descendants of King Cinead mac Alpin. The change in nomenclature reflects not so much the disappearance of the Picts as their linguistic and cultural assimilation by the Gaels.

Early medieval writers clearly recognized the existence of a Pictish language, though their comments are not such as to enable us to come to any conclusions about the nature of that language. We are told by Adamnán in his *Life of St Columba*, completed between 692 and 697, that Columba needed an interpreter in dealing with the Picts, which suggests that, whatever their language may have been, it was either not Gaelic or, if it was, then it was a very different kind of Gaelic from that spoken by Columba. Some forty years later, the Venerable Bede, in his *Ecclesiastical History of the English People*, which he completed in 731, refers to the existence in his day of four peoples, each speaking a different language, namely the English (*Angli*), the Scots (i.e. Gaels) (*Scotti*), the Britons (*Brettoni*) and the Picts (*Picti*) – though, again, this is not enough to warrant the conclusion that Pictish was necessarily unrelated to either Gaelic or Brittonic.

Classical and early medieval sources provide for Pictland, among a large number of certain or probable Celtic names, a few that cannot be shown to be Celtic and so may well be pre-Celtic. We shall return below to the question of whether a non-Celtic language may have been in use among the Picts. What is beyond dispute is that there is firm evidence for the existence in Pictland of a Celtic language, and we now turn to survey the little that is known of this language and its relations, if any, with other varieties of Celtic that are known to have existed in Scotland.

The evidence for this language is of two kinds.

First, there are names of places and people that occur in classical writers (see Jackson 1955, 134–8). Kenneth Jackson considers that sixteen names in northern Scotland occurring in Ptolemy's map (second century AD) are Celtic, and that all of these could be P-Celtic (see p. 4) and two of them, *Bannatia* ('probably the Roman fort at Dalingross, Perthshire' – Rivet and Smith 1979, 262) and *Decantae* (the name of a tribe), certainly are. Of the occasional Celtic names occurring in other texts, some (e.g. *Uepogenus*, a personal name that occurs in a third-century inscription) are certainly P-Celtic, while the remainder (e.g. *Calgacus*, whose name appears in Tacitus, and *Argentocoxos* 'Silver Leg', a third-century AD chief mentioned by Dio Cassius) could be either P-Celtic or Q-Celtic: none are necessarily Q-Celtic. Much later, the *Annals of Ulster* for AD 726 refer to a Pict by the name of *Tolarggan Maphan*, a name that in Jackson's view (ibid., 145) certainly contains the P-Celtic word for 'son', *map*. Finally, though some of the names given in the Pictish king-lists are not necessarily Celtic, others, such as *Drostan*, *Uuen*, *Tarain*, *Lutrin* and *Onuist* certainly *are* Celtic, and P-Celtic at that.

The other source of evidence for P-Celtic in northern Scotland is place-names. These provide such P-Celtic elements as *carden* (e.g. *Pluscarden*, *Kincardine*) (cognate with Welsh *cardden* 'thicket'), *pert* (*Perth*, *Larbert*, etc. – cf. Welsh *perth* 'hedge'), *lanerc* (*Lanrick*, *Lendrick*, etc. – cf. Welsh *llannerch* 'glade, clearing'), *pevr* (*Peffery*, *Strathpeffer*, etc. – cf. Welsh *pefr* 'shining'), *aber* (e.g. *Aberdeen* – cf. Welsh *aber* 'river mouth, confluence').[3]

Fragmentary though the evidence is, it is nevertheless enough to establish that, at some stage, a form of P-Celtic was in use throughout much of the area associated with the Picts. One might easily assume that one more or less homogeneous form of P-Celtic was spoken all over Scotland, and that it remained longest in the south-west, as Cumbric (see chapter 9). Jackson, however, argued (1955, 148–9) that there is some evidence for a differential distribution of certain P-Celtic place-names in Pictland on the one hand and in the Cumbric area on the other. While being careful not to overestimate the strength of the evidence, he goes so far as to suggest that there are 'slight indications' of possible affinities with Gaulish rather than Brittonic (from which, in most respects, Pictish was perhaps indistinguishable) and that these could lead us to recognize Pictish as 'a third dialect of the P-Celtic family, parallel to the other two, neither Gaulish nor Brittonic, though Gallo-Brittonic in descent and closely related to both' (ibid., 152). Even this cautiously expressed view has not, however, gone unchallenged. Nicolaisen, for example (1976, 164–71), stressed the fact that, as Jackson had already pointed out, a number of P-Celtic elements such as *carden, pert, lanerc, pevr* and *aber* (see above) occur both north and south of the Forth–Clyde line, i.e. in both Pictish and Cumbric territory (and indeed also in Welsh). So, while by no means rejecting Jackson's view that some features may seem to associate Pictish with Gaulish, he suggests that the separateness of Pictish from Brittonic may have been overstressed and that 'Pictish, although not simply a northern extension of British (or Cumbric), should rather be called a dialect of Northern Brittonic or of Brittonic in general, and not a separate language' (ibid., 171). John Koch, on the other hand, argues for greater differentiation. Adopting the term 'Pritenic' that, as we have seen, had been suggested by Jackson, he makes a distinction within the P-Celtic languages of Britain between Brittonic (covering Welsh, Cornish and Cumbric, together with Breton) on the one hand and Pritenic on the other. Whereas, he says (1983, 214), the four Brittonic languages 'were not geographically isolated from one another till the sixth century and show no detectable dialect separation before the fifth, Brittonic and Pritenic separated at a considerably earlier date, and intercourse between the two speech communities was much obstructed by the late heathenism of the Picts, Pictish matriliny, and – above all – the three-and-a-half-century occupation of the Brittonic half of the island by the Romans'. He fully recognizes that it is impossible to say precisely when Brittonic and Pritenic became 'mutually unintelligible, fully distinct languages', but, on the basis of the 'admittedly slight phonological evidence' that is all we have to go on, he concludes (ibid., 216) that the two were 'distinct dialects by the Roman period and quite probably by the last century of the pre-Roman Iron Age'.

The evidence and the arguments put forth by Jackson and others are surveyed and assessed by Katherine Forsyth (1997). Adopting the term 'Pritenic' for the language of the proto-Picts of the Iron Age period, i.e. for the ancestor of the Pictish language of the early Middle Ages, she agrees (ibid., 27) with Koch that a dialectal cleavage between Pritenic and British may have begun by the first century AD, and perhaps earlier, and that this was doubtless accentuated by the centuries during which Pritenic-speakers dwelt beyond the frontiers of the Roman Empire.

The evidence, as we have seen, is very slight. That some form of P-Celtic *was* indeed spoken in Pictland before the coming of the Gaels is certain. Its precise relationship to Brittonic and Gaulish is, and will probably always remain, problematic.

An intriguing aspect of the 'Pictish problem' is presented by a number of inscriptions found widely distributed over the north of Scotland and ranging in date from the sixth to the tenth century. Of these, a dozen are in Latin script but are brief and fragmentary and, as Forsyth puts it (1997, 32–3), 'have to be squeezed hard to extract any linguistic juice'. We have in addition some three dozen inscriptions in ogams (see pp. 12–13 and figure 1), mainly on carved stone monuments from various localities in those parts of Scotland known to have been occupied by the Picts, though a few are on pieces of silverware and other artefacts. These inscriptions, the most exhaustive description and analysis of which is provided in Katherine Forsyth's doctoral dissertation (Forsyth 1996), bristle with problems both of decipherment and of interpretation and have given rise to widely differing theories. As examples of these inscriptions where the transliteration of the ogams is more or less certain, we may quote IRATADDOARENS- and NEHTETRI- (or NEHTETRE-). Departing from the previously widely held assumption that the language thereof was Celtic (either P-Celtic or Q-Celtic), the eminent Celticist, Sir John Rhŷs, argued (1892–3) that the language of the inscriptions was not merely not Celtic but not even Indo-European. He at first propounded but later (1897–8) abandoned the view that it was an Iberian language related to Basque. Among later scholars who opted for the non-Celticity of the language in question[4] was R. A. S. Macalister who concluded (1940, 223) that 'the language of which a few disconnected scraps are recorded in the inscriptions [. . .], whatever it may be, is altogether independent of Celtic'. The most rigorous, authoritative and influential exposition of the case for the non-Indo-European nature of the language of the inscriptions was that argued by Kenneth Jackson who concluded (1955, 151) that 'the inscriptions, of which some certainly, probably all, date from the late-Pictish period, appear to be written in a quite unknown language, not Celtic and evidently not Indo-European at all; though they contain some Celtic names (both Gaelic and non-Gaelic) and two Gaelic loanwords' (the two words in question are *crroscc* 'cross' and *maqq* or *meqq* 'son'). He recognizes, however, that this problematic language was not necessarily still in normal spoken use at the period of the inscriptions; it is possible, he opines (ibid., 154), that the Celtic aristocracy of Pictland, or some of them, 'might actually have adopted the speech of the older population' or, on the other hand, that perhaps 'they took it over in the pagan period for certain ritual or magic purposes, thus consecrating it as the language of learning, and ultimately, when the ogam script reached Scotland, of epigraphy'. This is, of course, highly speculative.

Jackson's views were widely accepted and not seriously challenged for some forty years. In 1997 however, Katherine Forsyth, drawing on historical and archaeological as well as on linguistic evidence, argued cogently against them. While accepting that many problems remain, particularly in the interpretation of many of the inscriptions, and while regarding as virtually certain that Pictish was influenced by a pre-Celtic substratum, she comes down decisively (1997, 37) in favour of the view that 'from the time of our earliest historical sources, there was only one language spoken in Pictland, the most northerly reflex of Brittonic' and that 'those who wish to argue differently will have to adduce new evidence or fresh interpretations'.

Notes

1   Among a number of recent books devoted to the Picts, two that merit particular mention are Nicoll 1995 (which contains an article by Katherine Forsyth on 'Language in Pictland, spoken and written', pp. 7–10, and an extensive 'Pictish bibliography' by J. R. F. Burt, pp. 31–186), and Foster 1996.

2   On the Pictish symbols, see in particular J. Romilly Allen and J. Anderson, *The Early Christian Monuments of Scotland* (Edinburgh, 1903); R. B. K. Stevenson, 'Pictish art', in Wainwright (ed.) 1955, 97–128; and Charles Thomas, 'The interpretation of the Pictish symbols', *The Archaeological Journal*, 120 (1963):31–97.
3   For further examples of these elements, see Nicolaisen 1976, 158–65.
4   For brief but informative surveys of the views of some of those who argued whether the language of the inscriptions was P-Celtic, Q-Celtic or non-Indo-European, see Jackson 1955, 130–2, and Forsyth 1997, 7–10.

References

Forsyth, Katherine 1996. *The Ogham Inscriptions of Scotland. An Edited Corpus*. PhD dissertation, Harvard University.
——1997. *Language in Pictland*. Utrecht.
Foster, Sally, M. 1996. *Picts, Gaels and Scots*. London.
Henderson, I. 1971. The problem of the Picts. In Menzies, Gordon (ed.), *Who are the Scots?*, London, 51–65.
Jackson, K. 1955. The Pictish language. In Wainwright 1955, 129–66.
Koch, J. 1983. The loss of final syllables and loss of declension in Brittonic. *Bulletin of the Board of Celtic Studies*, 30:201–33 (on Pictish, see pp. 214–20).
Macalister, R. A. S. 1940. The inscriptions and language of the Picts. In Ryan, John (ed.), *Essays and Studies presented to Professor Eoin MacNeill*, Dublin, 184–226.
Nicolaisen, W. F. H. 1976. *Scottish Place-names. Their Study and Significance*. London.
Nicoll, Eric H. (ed.) 1995. *A Pictish Panorama*. Balgavies.
Rhŷs, J. 1892–3. The inscriptions and language of the northern Picts. *Proceedings of the Society of Antiquaries of Scotland*, 26:263–351; Addenda and corrigenda, 411–12.
——1897–8. A revised account of the inscriptions of the northern Picts. *Proceedings of the Society of Antiquaries of Scotland*, 32:324–98.
Rivet, A. L. F. and Smith, Colin 1979. *The Place-names of Roman Britain*. London.
Wainwright, F. T. (ed.) 1955. *The Problem of the Picts*. Edinburgh. (Reprinted Perth, 1980.)

11 Latin

Glanville Price

Roman Britain, in the sense of 'Britain as a part of the Roman Empire', lasted from the invasion of AD 43, in the reign of the Emperor Claudius, until 410, or perhaps a little longer. Part of the army was withdrawn in 401 to campaign against the Goths and in 407, Constantine III, who had been proclaimed emperor by the army in Britain (in opposition to the legitimate emperor, Honorius), crossed with most of his forces to Gaul to ward off a threat from Germanic tribes that had crossed the Rhine. Britain was left virtually unprotected. The history of the last years of Roman Britain is by no means clear, but it appears that in 408 there was a major Saxon raid on Britain to which the Britons reacted by rising in their own defence, expelling the Roman administrators of the island, and defeating the barbarians. It also appears that in 410 the Britons appealed to Honorius for protection but in vain. Rome no longer exercised any control in Britain.

In some respects, however, life for the to some extent Romanized population may have continued for a while much as before and the use of the Latin language may well have continued. Consideration of the position of Latin as a spoken language in Britain must therefore include the immediate post-Roman period.

For our purpose, the most important division within Roman and post-Roman Britain is the geographical one between the Lowland zone and the Highland zone (see map 4 and p. 70 above). Of the two, the Lowland zone was in Roman times the more prosperous, the more densely populated, and the more extensively Romanized.

That Latin was in widespread use as a *written* language in Roman Britain is beyond question though the extent to which it was spoken is far from clear. The written use of the language is well attested in the numerous inscriptions of various kinds that can plausibly be assumed to have been composed in Britain. *The Roman Inscriptions of Britain* (Collingwood and Wright 1965 and 1990–2) includes some 5,000 inscriptions, about half of them 'public' inscriptions on stone, the remainder being 'domestic' inscriptions. Most of the latter, found on wall plaster, tiles, pottery, wood, bone, metal and so on, are very brief (many consisting of only a letter or two). We now also have, however, the hundreds of wooden writing-tablets that have come to light since 1973 at the Roman fort at Vindolanda (Chesterholm) in Northumberland, just south of Hadrian's wall. The fort in fact predates the wall (construction of which probably began in AD 122 or 123), and the tablets date from the period 95–120. They include military documents relating to such matters as allocation of duties, construction work, lists of supplies, but also a number of private letters, and, altogether, they constitute one of the major collections of non-literary texts from anywhere in the Roman Empire.[1]

That Latin *was* used in speech, at least in some circles, can be proved on the basis of a variety of evidence.

First of all, we have the observations of contemporary writers, foremost among them the historian Tacitus who, in his biography of his father-in-law, Agricola, who was governor of Britain from AD 77 to 84, tells us that Agricola educated the sons of British chieftains, with the result that those who had previously rejected the Latin language were now anxious to achieve a mastery of it. In the early second century AD, the poet Juvenal tells us that Britons were trained by Gauls to plead (in Latin) in the law courts.

Then, though the 'public' inscriptions are usually in good classical Latin, some of the more informal ones reveal features that are characteristic of everyday spoken Latin (what is normally known as 'Vulgar Latin' – 'vulgar' meaning 'pertaining to the people'). Nevertheless, it must be borne in mind that, as Adams (1995, 87) points out, many of the Vindolanda tablets were written by trained scribes 'with a degree of education and numeracy' or by military or civilian personnel who were not British natives. He also points out, however (ibid., 127), that the fact that 'the tablets originate in a Celtic-influenced milieu is shown by the fact of the relative frequency of Celtic loanwords, most of them inactive in literary Latin', though these were not necessarily drawn from British Celtic since they could well have entered the Latin of Romanized natives of Gaul (the Celtic speech of Gaul being very closely related to British) who were now serving in Britain. The expression 'relative frequency' should not be misunderstood: there are, in fact, just four such words, namely a number of examples each of *bracis* (a cereal used in beer-making) and *ceruesa* 'beer', and one example each of *bedocem* (a textile) and *tosseas* 'blankets'.

Other inscriptions lead by their very existence to the conclusion that Latin was in everyday use. One that is often quoted is the following, scratched (while the clay was still wet) on a tile found at Newgate, London:

AVSTALIS DIBUS XIII VAGATVR SIB COTIDIM

i.e. 'Austalis has been going off on his own every day for thirteen days', which is generally assumed to be a comment by a workman on another workman's absenteeism. A fragment of a tile from Silchester bears the one word PVELLAM 'girl'. Some words scribbled (and no longer fully legible) on the plaster of a room at the tribal capital of the Silures at Venta Silurum (Caerwent, in Gwent) perhaps read DOMITILLA VICTORI SVO, i.e. 'Domitilla to her Victor', and may have meant something like 'Domitilla sends her love to her sweetheart Victor'; another hand has added the comment PVNIAMINI, 'For shame!' (Nash-Williams 1952–4, 162).

Finally, we have the evidence of the many words borrowed from Latin by the British language. About 800 of these survived in at least one, and in most cases more than one, of the Brittonic languages, Welsh, Cornish and Breton, though not all are still in use, and it is more than likely that these do not represent the sum total of such words borrowed but that others have since disappeared. It emerges from a classification made by Kenneth Jackson (1953, 78–80) that the great majority of the words in question fall into such categories as:

- Agriculture: e.g. *brassicae* 'cabbage', *fructus* 'fruit', *molina* 'mill', *oleum* 'oil' (giving Welsh *bresych, ffrwyth, melin, olew* respectively)
- Arts and crafts: *aurum* 'gold', *durus* 'hard', *plumbum* 'lead' (Welsh *aur, dur* 'steel', *plwm*)
- Building: *columna* 'column', *fenestra* 'window', *pontem* 'bridge' (Welsh *colofn, ffenestr, pont*)
- Calendar and time: *hora* 'hour' (Welsh *awr*), and the names of the days of the week and of some of the months (e.g. *(dies) Mercurii* 'Wednesday', *Aprilis* 'April', Welsh *(Dydd) Mercher, Ebrill*)
- Daily life: *catena* 'chain', *frenum* 'brake', *rete* 'net', *solidus* [type of coin] (Welsh *cadwyn, ffrwyn, rhwyd, swllt* 'shilling')
- Education and intellectual life: *auctor* 'author', *liber* 'book', *schola* 'school' (Welsh *awdur, llyfr, ysgol*)
- Household, kitchen, food and furniture: *caseum* 'cheese', *cathedra* 'chair', *coquina* 'kitchen', *cultellus* 'knife', *flamma* 'flame', *vinum* 'wine' (Welsh *caws, cadair, cegin, cyllell, fflam, gwin*)
- Military life: *arma* 'weapons', *legionem* 'legion', *sagitta* 'arrow', *vagina* 'sheath' (Welsh *arf, lleng, saeth, gwain*)
- Officialdom, administration, and communal life: *carcerem* 'prison', *medicus* 'doctor', *plebem* '[common] people', *testis* 'witness' (Welsh *carchar, meddyg, plwyf* 'parish', *tyst*)
- Parts of the body: *barba* 'beard', *bracchium* 'arm' (Welsh *barf, braich*)
- Religion: *altare* 'altar', *episcopus* 'bishop', *infernum* 'hell', *maledictio* 'curse', *peccatum* 'sin', *sanctus* 'holy', *spiritus* 'spirit' (Welsh *allor, esgob, uffern, melltith, pechod, sant, ysbryd*).

As Frere puts it (1978, 350), these words 'derive in the main from experience of the middle and upper classes rather than from the agricultural peasantry'. Colin Smith, however, points out (Rivet and Smith 1979, 17, note 1) that many of the Latinisms in the Celtic languages are not recorded in writing until the twelfth century or later and suggests that some of them may in fact have been borrowed 'not during the imperial period, but later, from written Latin and from Church sources'.[2]

This admittedly fragmentary evidence has led to widely differing conclusions.

First of all, it cannot reasonably be doubted that Latin was the language of military and civil administration, of the law courts and of the schools. But how much further did it extend? In particular, to what extent was it spoken by the lower classes in the towns and by country-dwellers?

One major problem is that, although it is a reasonable assumption that the rural population was very largely, perhaps almost entirely, made up of Britons, we cannot be at all sure of the ethnic composition of the army of occupation and we cannot even make an informed guess as to that of the population of the towns. We know that units of the army were frequently moved around, sometimes quite literally from one end of the Empire to the other. Jackson argues, however (1953, 98), that in the later stages of the occupation of Britain, there was a substantial amount both of local recruitment and of intermarriage with British women and that, in these ways, the rank and file may well have become to some degree British in speech, particularly in the Highland zone.

As for the civilian administration, there can be little doubt that some officials were of Roman or at least of Italian origin but, on the other hand, 'the native upper classes came to play a part in local self-government and official life, and were encouraged to do so' (ibid., 97). The language of administration and the law, however, can only have been Latin. But what of other sections of the community? As Salway puts it in his book on Roman Britain (1981, 506), 'there is some evidence that in Britain [Latin] remained a second language, but like English in India it was not only indispensable for public affairs but the only practical *lingua franca* in what was becoming a very mixed population'. Collingwood estimated that the Roman conquest itself brought into Britain at least 100,000 immigrants, of whom some 40,000 were soldiers, the rest being 'traders and camp-followers of every kind' and that 'during the generation that followed the landing of Claudius's army the influx of foreigners must have continued, though it probably declined and, by the end of the first century, was no longer very considerable' (Collingwood and Myres 1937, 181). The great majority of these early settlers, Collingwood considered, were either attached to the army or engaged in trade and may be supposed to have settled mainly in the south-east (ibid., 181–2). However, at a rough estimate (which is all that can be expected in the circumstances), the total population of more or less Romanized inhabitants of Britain was about half a million, out of a total population of perhaps about a million (ibid., 180). It follows therefore that, whatever language or languages they may have spoken, the greater part of the Romanized town-dwellers were probably of British origin.

This brings us back to our main concern: what language or languages did they in fact speak?[3] Some of those who have dealt with the problem seem to have built far too much on the data provided by the inscriptions and in particular on the assumption that some of the words and phrases scratched on tiles and pottery were written by workers. But even if one accepts this assumption – which is not an unreasonable one – all it proves is that some workers were able to write some Latin. It does *not* prove that Latin was their normal everyday language. There is no justification for concluding, for example, on the basis of a few inscriptions (including the PVELLAM one mentioned above) from Calleva Atrebatum (Silchester) that 'we may be sure that the lower classes of Calleva used Latin alike at their work and in their more frivolous moments' (Haverfield 1923, 30), or for supposing, on the basis of the absence of Celtic inscriptions, that it is highly likely that little (if any) Celtic was spoken (ibid., 31).

The interpretation to be placed on the fact that so many Latin words were borrowed by British is likewise open to contention. Henry Lewis's claim (1946, 22) that, in the course of time, Latin became the everyday speech of much of the south and east of the island, probably totally displacing British by the fourth century AD up to a line running, broadly speaking, from Exeter to York, seems excessive. At the other extreme, Myles Dillon and Nora Chadwick expressed the view (1972, 34) that 'Latin never gained wide currency in Britain'.

Enough has already been said to indicate that our knowledge of the place occupied by Latin in various aspects of public and private life in Britain during the centuries of the Roman occupation is limited and uncertain. We can, at best, consider, on the basis of the fragmentary and incomplete evidence at our disposal and of reasonable assumptions, what the situation was *likely* to have been.

In the towns and villas, there can be no reasonable doubt that Latin was the language of administration and, at least for 'elevated' purposes, of all literate sections of the community. This does not necessarily mean that their first language was Latin. It is quite possible that not only the artisans who, as we have seen, sometimes scratched a few words in Latin on tiles, pottery or wall plaster, but also many of the middle and upper classes acquired Latin only as a second language. Jackson plausibly suggests (1953, 110) that it was via this stratum of society that Latin words penetrated into the British speech first of the house serfs and labourers of the villas and then more generally into the speech of the rural lower classes. The following comment probably represents as good an assessment as we can hope for of the situation in the towns and villas:

> Most educated Romano-Britons were no doubt bilingual, Latin being the language of law, government, business and cultured life, British that of the intimate family circle and of intercourse with the lower orders. (Frere 1978, 350)

In other words, there existed a situation of diglossia, i.e. a situation in which two languages in a given community are distinguished primarily by function, one acting as a 'high language' for use in such contexts as administration, education, religion, the literary arts, and the other serving as a 'low language' for informal every-day use. How far this situation descended down the social scale in Roman Britain we can only guess.

Though there is room for difference of opinion about the extent to which Latin was spoken in the towns, we cannot doubt that it was spoken. But what kind of Latin was it? Certainly not the highly codified Classical Latin that we know from literary texts. It would perhaps be a reasonable assumption that the spoken Latin of Britain was much the same as the Vulgar Latin spoken in other parts of the Empire. In the first years of the occupation, this must have been so. However, after analysing the phonetic charac-teristics of the numerous Latin loan-words in the British language, Jackson argues (1953, 108) that they reflect a more conservative type of Latin than the Vulgar Latin of other parts of the Empire. The reason, he suggests, is that those Latin-speakers who were the channel through which loan-words were transmitted to British were neither 'the members of the army, nor the merchants, nor the middle and lower classes in the towns, all of whom no doubt spoke various types of the ordinary standard Vulgar Latin just as their counterparts did on the Continent', but rather 'the well-to-do landowners of the Lowland Zone, the native upper classes of town and country' (ibid., 109). And for them Latin would be a language acquired in the schools, a Latin characterized by features of pronunciation (and perhaps also of grammar and vocabulary) that would strike less well-educated speakers as archaic and pedantic. A thorough, balanced and shrewd examination of the evidence for Vulgar Latin in Britain and a critical assess-ment of previous work on the subject also leads Colin Smith (1983) to the conclusion that, though we may not perhaps have enough evidence to be able to claim a thorough knowledge of what the Vulgar Latin of Britain was like, it can be shown that it had a great many features in common with the Vulgar Latin of other parts of the Empire but that it was perhaps 'somewhat conservative' in character.[4]

However, A. S. Gratwick (1982) argues against the view that the Latin of Britain was any more archaic in either its phonology or its word-stock than that of Gaul or Spain. So perhaps even the term 'British Latin' is inappropriate.

So much for the at least partially Romanized population of the towns and villas. But what of the rural population of the Lowland zone, and those who dwelt in the High-land zone?

Some of the peasants of the Lowland zone, many of whom would have come into contact with the Romanized landowners and their families in the villas and, by way of trade, with the Latin-speaking town-dwellers, may well have acquired a fair amount of Latin, and many more may have had a smattering of it. There seems little reason, however, to suppose that Latin was in widespread use among them for any purpose whatsoever. It is significant that, as Colin Smith puts it (Rivet and Smith 1979, 18), 'when we turn to toponymy the balance is heavily tilted towards Celtic' – only some forty British place-names (excluding the names of provinces and seas) are wholly Latin.

If British remained the first, and probably for very many the only, language in the rural parts of the Lowland zone, this was even more true of the Highland zone. Remote from the possible Romanizing influence of the towns, with no villas set in their midst, with a military presence but little Roman civilian presence of any kind among them, the inhabitants of this area can but rarely, if ever, have heard Latin spoken during the whole time of the Roman occupation. Their British speech remained, intact and unassailed.

Archaeological evidence from a number of sites shows that, for some considerable time before the end of the Roman period, the standard of living in the towns had declined significantly and even catastrophically. Even the inhabitants of the best houses seem to have lived in squalor, and private and public buildings were allowed to decay or were not repaired when damaged by fire or suffering structural weakness. All this seems to have dated from the middle of the third century AD, and is paralleled all over the Empire. The reasons for this economic collapse are obscure. In all likelihood it was brought about by misguided financial policies that led to massive inflation, coupled perhaps with growing hostility towards the towns on the part of officialdom and peasantry alike. On the other hand:

> [W]e have a picture of country life and the villa economy flourishing and even expanding slowly in the third and fourth centuries. One may reasonably conclude that the decline of the towns, those centres of romanization, must have lessened the proportion of Latin to British spoken in the province by the end of the fourth century. (Jackson 1953, 112)

Neither this, however, nor the end of Roman administration in or around AD 410, meant an end to all traces of Romanization or even the immediate disappearance of Latin as a spoken language. In the first place, some kind of public administration inherited from the Roman period, and with it the use of Latin, persisted for some time. The Church, too, exercised a Latinizing influence.[5] As Jackson puts it (ibid., 117):

> It would be wrong [. . .] to suppose that Latin was suddenly forgotten at this stage. Celtic though they were, the Highland chiefs at the end of the Roman period, or some of them, were nevertheless identified with Rome.

But the reference here, it will be noted, is, paradoxically, to the Highland zone, the zone which was but lightly affected by Roman cultural influences (as distinct from the Roman military presence, which was well established in parts at least of the zone) throughout the period of the occupation. There is indeed good reason to believe that, in the fifth and sixth centuries AD, there was, for a variety of reasons, a considerable strengthening in the Highland zone of cultural influences derived from what had been in earlier centuries the more decisively Romanized Lowland zone.

Tangible evidence for the continued use of Latin is provided by the fact that the funerary inscriptions on the monuments that local British chieftains in Wales set up in the fifth and sixth centuries are all either in Latin (if on occasion a somewhat defective Latin) alone or else in Latin and Irish (i.e. in ogams – see pp. 12–13). It must, however, be recognized that this does not necessarily imply that their first language was Latin, which would be highly unlikely. Furthermore, the custom of erecting such monuments may have derived not from the Romanized Lowland zone but rather from Gaul, whence it is known that missionaries set out for Britain in the fifth century. Nevertheless, the very fact that such inscriptions are found only in the Highland zone is of great significance. It tends to confirm the view that, at this period, there were more traces of Roman influence there than in the Lowland zone. And the reason can only have been that, in the face of the advancing Angles and Saxons, Romanized or partly Romanized Britons from the Lowland zone had fled to the comparative safety of the Highland zone, taking with them some of their Romanized customs, a knowledge of the Latin language, and a form of British speech that had been much more deeply penetrated by Latin than that of the Highlanders.

All in all, then, the evidence seems to point to the conclusion that some knowledge and use of Latin persisted in the Highland zone of Britain, or at the very least in western parts, in what is now Wales, for perhaps a couple of hundred years after the island ceased to be a part of the Roman Empire. But it is a fair assumption that this knowledge was more or less limited to the educated and the aristocracy, and that even for them it was a second language, a prestige language, and that their first language, like that of the mass of those around them, was British. Even among the ruling class, the use of Latin for any kind of secular purposes seems to have ceased in the early seventh century (see Jackson 1953, 120).

The role of Latin as a spoken language in Britain seems, then, to have gone through three fairly clearly defined, but overlapping, stages.

First, Latin was brought to this island as the all-purpose language of an invading army which was soon to become an army of occupation, and of the associated administration and traders, and, in due course, of the urban civilization that quickly became established. The next stage was the at least partial Romanization of those Britons who dwelt in the towns and villas, and perhaps, though certainly not to the same extent, of the rural parts of the Lowland zone. In time, perhaps after two or three generations, some of these Romanized Britons may well have spoken Latin as their first language, but, for the community as a whole, it is likely that, in a diglossic situation, Latin occupied the role of a 'high language' and British that of a 'low language'. Finally, during the later years of the Roman occupation and for some considerable time (perhaps as long as two centuries) afterwards, the role of Latin even as a 'high language' became more and more artificial, Latin no longer had any real roots in the ordinary life of the community, and, around the year AD 600, perhaps even earlier, British re-established itself, in those areas not yet taken over by invading Germanic tribes, as the only language in use for secular purposes.

The use of Latin as the language of written communication in the post-Roman period is illustrated in particular by Gildas's *De excidio et conquestu Britanniae* 'On the Ruin and Conquest of Britain' (*c.* AD 540). And later, of course, as in the whole of western Christendom, Latin was to serve as a dominant cultural language, in the Anglo-Saxon period (one thinks, for example, of Bede's *Historia ecclesiastica gentis Anglorum* 'Ecclesiastical History of the English People', which he finished in 731) and throughout the medieval and Renaissance periods, and as late as 1687 Isaac Newton published his *Philosophiae naturalis principia mathematica* 'Mathematical Principles of Natural Philosophy' in Latin.

Notes

1   Some 400 tablets are published by Bowman and Thomas 1983 and 1994, together with descriptions of many others that are too fragmentary or illegible to provide much information. For a general account, see Bowman 1983.
2   This point is developed in Smith 1983.
3   A fine overall survey with a wealth of bibliographical references is provided by Evans 1983.
4   See especially Smith 1983, 947–8.
5   For a wide-ranging discussion of the role and possible influence of Latin as the language of Christianity in late Roman Britain, see Thomas's chapter 'Languages, literature and art' (1981, 61–95).

References

Adams, J. N. 1995. The language of the Vindolanda tablets: an interim report. *Journal of Roman Studies*, 85:86–134.

Bowman, Alan K. 1983. *The Roman Writing Tablets from Vindolanda*. London.

——and Thomas, J. D. 1983. *Vindolanda: The Latin Writing-Tablets (= Tabulae Vindolandenses I)*. London.

——1994. *The Vindolanda Tablets (Tabulae Vindolandenses II)*. London.

Collingwood, R. G. and Myres, J. N. L. 1937. *Roman Britain and the English Settlements*, 2nd edn. Oxford.

Collingwood, R. G. and Wright, R. P. 1965. *The Roman Inscriptions of Britain*, 1, *Inscriptions on Stone*. Oxford.

——1990–2. *The Roman Inscriptions of Britain*, 2, *Instrumentum Domesticum (Personal Belongings and the Like)* (ed. S. S. Frere and R. S. O. Tomlin). Gloucester.

Dillon, Myles and Chadwick, Nora K. 1972. *The Celtic Realms*, 2nd edn. London.

Evans, D. E. 1983. Language contact in pre-Roman and Roman Britain. In Temporini, H. and Haase, W. (eds), *Aufstieg und Niedergang der Römischen Welt*, 11, *Principat*, Berlin and New York, vol. 29.2, 949–87.

Frere, Sheppard 1978. *Britannia. A History of Roman Britain*, 2nd edn. London.

Gratwick, A. S. 1982. Latinitas Britannica: was British Latin archaic? In *Latin and the Vernacular Languages in Early Medieval Britain* (ed. Nicholas Brooks), Leicester, 1–79.

Haverfield, F. 1923. *The Romanization of Roman Britain*, 4th edn. Oxford.

Jackson, Kenneth 1953. *Language and History in Early Britain*. Edinburgh.

Lewis, H. 1946. *Datblygiad yr Iaith Gymraeg* ('The Development of the Welsh Language'), 2nd edn. Cardiff.

Nash-Williams, V. E. 1952–4. The Forum-and-Basilica and public baths of the Roman town of Venta Silurum at Caerwent in Monmouthshire. *Bulletin of the Board of Celtic Studies*, 15:159–67.

Rivet, A. L. F. and Smith, Colin 1979. *The Place-names of Roman Britain.* London.

Salway, Peter 1981. *Roman Britain.* Oxford.

Smith, Colin 1983. Vulgar Latin in Roman Britain: epigraphic and other evidence. In Temporini, H. and Haase, W. (eds), *Aufstieg und Niedergang der Römischen Welt*, 11, *Principat*, Berlin and New York, vol. 29.2, 893–948.

Thomas, Charles 1981. *Christianity in Roman Britain to AD 500.* London.

12 English

Glanville Price

English is central to the theme of this book. In nearly every other chapter, we find references again and again to English, to the relations between, say, Welsh, or Norse, or Anglo-Norman on the one hand and English on the other. Of all the languages dealt with in other chapters (and allowing for the fact that British is just an earlier stage of Welsh, Cumbric and Cornish, and that early Irish is continued as modern Irish and as Scottish Gaelic), the only one to which English is completely irrelevant is Pictish, which died out in northern Scotland centuries before English penetrated thus far.

For English is a killer. It is English that has killed off Cumbric, Cornish, Norn and Manx. There are still parts of these islands where sizeable communities speak languages that were there before English. Yet English is everywhere in everyday use and under-stood by all or virtually all, constituting such a threat to the three remaining Celtic lan-guages, Irish, Scottish Gaelic and Welsh, and to the indigenous French dialects of the Channel Islands (one of which, that of Alderney, is already extinct), that their long-term future must be considered to be very greatly at risk.

One could of course seek a more optimistic standpoint, and argue that, a millennium and a half after the English and their language came to these islands, and many cen-turies after they had established themselves as the numerically, militarily, politically, eco-nomically, socially and culturally dominant community, there *are* still, within only a few hours' distance of London, areas where other languages survive as the preferred medium of everyday life. Such a view is by no means indefensible. But one must remem-ber too that, recently enough for tape-recordings to be made, the last speakers of Manx were still alive, and that a century and a half before that one might still have found a few people who spoke Norn and, at the same period or a little earlier, Cornish still survived.

Who were the original English, where did they come from, and when? One of the best known 'facts' of English history – perhaps the best known apart from the date of the Norman invasion – is that Britain was invaded by the 'Angles, Saxons and Jutes'. And this belief has good documentary justification, since that is precisely what we are told by the Venerable Bede in his *Historia ecclesiastica gentis Anglorum* ('Ecclesiastical History of the English People'), which he completed in the year 731. But, unfortunately, Bede's account has to be treated with caution. In the first place it has to be remembered that he was writing not much less than three hundred years after the event. Further-more, there are discrepancies between his account of the origins of the invaders[1] and two briefer accounts, dating from the sixth century. The Byzantine historian,

Procopius,[2] mentions Angles and Frisians, but not Saxons or Jutes, whereas his Welsh contemporary, Gildas, in his *De excidio et conquestu Britanniae* ('On the Ruin and Conquest of Britain'), which is believed to have been written no later than 550, i.e. only a hundred years after the events referred to, calls all the invaders Saxons. As if that were not enough, 'another clue is provided by evidence such as the place-name Swaffham in Norfolk which suggests that at least one group of Suebians arrived. Archaeology also attests the Franks' (Laing and Laing 1979, 23). A further problem is that, though the names 'Jutes' and 'Jutland' must surely be connected, there is no archaeological evidence that the Jutes (if indeed there ever *were* any Jutes among the invaders) came from modern Jutland, i.e. mainland Denmark. Nor is there any certainty that the Angles came from present-day Angeln (in the German part of Schleswig), though these names too are presumably connected.

The most plausible conclusion one can arrive at in the face of the uncertain evidence is that the terms 'Angles', 'Saxons', 'Jutes' and 'Frisians' do not denote clearly differentiated tribes, but are somewhat vague and possibly synonymous or partly overlapping terms for the Germanic-speaking peoples who crossed the North Sea to Britain from an area corresponding more or less to the mainland of modern Friesland (divided between the Netherlands and Germany) and the Frisian Islands (stretching from the Netherlands to Denmark), and from the coastal areas of Saxony in north-west Germany.

The origins of the invaders are not the only problem in a period that is comparatively poorly documented and in relation to which many questions remain unanswered or only partially answered. Not only do we not know precisely who the original 'English' were or whence they came, we do not know for certain why they came, or in what strength. Germanic-speaking raiders had been attacking the coasts of Britain since long before the end of the Roman occupation, which is why the commander of the chain of coastal defences erected in the third century from the Wash to the Isle of Wight bore the title of *Comes litoris saxonici* 'Count of the Saxon Shore'. But the later and somewhat shadowy event that is traditionally termed *Adventus Saxonum*, 'the coming of the Saxons', did not, it appears, partake of the nature of a raid. The Romans sometimes adopted a policy in frontier areas of enlisting the help of one barbarian tribe, as mercenaries or *foederati* ('allies'), against attack from other tribes from without the Empire. It would appear that, after the Imperial authority had been withdrawn from Britain, the Romanized Britains followed a similar policy. According to the somewhat obscure account given by Gildas, and the later more circumstantial one by Bede (to whom we owe the names of the leaders concerned), the first Saxons to settle in Britain under their leaders Hengist and Horsa came at the invitation of a powerful British leader, Vortigern, as mercenaries (against, it seems, their former allies, the Picts and the Scots). Having once established themselves, the Saxons (and, for the moment, the term must serve to denote all and any of the incomers) declined to leave when their services were no longer required. Over a period of perhaps about a hundred years, other groups settled along various sections of the east and south coasts and, in due course, made themselves masters of the greater part of the island south of the Forth with the exception of the more mountainous western areas.

We shall not attempt to trace even in the broadest outline the stages by which the English occupied the island (see, for example, Blair 1956, 27–49). By way of indication of the speed with which they spread out, we need only mention that by the time Augustine arrived in the year 597, they controlled most of southern England east of Dorset and the lower Severn, together with much of Yorkshire and parts of Northumberland and Durham. By the mid-seventh century, the Northumbrians had probably reached the Forth, and by 722 Ine, king of Wessex, had reached Cornwall, though it was to be more than another hundred years before the Britons of Cornwall were finally subdued.

Nor shall we attempt to follow the shifting, kaleidoscopic pattern of the early English kingdoms, which by the eighth century had been reduced to three, namely, Northumbria, Mercia and Wessex.

Where the English went, their language went with them. As we have seen (pp. 75–6), British-speaking enclaves may well have remained here and there, particularly, but not necessarily only, in what is now southern Yorkshire, far removed from the main British-speaking territories of Cornwall, Wales and Cumbria. But, in general, the territory of modern England (with the exception of the extreme south-west and north-west) together with south-east Scotland was English-speaking well before the Norse raids began in the eighth century.

The English language of the period up to the early twelfth century, i.e. until some fifty years after the Norman Conquest, is conventionally known as 'Old English'. Though there is no disagreement among scholars that, from the Forth to the Tamar, the language spoken was English – i.e., it was one language and not several – it is also beyond dispute that there were dialectal differences within Old English.[3] It is not possible to draw clear lines on a map marking off dialectal divisions, but, provided we do not seek to be too rigorous in defining the zones in question, we can identify four main dialects of Old English. The northernmost, Northumbrian, was the dialect of England north of the Humber and of south-east Scotland. Further south, there is the Mercian or Midland dialect – with two main subdialects, West Midland and East Midland. (Northumbrian and Mercian are sometimes grouped together as 'Anglian'.) In the south-east we have the Kentish dialect, the dialect not only of the modern county of Kent but also of an area corresponding more or less to Surrey. The fourth dialect – i.e. that of the remainder of England south of the Thames, from Sussex to Devon, but excluding the Cornish-speaking area – is usually known as West Saxon.

The origins of the different dialects are far from clear. The most obvious explanation, and one that used to be widely accepted, is that they correspond to linguistic differences among the various groups that migrated to England. This implies that these dialectal differences were already in existence before the Angles, Saxons and others migrated from mainland Europe. But this is merely an assumption, albeit not an implausible one. As we have seen, however, it is by no means certain that the terms 'Angles', 'Saxons' and so on in fact corresponded to tribal (and, consequently, linguistic) divisions among the incomers. It has therefore been argued (DeCamp 1958) that the dialectal divisions of Old English could have developed in England itself as a result of various political, social and economic factors and relationships. In particular, it is suggested that Kent maintained trade and cultural links with continental Friesland, that Frisian influence was therefore strong on the English of the south-eastern area, and that the varying extent to which features of Kentish-Frisian pronunciation spread to other parts of England accounts in part for the dialectal divisions of Old English.

A substantial amount of pre-Conquest – i.e. Old English – material has come down to us. By far the greater part of it is in the West Saxon dialect, in which we have – to mention only a few of the more important texts – the *Anglo-Saxon Chronicle*, the writings of Abbot Ælfric (including many homilies and a grammar of Old English) and of Archbishop Wulfstan, and translations of a number of Late Latin texts (including St Augustine's *Soliloquies*, Boethius's *On the Consolations of Philosophy*, and Pope Gregory I's *Pastoral Care*, all of them translated by King Alfred). One of the major works of Western European medieval literature, the epic poem *Beowulf*, is also preserved for us in a predominantly West Saxon dress, in a manuscript dating from around the year 1000, though both the area in which and the period when it was originally written are unknown.

The other Old English dialects are, in comparison, poorly represented. In Northumbrian we have four fragmentary poems and some interlinear glosses (word-for-word translations) of parts of the Gospels added to Latin manuscripts thereof. Mercian is represented by similar glosses to a psalter and to parts of a Gospel manuscript, by some alphabetical glossaries giving (as in a bilingual dictionary) the English equivalents of Latin words, and by a short prayer, while in Kentish there is little other than a paraphrase of one of the psalms and a number of charters (i.e. legal documents).

The distance that separates Old English from Modern English can be illustrated by a couple of brief extracts; note that the characters þ (known as 'thorn') and ð ('edh' or 'eth') are both the equivalent of modern *th* (and note that, curiously, each is used either for voiceless *th*, as in *thin*, or for voiced *th*, as in *this*):

(a) Matthew 25.20–21:
Witodlīce æfter miclum fierste cōm þāra þēowa hlāford, and dihte him gerād. þā cōm sē þe þā fīf pund underfēng, and brōhte ōþru fīfe, and cwæþ: 'Hlāford, fīf pund þū sealdest mē; nū ic gestrīende ōþru fīfe.'
'Indeed after much time the lord of those servants came, and made reckoning with them: then he who received five pounds came and brought five more (others), and said: "Lord, five pounds thou gavest me; now I have gained five more." '

(b) The beginning of *Beowulf*:
Hwæt, wē Gar-Dena in geār-dagum,
þēod-cyninga, þrym gefrūnon,
hū ðā æþelingas ellen fremedon.
'What [i.e. 'Listen to what I have to say!'], we have heard of the glory of the Spear-Danes in olden days, kings of peoples, how those princes performed valiant deeds.'

Contact from the ninth century on with the Danes and with their language, which was closely related to Old English (see chapter 14, 'Norse and Norn'), was to leave a permanent mark on the vocabulary of English, giving it not only a large number of everyday nouns, adjectives and verbs but even the pronouns *they* and *them* and the possessive *their*. An even more extensive influence was to be exercised by French, in particular after the Norman Conquest (see chapter 17, 'Anglo-Norman'). Since French is a Romance language, rather than a language closely related to English as Norse was, borrowings from French were less easily assimilated and the presence of large numbers of them on a page of English – and it was, at first, the written language that was principally affected – had the effect of changing markedly the appearance and, indeed, the character of the language. Baugh and Cable estimate (1993, 168) that some 900 French words had already appeared in English before 1250, and thereafter they were to come in in their thousands. They include, to mention only a few of those quoted by Baugh and Cable (ibid., 167–74), many in the fields of government and administration (*govern(ment)*, *crown*, *state*, *realm*, *royal*, *court*, *council*, *assembly*, *tax*, *noble*, *prince*), of the church (*religion*, *sermon*, *prayer*, *clergy*, *parson*, *vicar*, *image*, *abbey*, *cloister*, *saint*, *miracle*, *redemption*, *mercy*, *charity*, *solemn*, *preach*, *ordain*), of the law (*justice*, *judge*, *plea*, *advocate*, *jury*, *proof*, *verdict*, *accuse*, *acquit*, *condemn*, *felony*, *property*, *heir*), of the army and navy (*army*, *navy*, *peace*, *battle*, *retreat*, *soldier*, *guard*, *captain*, *besiege*, *defend*), of fashion, meals and social life (*habit*, *gown*, *coat*, *button*, *fur*, *blue*, *brown*, *scarlet*, *jewel*, *brooch*, *pearl*, *diamond*, *feast*, *dinner*, *supper*, *taste*, *salmon*, *beef*, *veal*, *mutton*, *pork*, *bacon*, *gravy*, *poultry*, *toast*, *cream*, *raisin*, *tart*, *jelly*, *spice*, *mustard*, *roast*, *boil*, *plate*, *curtain*, *chair*, *lamp*, *blanket*, *leisure*, *dance*, *stable*, *harness*, *terrier*, *pheasant*, *forest*, *park*), and of art, learning and medicine (*art*, *painting*, *music*, *beauty*, *chimney*, *tower*, *prose*, *story*, *title*, *paper*, *pen*, *grammar*, *copy*, *medicine*, *surgeon*, *pain*, *plague*, *remedy*, *ointment*). Among the vast quantities of everyday words that were already current by 1300 are nouns such as *age*, *air*, *city*, *flower*, *noise*, *people*, adjectives such as *brief*, *easy*, *feeble*, *hasty*, *large*, *nice*, *poor*, *proper*, *real*, *sure*, and verbs such as *allow*, *arrive*, *carry*, *change*, *cry*, *enter*, *form*, *move*, *pass*, *pay*, *please*, *push*, *save*, *serve*, *travel*, *waste*, *wince*.

Anglo-Norman also served as a channel for large numbers of Latin loan-words to pass into English, and once the practice of borrowing Latin words through French had become established, then, inevitably, others were taken directly from Latin.[4] Among the hundreds of Latin words borrowed into English directly, not through French, in the Middle English period, i.e. the period from the early twelfth century to the mid-fifteenth century, are *conspiracy*, *contempt*, *distract*, *frustrate*, *gesture*, *history*, *include*, *index*, *individual*, *infancy*, *inferior*, *intellect*, *interrupt*, *legal*, *lucrative*, *magnify*, *mechanical*, *minor*, *moderate*, *necessary*, *nervous*, *picture*, *polite*, *popular*, *prevent*, *private*, *quiet*, *reject*, *solitary*, *submit*, *summary*, *suppress*, *temperate*, *tract*, *tributary*, *ulcer* (see Baugh and Cable 1993, 184–5).

It is largely because of the effect of this massive French and Latin element that English no longer gives the impression of being as closely related to its sister Germanic languages, German, Dutch and the Scandinavian languages, as they are to one another.

As we have seen, before the Conquest the West Saxon dialect had established itself as the principal written variety of English:

> The history of the country caused this West-Saxon to become by the tenth century the accepted language for most vernacular literary purposes. Even the literature of other dialects, such as was most of the poetry, was re-copied into the 'standard' West-Saxon which, with local modifications, had become a sort of common literary language all over the country. (Wrenn 1949, 24)

But the fact that English was replaced for a time by French as the dominant vernacular in the cultural field dealt a death-blow to literary West Saxon:

> The use of Latin for learned work, and of Norman French for aristocratic entertainment, reduced the English vernacular to a set of spoken dialects with little common impetus towards a norm or standard, and West-Saxon had no successor as a common literary vehicle. (ibid., 26)

When in the late Middle English period a standard was gradually to emerge, it was to be on the basis of a different dialect. But which? Strangely, there is some uncertainty about this.

The first point to be made is that, if it is legitimate to refer to West Saxon as having represented, to some extent at least, a 'standard' language, then, in the early Middle English period, the language suffered, among other setbacks, that of going through a time of 'destandardization':

> One of the striking characteristics of Middle English is its great variety in the different parts of England. This variety was not confined to the forms of the spoken language, as it is to a great extent today, but appears equally in the written literature. In the absence of any recognized literary standard before the close of the period, writers naturally wrote in the dialect of that part of the country to which they belonged. (Baugh and Cable 1993, 184)

Not only was there no standard, but even the 'idea of a kind of standard or common literary dialect which had been a feature of later Old English' had been lost (Wrenn 1949, 26).

The main Middle English dialectal areas did not differ greatly from those of the Old English period, except perhaps that West Midland and East Midland are often regarded not as subdialects of Mercian but as distinct dialects on a par with Northumbrian, West Saxon and Kentish (or Northern, South Western and South Eastern as they are often termed in relation to Middle English).

When English first re-emerged from the shadow of French as a literary language (though it had never entirely ceased to be written), no one dialect enjoyed supremacy. There are important Middle English texts in every one of the five main dialects.

The best-known Middle English works in Southern dialects are the poem *The Owl and the Nightingale* (*c*.1250), attributed (perhaps wrongly) to Nicholas of Guildford, from Portisham in Dorset, and John of Trevisa's translation (1387) into a Gloucestershire dialect of Higden's *Polychronicon* (a history of Britain and the world), after which there is virtually nothing in Southern English. Kentish is best represented by *The Ayenbite of Inwyt*, 'Remorse of Conscience', translated from French by Michael of Northgate (Canterbury).

The various Midland dialects are well represented. West Midland has such major texts as the *Brut* (a poem of over 32,000 lines) by Layamon, and the *Ancrene Riwle* or *Ancrene Wisse* (a manual of devotion for anchorite nuns), both from the early thirteenth century. There is also one of the most important Middle English texts, *Piers Plowman*, probably written by William Langland, who hailed from near Malvern, in the second half of the fourteenth century, and the verse Romance *Sir Gawain and the Green Knight* and other poems, also from the late fourteenth century. In the East Midland dialect we have the later parts of the *Anglo-Saxon Chronicle*, which was continued at Peterborough until 1154, and, as early as 1200 if not before, a lengthy poem by one Orm, known (from its author's name) as *The Ormulum*, which, though of little literary significance, is of particular linguistic interest in that Orm uses a phonetic spelling of his own devising. Among later East Midland texts are, from the early fourteenth century, *The Lay of Havelock the Dane*, and, from later in the century, the important works of John Gower (in particular, his *Confessio Amantis*) and Chaucer, both of whom wrote in what is basically the dialect of London, but who did not hesitate to adopt Kentish forms when these could provide a useful rhyme – Chaucer, for example,

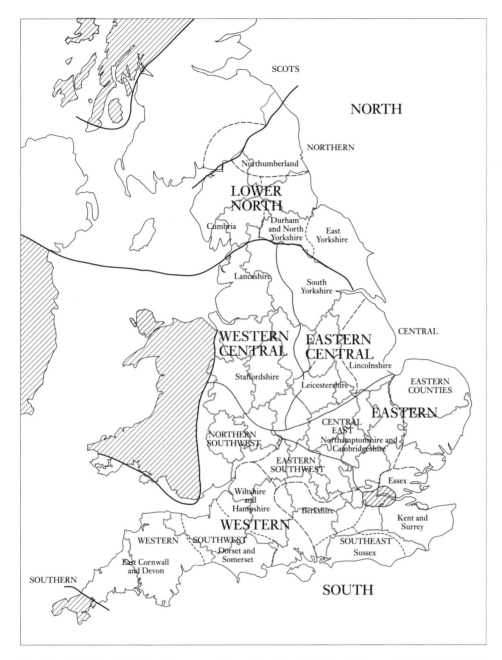

Map 7 *Traditional English dialect areas. From Peter Trudgill,* The Dialects of England *(Oxford, Blackwell, 1990).*

uses Kentish *ken* and *kesse*, instead of *kin* and *kisse*, when he wants rhymes for *ten* and *stedfastnesse*.

The following lines from the 'Prologue' to the *Canterbury Tales* illustrate the gulf that separates Middle English from pre-Conquest Old English:

Bifil that in that seson on a day,
In Southwerk at the Tabard as I lay
Redy to wenden on my pilgrymage
To Caunterbury with ful devout corage,
At nyght was come into that hostelrye
Wel nyne and twenty in a compaignye,
Of sondry folk, by aventure yfalle
In felaweshipe, and pilgrimes were they alle,
That towards Caunterbury wolden ryde.

The language is by now recognizably English – and indeed, one suspects that the language of *Beowulf* would be almost as unintelligible to a man of Chaucer's time as it is to the modern reader.

There is practically nothing in the Northern dialect before about 1300, after which, even leaving aside for a moment the early works in the dialect now referred to as Scots (see chapter 13), there are a number of important texts. Among the earliest of these are the *Cursor Mundi*, a poem probably from the Durham area, surveying the history of the world in some 30,000 lines, and a Yorkshire translation of the psalms. Also from Yorkshire are the poem *The Prick of Conscience* (*c.*1340), by Richard Rolle of Hampole, near Doncaster, and, somewhat later, the cycles of religious plays known as 'Miracles' or 'Mystery Plays' from York and Wakefield. It is worth stressing that, though it was spoken over such a wide area (including much of Scotland), the Northern dialect at this time was remarkably homogeneous. Writing of the texts we have from before 1400, Skeat for example says (1911, 33) that 'the Durham dialect of the *Cursor Mundi* and the Aberdeen Scotch of Barbour are hardly distinguishable by grammatical or orthographical tests; and both bear a remarkable resemblance to the Yorkshire dialect as found in Hampole'. However, there are still enough minor differences to make distinction possible.

In the course of the fifteenth century, we see the emergence of a fairly uniform or 'standard' kind of English that gradually comes to be used all over the kingdom for both official and literary purposes. (The terms 'standard language', 'literary language' and 'official language', though sometimes used as if they were virtually interchangeable, in fact express different concepts. Since, however, in the case of English the 'standard language' also serves as a literary and as an official language, we shall here use that term without further qualification.)

It used to be held that modern standard English is based on the East Midlands dialect, and in particular on the East Midlands dialect as spoken in London (for it stretched that far south), Oxford and Cambridge. Three main and, indeed, plausible reasons are usually given for this. One is that it enjoyed a special prestige as the language of the capital and the two university cities. Another is that, as a geographically central dialect, it was well placed to serve as the basis of a common means of communication for the entire country, being less unfamiliar and hence more acceptable to speakers of southern dialects than a northern form of English would be and vice versa. Thirdly, there was the influence of Chaucer (1340?–1400?) and perhaps also of Wyclif (whose translation of the Bible dates from the 1380s) and his followers.

However, all this was perhaps something of an oversimplification. M. L. Samuels drew attention several years ago to the likelihood that the survey of Middle English dialects, begun in 1952 under the direction of Angus McIntosh, could 'cast light on the probable sources of the written standard English that appears in the fifteenth century' (Samuels 1963, 84). Having first shown that the written language of Wyclif and his followers (which used to be regarded as the language of Oxford, and then of London) is 'obviously [. . .] not "Wyclif's dialect"', he demonstrates, on the basis of various linguistic features (such as *sich* 'such', *ony* 'any', *stide* 'stead'), that 'this is a standard literary language based on the dialects of the Central Midland counties, especially Northamptonshire, Huntingdonshire and Bedfordshire' (ibid., 85) and that it was copied in areas as far removed from the Central Midlands as Somerset and Devon. Though Wyclif's followers, the Lollards, did not invent this 'literary standard', they were, he argues, 'a powerful influence in spreading it, in their bibles, sermons and tracts'. Samuels goes on to assert, plausibly, that the spread of a standard written English depends primarily on the *quantity* written. He stresses in this connection the fact that, whereas up to 1430–5 English is the exception rather than the rule in the administrative documents preserved in the Public Record Office, thereafter there is a sudden change 'from a mere trickle of English documents among thousands in Latin and French, to a spate of English documents' (ibid., 87). And this written language is significantly different from that of Chaucer's London (i.e. East Midlands) English (for example, whereas Chaucer writes *yaf* 'gave', *nat* 'not', *hir* 'their', *swich* 'such', etc., the 'Chancery Standard', as Samuels terms it, usually has *gaf, not, theyre, such*, etc. – ibid., 89, n. 10). So, if this is a form of London English at all, then it is 'a stage of London English changed beyond all recognition from that of a century previous' (ibid., 89). Samuels goes on to argue that the previously popular theory of East Midland influence is not supported by what we know of the dialect in question, and that the source of new influences on London English is the Central Midlands dialect which was 'the only one that achieved the status of literary standard' (ibid.).[5] The plausibility of this case is strengthened when Samuels is able to show that, whereas in the thirteenth and early fourteenth centuries, immigration to London had mainly been from East Anglia and neighbouring counties, thereafter immigration from Northamptonshire and Bedfordshire increased. The immigrants would bring with them a form of English that, being geographically central, was more widely accessible than peripheral dialects, including that of the capital itself. The standard language, therefore, developed 'from a combination of spoken London English and certain Central Midland elements, which themselves would be transmitted in the spoken, not the written language. But the result was a written, not a spoken, standard, which was to spread considerably in use by 1470' (ibid., 93).

The case for a 'Chancery Standard' was taken up and persuasively argued by John H. Fisher who points out (1977, 872) that, until the end of the fifteenth century, 'Chancery comprised virtually all of the national bureaucracy of England except for the closely allied Exchequer' and that, by 1400:

> the use of English in speaking and Latin and French in administrative writing had established a clear dichotomy between the colloquial language and the official written language, which must have made it easier to create an artificial written standard independent of the spoken dialects when the clerks in Chancery began to use English in their official writing after 1420. (ibid., 874)

The estimated 120 or so civil servants of whom Chancery was composed were therefore responsible for introducing English as an official language of central administration in the mid-fifteenth century and so played a major part in the evolution of standard written English.

This variety of 'fairly modern, fairly standard prose' (ibid., 887) was in fairly wide use at Westminster by the 1430s, and 'in view of the enormous prestige and ubiquitous presence of Chancery writing, it is not surprising that Chancery set the fashion for business and private correspondence' (ibid., 891). The success of this particular variety of written English was assured when Caxton set up his press in 1476 at Westminster, close to the government offices, and, almost inevitably, adopted in his publications the type of English that was in normal use in official circles. It is true that printers gradually introduced a few London features for Chancery features (e.g. *are* for *be*, verb forms in *-s* instead of *-th*), and that 'Modern English is not Chancery English', and has continued to evolve. Nevertheless:

> Chancery English of the early fifteenth century is the starting point for this evolution, and has left an indelible impression upon the spelling, grammar, and idiom of Modern English. (ibid., 899)

Spelling has changed little in the last four or five hundred years, failing to keep up with the evolution of pronunciation. The following extract is from Tyndale's translation of the Bible (1525):

> Ye can nott serve God and mammon. Therefore I saye vnto you, be not carefull for youre lyfe, what ye shall eate, or what ye shall dryncke, nor yet for youre boddy, what rayment ye shall weare. Ys not the lyfe, more worth then meate?[6]

By the early eighteenth century, the orthography was virtually completely stabilized, since when there have been no more than minor changes (see Scragg 1974, 80–1).

The grammar has evolved in some respects. Among the most immediately striking differences when one compares the language of, say, the Authorized Version of the Bible (1611) with contemporary English are the abandonment of the second person singular (*thou, thee, thy*), the replacement of the subject pronoun *ye* by *you* and of the possessive determiner *mine* (which was already restricted to pre-vocalic positions, e.g. *mine eyes*) by *my*, the substitution of the (originally northern) verb ending *-s* (*comes*) for the southern *-th* (*cometh*), the generalization of the auxiliary 'do' in questions ('When did we see you sick?' for 'When saw we thee sick?') and negative constructions ('I do not know you', 'Do not fear' for 'I know you not', 'Fear not'), and an increasing tendency to avoid inversion of the subject (i.e. putting it after the verb), as in 'Then came she and worshipped him'.[7]

And there have inevitably been far-reaching changes in the word-stock as civilization and lifestyle have evolved. Every year we all acquire new words, or new meanings for old words. Among the many recent innovations given in Strang's chapter 'Changes within living memory' (1970, 23–69) are *apartheid, chromatograph, collage, couchette, entrepreneurial, fail-safe, gimmickry, to hospitalize, marijuana, to monopolize, motorway, non-event, ombudsman, pizza, quasar, stop-go, teenager, terylene, voyeur, with-it*; other, older, words that had acquired additional meanings include *to commute, to escalate, gear* (= 'clothing'), *nucleus, redundancy*, and *square*. But Strang was writing a generation ago and the vocabulary continues to expand at an astonishing rate. Even between the 1991 and the 1997 editions of *The Oxford Dictionary of New Words* (see Tulloch 1991, and

Knowles 1997), some hundreds of new words, phrases and meanings had been added (some of them dating, however, from the 1980s), including *applet, bad hair day, bonk-buster, commonhold, decaf, edutainment, ethnic cleansing, flying bishop, fundholder, golden goal, happy-clappy, helpdesk, lipstick lesbian, orzo, snowboarding, superunleaded, through-ticketing, tiramisu, upgradability* and *Wessi*.

The 'standard' we have just been discussing is primarily a *written* standard. But the written language and the spoken language, though not identical, are not by any means independent of one another, rather each influences the other, and so many of the conventions, and particularly the grammatical conventions, of the written language may well act as constraints upon the spoken language, at least of educated speakers when they are at pains to express themselves carefully. (However, speech that models itself too closely on the written standard is apt to sound stiff or pretentious – most of us, for example, would say 'Who did you see?' even if we were sufficiently observant of written standards to write 'Whom did you see?'.)

Although the term 'standard English' is sometimes applied to pronunciation as well as to aspects of the written language, it is perhaps not strictly applicable, or at least not in the way in which it is applied to written English. For example, we can say without contradiction that forms like *I seen it*, or spellings like *accomodate* are 'wrong'. This does not mean that they are any less efficient than the 'correct' *I saw it* and *accommodate*, but merely that they are excluded by the accepted conventions of standard English grammar and spelling. While it is also sometimes possible to label certain pronunciation features as 'wrong' (as when, for example, a foreigner pronounces the *-u-* of *guard* as a *w*), a considerable degree of latitude in pronunciation is tolerated, particularly in respect of regional varieties. We shall return to this point.

What *is* beyond dispute is that, as far as British English is concerned, one particular type of pronunciation came to enjoy a certain special prestige. This is what is generally known by the somewhat vague term 'Received Pronunciation' or 'RP' (by whom it is 'received' is not clear – by those who adopt it, perhaps?) and we must now briefly trace its origins and development.[8] With the reservations expressed above, we can, provisionally and for convenience, refer to it as a 'standard'.

The existence of a *spoken* standard seems to be first recognized in the sixteenth century. E. J. Dobson, the author of a thorough study of English pronunciation in the sixteenth and seventeenth centuries (Dobson 1968), draws attention (1955, 27) to comments such as those made by Sir Thomas Elyot, who urged in his treatise, *The Boke named the Governor* (1531), that the children of noblemen should be taught only the type of English 'which is cleane, polite, perfectly and articulately pronounced'. This recommendation and others like it from other sources allow us to draw the conclusion that 'by Henry VIII's reign there was already a clear idea that there was a correct way of pronouncing English, that some form of speech had already become a criterion of good birth and education, and that it was deliberately fostered and taught' (Dobson 1955, 27). The spoken standard in question was defined not merely geographically but socially, as being the language of the highest social classes and of those who had studied at the universities of Oxford and Cambridge: in brief, the language 'in use among well-bred and well-educated people in the Home Counties' (ibid., 30). It is uncertain, however, how widely (in either a geographical or a social sense) this standard was spoken in the sixteenth and seventeenth centuries, but Dobson concludes (ibid., 33) that a reasonable interpretation of the evidence is that:

the common people everywhere spoke dialect and the standard language was the possession only of the well-born and the well-educated, that in the Court and the Home Counties one might expect all well-born and well-educated people to use this standard language,
but beyond those limits, though one might still find men who spoke pure standard English,
the greater part of the gentry and scholars were influenced by the speech of the common
people (i.e. they spoke 'modified Standard'), and finally that in the far West and the North
the standard did not apply at all.

Although regional accents were by no means excluded from the Court (it is related,
for example, that Sir Walter Raleigh spoke with a Devon accent), nevertheless, for the
reasons mentioned above, the pronunciation of the Court, based on that of the London
area (though in the course of time it shed some features of London pronunciation),
acquired the status of a prestige variety:

> It may be said to have been finally fixed, as the speech of the ruling class, through the con-
> formist influence of the public schools of the nineteenth century. Moreover, its dis-
> semination as a class pronunciation throughout the country caused it to be recognized as
> characteristic not so much of a region as of a social stratum. With the spread of educa-
> tion, the situation arose in which an educated man might not belong to the upper classes
> and might retain his regional characteristics; on the other hand, those eager for social
> advancement felt obliged to modify their accent in the direction of the social standard.
> Pronunciation became, therefore, a marker of position in society. (Gimson 1994, 78)

This prestige it retains to some extent, though far less than even two or three decades
ago. Its role is perhaps that of a yardstick against which other varieties of pronunciation may be measured rather than that of a standard, all deviations from which are to
be considered as incorrect. The eminent authority on English pronunciation, Daniel
Jones, while stating his intention of basing his description of English pronunciation
on RP which he regards as 'useful' and having the advantage of being perhaps more
widely understood than any other type throughout the English-speaking world, is
careful to make it clear that he does not 'consider it possible at the present time to
regard any special type as "standard" or as intrinsically "better" than other types' (Jones
1960, 12).

There seem, in fact, to be two contrary tendencies at work at the present time. It is
true, on the one hand, that 'the more marked characteristics of regional speech and, in
the London region, the popular forms of pronunciation, are tending to be modified in
the direction of RP, which is equated with the "correct" pronunciation of English'
(Gimson 1994, 79). On the other hand, it seems to be increasingly accepted that, provided intelligibility is not impaired, regional pronunciations are neither 'inferior' (or
indicative of a lack of education) nor 'ugly'. It is worth mentioning in this context that
Daniel Jones, in both of his authoritative works on the pronunciation of English (1958,
1960) not only makes this specific point but, though giving priority of attention to RP,
refers throughout to 'some of the more outstanding [British and other] divergences
commonly heard in various localities' (Jones 1958, 4). Indeed, the demotion of RP from
its privileged position seems to be already in train. Not only is it indisputably true that
'RP no longer has the unique authority it had in the first half of the twentieth century'
(Quirk et al. 1972, 20; Quirk and Greenbaum 1973, 6), but, as Gimson points out
(1994, 79):

some members of the present younger generation reject RP because of its association with the 'Establishment' in the same way that they question the validity of other forms of traditional authority. For them a real or assumed regional or popular accent has a greater (and less committed) prestige.

This leads him to speculate (ibid.) on the possibility that:

> if this tendency were to become more widespread and permanent, the result could be that, within the next century, RP might be so diluted that it could lose its historic identity, and that a new standard with a wider popular and regional base would emerge.

The late twentieth century has in fact seen what are perhaps the first significant developments in such a direction with the coming into public awareness and discussion of what is widely referred to as 'Estuary English'. The origin and introduction of the term can be precisely dated: it was launched in an article having that as its title published by David Rosewarne in *The Times Educational Supplement* of 19 October 1984, and was quickly taken up by others. What Rosewarne seeks to characterize is a type of modified regional speech that is 'a mixture of non-regional and local south-eastern pronunciation and intonation'. Its heartland he sees as the area around the Thames and its estuary (which would seem to imply that it extends at least as far as northern Kent and southern Essex). Among some of its more salient features are a tendency for final or preconsonantal /l/ to become /w/ in such words as 'will', 'build', the widespread use of a glottal stop instead of a /t/ in such pronunciations as 'Sco'land', 'tha' one', 'trea'ment' for 'Scotland', 'that one', 'treatment', and a degree of diphthongization of the final vowel in words such as 'me' and 'city'. Socially, Estuary English is to be heard, Rosewarne asserts, in both Houses of Parliament and it is 'well established in the City, business circles, the Civil Service, local government, the media, advertising as well as the medical and teaching professions in the south-east'. It is perhaps well placed to be 'now and for the foreseeable future [. . .] the strongest native influence on RP'. As for the reasons for the development and spread of Estuary English, Rosewarne refers to Gimson's 'Conservative RP' and 'Advanced RP' and thinks it likely that those RP-speakers who are now switching to Estuary English do so because they are 'aware that "Conservative" and more so "Advanced" RP can arouse hostility'. So, 'what for many starts as an adaptation first to school and then working life, can lead to progressive adoption of "Estuary English" into private life as well'. He even goes so far as to suggest that Estuary English may be in the process of taking over RP's function of disguising social origins and of becoming the RP of the future.

In reality, there are as many varieties of English (and of all other languages) as there are speakers – each of us has his or her own idiolect – and any attempt to reduce the varieties even of British English to a small number of categories is bound to be an over-simplification. Even if we restrict ourselves to dialects rather than to idiolects, we have to agree with Quirk et al. (1972, 15; 1973, 2) that 'it is pointless to ask how many dialects of English there are: there are indefinitely many, depending solely on how detailed we wish to be in our observations'. Fortunately, however, within the innumerable varieties of English there is what Quirk et al. call (1972, 13–14; 1973, 1) 'a common core or nucleus' which 'dominates all the varieties' and means that 'however esoteric or remote a variety may be, it has running through it a set of grammatical and other characteristics that are common to all', and this 'justifies the application of the name "English" to all the varieties'.

However, if any manageable account of pronunciation is to be given, an attempt must be made to reduce the literally countless varieties to a small number of well-defined categories, taking account of at least two main dimensions, namely the social and the geographical. The problem is that there is no simple correlation between the two: an individual's pronunciation is determined both by his regional origins and by his level of education and his social position (see Quirk et al. 1972, 15–16; 1973, 3). Gimson (1980, 91–2) distinguished three grades of RP, namely 'conservative' (characteristic of the elderly and of certain professions or social groups), 'general' (typified by what is generally considered to be 'BBC pronunciation'), and 'advanced' (or 'affected'), and three grades of regional pronunciation, namely 'educated', 'popular' (or less educated), and 'modified' (i.e. a basically regional pronunciation modified by the adoption of certain RP characteristics).[9] In his 1994 revision of Gimson's book, Alan Cruttenden modifies this classification, distinguishing three main types of RP, viz. General RP, Refined RP ('that type which is commonly considered to be upper-class, and it does indeed seem to be mainly associated in some way with upper-class families and with professions which have traditionally recruited from such families, e.g. officers in the navy and some regiments'), and Regional RP ('which is basically RP except for the presence of a few regional characteristics which go unnoticed even by other speakers of RP') (Cruttenden 1994, 80). He adds that 'the concept of Regional RP reflects the fact that there is nowadays a far greater tolerance of dialectal variation in all walks of life, although, where RP is the norm, only certain types of regional dilution of RP are acceptable' (ibid., 81). It is noticeable, too, that, whereas Gimson says of RP that 'great prestige is still attached to this implicitly accepted social standard of pronunciation' (1980, 85), Cruttenden, in a paragraph which is otherwise little changed, comments that 'some prestige is still attached [. . .]' (Cruttenden 1994, 78).[10]

Although many, or most, people speak with a regional accent (and it has been estimated that only about 3 per cent even of English people – 'English', not 'English-speaking' – speak RP: Hughes and Trudgill 1996, 3), very few nowadays speak what can properly be termed 'dialect' (the distinction being that the term 'dialect' covers much more than the term 'accent' – a dialect has not only its own characteristic pronunciation but also, to a greater or lesser extent, its own grammar and its own vocabulary):

> the English of most English (and English-speaking Welsh) people is neither RP Standard English nor a rural dialect. The vast mass of urban working-class and lower-middle-class speakers use a pronunciation nearer to RP, and lexical and grammatical forms much nearer to Standard English, than the archaic rural dialects recorded by the dialectologists. (Wells 1970, 231)

As we have seen above, the regional dialects of English virtually ceased to be written after the fifteenth century. The exceptions are all the more noticeable because they are so highly exceptional – like, for example, William Barnes's *Poems of Rural Life in the Dorset Dialect* (1844), the language of which can be illustrated by the following extract:

The gre't woak tree that's in the dell!
There's noo tree I do love so well;
Vor times an' times when I wer young
I there've a-climb'd, an' there've a-zwung
An' pick'd the eäcorns green, a-shed
In wrestlèn storms from his broad head.

Dialectal studies in England can perhaps be said to have begun as far back as 1674 when John Ray published his *Collection of Words not Generally Used*. The late eighteenth century[11] saw the appearance of Francis Grose's *Provincial Glossary* (1787), followed in the nineteenth century by others (none of which, however, stand comparison with Jamieson's *Etymological Dictionary of the Scottish Language* (1808–25)). An important advance came with the foundation of the English Dialect Society by William Skeat in 1873. This led to the publication of some eighty dialectal glossaries, but unfortunately, 'by 1896, when the *English Dialect Dictionary* was commenced, it was considered that the Society's function had been fulfilled and it was wound up' (Wakelin 1972, 46). Joseph Wright's *English Dialect Dictionary*, published in six volumes, 1898–1905, and including (in vol. 6) an 'English Dialect Grammar' (also published separately), contained some 100,000 entries and was to remain for over half a century the principal monument of English dialectological research. Thereafter, serious work on the dialects of England lagged far behind what was going on in many other European countries. Skeat's comment (1911, 105) that 'certainly no other country can give so good an account [as England] of its dialects' may perhaps have been true when it was written, but it was already out-of-date when it appeared in print, since publication of Jules Gilliéron's monumental *Atlas linguistique de la France*, the first great linguistic atlas of any area in the world, was completed in 1910. Recent years have seen the appearance of a number of French regional linguistic atlases, and meanwhile every major linguistic area and many minor ones on the mainland of Europe had been provided with a linguistic atlas. That of England (to which we shall return) did not appear until 1978, and, admirable though it is, it cannot compare in scope with many of the Continental atlases. And, regrettably, it is now too late. The steady decline of dialects in the course of the twentieth century and the escalating costs of dialectological research (not least in the costs of printing) must mean that there will never be a really major atlas of the English dialects.

A number of dialectal monographs, many of them of great value, have indeed appeared since the early years of the twentieth century (a useful listing is given by Wakelin 1972, 173). But there was no worthy successor to the work of the English Dialect Society and Wright's dictionary until the *Survey of English Dialects (SED)* (see Orton 1960 and 1962, and Petyt 1980, 88–93), based at the University of Leeds, was initiated in 1946 by Harold Orton and Eugen Dieth (Dieth, who was Professor of English Language at Zurich, died in 1956, and the bulk of the work was directed by Orton). The ultimate aim of the *SED* was the compilation of a linguistic atlas of England, on the basis of direct investigation carried on between 1950 and 1961 by trained field-workers, using a questionnaire designed for the purpose by Orton and Dieth (and reproduced in Orton 1962, 39–113). Lack of 'the vitally necessary editorial and financial assistance' (ibid., 22) unfortunately meant that the plans for the atlas, which was to have provided 'interpretative maps of the whole country' showing 'important lexical, phonological and grammatical distributions' (Wakelin 1972, 56), had to be drastically revised. It did not prove necessary to abandon the idea entirely, but, as we saw above, what was eventually produced (Orton, Sanderson and Widdowson 1978) was, by comparison with other linguistic atlases, a relatively modest volume: 406 small-scale maps, of which the great majority (249) are of phonological interest, while 65 relate to vocabulary and 92 to grammar (83 to morphology, 9 to syntax). It is a tragedy that it was not possible to achieve Orton and Dieth's ambition: as one of Orton's associates put it, 'although this work is styled "Linguistic Atlas of England", it is not [. . .] the full linguistic atlas planned as the crowning achievement of the *SED*' (Wakelin 1972, 57).

A subsidiary but nevertheless important aim of the *SED* has, however, been fully attained with the publication in tabular form of the 'basic materials' obtained by means of the questionnaire and on which the projected atlas was to have been based. This has appeared in four volumes, each in three parts, covering respectively the North of England and the Isle of Man (Orton and Halliday 1962–3), the West Midlands (Orton and Barry 1969–77), the East Midlands and East Anglia (Orton and Tilling 1969–71), and the South of England (Orton and Wakelin 1967–8).

The *SED* has also had the belated but nevertheless very welcome effect of triggering an enhanced interest in the dialects of English which has led to the publication of a number of works that are likely to appeal both to scholars and to those members of the general reading public with an interest in such matters (see in particular Wakelin 1972; Hughes and Trudgill 1996; Trudgill 1990; Trudgill and Chambers 1991; Upton, Sanderson and Widdowson 1987; Upton and Widdowson 1996).

We began this chapter by referring to the role that English has played in killing off other languages with which it has shared these islands. It is ironic to have to end with a discussion of the efforts made to rescue from oblivion the remnants of the dialects of English itself before they too decline to the point of extinction.

Notes

1   For the full text of his account (Book 1, Chapter XV), see the edition and translation of the *Ecclesiastical History* by Bertram Colgrave and R. A. B. Mynors, Oxford, 1969, pp. 48–51.

2   A Byzantine historian may seem a strange source for English history, but Myres points out (1937, 337) that Procopius 'probably derived his information from Angles who are known to have accompanied a Frankish embassy to Constantinople in his day'.

3   For a recent survey, see Thomas A. Toon, 'Old English dialects', in Hogg 1992, 409–51.

4   For a recent survey of Scandinavian, French, Latin and other foreign loan-words, see David Burnley, 'Lexis and semantics', in Blake 1992, 409–99 (especially pp. 414–39).

5   On the evolution of London English up to the fifteenth century and the decisive influence of the changing pattern of immigration, see Samuels 1972, 165–70.

6   For the whole of this parable, Matthew 6.24–34, in various English versions, beginning with one dating from the tenth century, see Bolton 1972, 68–77.

7   On changes in the grammar of English in the last four hundred years, see Barbara Strang's *A History of English*, 1970, which adopts the strikingly original procedure of tracing the history of the language backwards, by two-century periods, from '1970–1770' to 'Before 370'; see especially, on '1970–1770', pp. 96–101, and on '1770–1570', pp. 136–53.

8   For a full and authoritative historical survey of the notion of a standard, covering the time from the late Middle Ages onwards but concentrating necessarily on the period from the sixteenth and more especially from the eighteenth century onwards, the reader is referred to Lynda Mugglestone's book (1995). Blake (1996) also devotes several chapters to the development of a standard language (with reference to grammatical and lexical as well as phonetic features) and to deviations from it.

9   A useful and readable introduction to social and regional varieties of contemporary English is provided by Hughes and Trudgill 1996. See also Petyt 1980, ch. 7, 'Social and urban dialectology: Britain'.

10 An informative survey of the origins and present status of RP, and of changing attitudes towards it, is provided by Honey 1989.

11 For a survey of English dialects in the last two hundred years, see Ossi Ibalainen, 'The dialects of England since 1776', in Burchfield 1994, 197–274.

References

Baugh, Albert C. and Cable, Thomas 1993. *A History of the English Language*, 4th edn. London.

Blair, Peter Hunter 1956. *An Introduction to Anglo-Saxon England*. Cambridge.

Blake, Norman (ed.) 1992. *The Cambridge History of the English Language*, II, *1066–1476*. Cambridge.

Blake, N. F. 1996. *A History of the English Language*. Basingstoke and London.

Bolton, W. F. 1972. *A Short History of Literary English*, 2nd edn. London.

Burchfield, Robert (ed.) 1994. *The Cambridge History of the English Language*, IV, *English in Britain and Overseas: Origins and Development*. Cambridge.

Cruttenden, Alan 1994. *Gimson's Pronunciation of English*, 5th edn, revised by Alan Cruttenden. London.

DeCamp, David 1958. The genesis of the Old English dialects. A new hypothesis. *Language*, 34:232–44.

Dobson, E. J. 1955. Early modern standard English. *Transactions of the Philological Society*, 25–54.

——1968. *English Pronunciation, 1500–1700*, 2nd edn. Oxford.

Fisher, John H. 1977. Chancery and the emergence of standard written English in the fifteenth century. *Speculum*, 52:870–99.

Gimson, A. C. 1980. *An Introduction to the Pronunciation of English*, 3rd edn. London.

——1994. (see Cruttenden 1994).

Hogg, Richard M. (ed.) 1992. *The Cambridge History of the English Language*, I, *The Beginnings to 1066*. Cambridge.

Honey, John 1989. *Does Accent Matter? The Pygmalion Factor*. London.

Hughes, Arthur and Trudgill, Peter 1996. *English Accents and Dialects. An Introduction to Social and Regional Varieties of English in the British Isles*, 3rd edn. London.

Jones, Daniel 1958. *The Pronunciation of English*. Cambridge.

——1960. *An Outline of English Phonetics*, 9th edn. Cambridge.

Knowles, Elizabeth (ed.), with Elliott, Julia 1997. *The Oxford Dictionary of New Words*. Oxford.

Laing, Lloyd and Laing, Jennifer 1979. *Anglo-Saxon England*. London.

Mugglestone, Lynda 1995. *'Talking Proper.' The Rise of Accent as a Social Symbol*. Oxford.

Myres, J. N. L. 1937. The English settlements, Book V of R. G. Collingwood and J. N. L. Myres, *Roman Britain and the English Settlements*, 2nd edn. Oxford.

Orton, Harold 1960. An English Dialect Survey: Linguistic Atlas of England. *Orbis*, 9:331–48.

——1962. *Survey of English Dialects*. (A) *Introduction*. Leeds.

Orton, Harold and Halliday, Wilfred J. 1962–3. *Survey of English Dialects.* (B) *The Basic Material.* Vol. 1, *The Six Northern Counties and the Isle of Man*, Parts 1–3. Leeds.

Orton, Harold and Barry, Michael V. 1969–77. *Survey of English Dialects.* (B) *The Basic Material.* Vol. 2, *The West Midland Counties*, Parts 1–3. Leeds.

Orton, Harold and Tilling, Philip M. 1969–71. *Survey of English Dialects.* (B) *The Basic Material.* Vol. 3, *The East Midland Counties and East Anglia*, Parts 1–3. Leeds.

Orton, Harold and Wakelin, Martyn F. 1967–8. *Survey of English Dialects.* (B) *The Basic Material.* Vol. 4, *The Southern Counties*, Parts 1–3. Leeds.

Orton, Harold, Sanderson, Stewart and Widdowson, John 1978. *The Linguistic Atlas of England.* London.

Petyt, K. M. 1980. *The Study of Dialect.* London.

Quirk, Randolph, Greenbaum, Sidney, Leech, Geoffrey and Svartik, Jan 1972. *A Grammar of Contemporary English.* London.

Quirk, Randolph and Greenbaum, Sidney 1973. *A University Grammar.* London.

Samuels, M. L. 1963. Some applications of Middle English dialectology. *English Studies,* 44:81–94.

——1972. *Linguistic Evolution with Special Reference to English.* London.

Scragg, D. G. 1974. *A History of English Spelling.* Manchester and New York.

Skeat, Walter W. 1911. *English Dialects from the Eighth Century to the Present Day.* Cambridge.

Strang, Barbara M. H. 1970. *A History of English.* London.

Trudgill, Peter 1990. *English Dialects.* Oxford.

——and Chambers, J. K. (eds) 1991. *Dialects of English: Studies in Grammatical Variation.* London.

Tulloch, Sara (ed.) 1991. *The Oxford Dictionary of New Words.* Oxford.

Upton, Clive, Sanderson, Stewart and Widdowson, John 1987. *Word Maps: A Dialect Atlas of England.* London.

Upton, Clive and Widdowson, D. A. 1996. *An Atlas of English Dialects.* Oxford.

Wakelin, Martyn F. 1972. *English Dialects: An Introduction.* London.

Wells, J. C. 1970. Local accents in England and Wales. *Journal of Linguistics*, 6:231–52.

Wrenn, C. L. 1949. *The English Language.* London.

13 Scots

Jeremy J. Smith

Whether Scots[1] is a distinct language from English, or simply a markedly differentiated variety of English, is hard to decide. Indeed, any question about the precise status of Scots in relation to the English used in England is probably unanswerable in clear-cut terms. The problem, of course, is that languages are dynamic, evolving phenomena. English, after all, was originally a dialect of West Germanic, only gradually becoming distinguished from the other dialects which eventually became Dutch, German and so on. The precise moment when English ceased to be a dialect and became a language is impossible to determine; the distinction is one of the 'more/less' rather than of the 'either/or' kind.

The Scots/English distinction seems similar. An extra problem is that languages evolve through interaction with their geographical neighbours, and Scots and English have been neighbours for a long time. It is often said that a language is a 'dialect with a flag', and there is much truth in this statement. After all, Danish, Norwegian and Swedish are, objectively considered, in some ways as close to each other as (say) the broad Yorkshire and Devonshire dialects of English, yet all are counted as distinct languages for political reasons. And Scotland has a flag of her own, even though her flag is also included – at least at present – in that of a larger entity, the United Kingdom.

The twentieth-century border between Scotland and England certainly correlates with a frequent correspondence of isoglosses in non-standard speech. This correspondence has been steadily developing since the Middle Ages, as non-standard usage in England was affected by a process of standardization which for some time did not spread north of the border. Especially on the level of lexis (Glauser 1974; Smith 1994; Smith 1996a, 177–86), a dialectal distinction is probably more marked here than anywhere else in Britain, although a fair case could be made for a similar North–South divide in the Midlands of England.

It is probably fairest to state that the relationship between Scots and English is in linguistic terms much the same as that between Dutch and certain varieties of German, or that between some of the Scandinavian languages; that is, they are part of the same dialect continuum and are to a large extent mutually comprehensible. Thus whether you count Scots as a language or a dialect depends on your political viewpoint.[2]

The remainder of this chapter is divided into four parts: a more detailed sketch of the present-day linguistic situation in Scotland; an external history of Scots; an internal history; and futures for Scots.

In what follows, the following comparative chronology, taken with slight modifications from the *Concise Scots Dictionary* (hereafter, *CSD*) (1985, xiii), might be a helpful point of reference. All dates are approximate.

Old English (Anglian):	to 1100
Older Scots:	1100 to 1700
Older Scots is generally subdivided into the following periods:	
Pre-literary Scots:	to 1375
Early Scots:	to 1450
Middle Scots:	1450–1700
Early Middle Scots:	1450–1550
Later Middle Scots:	1550–1700
Modern Scots:	1700 onwards

A corresponding list of the periods for English is as follows:

Old English:	to 1100
Middle English:	1100–1475
Early Middle English:	1100–1350
Late Middle English:	1350–1475
Modern English:	1475 onwards
Early Modern English:	1475–1700
Later Modern English:	1700 onwards

Present-day Scotland is a multilingual society. Gaelic (see chapter 4), the language which has been spoken for longest in Scotland, continues to be used in the Highlands and Islands of Scotland, but it is not restricted to those areas; indeed, Glasgow, Scotland's largest city, has such a substantial population of immigrants from the Highlands that it is occasionally referred to as the largest Gaelic-speaking city in the world. At the other end of the chronological scale, languages new to Scotland, such as Urdu, Panjabi and Cantonese (see chapter 19, 'Community Languages'), are now spoken by substantial communities throughout the country, especially in the 'central belt' of settlement stretching from Edinburgh in the east to Glasgow in the west.

However, most folk living in present-day Scotland speak a language which ultimately derives from Old English. These people form not one but several overlapping speech communities. Very roughly speaking, three groups may be distinguished.

First, there are those who speak non-Scottish varieties of English, notably English as spoken in England. Of these the most socially salient variety is what might be termed Standard Southern English, a usage consisting of the grammar and vocabulary of Standard English transmitted in an accent focused on Received Pronunciation, the prestigious accent of England. This variety is spoken in particular by two groups of speakers living in Scotland: some English immigrants, and members of the Scottish aristocracy. Scottish people most regularly encounter Southern Standard English through radio and TV.

Second, there are speakers of Scots, a variety derived from Old English but with a separate history since the late Middle Ages. Spoken Scots can be divided into subvarieties (map 8). It is used throughout the Lowlands of Scotland; it has spread into the north-east of Scotland (where it is often referred to as 'Doric') and Orkney and Shetland, and a derived variety, Ulster Scots, arrived in Northern Ireland in the sixteenth century and has remained there ever since. Scots today has become in general

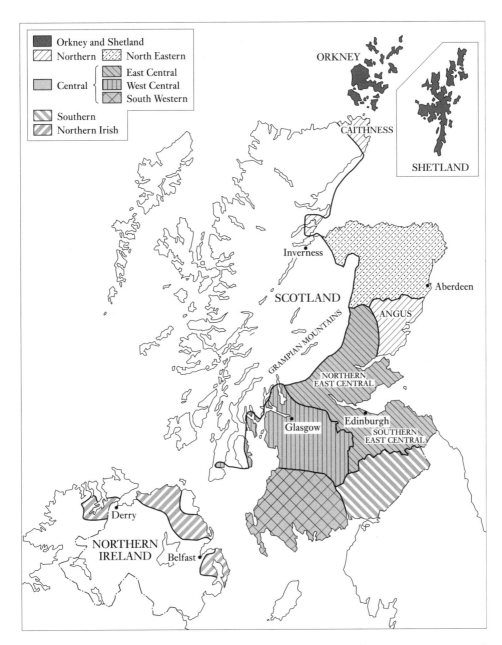

Map 8 *Scots. The territory of Scots in Scotland and Ulster in the 19th and 20th centuries, with major dialectal divisions. Based, by permission of the Scottish National Dictionary Association, on a map in Mairi Robinson (editor-in-chief),* The Concise Scots Dictionary *(Aberdeen, Aberdeen University Press, 1985) and, by permission of Mrs Millicent Gregg, on Robert J. Gregg,* The Scotch-Irish Dialect Boundaries in the Province of Ulster *(Port Credit, Ont., Canadian Federation for the Humanities, 1985).*

Legend:
- Orkney and Shetland
- Northern
- North Eastern
- Central
  - East Central
  - West Central
  - South Western
- Southern
- Northern Irish

Map labels: ORKNEY, SHETLAND, CAITHNESS, Inverness, SCOTLAND, GRAMPIAN MOUNTAINS, Aberdeen, ANGUS, NORTHERN EAST CENTRAL, Glasgow, Edinburgh, SOUTHERN EAST CENTRAL, Derry, NORTHERN IRELAND, Belfast

the preserve of the working classes, either rural or urban, and is still frequently subjected to correction in the classroom. Especially in urban usage, it is losing a good deal
of its lexical (although not accentual or grammatical) distinctiveness. This bleaching of
many distinctively Scots features is partially, no doubt, the result of exposure to UK-
wide radio and television, but more probably is mainly to do with the greater range of
social interaction taking place in towns. Nevertheless, those signalling their identity with
Scottish working-class culture continue to do so by using this variety. There have been
and are developments which are favourable to the elaboration of Scots as available for
more than a restricted register of spoken use (see pp. 167–8 below).

Finally, there are speakers of what is usually called Scottish Standard English
(Abercrombie 1979). This prestigious variety is frequently defined as Standard English
with a Scottish accent. It has a grammar and vocabulary almost (although not quite) the
same as that used by high-prestige speakers of Standard English in England, but it com-
bines these characteristics with an essentially Scots pronunciation, albeit modified somewhat in the direction of Received Pronunciation. It thus lies between English and Scots
on the same linguistic continuum as Scots; many middle-class speakers in less formal
situations use Scots items as opposed to those more characteristic of Scottish Standard
English. However, the fact that it can be modified also in the direction of Southern
English is also significant; evidently, middle-class people feel the centripetal pull of
two different linguistic centres of gravity. In such circumstances it is unsurprising that
Scottish Standard English is a somewhat fluid phenomenon, hard to categorize precisely.

Of course, this outline of Scottish usages is a crude categorization; and it is important to bear in mind that the relationship between these three groups is not one of clear-
cut division, but clinal; many speakers shift from one group to another in different social
situations. Nevertheless, the description given above is perhaps enough to show that
class and language have an intimate relationship.

The present-day configuration just described derives from historical developments
over the last millennium. English has overt prestige in present-day Scotland because,
since the seventeenth century, Scotland has been governed from England as a subordinate part of the United Kingdom. But Scots has covert prestige in Scotland, notably
among the working classes, in part because Scottish workers have resisted perceived
English oppression much more strongly than those who have prospered under the union.
It is no coincidence that Scottish nationalism as a political movement is most deeply
rooted among the Scottish working classes, and has a powerful radical edge to it.

Varieties of present-day Scots are of course, like all natural languages, the result of
interaction between inherited and borrowed linguistic material. Ultimately these varieties derive from Anglo-Saxon or Old English, brought to Britain from northern
Germany by Anglo-Saxon invaders in the fifth century AD. These invaders spread across
Britain, pushing the Celtic inhabitants of the island into the north and west, where they
still remain, notably in Wales and in the Highlands of Scotland. In general, the Angles
spread north and north-west, whereas the Saxons spread south and south-west.
Anglian, the speech-variety of the Angles, was almost certainly distinct from the Saxon
dialects even before the Anglo-Saxons arrived in Britain, although subsequent interaction between Anglian and Saxon is important for the later history of English.

In the early seventh century the Angles, having crossed the River Tweed, established
themselves in what is now Scotland, and in 638 they captured the strongpoint called

Din Eidyn 'sloping-ridge fortress'. They changed the name, replacing Celtic *din* 'fortress' with its Germanic equivalent *burgh*, and reversing the element order in the place-name (generic + qualifier) to conform to Germanic patterns of word-formation (qualifier + generic): the result was the form 'Edinburgh'. Any medieval ruler of Scotland had to hold at least one of the great strongpoints in the Forth–Clyde valley: Edinburgh in the east, Stirling in the centre and Dumbarton in the west. The possession of Edinburgh made the Angles an important grouping in contemporary Scottish power-politics. A new hegemony spread over the Lowlands of Scotland into northern England, forming the Anglian kingdom of Northumbria.[3]

Northumbrian kings of the period, of whom the most famous is probably St Oswald (reigned 633–651), were active Christian proselytizers, and left symbols of their power throughout their kingdom. They had a particular veneration for the cult of the True Cross – Oswald made a point of erecting a wooden cross before his victory against the pagans at 'Heavenfield' – and perhaps the best-known of their monuments are the great stone crosses such as that at Ruthwell in Dumfriesshire. Such objects were not simply religious statements; they were a public attestation of the hegemony of Christianized Germanic kings. It is no coincidence that the Ruthwell Cross, erected originally on a hill overlooking the Solway Firth, would have been visible for a long way. On this cross appears part of an Old English poem on Christ's crucifixion carved in runes, the ancient Germanic alphabet (see figure 2 in chapter 14). This poem, which is related to a much fuller poem, 'The Dream of the Rood', which has survived in a West Saxon manuscript from the tenth century, is occasionally claimed as the earliest piece of Scottish literature. The claim is of course anachronistic (but see McClure 1988, 8; Murison 1978, 1).

However, Gaelic continued to be spoken and written throughout what is now Scotland, even in the south-east Lowlands, and even seems to have become resurgent in the tenth century with the emergence of the Celtic kingdom of Alba, a precursor of present-day Scotland which was focused on the ancient kingdom of Fife.

The Anglo-Saxon area was considerably affected by a later wave of invasions: the arrival of Norse (Norwegian and Danish) peoples in the British Isles from the eighth century onwards. The primary Norse settlement was focused on the so-called 'Great Scandinavian Belt' across Northern England (especially Lancashire and Yorkshire where interaction between Anglian and Norse brought about significant linguistic change), in eastern Ireland and in the Northern and Western Isles and Caithness. But the impact of the Norse settlements extended far beyond these areas. For instance, Scandinavianized people whose origins lay in Northern England settled early in south-west Scotland, bringing place-name elements such as *kirk* 'church' with them. An interesting point is that, contrary to popular belief, they seem to have mixed fairly peacefully with the Celtic-speaking inhabitants of that area; thus blend-forms appear, such as *Kirkcudbright* 'Cuthbert's church'. In this name, a Northumbrian saint, a Celtic element-order (generic + qualifier) and a Scandinavian word (*kirk*) have been brought together.[4]

Norse had comparatively little effect on the evolution of Scots until the Norman Conquest of England in 1066. In Scotland, a major effect of the Norman Conquest, albeit somewhat delayed, was, oddly enough, the expansion of Anglian usage at the expense of Gaelic. The accession in Alba of Normanized kings, especially David I

(1124–53) and his successors, who held lands in northern England of the English king, meant that Gaelic was no longer so widely used. The king and his immediate circle habitually seem to have spoken in Anglo-Norman (see chapter 17). As the English author Walter of Coventry wrote (in Latin) in the thirteenth century: 'The more recent kings of Scots profess themselves to be rather Frenchmen, both in race and in manners, language and culture; and, after reducing the Scots [i.e. Gaels] to utter servitude, they admit only Frenchmen to their friendship and service' (cited in Dickinson and Duncan 1977, 83; see also Macafee 1988, 4). Noble Anglo-Norman families from England brought with them English-speaking servants and retainers.

Another important group of English-speakers were so-called 'pioneer burgesses' (*CSD*, ix) from Northern England who settled in the new royal and baronial burghs which were established during the period. The English of these burgesses from the 'Great Scandinavian Belt' was heavily marked by the impact of the earlier Scandinavian invasions, and it blended with the Anglian speech of south-east Scotland. By the twelfth century this variety of English, heavily influenced by Norse, was strongly established in the eastern Lowlands; by the mid-fourteenth century it had replaced Gaelic throughout eastern Scotland as far north as the Moray Firth, and also in much of the south-west of the country. From the major port of Aberdeen, Scots spread into Caithness and the Northern Isles to replace Norn.

Written records in Scots begin to appear from the late fourteenth century onwards; before that date, the only evidence of any significance for this variety is to be found in place-names and in occasional glosses on Latin material. The extent of the divergence of this pre-literary material from Northern Middle English, however, is unclear; and when we move into the Early Scots period (*c*.1375–1450) it seems that the Anglian-derived variety spoken in Scotland was not viewed by contemporaries as a language distinct from English. Even later fifteenth-century writers from the Early Middle Scots period (*c*.1450–1550) such as William Dunbar refer to Londoners such as Chaucer as using 'our' language. The term 'Inglis', used to describe the non-Celtic language of the Lowlands of Scotland, was only joined (and not replaced) by 'Scottis' in the late fifteenth century; until that date, the term 'Scottis' was used to refer to Gaelic (Templeton 1973, 6).

Whatever its precise relationship to English, Early and Early Middle Scots developed as an elaborated language, i.e. a variety which could be used in more than one register. In 1398, the Scottish Parliament began to legislate in Early Scots rather than in Latin, and the Middle Scots period saw an efflorescence of literary activity. Barbour's national epic-romance, *The Brus*, was composed in 1375 but survives earliest in two late-fifteenth-century copies. James I of Scotland composed *The Kingis Quair* in the vernacular while in exile in England, and major poets, such as Robert Henryson, William Dunbar, Gavin Douglas and David Lindsay followed after him. Many of these writers were associated with the sophisticated court culture of the later Stuart kings. Somewhat later a flourishing prose tradition emerged.[5] As in England, the elaboration of the vernacular meant that contemporaries embellished their Scots with vocabulary derived from the high-status languages of the late medieval period, French and Latin, a practice encouraged by close contacts with France under the 'Auld Alliance' against England, and by the evolution of Scots law in accordance with Continental rather than English customs. Even present-day Scottish law-texts are filled with Latin-derived terminology which is not used in England.

As Scots became elaborated, it underwent some of the formal changes also found in Middle English. Dialectal diversity, which seems to have been a feature of Early Scots, seems to have been muted for communicative reasons as the Middle Scots period progressed. This muting may be termed 'standardization', even though a fixed form of Middle Scots was never fully achieved (Agutter 1989; Aitken 1971; Meurmann-Solin 1997).

Whereas standardized written English subsequently became the educationally enforced (and fixed) norm, socio-political and cultural events meant Scots did not develop similarly. England was always the big neighbour, and there was a continuing cultural gravity effect which could not be ignored; a parallel may be drawn with the present-day relationship between the United States and Canada. The most significant specific cultural event of the sixteenth century, of course, was the Reformation, which took place in Scotland in 1560. A Scots version of the New Testament, that of Murdoch Nisbet from *c*.1520, did exist, but this text was not printed until the twentieth century. It was based on the English Wycliffite Bible from the late fourteenth century, itself a translation from the Latin Vulgate of St Jerome, and contemporary biblical scholarship demanded a return to the original Greek (as in William Tyndale's English Bible of 1525–6). Throughout the sixteenth century, Protestant religious writers looked to England for their cultural models; indeed, the use of written Scots became in certain registers identified with Catholicism. It was the Catholic writer Ninian Winget who attacked the great Reformer John Knox in the following terms: 'Gif ze, throw curiositie of nouationis, hes forzet our auld plane Scottis quhilk zour mother lerit zou[,] in tymes cuming, I sall wryte to zou my mynd in Latin, for I am nocht acquyntit with zour Southeron' ('If you, through excessive attention to novelties, have forgotten our old plain Scots which your mother taught you, in times to come, I must write to you concerning my thinking in Latin, because I am not acquainted with your Southern [speech]') (cited in Tulloch 1989, 14).[6]

This Anglicizing tendency was reinforced by the major political events of the seventeenth and eighteenth centuries: the Union of the Crowns of 1603, when James VI of Scots succeeded Elizabeth I as James I of England, and the Union of Parliaments of 1707. James VI had been a patron of Scots poets but they, like himself, began to write in English when they moved to London; and recent research has drawn attention to the evolution of Scottish Standard English (not Scots) as a prestigious variety in the Scottish Enlightenment culture of the eighteenth century (Jones 1995).

Late Middle Scots was therefore under cultural pressure, and both A. Devitt (1989) and more recently A. Meurmann-Solin (1997) have charted the increasingly restricted use of written Scots as the sixteenth and seventeenth centuries progressed. By 1700 and the beginning of the Modern Scots period, written Scots was confined to material with a local or private currency, such as letters between members of the same family, and even there was under pressure as the Bible provided a written model for all literate classes in society. Written (as opposed to spoken) Scots became during the eighteenth century essentially a curiosity, albeit sometimes a fashionable one, in (for instance) the poetry of Robert Burns, or one with a surreptitious political connotation (as in the verse of Robert Fergusson). Burns, in poems like 'Tam O'Shanter' or 'The Cotter's Saturday Night', notoriously used Scots for conversation and narrative but his own version of written Augustan English for more elevated discourse.[7]

In the nineteenth century, however, a Scots prose tradition flourished in the developing popular press and in fiction generally (Donaldson 1986, 1989), and in the twentieth century there was an attempt to create a prestigious written Scots, in the shape of Lallans (= 'Lowlands'), a synthetic mixture of Scots varieties, invented by the poet Hugh MacDiarmid and others, and given normative form by a published style-sheet. However, the use of this so-called 'plastic' variety has never become common. A comparison is sometimes made between Lallans and Norwegian Nynorsk, which emerged in the nineteenth century in a similar way; interestingly, both varieties have developed strong political associations, especially radical ones. Unlike Lallans, Nynorsk has received a fair degree of state support, and has developed as an everyday language, spoken as well as written by persons with some social prestige. However, both Lallans and Nynorsk are marked by artificiality and, especially in the case of the former, restriction to a particular kind of literary usage, and their long-term prospects outside this register do not look good (despite McClure 1981). Even in poetic use, Lallans seems now to be declining, to be replaced by an attempt to reflect working-class urban speech in writing, for example in the poetry of Tom Leonard, or in the novels of James Kelman and Irvine Welsh. However, even in the work of some of these writers Scots, as opposed to English, is sustained only fitfully. Thus Welsh's 1986 novel *Trainspotting*, which had a considerable vogue in the 1990s, arguably distinguishes Scots and English in a way which parallels Burns's distinction.[8]

The external history of the language just described has left its mark on its internal history, i.e. the formal evolution of Scots over time. Scots has developed distinctive characteristics in every level of language: in transmission (spelling in writing, accent in speech), in grammar and vocabulary. The details of these characteristics are technical, and it is perhaps not appropriate to give an exhaustive account of each element here; readers are referred to standard accounts such as those contained in the major history edited by C. Jones (1997).

Thus Scots orthography seems to have developed as a regionally standardized form at the end of the Middle Ages, and an approximation to this usage has been sustained since then to represent Scots usage. Spellings such as *guid* 'good', *hame* 'home', *deil* 'devil' and *fu* 'full' correspond to sound-changes which have emerged as prototypical of Scots speech (Aitken 1977; Jones 1997). In grammar, several constructions are characteristic of Scots, especially in the modal verbs and in negation (Jones 1997).

But perhaps the most obviously distinctive Scots features are to do with vocabulary, where all the languages with which Scots has come into contact have left their mark. The major sources of Scots vocabulary are as follows:

- There are, perhaps surprisingly, comparatively few loan-words from Gaelic in Scots; examples quoted in *CSD* are *cairn, glen, loch, capercailzie, quaich* 'drinking-cup', *tocher* 'dowry', *sonse* 'plenty, prosperity'. Gaelic loans tend to refer to culture-specific objects (e.g. *quaich, tocher*) or to topographical features (e.g. *glen, loch*).
- Some Scots words of Old English origin no longer survive south of the border, e.g. *bannock* 'meal-cake', *gloamin* 'twilight', *haugh* 'level ground'.
- Norse words in Scots entered the language with the Anglo-Scandinavian immigration from northern England; examples include *gate* 'road', *bairn, flit* 'to (re)move (house)', *lass, kirk, dreich* 'dreary'. A number have survived in present-day Scots but

not in present-day Northern English; their disappearance in the latter variety is the result of standardizing pressures which have not extended into Scotland.

- French was the mother tongue of the kings and magnates of Scotland from the time of David I until probably the fourteenth century, and it remained one of the two languages of prestige (the other being Latin) in Britain for much of the Middle Ages. Many French words in Scots are also found in English, but some are restricted to Scots, e.g. such common expressions as *fash* 'anger, trouble' and *Hogmanay*.
- Latin was the language of learning and the church. Loan-words in Scots tend to be rather restricted until the 'aureate' poets of the fifteenth century, such as William Dunbar, borrowed many Latin words into Scots for decorative effect. A special set of Latin borrowings are to do with Scots law, e.g. *narrative* 'statement of alleged facts as the basis of a legal action', *executor-dative* 'person who serves a writ at the order of a court of law', *homologate* 'render valid a legal document which is informal or defective', *nimious* 'vexatiously burdensome in a legal sense'.
- Other languages also came into contact with Scots through trade, etc., the most important of which were Dutch and Flemish, yielding words such as *golf*, *scone*, but for the most part their influence on the Scots lexicon was comparatively small.

In a previous volume, the editor of this present book considered that the future prospects for Scots were rather bleak (Price 1984, 192). Great projects of linguistic record were discussed there: the *Dictionary of the Older Scottish Tongue* (Craigie et al. 1937–), dealing with Older Scots, now nearing completion; the *Scottish National Dictionary* (Grant and Murison 1931–76), designed to record Modern Scots; and the continuing Linguistic Survey of Scotland (see Catford 1957; McIntosh 1952; Mather and Speitel 1975–). The implication of the discussion was that these projects were hastening to record a variety which was dying out. It is possible that this was an over-pessimistic view. Like all living languages, Scots continues to change; indeed, it is arguable that, if it did not change, it would be truly dead, like Latin. Some have suggested that it is losing a good deal of its lexical distinctiveness as a result of exposure to UK-wide radio and television, but there is evidence that Scots is continuing to be a creative language, developing its own distinctive forms. The urban vernaculars of the great cities of Scotland, for instance, may have lost many traditional dialect usages but continually develop their own new forms. Michael Munro's fascinating study of Glasgow vocabulary, *The Patter* (Munro 1985), is marketed as a humorous book, but it contains numerous examples of the productiveness of Glaswegian vernacular and has a serious side to it (see further Macafee 1983).

Such 'bottom-up' developments are currently being complemented by 'top-down' initiatives, part of a reassertion of Scottish nationhood which was also expressed in the reconvening in 1999 of the Scottish Parliament – the first since 1707. The Scottish National Dictionary Association continues to flourish and has recently had an access of new funding. Recent initiatives in Scottish schools and universities, such as the development of the children's Scots language resource *The Kist* and the establishment of Scottish Language courses in university curricula, have tried to reaffirm the value of Scots in Scottish culture (Niven and Jackson 1998). The interest in Scots in other European universities (notably in Germany and Scandinavia) is indicative of its recognition as an important variety in its own right.

How effective such official initiatives will be remains to be seen. It is perhaps worth pondering on the truism that the cultural value placed upon any linguistic variety cannot be divorced from the cultural status allotted to those who use it. Languages are a human tool; it is arguable that Scots will be valued only when the human users of Scots are valued.

Notes

1 This chapter derives orientation and information from standard surveys of the subject: the essays in Aitken and McArthur 1979 (especially Aitken 1979 and Murison 1979), in Jones 1997 and in McClure and Spiller 1989; Barber 1997; McClure 1988, 1994; Murison 1978; Templeton 1973; and the important introductory essay by A. J. Aitken in *CSD*. These surveys all give extensive bibliography and suggestions for further reading. Articles on topics to do with Scots are published in the journal *Scottish Language*, published by the Language Committee of the Association for Scottish Literary Studies. Information about the work of the Scottish National Dictionary Association is obtainable from the Secretary, SNDA, 27 George Square, Edinburgh EH8 9LD. An invaluable new resource is the machine-readable *Helsinki Corpus of Older Scots*, compiled by A. Meurmann-Solin; further related machine-readable corpora are currently being developed.
2 On all these issues, see Kay 1990, McClure 1988, for views from a nationalist perspective; perhaps more dispassionate is Wells 1982, 393–6, although the focus there is primarily on accent.
3 An excellent one-volume history of Scotland is Lynch 1991; Dickinson and Duncan 1977 can also be recommended. For information about Scottish place-names, see in the first instance Nicolaisen 1976.
4 The Scandinavian settlement in the south-west of Scotland should be kept separate from that in the far north of Scotland and in the Northern and Western Isles. Settlers in these latter areas had come directly from Scandinavia, and their presence, although it did affect Gaelic, had little or no effect on the subsequent development of Scots. The Scandinavian language of these settlers is often referred to as Norn (see chapter 14). See further Macrae-Gibson 1989 and references there cited; also Smith 1994. On the 'Great Scandinavian Belt' see Samuels 1985.
5 On the literary history of Scotland, see in the first instance the authoritative series edited by Cairns Craig 1987. Still useful as a single-volume account is Wittig 1958. On literary language in Older Scots times, see Agutter 1987; a more recent general account is Corbett 1997.
6 The standard account of the history of the Bible in Scots, on which this discussion depends, is Tulloch 1989. Perhaps the best-known translation into Scots is that undertaken in the twentieth century by W. Lorimer (see Lorimer 1983).
7 Recent analysis of some of Burns's Augustan writing reveals a more subtle interplay between spoken and written modes than he has sometimes been credited with; see Smith 1996a, 170–6, and 1996b.
8 See for instance the distinction between prose description and dialogue in the passage 'There is a light that never goes out' (Welsh 1996, 262–73).

References

Abercrombie, D. 1979. The accents of Standard English in Scotland. In Aitken and McArthur, 68–81.
Agutter, A. 1987. Middle Scots as a literary language. In Jack, R. D. S. (ed.), *The History of Scottish Literature*, I, Aberdeen, 13–25.

—— 1989. Restandardisation in Middle Scots. In Adamson, Sylvia et al. (eds), *Papers from the Fifth International Conference on English Historical Linguistics 1987*, Amsterdam, 1–11.

Aitken, A. J. 1971. Variation and variety in written Middle Scots. In Aitken, A. J. et al. (eds), *Edinburgh Studies in English and Scots*, London, 177–209.

—— 1977. How to pronounce Older Scots. In Aitken, A. J. et al. (eds), *Bards and Makars*, Glasgow, 1–21.

—— 1979. Scottish speech: a historical view, with special reference to the standard English of Scotland. In Aitken and McArthur, 85–119.

—— and McArthur, Tom (eds) 1979. *Languages of Scotland*. Edinburgh.

Barber, C. L. 1997. *Early Modern English*. Edinburgh.

Catford, J. 1957. The Linguistic Survey of Scotland. *Orbis*, 6:105–21.

Corbett, John 1997. *Language and Scottish Literature*. Edinburgh.

Craig, Cairns (gen. ed.) 1987. *The History of Scottish Literature*. Aberdeen.

Craigie, Sir William et al. (eds) 1937– . *Dictionary of the Older Scottish Tongue*. London.

CSD = Robinson, Mairi (ed.) 1985. *The Concise Scots Dictionary*. Edinburgh.

Devitt, Amy 1989. *Standardizing Written English: Diffusion in the Case of Scotland 1520–1659*. Cambridge.

Dickinson, W. Croft and Duncan, Archibald A. M. 1977. *Scotland from the Earliest Times to 1603*. Oxford.

Donaldson, William 1986. *Popular Literature in Victorian Scotland*. Aberdeen.

—— 1989. *The Language of the People*. Aberdeen.

Glauser, Beat 1974. *The Scottish–English Linguistic Border: Lexical Aspects*. Bern.

Grant, W. and Murison, David (eds) 1931–76. *The Scottish National Dictionary*. Edinburgh.

Jones, Charles 1995. *A Language Suppressed: The Pronunciation of the Scots Language in the Eighteenth Century*. Edinburgh.

—— (ed.) 1997. *The Edinburgh History of the Scots Language*. Edinburgh.

Kay, Billy 1990. *The Mither Tongue*. Glasgow.

Lorimer, W. L. 1983. *The New Testament in Scots*. Edinburgh.

Lynch, Michael 1991. *Scotland: A New History*. London.

Macafee, Caroline 1983. *Glasgow*. Amsterdam.

—— 1988. *Origins and Development of Older Scots*. Glasgow.

McClure, J. Derrick 1981. The synthesizers of Scots. In Haugen, Einar et al. (eds), *Minority Languages Today*, Edinburgh, 91–9.

—— 1988. *Why Scots Matters*. Edinburgh.

—— 1994. English in Scotland. In Burchfield, Robert (ed.), *The Cambridge History of the English Language*, IV, *English in Britain and Overseas*, Cambridge, 23–93.

—— and Spiller, Michael (eds) 1989. *Bryght Lanternis*. Aberdeen.

McIntosh, Angus 1952. *Introduction to a Survey of Scottish Dialects*. Edinburgh.

Macrae-Gibson, O. D. 1989. The other Scottish language – *Orkneyinga saga*. In McClure and Spiller, 420–8.

Mather, J. Y. and Speitel, Hans 1975– . *The Linguistic Atlas of Scotland*. London.

Meurmann-Solin, Anneli 1997. Differentiation and standardisation in Early Scots. In Jones (ed.), 3–23.

Munro, Michael 1985. *The Patter: A Guide to Current Glasgow Usage*. Glasgow.

Murison, David 1978. *The Guid Scots Tongue*. Edinburgh.

—— 1979. The historical background. In Aitken and McArthur, 2–13.

Nicolaisen, W. 1976. *Scottish Place-names*. London.

Niven, Liz and Jackson, Robert (eds) 1998. *Scots Language: Its Place in Education*. Dumfries.

Price, Glanville 1984. *The Languages of Britain*. London.

Samuels, M. L. 1985. The Great Scandinavian Belt. In Eaton, Roger et al. (eds), *Papers from the Fourth International Conference on English Historical Linguistics*, Amsterdam, 269–81.

Smith, Jeremy J. 1994. Norse in Scotland. *Scottish Language*, 13:18–33.

——1996a. *An Historical Study of English*. London.

——1996b. Ear-rhyme, eye-rhyme and traditional rhyme: English and Scots in Robert Burns's 'Brigs of Ayr'. *Glasgow Review*, 4:74–85.

SND = Grant and Murison (eds) 1931–76. *The Scottish National Dictionary*. Edinburgh.

Templeton, J. M. 1973. Scots: an outline history. In Aitken, A. J. *Lowland Scots*, Edinburgh, (ed.), 4–19.

Tulloch, Graham 1989. *A History of the Scots Bible*. Aberdeen.

Wells, J. C. 1982. *Accents of English*. Cambridge.

Welsh, Irvine 1996. *Trainspotting* (paperback edn). London.

Wittig, Kurt 1958. *The Scottish Tradition in Literature*. Edinburgh.

14 Norse and Norn

Michael P. Barnes

Viking raids against Britain and Ireland seem to have begun late in the eighth century, though there is evidence that contact between Scandinavia and parts of the British Isles had existed for some time before this. For a while the invaders appear to have been content to harry and plunder, but as the ninth century advanced they started to settle – in some areas in considerable numbers.

Settlement probably took place first in Orkney and Shetland, the area of Britain closest to Norway and an important staging-post on voyages further south and west. A date in the early ninth century, arrived at on the basis of literary, archaeological and onomastic evidence, is generally accepted as the starting point for Norse[1] immigration into the Northern isles, but it is uncertain how quickly the numbers built up. The time at which Norsemen first began to settle in the Hebrides and Man is even less clear, but it was probably not very long after they had established a permanent presence in Orkney and Shetland. Small islands are easier targets than large ones for conquest and settlement, and Man in particular was doubtless seen as an attractive base for raids on adjacent coasts. The northern and western littoral of Scotland was also affected, particularly north-east Caithness, but precisely when Norsemen began to live permanently in these areas is uncertain.

The Viking kingdom of Dublin appears to have come into being in the 850s, and in the course of the next hundred years the Norse invaders founded a number of other coastal settlements such as Wexford, Waterford and Limerick. They also established a presence in the hinterland of these developing towns, although the majority seem to have lived close to the coast or to navigable waterways.

Despite sporadic raids on the east and south coasts starting in the late eighth century, Viking settlement in eastern England did not really begin until the arrival of the *mycel hæðen here* 'great heathen army' in 865–6. The immigration that followed culminated in the treaty of 886 or thereabouts between Guthrum, a Viking leader, and King Alfred of Wessex by which a Norse sphere of influence known later as the Danelaw was established north of a line running roughly from the mouth of the Thames to Staffordshire (see map 9). A second wave of Viking activity afflicted England towards the end of the tenth century, reaching its climax in the conquest of the whole country by the Danish king, Sveinn Forkbeard, in 1013. On his death in the following year, Sveinn was succeeded by his son, Knútr the Great, who ruled until 1035.

Viking involvement in English affairs ended abruptly in 1066: in September the Norwegian king Haraldr the Hard-Ruler, who had also had his eye on the English throne, was defeated and slain at the Battle of Stamford Bridge; less than a month later the

Map 9 *Viking settlements in Britain and Ireland.*

Battle of Hastings had ushered in the Norman Conquest. In Ireland it was also the Normans who put an end to the Hiberno-Norse culture of the coastal towns with their invasion of 1166–72. Norse predominance in Man and the Hebrides seems likely to have suffered a more gradual decline. Norwegian claims to supremacy over the islands ended with the defeat of their forces at the Battle of Largs in 1263 and the ceding of the territory to the King of Scotland in 1266, but the descendants of the Viking settlers may well have formed a large and influential enough segment of the population for their language and culture to persist for some time afterwards, at least in the Hebrides. Norse speech on the Scottish mainland is unlikely to have survived beyond the thirteenth century, except in north-east Caithness – for a time part of the Earldom of Orkney and to judge from place-name and other evidence an entirely Norse province in the Viking and early Middle Ages. The Northern Isles themselves remained politically Scandinavian until their pledging in 1468–9 to King James III of Scotland; culturally they retained their Scandinavian character for considerably longer.

The ninth-century settlers in Orkney, Shetland and Caithness seem on the evidence of language, place-names and later literary sources to have hailed chiefly from western Norway (the area stretching from present-day Trøndelag to Agder; cf. Barnes 1998, 2–4). The nature of the relations between the settlers and the indigenous population has been a matter of controversy. It has been variously claimed that the Northern Isles were all but deserted before the Norsemen arrived, that the pre-Viking inhabitants were exterminated or driven out, or that they were assimilated. There is little evidence to support the idea of a depopulated Orkney and Shetland. Recent archaeological discoveries point to a degree of co-existence between Viking invaders and natives, but the total obliteration of pre-Norse place-nomenclature in the Northern Isles and Caithness is perhaps suggestive of a more dramatic turn of events. Whatever the truth, it is clear that indigenous speech rapidly withered away as a form of Scandinavian based on the ninth-century dialects of western Norway became dominant. Because it has left so few traces, the nature of this indigenous speech has also proved a controversial subject. Recent scholarly opinion favours a P-Celtic tongue (see p. 4), that is, one most closely related to the Celtic of Strathclyde, Cumbria, Wales and south-west England, but persuasive arguments have also been advanced for the existence of a pre-Indo-European language side-by-side with the P-Celtic.

The Vikings who harried and ultimately settled the Hebrides and Man seem also to have hailed chiefly from western Norway. Unlike Orkney and Shetland, these more southerly islands, together with most of the Scottish Highlands, were mainly if not completely Gaelic-speaking, the result of a steady migration from Ireland going back to AD 500 or even earlier. What happened in the meeting between Norse and Gael in this region is far from clear. In Man and the outer Hebrides – the areas of densest Norse settlement – the invaders seem for a time to have become the dominant element in the population. Some have claimed or implied that here Norse speech superseded Gaelic almost entirely, an inference drawn not least from the alleged circumstance that few of the Gaelic place-names in either area can be proved to be of pre-Viking date (e.g. Gelling 1970–1, especially 1970, 137–9, and 1971, 173–4; Fraser 1984, 40). Against this it has been argued that in Man the totality of the evidence, archaeological, historical, literary and linguistic, points to the widespread survival of Gaelic, certainly among the peasant population, and probably at a higher social level too, during a period of dominance by a small Norse aristocracy (Megaw 1978). Evidence for the continuous use of

Gaelic in the outer Hebrides is sparser, but a detailed study of nearly 3,000 place-names from an area of about 150 square kilometres in the west of Lewis led its author to the conclusion that many were in fact of pre-Viking origin (Cox 1991). The issue is far from resolved, but most would probably now accept (a) that the Norse settlement in both Man and the Hebrides was considerable and involved not just a ruling elite but different levels of society, (b) that there is no incontrovertible evidence that Gaelic ceased to be spoken in either area, and no reason short of the total extermination or expulsion of the native population to expect such an outcome (see e.g. Fellows-Jensen 1983, 42–5).

The pattern of Norse settlement in Ireland differed considerably from that in the islands. It involved both Norwegians and Danes (to the extent such terms are meaningful in a ninth-century context), and was limited, as we have seen, to a few small coastal enclaves with towns at their centres. The question of the linguistic dominance of Norse over Gaelic does not thus arise, although it could well be that during the Viking Age the Irish towns had a preponderance of Norse-speakers (of different origins and with different dialects). The country at large, however, remained uniformly Gaelic in language and custom, as witness, for example, the extreme paucity of Scandinavian place-names in Ireland.

Viking settlement in eastern England was mainly from Denmark; Norwegians participated as well, and possibly even Swedes, but in nothing like such numbers as the Danes (again to the extent these terms are meaningful). In the north-west the immigrants tended to be of Norwegian language and custom, though most of them, it is thought, came by way of Ireland, Man and Scotland, rather than direct from Norway. The linguistic situation the settlers encountered in most areas of England was different from the one that faced them in other parts of the British Isles. Old English (i.e. Anglo-Saxon) was a Germanic language, closely related to Norse. Some have argued the relationship was so close that mutual comprehension was possible (e.g. Kisbye 1982, 138–9); others have denied this, either directly (e.g. Hansen 1984, 88–9) or by implication (e.g. Thomason and Kaufman 1988, 302–4). For the most part the debate has had an abstract quality since mutual comprehension is seldom defined and could mean anything from the uttering of single words accompanied by gesticulation to the ability of Anglo-Saxons and Vikings to hold lengthy conversations each speaking their own language. From what we know of Norse dialects and northern and eastern varieties of Old English in the ninth century – comparatively little, it must be said – lengthy conversations seem unlikely, not least because of differences in vocabulary. The size of the Viking settlement in England and the status of the settlers are also matters that have provoked disagreement. The traditional view, based chiefly on a literal interpretation of the *Anglo-Saxon Chronicle*, the density of Scandinavian place-names in parts of England, and the strong Scandinavian element in later English, was that immigrants arrived in vast numbers (e.g. Ekwall 1937–45). Challenging this notion, various historians (e.g. Sawyer 1958) have proposed far-reaching linguistic influence by a small group of prestigious settlers. Philologists are on the whole still of the opinion that the nature and depth of Norse influence on English can only be explained by prolonged linguistic contact with sizeable numbers of Norse-speakers (for a recent survey of the debate and the evidence, see Nielsen 1998, 165–88).

The position, development and ultimate fate of Norse speech in England following the settlement is difficult to reconstruct and has likewise been subject to a range of interpretations. Evidence is drawn broadly from place-names, Norse elements borrowed into English, inscriptions in the runic and roman alphabets, and the increasing body of knowledge about language survival and language death.

The greatest concentrations of Scandinavian names in England are to be found in the east and north (the Danelaw) or in the north-west. The most common types are compounds often having a Scandinavian personal name as the first element and a settlement name, e.g. Scandinavian *-by*, *-garth*, *-holm/-hulme*, *-thorp*, *-thwait*, English *-ton*, as the second. Many of the Danelaw names betray their specifically Danish origin (e.g. those with second element *-by* or *-thorp*), while some of those in the north-west point to a West Norse milieu (e.g. those containing the elements *garth*, *gil*, *scale*). Apart from such indications of provenance, however, Norse place-names have been unable to shed much light on the position of Norse speech in England. Their abundance has been taken by some as evidence of massive immigration, and thus of widespread and sustained use of the Norse language, but others have pointed out that large numbers of names do not necessarily equal large numbers of settlers: Scandinavian personal and place-names may have become fashionable and been adopted by the native English.

Norse loan-words in Old English would seem to have been limited to a small number of technical terms to do chiefly with seafaring and the law for which English had no precise equivalents (e.g. OE *steoresmann* < ON *stýri(s)maðr* 'ship's captain', OE *sacleas* < ON *saklauss* 'innocent'). However, most of our Old English texts come from Wessex. Effectively, texts from the Danelaw region only appear in Middle English (which can be considered to have begun *c.*1130), but from these it is apparent that Norse influence on the native language was profound, affecting all word classes (even pronouns) and involving the replacement of scores of everyday English words with Norse equivalents (e.g. *window* < ON *vindauga*, *take* < ON *taka*, *ill* < ON *illr*, *till* < ON *til*, *they* < ON *þeir*, *though* < ON **þóh*; contrast, e.g., OE *eagþyrel* 'window', *niman* 'take', *hi(e)* 'they'). The Norse impact on English went further than this, affecting phonology, morphology and arguably also syntax. Plosive [g] and [k], for example, were reintroduced in positions where in OE they had become palatalized (cf., e.g., Norse *Skipton* vs. English *Shipham* 'sheep farm', *give* < ON *gefa* vs. ME *yive*, *yeve*); the 3rd person singular *-s* ending, as in *he sings*, is thought to have spread from the Danelaw area, replacing English *-th*, as in *he singeth*; and it is a common view that the change from synthetic (highly inflected) to analytic structure that English underwent at the end of the Old English period was due at least in part to simplified forms of contact speech used between the Norse and English. In spite of this abundance of evidence and deduction, we know little of the circumstances in which Norse elements entered English, the chief problem being the lack of texts from the time and the areas of the settlement.

Inscriptions in the runic alphabet add little to the overall picture. Sixteen Scandinavian runic inscriptions are known from England: seven from the north-west, only one older than the eleventh century, and most from the twelfth (one also apparently modern), six from the south-east, all probably stemming from the period of Scandinavian rule early in the eleventh century, and three from areas of Norse settlement in the east, of somewhat uncertain date. Insofar as they contain diagnostic features, the inscriptions of the north-west by and large reflect a West, those of the south-east an East Scandinavian milieu. Of the three from the east, one appears to be Danish, one West Scandinavian, while the third lacks diagnostic features. The inscriptions are of

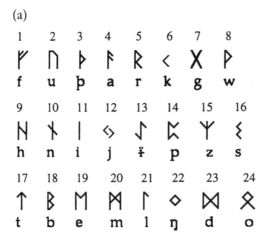

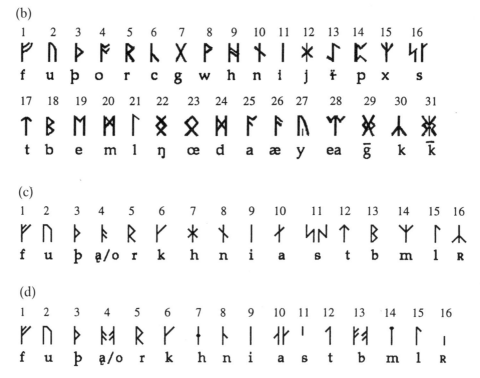

Figure 2 *Forms of the runic alphabet (the Norse is also known as the fuþark and the Anglo-Saxon as the fuþorc (þ = 'th') after their first six letters): (a) the older fuþark; (b) the Anglo-Saxon fuþorc; (c) the long-branch younger fuþark; (d) the short-twig younger fuþark. Illustration by courtesy of Anne Haavaldsen, University of Bergen.*

different types. All but one of those in the north-west are on stone and some of them imply a settled, rune-using community. Most of the south-east group are likely to be the work of Scandinavians who came over with Sveinn or Knútr's armies. Of the three from the east two are on loose objects and do not necessarily represent local usage. The language of the inscriptions is perfectly reasonable Old Norse, as far as can be determined, except when we come to the north-west. Three of the inscriptions from this area are long and coherent enough for a view to be taken about the form of language in which they are written: one is in ungrammatical Old Norse, one in what appears to be a mixture of English and Norse, and one in Middle English. None of the roman alphabet inscriptions is in Norse, except perhaps the fragmentary text on the Skelton sundial (which also bears a runic legend), but some contain Norse names, and occasional Norse words and forms are found.

Current knowledge about language survival and language death suggests that only if the number of Norse settlers in England was very large – which most would now discount – or if they established isolated, tight-knit communities, could their distinctive idiom have survived for more than a couple of generations. Some have suggested that linguistic survival was helped by a good deal of secondary immigration, which is possible but hard to document. The conquests of Sveinn and Knútr in the early eleventh century certainly meant a renewed influx of Scandinavians, chiefly Danes, into England, but for most of these the stay was temporary. However, the pattern and extent of Norse influence on English implies prolonged contact, and thus presupposes the existence of some form of Scandinavian speech for a fair length of time.

A possible scenario is relatively extensive settlement, dense enough in places for Norse to become the principal language for a while, leading to attempts by the English to speak it, resulting – because of the similarity of the two languages – in an Anglo-Scandinavian pidgin. The pidgin may then in time have become a creole, and it could be elements of this Anglo-Scandinavian dialect that were eventually carried into southern English and the developing standard – at a time when English enjoyed little prestige. Possibly the Scandinavian runic inscriptions of the north-west reflect a linguistic and cultural mix of this type. They certainly bear witness to the late survival of some form of Scandinavian in England. It has, however, been suggested that the late Scandinavian of the north-west, rather than being a direct descendant of the language of ninth-century settlers, represents the speech of a new wave of immigrants first from Ireland and then from Man, as Scandinavian power in these areas waned (e.g. Fellows-Jensen 1975, 194–5; Page 1971, 174). This presupposes, of course, that such secondary immigration took place well before the twelfth century, since it is implausible that settlers fresh from Gaelic-speaking Ireland or Man could be responsible for a runic inscription in a mixed English–Norse idiom, let alone one in Middle English (see further below).

It seems unlikely that pure Scandinavian speech can have survived for very long anywhere in England, with the possible exception of the north-west (perhaps because no other language was in the ascendancy there until English began to dominate in the eleventh century). Pockets of Scandinavian may well have persisted in the areas of densest settlement for a few generations, but it is hard to conceive of 'English Norse' as a distinct language on that basis alone. If such a language did exist, perhaps in the north-west, we certainly have no knowledge of it. The runic inscriptions of the area offer us at best glimpses of how it died.

In Ireland, in contrast to England, Norse had only the most modest influence on the native language. Scholars have not managed to find more than a handful of Scandinavian loan-words in Gaelic (e.g. *bád* 'boat' < ON *bátr*, *trosc* 'cod' < ON *þorskr*, *pinginn* 'penny', 'money' < ON *peningr*, *margadh* 'market', 'bargain' < ON *markaðr*), and while the Irish did take over a fair number of Norse personal names (e.g. *Amlaibh, Caittil* < ON *Óláfr, Ketill*), some of which still survive in surnames (e.g. *MacManus, MacAulay* < ON *Magnús, Óli*), the impact of the settlers on Irish place-nomenclature was small indeed.

In spite of this, there are grounds for suspecting that Scandinavian speech may have survived intact in the Irish towns from the time of their founding to the English invasions in the mid-twelfth century. First, it is likely that these urban settlements formed relatively self-contained Scandinavian-speaking communities. Second, their place-names have by and large passed directly from Scandinavian into English (e.g. *Howth, Dalkey*, near Dublin, < ON **hǫfði* 'head' (Irish name: *Beann Éadair*), **Dálkey* 'cloak-pin island' or 'dagger island' (Irish name: *Deilginis Cualann*), *Waterford* (early Irish-English *Vadrefiord*) < ON *Veðra(r)fjǫrðr* 'ram fjord' or 'windy fjord' (* indicates that the Norse names are confidently assumed rather than actually attested). Third, excavations in Dublin have revealed a number of Scandinavian runic inscriptions spanning the period *c*.950–1125. These are all on loose objects so it is difficult to know whether they were carved by residents or visitors from abroad, but they testify to a Scandinavian milieu – albeit a fairly mixed one, exhibiting as they do both West and East Scandinavian features. Beyond this it is impossible to form an impression of Scandinavian speech in the Irish towns. Even if we could be sure the Dublin inscriptions were carved by permanent residents, they are too laconic to provide insights into 'Dublin Norse' – indeed, many are incomprehensible.

In England and Ireland, speakers of Scandinavian can only ever have formed a small percentage of the population. In the Isle of Man, by contrast, Norse – of a relatively homogeneous western variety – may for a century or two after the settlement have been the majority tongue. Certainly it seems likely to have enjoyed greater prestige than any other language on the island. Even so, the evidence of historical sources and not least of the thirty-three (chiefly tenth-century) Scandinavian runic memorial inscriptions found in Man is of intermarriage with the native population and the fairly rapid development of a local variant of Norse, perhaps under the influence of Gaelic.

The majority of the inscriptions, even those commissioned by or commemorating people with Gaelic names, are in irreproachable Norse, but there are a few that exhibit aberrant grammar, one to the extent that the sense is impaired (cf. *mallymkun raisti krus þena efter malmury fustra sine totor tufkals kona is apisl ati* 'Mallymkun [male?] raised this cross after Malmury [female?] his foster son(?), the daughter [object] of Dufgal, the wife [subject] whom Aðísl married'). Two of the ungrammatical inscriptions, apparently by the same man and dated considerably later than the generality of Manx runic epigraphy, exhibit further peculiarities, and it has recently been argued (Page 1992, 134–7) that these represent attempts by someone with an antiquarian interest in archaic scripts but little knowledge of runes, or possibly even of Norse, to imitate older tradition. If that is true, it suggests that at the time the two inscriptions were carved (probably the late twelfth century) runes had ceased to be a common script in

Man and that the Norse language itself was in a very parlous state, if it had not already died out.

The picture of post-settlement linguistic development in Man that emerges is in keeping with the idea of a native population that remained numerous and relatively influential. The runic evidence is also suggestive of close links with Norway until early in the eleventh century and of relative isolation from the Scandinavian world thereafter. If this gives anything like an accurate reflection of events, it is easy to see how Norse in Man may have succumbed to the encroachment of Gaelic as early as the twelfth century.

The Hebrides is the area of Norse settlement in the British Isles with the scantiest documentation of Norse speech. A large number of place-names survive, particularly in Lewis, and there are loan-words in Scottish Gaelic, but neither of these has been as intensely studied as their counterparts in England, Man or the Northern Isles (cf. Fraser 1984; Cox 1991, 479–80, 490). Eleven runic inscriptions have been found in the region, but eight of these are casual graffiti, chiefly the names of thirteenth-century Norwegian passers-by carved into a rock overhang on Holy Island (Arran). The three others, from Barra, Inchmarnock and Iona, seem to be the work of locals, and exhibit one or two peculiarities of language, but far too little for us to form a view about the nature of Hebridean Norse. Phonological influence on Gaelic of the type mooted by one scholar (Borgstrøm 1974) might add a little to the picture, but there is uncertainty whether the features concerned, pre-aspiration and a particular pitch pattern, existed in Norse at the time.

In the areas of densest settlement in the Hebrides it is not unlikely that Norse developed much as it seems to have done in Man. The external conditions were probably very similar – Gaelic-speaking (for the most part, at least) island communities overrun by invaders from Norway, but retaining a substantial native element. With their greater proximity to the North, however, it is unlikely that the Norse communities in the Hebrides became isolated from Scandinavian influence as early as the eleventh century, and thus possible that they retained (a local variant of) Norse speech for a while longer than in Man. For what it is worth, the concept of a Norse language seems still to have been alive in the Hebrides in the middle of the sixteenth century. Then we find Donald Monro, 'High Dean of the Isles', using the phrase *in norn leid* 'in Norn language' (see below) in the course of a discussion about the etymology of the island name Jura (< ON *Dýrey*; Munro 1961, 50).

Following the Viking settlement, Orkney and Shetland – for a time doubtless northeast Caithness too – became a totally Norse province, and by the middle of the eleventh century, if not before, the region is likely to have been as monolingually Norse as the Faroes or Iceland. In spite of its unchallenged supremacy, we know little of how Northern-Isles Norse developed. The settlers and their descendants do not seem to have set much store by writing, either in runes or the roman alphabet, and the few texts that exist tend to mirror faithfully the contemporary idiom of Norway. The result is a scarcity of linguistic evidence. What we do learn is that Scandinavian in Orkney and Shetland came to be called 'Norn', from Old Norse *norrœna* '(West) Norse language', 'Norwegian language' or *norrœnn* '(West) Norse', 'Norwegian' – a term first recorded in an endorsement in Scots appended to a Norwegian document of 1485 dealing with a Shetland matter. Although occasionally applied to Norse speech elsewhere in

Scotland (cf. Barnes 1989, 21 and above), Norn is in most contexts used exclusively of the Northern-Isles variety.

Unlike the Faroes and Iceland, which were geographically isolated, Orkney and Shetland lay close to the Scottish mainland. This meant that influence from the south was bound sooner or later to make itself felt. Scots linguistic infiltration probably began in earnest with the succession to the Earldom of Orkney in 1379 of the Scots-speaking Sinclairs. The first surviving document in Scots from Orkney is dated 1433 and as early as 1438 we find the native Lawman (judge and legal adviser) using the new language on internal Orcadian business. In the more remote Shetland change did not come so quickly. The earliest extant letter in Scots from these islands bears the date 1488, but until late in the sixteenth century Danish (by then the written language of Norway) was used as well, whereas in Orkney the last preserved Scandinavian-language document (in what appears to be Swedicized Middle Norwegian) is from about 1425.

None of this tells us much about the directions in which the spoken Scandinavian of the Northern Isles developed – the language or, perhaps more accurately, group of related dialects, to which the name Norn is most appositely applied. Beginning in the early sixteenth century we have a fair number of references to Norn-speakers in the islands, but frustratingly little detail on how they spoke. More forthcoming than many is 'Jo Ben', writing of the situation in Orkney in 1529 (Marwick 1929, 224):

> Utuntur idiomate proprio, veluti cum dicimus Guid day Guidman, illi dicunt goand da boundæ, &c.[2]

This snippet suggests not only that Norn was commonly spoken, but that the case system of medieval Scandinavian was still intact (*goand* reflecting the ON accusative masculine singular adjective ending *-an*). The '&c.' is exasperating, but no more so than the complete dearth of linguistic information in the reports of seventeenth-, eighteenth- and early nineteenth-century writers, almost all of whom are content simply to note the continued existence in either Orkney or Shetland of what they term variously 'Gothick', 'Norwegian', 'Norse', 'Noords', 'Norn(s)' and 'rude' or 'corrupt Danish' (the chief sources are quoted with references in Marwick 1929, 224–7; Stewart 1964, 163–6).

There are two exceptions to this woeful lack of curiosity, and without them we should have virtually no record of Norn from the period when it can be presumed still to have been a living language. James Wallace's son printed an Orkney version of the Lord's Prayer in the second edition of his father's *An Account of the Islands of Orkney* (1700), though with no indication of where he got it from. More importantly, the Revd George Low, an amateur student of natural history, and much else besides, from Edzell in Angus, but resident in Orkney, recorded samples of Norn from the Shetland island of Foula during a visit there in 1774 and included them in his *A Tour through the Islands of Orkney and Schetland* (first published 1879).

Low's texts – a Lord's Prayer from an unknown source, a list of thirty English words translated into Norn, presumably by different informants, and a 35-stanza ballad obtained from an old man 'William Henry, a farmer in Guttorm, in Foula', provide insights into Norn phonology, morphology, syntax and vocabulary. The Lord's Prayer and the first stanza of the ballad are as follows (Low 1879, 105, 108):

Fy vor o er i Chimeri. Halaght vara nam dit. La konungdum din cumma. La vill din vera guerde i vrildin sindaeri chimeri. Gav vs dagh u dagloght brau. Forgive sindorwara sin vi forgiva gem ao sinda gainst wus. Lia wus ikè o vera tempa, but delivra wus fro adlu idlu for do i ir konungdum, u puri, u glori, Amen.

Da vara Iarlin d' Orkneyar
For frinda sin spir de ro
Whirdè ane skildè meun
Our glas buryon burtaga.[3]

Important as these specimens are, they suffer from several drawbacks. First, Low himself, it is clear, knew no Scandinavian, so what we have is his record of what he heard, presented through the medium of English, and to a limited extent French, orthography. Second, although it has often been assumed that Norn was still a living language on Foula in 1774, Low's account is sufficiently imprecise to enable the opposite inference to be drawn (1879, 105):

> None of them can write their ancient language, and but very few speak it; the best phrases are all gone, and nothing remains but a few names of things and two or three remnants of songs which one old man can repeat, and that but indistinctly.

Third, since we have no Norn of a similar period from anywhere else in Shetland, it is impossible to say how representative Low's material is of the language in general. Stylistically, one would not expect either the Lord's Prayer or a (medieval?) ballad to reflect everyday speech. More crucial than this, though, is the extent to which Foula Norn may have deviated from Norn elsewhere. Several of its most characteristic phonological features, reminiscent of Faroese and to a lesser extent west Norwegian dialects and Icelandic, do not recur in other sources (e.g. /dn/ for earlier /n:/ and /rn/, as in *eidnar* from ON *hennar*; /dl/ for /l:/, as in *adlu idlu* (in the Norn Lord's Prayer quoted above) from ON *ǫllu illu*; intercalation of /g/ as in *Sheug* from ON *sjó(r)* (Faroese *sjógv*); loss of initial /þ/ (= *th*) in pronouns, as in *eso* from ON *þessi*, doubtless via *heso* (Faroese *hesin*), cf. loss of initial /h/ in *eidnar*).

The only material extensive enough to allow comparison with Low's texts comes from the period when Norn was no longer a living language. Most of it is to be found in the collections of Jakob Jakobsen (see in particular 1928–32) and Hugh Marwick (1929). Jakobsen spent the years 1893–5 in Shetland, during which period he visited numerous informants who remembered something of the old language and as a result was able to gather a substantial amount of information on pronunciation and vocabulary. His 1928–32 dictionary contains some 10,000 items. As well as individual words, certain informants provided him with complete phrases or sentences and some even with rhymes, riddles, and fragments of songs and ballads. Marwick's field-work took place in Orkney in the early part of the twentieth century. Because he was active twenty to thirty years after Jakobsen and Orkney was more Scotticized than Shetland, he obtained less extensive and less varied results. Nevertheless, his 'glossary' of Norn words runs to some 3,000 items.

Although these two collections demonstrate the size and nature of the early-to-mid nineteenth-century Norn substratum in Shetland and Orkney speech (most of the informants were of considerable age), and provide something of a corrective to Low's records from Foula, they give nothing like a comprehensive picture of the language. Much of the data consists of individual lexical items. These can tell us something of Norn's relationship to other forms of Scandinavian, and reveal differences between the Shetland and the Orkney variety; taken as a whole they can perhaps also offer an insight into Norn in its dying stages: the surviving vocabulary suggests it had retreated to the point where it was purely a language of work and the home. It is impossible, however, to use Jakobsen's and Marwick's material to establish the phonological and morphological system or systems of Norn, or to gain an understanding of the syntax. The pronunciations recorded do not relate clearly enough to Old Norse phonology, and where complete sentences are given the grammatical endings of earlier Scandinavian have in many cases been levelled to *-(en)a* (e.g. *bodena komena rontena Komba* 'the boat has come round de Kaim [a hill in Foula]'). These nineteenth-century relics are also a poor guide to the present-day Norn substratum in Shetland and Orkney speech. Investigations have shown that in Shetland only about a tenth of the words Jakobsen recorded are now likely to be recognized, and the same would almost certainly prove the case if Marwick's glossary were tested on 1990s Orcadians.

In one area Norn is still very visible in the Northern Isles, as also in north-east Caithness. The vast majority of place-names in the erstwhile Earldom of Orkney are still of Norse origin (cf., e.g., *Kirkwall* < *Kirkjuvágr*, *Lerwick* < *Leirvík*, *Hoy* < *Háey*, *Foula* < *Fugley*, *Twatt* < *þveit*, *Collafirth* < *Kollafjorðr*). A recent onomastic study of Foula showed there to be about 80 Scots or hybrid names to 800 Norn (Stewart 1970, 318–19). It is likely the proportion would be fairly similar throughout the Northern Isles.

Regarding the death of Norn, little is certain. The socio-political, literary and linguistic evidence suggests the following scenario. A period of bilingualism in the fifteenth(?), sixteenth and seventeenth centuries was followed by the collapse of Norn – by then a low-prestige vernacular heavily influenced by Scots – in the late seventeenth and early eighteenth centuries, as ties with Scandinavia were weakened and the population turned its attention firmly towards Scotland. The collapse came about chiefly through the failure of parents to speak Norn to their children. The last native speakers (those whose first language had been Norn) probably passed away around the middle of the eighteenth century in Orkney, perhaps as late as 1800 in Shetland.

Notes

1 'Norse' in this chapter is used synonymously with Viking-Age and early medieval Scandinavian.
2 'They have their own way of speaking, for example when we say *Guid day Guidman*, they say *goand da boundæ*, etc.'
3 'It was the Earl of Orkney, asked advice of his kinsman: whether he should take the maiden out of the glass palace.'

References

Barnes, Michael P. 1989. The death of Norn. In Beck, Heinrich (ed.), *Germanische Rest- und Trümmersprachen*, Berlin, 21–43.

——1998. *The Norn Language of Orkney and Shetland*. Lerwick.

Borgstrøm, C. H. 1974. On the influence of Norse on Scottish Gaelic. *Lochlann*, 6:91–103.

Cox, R. A. V. 1991. Norse–Gaelic contact in the west of Lewis: the place-name evidence. In Ureland, P. Sture and Broderick, George (eds), *Language Contact in the British Isles*, Tübingen, 479–94.

Ekwall, E. 1937–45. The proportion of the Scandinavian settlers in the Danelaw. *Saga-Book*, 12:19–34.

Fellows-Jensen, G. 1975. The Vikings in England: a review. *Anglo-Saxon England*, 4:181–206.

——1983. Scandinavian settlement in the Isle of Man and North-west England: the place-name evidence. In Fell, Christine et al. (eds), *The Viking Age in the Isle of Man*, London, 37–52.

Fraser, I. A. 1984. Some further thoughts on Scandinavian place-names in Lewis. *Northern Studies*, 21:34–41.

Gelling, M. 1970–1. The place-names of the Isle of Man. *Journal of the Manx Museum*, 7:130–9, 168–75.

Hansen, B. H. 1984. The historical implications of the Scandinavian linguistic element in English: a theoretical evaluation. *NOWELE*, 4:53–95.

Jakobsen, Jakob 1928–32. *An Etymological Dictionary of the Norn Language in Shetland*. London.

Kisbye, Torben 1982. *Vikingerne i England – sproglige spor*. Copenhagen.

Low, George 1879. *A Tour through the Islands of Orkney and Schetland*. Kirkwall.

Marwick, Hugh 1929. *The Orkney Norn*. London.

Megaw, B. 1978. Norseman and native in the Kingdom of the Isles: a re-assessment of the Manx evidence. In Davey, Peter (ed.), *Man and Environment in the Isle of Man 2* (*British Archaeological Reports* (British Series) 54(ii)), Oxford, 265–314.

Munro, R. W. 1961. *Monro's Western Isles of Scotland and Genealogies of the Clans 1549*. Edinburgh.

Nielsen, Hans Frede 1998. *The Continental Backgrounds of English and its Insular Development until 1154*. Odense.

Page, R. I. 1971. How long did the Scandinavian language survive in England? The epigraphical evidence. In Clemoes, Peter and Hughes, Kathleen (eds), *England before the Conquest*, Cambridge, 165–81.

——1992. Celtic and Norse on the Manx rune-stones. In Tristram, Hildegard L. C. (ed.), *Medialität und mittelalterliche insulare Literatur*, Tübingen, 131–47.

Sawyer, P. 1958. The density of the Danish settlement in England. *University of Birmingham Historical Journal*, 6:1–17.

Stewart, J. 1964. Norn in Shetland. *Fróðskaparrit*, 13:158–75.

——1970. Place-names of Fula. *Fróðskaparrit*, 18:307–19.

Thomason, Sarah Grey and Kaufman, Terrence 1988. *Language Contact, Creolization, and Genetic Linguistics*. Berkeley.

Wallace, James 1700. *An Account of the Islands of Orkney*. London.

15 Flemish in Wales

Lauran Toorians

'[. . .] and I have also spoken with some who still spoke Flemish well, as they have learned it from their parents and from father to son.' Lucas de Heere (1534–84), a lesser known painter from Ghent, wrote these words, in Flemish and partly in the margin, in his manuscript 'A short description of England, Scotland and Ireland, gathered from the best authors by L.D.H.' (Chotzen and Draak 1937, 48; Chotzen 1937, 102). As a Protestant, de Heere was formally banned from Flanders in 1568, by which time he was already in England where he remained in exile until early 1577.

De Heere probably wrote his 'Short description' in the early 1570s and added the words quoted above to his brief account of how Flemings came to eastern England in 1106 and were transferred from there to *West Wallia* by the English king. As a source of this historical information he refers to Humphry Lhuyd. Apparently de Heere travelled a great deal and visited Pembrokeshire in person. His remark that some people there still spoke Flemish in his own time should be taken seriously. After all, Flemish was de Heere's own mother tongue.

How did people from Flanders come to south-western Wales and how did they manage to keep their own cultural identity, including their language? Scarcity of historical sources makes these questions hard to answer in great detail, but an outline is possible. Tradition has it that a large group of people was forced out of Flanders by flooding, but this detail seems to rest mainly on folk-tradition. Though inundations were frequent in the Low Countries, in the period in question no such flooding was disastrous enough to force a substantial part of the population to emigrate. In fact, large numbers of Flemings had already come to England in the army of William the Conqueror. Later they were welcomed as merchants, as citizens for new boroughs or as colonists in new settlements. It seems true that Henry II found the influence which Flemings gained in his kingdom threatening and banished them to south-western Wales. The details, however, are not very clear.

In reality these people seem to have left the Low Countries for various reasons. For the nobility this was a means of acquiring land and opportunities for their younger sons. Other adventurers, and especially farmers, escaped the over-populated and highly urbanized county of Flanders and found a new frontier in the Anglo–Norman kingdom in Britain. Merchants were welcomed with their expertise, which was unrivalled in north-western Europe. They could secure trade of, especially, wool and fleeces for the Flemish market. This way Flemings ended up not only in England and in Wales but also in Scotland and even in Ireland (Toorians 1996, 1998).

What makes Pembrokeshire special among the areas with Flemish settlers is the fact that it was only here (and perhaps, but surely on a lesser scale, in upper Clydesdale south of Glasgow) that they retained their identity as a group for several generations and even managed to cling on to their own language. Closer in time to their arrival than Lucas de Heere we have the important comment by the Welsh historian and geographer Giraldus Cambrensis or Gerald of Wales (*c*.1146–1223) that his brother, Philip de Barri, was once addressed in Flemish by a local knight in Haverfordwest, and apparently was able to understand the language.

Strictly in relation to the language, this is all the evidence we have. Neither the English nor the Welsh dialects of the area have preserved elements which could with any certainty be labelled Flemish. Only place-names reveal the presence of the sturdy settlers who once conquered and kept this area from the Welsh. In the course of time their language became English and the area became known as 'Little England beyond Wales'. Places with names like Flemingston or Flimston clearly recall the Flemings. Wiston is *Wizo's town* and can boast one of the best-preserved motte-and-bailey castles in Britain. Because of its bloody history this is also the best-documented place in the written history of the Flemish settlement in Pembrokeshire (Chotzen 1933; Toorians 1990, 1998).

Especially interesting is Walwyn's Castle, where early spellings of the place-name, like *Walewynecastle* from 1307, suggest a Dutch/Flemish pronunciation of the name. As I have argued earlier (Toorians 1995, 99–103) this may be the place where the Welsh personal name *Gwalchmai* was equated with the Continental name *Wal(e)wain*, thus laying the foundation for the Gawain of Arthurian romance. Since also a mysteriously lost book by the author of the Middle Dutch *Reynard* may have had a Welsh connection (all we know is the title *Madoc*, which is a Welsh personal name), the most lasting influence of the Flemish presence in Wales may well be of a literary kind.

That, on the other hand, fighting remained an important occupation for the Flemings in Pembrokeshire explains how Irish annals can describe Strongbow's invasion army in 1169 as 'a fleet of Flemings'. Probably all the Flemings we find in twelfth- and thirteenth-century Ireland will have come from (or through) south-western Wales. Wool from the area remained important for the Flemish cloth industry well into the fourteenth century and when in 1353 Carmarthen was made the sole staple town for the wool trade in Wales, Haverfordwest was recognized as an 'English town' and as such was exempt from this new regulation. Thus the Flemings created their own 'Little England beyond Wales'.

References

Chotzen, Th. 1933 1934. Willem van Brabant en Owain ap Cadwgan. *Annales de la Société d'Émulation de Bruges*, 76:65–82.

——1937. Some sidelights on Cambro-Dutch relations. *Transactions of the Honourable Society of Cymmrodorion*, 101–44.

——and Draak, A. M. E. (eds) 1937. *Beschrijving der Britsche Eilanden door Lucas de Heere. Een geïllustreerd geschrift uit zijn Engelsche ballingschap*. Antwerp.

Toorians, L. 1990. Wizo Flandrensis and the Flemish settlement in Pembrokeshire. *Cambridge Medieval Celtic Studies*, 20:99–118.

—— 1995. Nogmaals 'Walewein van Melle' en de Vlaams-Keltische contacten. *Queeste*, 2:97–112.

—— 1996. Flemish settlements in twelfth-century Scotland (with an Appendix: Handlist of Flemings in Scotland in the twelfth and thirteenth century). *Revue belge de philologie et d'histoire*, 74:659–93.

—— 1998. Vlaamse nederzettingen in Keltische gebieden. In Toorians, Lauran (ed.), *Kelten en de Nederlanden van prehistorie tot heden*, Louvain, 69–88.

16 French in the Channel Islands

Glanville Price

The Channel Islands, known in French as 'les Îles Anglo-Normandes', lie off the west coast of the Cotentin peninsula in Normandy, and, in the Middle Ages, formed part of the Duchy of Normandy (as in a sense they still do).[1] The duchy itself, as a distinct political entity, came into being in 911 when the French king, Charles the Simple, ceded an area around the lower reaches of the river Seine, including the town of Rouen, to Rollo, the leader of a Viking band that had settled there. In the course of the next quarter of a century, the 'Northmen' – whence the name 'Normans' – had extended their duchy to take in first Bayeux and its hinterland, then the Cotentin peninsula, and finally the offshore islands of which Rollo's son, William Longsword, took possession in 933.

There can be no doubt that the original Normans, like those other Norwegians and Danes who settled in Britain and elsewhere, spoke Norse. There are indeed still a number of Norse elements, particularly seafaring terms, in the French dialect of Normandy, and some of them have become established in standard French (i.e. *crique* 'creek', *vague* 'wave', *marsouin* 'porpoise'). However, in the course of a very few generations the Normans abandoned their traditional Norse speech and when, only a century and a half after the foundation of the duchy, Duke William invaded England in 1066, the language he and his men took with them was Norman French. Its later fortunes in England are discussed in chapter 17, 'Anglo-Norman'.

After the Conquest, William reigned in England as King and in Normandy as Duke, and at that period the Channel Islands remained as part of the Duchy of Normandy, not of the Kingdom of England. At the death of the Conqueror, his eldest son, Robert, became Duke of Normandy, and his second son, William Rufus, King of England. In 1100, Rufus was succeeded as king by his brother Henry who by 1106 also gained possession of Normandy. England and Normandy were once more separated during the reign of his successor, Stephen, but when he was succeeded in 1154 by Henry II, who was already Duke of Normandy, the two domains were united, in the person of the ruler if in no other sense.

The Channel Islands were finally severed administratively from mainland Normandy in 1204 when the French king, Philippe Auguste, conquered the rest of the duchy after King John had refused to do homage to him in respect of his lands in Normandy. John then established a jurisdiction of its own in each island and so has a claim to be considered as the originator of the separate political identity of the islands and of the extensive degree of autonomy that they still enjoy. This separateness was duly recognized in 1360 when England formally ceded Normandy, with the specific exception of the Channel Islands, by treaty to France.

The term 'French' in relation to the Channel Islands refers to what are variously considered as two different languages or as two markedly different forms of the same language. On the one hand, there are the traditional spoken vernaculars of the islands. These, as we shall see, are varieties of Norman French and the idea that they are a 'corruption' of standard French is devoid of all foundation. On the other hand, standard French, though it has never been an everyday spoken language in any of the islands, has served, and to some extent still serves, as an official language. For that reason, and although our concern in this book is primarily with spoken languages, a few brief paragraphs are devoted at the end of this chapter to the role of French as an official language.

We know nothing of the linguistic history of the Channel Islands in the pre-French period, and there is indeed relatively little direct evidence even for the French-speaking period before the nineteenth century. It is, however, certain not only that Channel Islands French in the Middle Ages was basically Norman French, not Parisian French, but also that the modern dialects of the Islands are Norman dialects (see Collas 1933–6; Spence 1957; Brasseur 1978). For example, a Latin *c-* became *ch-* (like English *ch*, but later simplified to English *sh*) before *a* in Parisian French, but remained (i.e. pronounced *k*) in the Norman dialect – so, for example, corresponding to standard French *chaleur* (from Latin *calorem*) 'heat', *château* (from *castellum*) 'castle', we find in Jersey the forms *caleu* (only in eastern Jersey, but *chaleu* in the west) and *câté*.[2] On the other hand, Latin *c-* before an *e* came to be pronounced *s* in Parisian French, but like English *ch* and later *sh* (or French *ch*) in Norman – so, corresponding to French *cent* 'a hundred' (from *centum*) and *cerveau* (from *cerebellum*), we have *chent, chèrvé*.

The four main islands are, in decreasing order of size, Jersey, Guernsey (in French, Guernesey), Alderney (Aurigny) and Sark (Sercq). Not only are there differences (sometimes major ones) between the dialects of the various islands, but it is also possible to distinguish local varieties within both Jèrriais[3] (in French, *jersiais*) or Jersey French (in particular, between eastern and western varieties)[4] and Guernesiais or Guernsey French (in particular, between the speech of the Upper Parishes, i.e. the south of the island, and that of the Lower Parishes, i.e. the north of the island). The dialect of Sark (see Liddicoat 1989) is basically a dialect of Jersey French, as the island was colonized from Jersey in 1565.

One important Old French writer is known to have hailed from Jersey, namely Wace (*c*.1100–75), the author of two lengthy historical poems, the *Roman de Brut* and the *Roman de Rou* (Rou being the Duke Rollo who gained possession of Normandy in 911). The following is an extract, in which he identifies himself, from the *Roman de Rou*:[5]

> Se l'on demande qui ço dist,
> Qui ceste estoire en romanz fist,
> Jo di e dirai que jo sui
> Wace de l'isle de Gersui,
> Qui est en mer vers occident,
> Al fieu de Normendie apent.

('If one asks who said this, who put this story into French ["Romance"], I say and shall say that I am Wace of the Isle of Jersey, which is in the sea towards the west, and belongs to the fief of Normandy.')

Thereafter, there is nothing until the nineteenth century when a certain amount of verse was produced, in particular in Guernsey French which was used by such writers as Georges Métivier[6] (*Rimes guernesiaises*, 1831; *Fantaisies guernesiaises*, 1866; *Poësies guernesiaises et françaises*, 1883), Denys Corbet (*Les Feuilles de la forêt* [poems in Guernesiais, French and English], 1871; *Les Chants du draïn Rimeux* [Guernesiais and French], 1884) and Thomas Lenfestey (*Le Chant des fontaines*, 1875). Jersey French was mainly represented by A. Mourant's collection of *Rimes et poésies jersiaises* of 1865 and an anonymous and undated volume of *Rimes jersiaises*. More recently, Jean Du Nord has written Guernesiais plays for local drama contests and, in the 1960s, Marjorie Ozanne published tales in Guernesiais in the local press (see Tomlinson 1981, 354), while George F. Le Feuvre produced the first ever volumes of prose to be published in Jèrriais, *Jèrri Jadis* (1973) and *Histouaithes et Gens d'Jèrri* (1976).

Métivier also translated the Gospel according to St Matthew into Guernesiais in 1863. The following is his version of chapter 8, verses 1–4:

1 Quànd Jésus aeut d'vallaï avaû la montàigne, une grànd route de gens l'siévit:

2 Et en même temps ùn lépraeux vìnt à li et l'adorit, et lli dìt: Signeur, s'ous voulaïz, vous pouvaïz m'guérìr.

3 Jésus étèndit sa maïn, l'touquit, et lli dìt: Je l'veurs; séyiz guéri; et dans ùn môment sa lèpre fut guérie.

4 Et Jésus lli dìt: Gardons bien d'pâlaïr d'chunchin à persounne; mais allaïz vous mourtraïr au prêtre, et offraïz l'don ordounnaï par Moïse, A ceulle fin qu' vlà qui leû serve de témouégnage.

As an example of Jersey French here is F. Le Maistre's rendering of the Gospel according to St Luke, chapter 2, verses 8–10 (quoted after Don Balleine Trust 1979, 5:2):

Eh bien, i' y'avait dans la même contrée des bèrgers tchi couochaient dans les clios, et y gardaient lus troupieaux en villiant d'ssus la niet.

Et tout à co un aunge du Seigneu sé préthentit à ieux, et la glouaithe du Seigneu brilyit à l'entou d'ieux, et i' fûdrent saisis d'eune grant' peux.

Et l'ange lus dit: N'ayiz pon d'peux; car jé vouos annonce des bouonnes nouvelles dé grand' jouaie tchi s'sont pouor tout l'monde.

The first lexicographical work on Channel Islands French was also due to Georges Métivier, who in 1870 published a *Dictionnaire franco-normand ou recueil des mots particuliers au dialecte de Guernesey* (London). As only Vol. 1, the French–Guernesiais section, of Sjögren's much more scholarly dictionary (1964) has appeared, and as there is as yet no companion volume to the English–Guernesiais dictionary by Marie de Garis and others (1967; revised edition, 1982), Métivier's now aged work has not been superseded. For Jersey French we have two glossaries, namely a *Glossaire du patois jersiais* of 1924 and the much more recent one by Spence (1960), and Le Maistre's monumental dictionary (1966).[7] Items on pronunciation and grammar of Jersey French include Le Maistre's introductory sections on pronunciation and the morphology of verbs (1966, xxvii–xxxiii), Birt's course-book on Jèrriais (1985), two articles by Spence (1957, 1985–7) and chapters on the contemporary language (including a section on phonetic variation) and on grammatical forms and phonetic development in his history of Jèrriais (Spence 1993); five cassettes of passages of Jersey French have also been produced (see Don Balleine Trust 1979). For Guernsey French we are largely dependent on an article by de Garis (1983) on the grammatical structure of the language.[8] There is relatively little on Alderney and Sark, though both figure (as do Guernsey and Jersey) as points in the *Atlas linguistique de la France* (1903–10) by Jules Gilliéron and Edmond Edmont, and Sark also figures, together with Guernsey and Jersey (but not Alderney, where the dialect is now extinct), in the much more recent linguistic atlas of Normandy (Brasseur 1980–97) and is the subject of an article by Liddicoat (1989).

Societies have been formed in both Jersey and Guernsey for the purpose of encouraging the use of the rapidly declining local speech. The *Assembliée d'Jèrriais* (founded in 1951) and the *Assemblaïe d'Guernesiais* (founded in 1956) each seems to have the support of a small but devoted band of enthusiasts. The former published from 1952 to 1977 a quarterly bulletin (*Bulletin d'Quart d'An*, entirely in Jèrriais)[9] and the latter publishes an annual bulletin.[10] Neither society, however, has succeeded in touching the mass of speakers, who tend to hold their traditional tongue in low esteem and who (like many speakers of other minority languages under pressure from a more prestigious language) are often indifferent as to its survival and sometimes overtly hostile. The Swedish scholar Albert Sjögren, for example (1964, xiv–xviii), had the experience in 1926 of hearing local Guernsey children refer to the dialect as 'Guernsey gibberish', and a quarter of a century later Spence (1960, 10) was to find in Jersey that 'although many dialect-speakers have shown an increased interest in and affection for "Jerriais" in recent years, there are many who are somewhat ashamed of it, considering it a corruption of "good French"'. Le Maistre too (1966, xviii) mentions the scorn in which it is held by the younger generation ('notre vieil idiome chancelant, méprisé par les jeunes').

It is difficult to estimate with any great degree of precision how many still speak the various dialects of Channel Islands French. The decennial census reports, apart from the 1989 report on Jersey (see below), provide no information on the subject. It is clear, however, that it is everywhere in an advanced state of decline. Indeed, in Alderney, where some thirty people were still able to speak Auregnais in the 1930s (Le Maistre 1947, 3), it is already extinct.[11] The process of Anglicization probably began in Alderney when large numbers of Irish and other English-speaking labourers were brought in for the construction between 1845 and 1864 of extensive naval and military installations, and was further encouraged by the permanent presence thereafter in the island of a large English-speaking garrison. The main factors in familiarizing the inhabitants of Sark (where, so a Methodist missionary reported to John Wesley in 1787, not a single family at that time understood English) with English were the importation of English-speaking miners from 1835 onwards, and then, during and after the 1850s, the growth of a flourishing tourist traffic (see Ewen and de Carteret 1969, 105–6). Although as recently as 1935 Le Maistre found the local Norman French 'excellent et bien vivant' (1949, 211), it is likely that fewer than 10 per cent of the resident population of some 600, and no children, now speak Sercquiais.

The Anglicization of Guernsey began with the growth of tourism and trade in the nineteenth century, leading to a marked increase in the use of English in and around the capital, St Peter Port. However, in spite of the generalization of education through the medium of English towards the end of the century, Guernesiais remained the language of the home in most parts of the island (see Tomlinson 1981, 13). But when Sjögren investigated the situation of Guernesiais in 1926, he discovered that it was already seriously undermined by English, particularly in the north of the island (see Sjögren 1964, xiv–xviii). In St Peter Port and the island's second town, St Sampson, English had already triumphed – those who spoke Guernesiais could be counted on one's fingers, and the number of those who understood it was not much greater. The local dialect was still spoken by some families in the rural parts of the parish of St Sampson, though not generally by the children. In the northernmost parish of the Vale, few of those under 30 spoke Guernesiais. In St Martin (adjoining St Peter Port to the south), the young people spoke almost exclusively English, and in the central parish of St Andrew only seven of a class of forty 10- to 12-year-olds spoke Guernesiais at home (though some of the others used it with grandparents). Sjögren concluded, however, that the Anglicization of St Andrew was a recent phenomenon, and in the northern rural parish of Câtel and in the south-western parishes of St Saviour, Forest, St Peter in the Wood and Torteval, Guernesiais still flourished throughout the population, and there even remained a very few elderly people who did not speak English. Furthermore, the pronunciation in the south was still authentic, whereas in the north it had been much influenced by English, as had the vocabulary and the syntax.

The linguistic situation in Guernsey was to deteriorate considerably in the half-century after Sjögren's visit.[12] As late as the beginning of the Second World War, there were some who could not express themselves in English, but the evacuation of the majority of the island's children to England in 1940 dealt the language a blow from which it did not recover, for when they returned, the children were more at home in English than in Guernesiais. Consequently, when they were restored to their families, the language used tended to be English. For most of those of the succeeding generation, Guernesiais is unintelligible and often looked down on. The influx in recent years of large numbers of outsiders, either as residents or as tourists, and the influence of radio and television have served to encourage the progressive Anglicization of all parts of the island. Although there are some rural areas, particularly in the north and the south-west of the island, where Guernesiais is still the first language of a number of elderly people, there is now no one who does not understand English, and in and around St Peter Port Guernesiais has completely disappeared. Tomlinson's estimate – which in the circumstances could not be more than a well-informed guess – was that in 1981 there were perhaps some 6,000 speakers left (i.e. only about 11 per cent of the population, according to the 1981 census, of 53,268), but more recently (in Domaille 1996) he has revised this downwards to some 3,000.

Things are little better in Jersey. Here, the beginnings of Anglicization probably go back earlier than in Guernsey, and in particular to the early nineteenth century when, on the one hand, some 2,000 workers were brought in from England and Ireland to work in the fisheries at Grouville Bay and, on the other hand, numerous veterans of the Napoleonic wars settled on the island. Increasing contacts with English throughout the century, with the development of steamer services and the beginnings of tourism, were to hasten the process, as was later the dominance of English in the fields of trade and education (see Hublart 1979, 26–30). As early as 1863, a French writer reported that, in Jersey, 'la langue anglaise est presque généralement employée dans les rapports de société et dans les relations de commerce' (Le Cerf 1863, 109).

Frank Le Maistre, a life-long student of and enthusiast for Jèrriais, declared shortly after the Second World War (1947, 3) that it was dying and that the disappearance of Norman French there, as also in Guernsey and in Sark, was only a matter of years. He estimated that, if a few elderly natives of the capital, St Helier, were still able to speak Jèrriais, no-one under 50 could do so. It was unlikely that there were any Jèrriais-speaking children left in the other southern parishes of St Brelade, St Saviour, St Clement and Grouville, and they were becoming fewer and fewer in the inland parishes of St Lawrence and St Peter, though there were more in the north-central parishes of St Mary and St John. The language was also declining rapidly in the north-eastern parishes of St Martin and Trinity. It was best preserved in St Ouen, in the north-west of the island, where it was still widely spoken, even by the children (though there were few who could not already speak English when they first attended school). It is there, says Le Maistre, that, at some future date, the funeral of 'la langue Jèrriaise' will take place. In 1982, he estimated that there were some 10,000 speakers of Jèrriais (out of a total population, according to the 1981 census, of some 76,000, so about 13%), many of whom rarely used the language, and that there was probably no-one under the age of 20 who could speak it and perhaps not more than three or four under the age of 30 who could so so. This was perhaps an overestimate. According to the 1989 census (the only time a question on ability to speak 'Jersey-Norman French', as it was termed, has been included on the census form), the language was spoken by only 5,700 (6.9%) of the resident population of 82,809. In only five (predominantly rural) parishes out of twelve was it spoken by up to 12% to 14% of the population, with the highest proportion, 13.8%, in St Ouen. The great majority of speakers (89%) were aged 40 or over while, of those who spoke the language, only 10% were in the age-group 15–39 and only 1% were aged under 15.[13]

Before we can consider the role of French (i.e. standard French, not the local Norman French dialects) as an official language, we must take a brief look at the constitutional position of the various islands. They comprise two Bailiwicks, namely Jersey and Guernsey. In each Bailiwick, the legislative assembly is known as the States. There is, however, a further complication in the case of the Bailiwick of Guernsey, which, in addition to the main island, includes the islands of Alderney and Sark, each of which is to some extent self-governing, and the smaller islands of Herm and Jethou which are administratively part of Guernsey. In Alderney, the legislative assembly (which sends two of its members to sit as deputies in the States of Guernsey) is also known as the States. That in Sark (which is not represented in the States of Guernsey) is known as the Chief Pleas. The highest judicial body in each Bailiwick is the Royal Court.

Technically, French is still an official language in both Bailiwicks. In practice, its role is almost entirely restricted to certain purely formal and ceremonial functions. The one exception, i.e. the one field in which it still serves, so to speak, a productive role, is that of property conveyancing in Jersey (where moves in 1982 to adopt English for the purpose were successfully resisted by the legal profession) and in Sark. English was adopted as the language of conveyancing in Alderney under the new Constitution that came into force in 1949, and in Guernsey in 1969.

It is only within living memory that English has replaced French as the language of legislation and debate in the legislative assemblies. The former Bailiff[14] of Jersey, Lord Coutanche, commented in 1963 (1963, 404) that, when he first entered the States as a

Deputy some forty years earlier, 'French was the language largely in use in debate and almost exclusively for legislation'. In fact, a motion that members should have the right to address the States in English had been adopted in 1900 by the States of Jersey, which seven years earlier had thrown out a similar proposal by a large majority. The first law in Jersey to be drafted in English ('because no-one could draft it in French', ibid.) was the Income Tax Law of 1928. Throughout the 1930s there was a gradual increase in legislation in English. Formal recognition of the *de facto* role of English was given when the States approved the view, almost unanimously expressed by those of its members who appeared before a Privy Council committee in 1946, that English should be the recognized language of the States, French being retained only for formal and official occasions (see Le Hérissier (n.d.), 149). Nevertheless, it was not until States procedure was revised in 1966 that French, which had gradually been falling into disuse as the language in which the official record of States proceedings was kept, was finally supplanted here too by English (see Bois 1976). In Guernsey, the States resolved in 1898 that the use of English should be permitted in debate, and in 1926 that English should rank with French as an official language of the States for the purpose of written records. Legislation was rarely drafted in English before 1914, but since 1945 has invariably been drafted in English apart from amendments to existing laws the text of which is in French (and even here, where major amendments are involved, the practice is sometimes adopted of repealing the earlier legislation and re-enacting it in English). States minutes, which for some years before 1946 had been kept partly in one language and partly in the other, since that date have been kept entirely in English.

In Alderney, the most thoroughly Anglicized of the islands, bills were usually drafted in French (with an English translation) until the new Constitution came into force in January 1949.

In the Royal Courts, too, the working language is now no longer French, as used to be the case, but English. In Jersey, where the language used in the Court at the beginning of the century was normally, though not invariably, French, it had become rare by the 1930s for a trial to be conducted in that language, though it was not until 1963 that this *fait accompli* was recognized when English was adopted as the language of record (Bois 1976). However, the formal record of instruction by the Royal Court that Orders in Council and other texts be entered in the records of the Island ('enregistrés sur les records de l'Île') was still expressed in French up to June 1972, since which date such formal notification has no longer been printed as a preamble to each such Order.[15] In Guernsey, a long-standing practice was formally recognized and regularized in 1946 when the States approved proposals made by the Royal Court that legal proceedings and documents should be either in English or in French at the option of the parties concerned. Since 1946 English has gradually come to replace French as the day-to-day language of record. The last entry in French in the Orders in Council dates from June 1948.[16]

Although French no longer functions as a working language (apart from serving as the language of conveyancing in Jersey and Sark), it retains a residual role for certain purely formal and ceremonial purposes. It is still, for example, the language in which opening prayers are said at meetings of the States in Jersey, Guernsey and even Alderney, and of the Chief Pleas in Sark, and at sessions of the Royal Court in each Bailiwick. In the legislative assemblies (except the States of Alderney), when a vote by *appel nominal* is taken (i.e. when each member in turn gives his vote orally), members vote 'pour' or 'contre'. Also, in the States of Jersey and Guernsey, when the roll is taken at the beginning of each sitting, each member answers 'présent' or, if absent for good cause, is declared 'absent de l'Île', 'malade' (Jersey) or 'indisposé' (Guernsey), or 'excusé' (Jersey), or, in Jersey, if absent without good cause is pronounced 'en défaut'. Among other formal or ceremonial uses of French, we may note the usher's call 'La Cour!', when bidding the public rise when the Bailiff or Deputy Bailiff enters the court-room for sittings of the Royal Court in either Bailiwick, and the use of occasional French phrases in the course of the proceedings, as when, in the Royal Court in Guernsey, an advocate making an *ex parte* application to the Court ends with the phrase 'J'en supplie' ('May the application be granted').[17] In Sark, public notices, signed by the Seigneur and the Seneschal, summoning meetings of Chief Pleas are still put up in French only.

In other public contexts, the use of French has to all practical intents and purposes ceased. Travelling around the islands, one occasionally sees the words 'École élémentaire' or 'Salle paroissiale' on the buildings in question, but what goes on inside is now in English. Le Maistre commented just after the Second World War (1947, 9) that Wesleyan Methodism had 'contributed considerably to preserve the French language', but that, by then, very few services were in French. Now, apart from Roman Catholic masses held at one church in St Helier and one in St Peter Port (in the interests of French residents and visitors, not for the local population), there are now no regular services in French in the churches of any denomination. Nor is there any periodical press – the *Gazette de Guernesey* ceased publication in 1936 and the last remaining French-language newspaper, *Les Chroniques de Jersey*, at the end of 1959.

The prevailing pessimism one encounters everywhere in the islands among those who still retain an interest in the maintenance there of French, whether it be the traditional native Norman French or standard French, seems all too well founded. It can only be a matter of a few decades at most before Jersey, Guernsey and Sark are as Anglicized as Alderney already is.

Notes

1   The reigning King or Queen of England is still referred to in the islands as 'Duke of Normandy', although this is not in fact one of the recognized titles of the sovereign.
2   The form *câté* now survives only in place-names (Le Maistre 1966, 89). English *castle* also derives from Old Norman French *castel* (corresponding to *chastel* in the Old French of the Parisian and other areas).
3   Whereas standard French uses a lower-case initial for names of languages and dialects (*le français*, *le jersiais*), it is customary in written Jèrriais and Guernesiais to use capitals.
4   On dialectal differences in Jersey, see Spence 1993, 20–3.
5   Here quoted after the edition by A. J. Holden, Paris (Société des Anciens Textes Français), 3 vols, 1970–3. The *Roman de Brut* was edited in the same series by I. Arnold, 2 vols, 1938–40.
6   On Métivier and other poets, see R. J. Lebarbenchon, *Des Filles, Une Sorcière, Dame Toumasse et quelques autres*, Azeville, 1980.
7   Le Maistre's dictionary also contains a French–Jersiais vocabulary by Albert L. Carré who has since published an *English–Jersey Language Vocabulary*, Jersey, 1972.

8   H. Tomlinson's doctoral thesis (1981) on the grammar and vocabulary of Guernesiais is unpublished.

9   This was the first regular periodical publication in Jèrriais. It was succeeded in 1979 by the half-yearly *Chroniques du Don Balleine*, also entirely in Jèrriais. There has never been anything resembling a newspaper or popular magazine in Jèrriais, but the *Jersey Evening Post* has for many years given it house-room, publishing occasional articles in the language.

10 The Société Jersiaise also has a 'Section de la langue' and, in Guernsey, Les Ravigoteurs ('The Revivalists') organize social events and evening classes.

11 Although the last native speakers of Auregnais probably died in the 1970s, Frank Le Maistre, who, before the Second World War, knew well the island, its dialect and a number of the remaining speakers, recorded in 1982 a passage of some 400 words in Auregnais (Le Maistre 1982).

12 The following comments are based mainly on the introduction to Tomlinson's thesis (1981, 11–18).

13 Some encouragement is perhaps to be found in the fact that, though Jèrriais has never before been taught in schools, the island's Education Committee decided in 1998 to support a two-year trial programme for the teaching of the language, on an extra-curricular basis, to pupils aged 7–11.

14 The Bailiff of each Bailiwick presides both over the States and over the Royal Court.

15 The title of the volume (published by the States Greffe of the States of Jersey) in which Orders in Council, etc., are collected was in French, viz. *Île de Jersey, Ordres en Conseil, Lois, etc.*, up to and including the volume for 1963–5 (published 1966). Thereafter, i.e. from the volume for 1966–7 (published 1968), it was *Jersey, Orders in Council, Laws, etc.*

16 The change in title from *Recueil d'Ordres en Conseil et d'autres matières d'un intérêt général enregistrés sur les records de l'Île de Guernesey, rédigé sous l'autorité de la Cour Royale* to *Orders in Council and other matters of general interest registered on the records of the Isle of Guernsey, compiled under the authority of the Royal Court*, was made even earlier, between Volumes IX (1931–4) and X (1935–6).

17 It is worth noting that advocates wishing to practise in Guernsey (but not Jersey) are required to study law for one year at the University of Caen.

References

Birt, Paul 1985. *Lé Jèrriais pour tous. A Complete Course on the Jersey Language.* Jersey.

Bois, F., de L. 1976. The disappearance of official French. *Jersey Evening Post*, 9 January 1976, p. 8.

Brasseur, Patrice 1978. Les principales caractéristiques phonétiques des parlers normands de Jersey, Sercq, Guernesey et Magneville (canton de Bricquebec, Manche). *Annales de Normandie*, 28:49–64, 275–306.

——1980–97. *Atlas linguistique et ethnographique normand*, 3 vols (1, 1980; 2, 1984; 3, 1997). Paris.

Collas, J. P. 1933–6. Some aspects of the Norman dialect in the Channel Islands, with special reference to Guernsey. *Transactions of La Société Guernesiaise*, 12:213–25.

Coutanche, Lord 1963. A glance at the past ninety years. Société Jersiaise, *Bulletin*, 18 (1961–4):401–8.

de Garis, Marie 1983. Guernesiais: a grammatical survey. Société Guernesiaise, *Report and Transactions*, 21:319–53.

——et al. 1967. *Dictionnaire angllais–guernesiais.* Guernsey (with a Supplement, 1973; revised edn, 1982, Chichester).

Domaille, D. R. F. 1996. Analyse sociolinguistique du guernesiais. Unpublished MPhil thesis, University of Bristol.

Don Balleine Trust 1979. *The Jersey Language.* Five cassettes and accompanying booklets. St Helier.

Ewen, A. H. and de Carteret, Allan R. 1969. *The Fief of Sark.* Guernsey.

Hublart, Claude 1979. Le français de Jersey. Unpublished dissertation, University of Mons.

Le Cerf, Théodore 1863. *L'Archipel des Îles Normandes.* Paris.

Le Hérissier, R. G. (n.d.). *The Development of the Government of Jersey, 1771–1972.* Jersey.

Le Maistre, Frank 1947. *The Jersey Language in its Present State. The Passing of a Norman Heritage.* London.

—— 1949. Le normand dans les îles Anglo-Normandes. *Le Français moderne*, 17:211–18.

—— 1966. *Dictionnaire jersiais–français.* Jersey.

—— 1982. *The Language of Auregny: La Langue normande d'Auregny.* Jersey, Alderney.

Liddicoat, A. J. 1989. A brief survey of the dialect of Sark. *Transactions of La Société Guernesiaise*, 22:689–704.

Sjögren, Albert 1964. *Les parlers bas-normands de l'île de Guernesey.* 1, *Lexique français–guernesiais.* Paris.

Spence, N. C. W. 1957. Jerriais and the dialects of the Norman mainland. Société Jersiaise, *Bulletin*, 17:81–90.

—— 1960. A *Glossary of Jersey French.* Oxford.

—— 1985–7. Phonologie descriptive des parters jersiais. *Revue de linguistique romane*, 49:151–65, 51:119–33.

—— 1993. *A Brief History of Jèrriais.* St Lawrence, Jersey.

Tomlinson, Harry 1981. Le Guernesiais – étude grammaticale et lexicale du parler normand de l'île de Guernesey. Unpublished PhD dissertation, University of Edinburgh.

17 Anglo-Norman

D. A. Trotter

The aim of this chapter is threefold: to outline the establishment, and subsequent distribution socially and spatially, of Anglo-Norman from 1066 until the end of the Middle Ages; to offer an account of the development of the language thereafter in terms of the functional roles it was called upon to play in speech and writing; and, finally, to discuss the implications of the arrival and expansion of Anglo-Norman for the other languages with which it was in contact throughout the Middle Ages, and upon which it has exerted considerable influence. It will be apparent from the last of these three objectives that it makes no sense at all to deal with Anglo-Norman in splendid isolation, as though it were simply an offshoot of Continental French exported across the Channel and allowed to develop into an eccentric and aberrant dialect, hermetically sealed from the adjacent languages which it encountered in these islands and cut off from its parent French (Trotter 1997; Rothwell 1993).

The question of sources raises a problem. By definition, all our records of Anglo-Norman are written: anything that can be said about the spoken language is the result of more or less speculative reconstruction. Other evidence derives from information concerning the later development of French and English, and from what is understood about the development of Latin into modern Romance. In short, it must always be borne in mind that anything that is said about spoken Anglo-Norman and most of what is said about the extent to which Anglo-Norman *was* indeed spoken throughout the British Isles, is supported at best by very limited evidence. The elaborate detail into which traditional treatises go in their discussions of the arcana of the phonology, morphology and orthography of (especially) earlier Anglo-Norman have more to do with late nineteenth-century Neo-Grammarian theory than the reality of twelfth-, thirteenth-, or fourteenth-century language use (Cerquiglini 1993; Rothwell 1985). From the point of view of anyone interested in real language distribution and functional use within the British Isles, the standard manuals are almost wholly useless. Nor are they helpful when it comes to actually understanding texts. The reader confronted with documentary sources of a non-literary type will find little solace in a learned exposition of twelfth-century phonology (Rothwell 2000b).

One of the most conspicuous advances in recent years in the study of Anglo-Norman has been the broadening of the compass of documentary evidence to bring within the fold a vast range of material which was excluded from the purview of earlier scholars.[1] There is, of course, no possible dispute about the value and interest of studying Anglo-Norman literature. Anglo-Norman literary texts antedate those produced in Continental French. In the first century after the Norman Conquest, and indeed well into the middle of the thirteenth century, a profusion of imaginative literature in Anglo-Norman, written predominantly although not exclusively in England, offers a fine example of an early and highly developed Romance tradition which subsequently feeds with lasting effect into the development of Middle English literature (Legge 1963; Crane 1986; Calin 1995). But this material can at best be but an incomplete and inaccurate guide even to written language use in general, let alone to the reality of speech. To continue to rely on it for the purposes of strictly linguistic analysis is unsatisfactory.

Why Anglo-Norman literature should have emerged so early has been a matter for some debate (Legge 1961). One conventional explanation is that there existed, certainly in England (and the discussion of Anglo-Norman in general has rarely gone beyond England), a prior tradition of vernacular writing established by the Anglo-Saxons. The Normans, just as they assimilated much of Anglo-Saxon administrative practice, law, and culture, also adopted the tradition whereby the vernacular (in their case now Anglo-Norman) was entitled to enjoy the status of 'high' or prestige variety and thus be used in writing. It has been persuasively argued that this vernacular tradition in England may be traced back to Ireland and Wales, as part of the general transmission of knowledge during the so-called Dark Ages, in which Irish and Welsh scholars played a crucial role. More audaciously, it is proposed that French literature as a whole originated in Anglo-Norman England (Howlett 1992). It remains for those who will undoubtedly oppose this view to refute it; and, since the implication is that the Anglo-Norman regnum was the driving force behind much of vernacular literature across the whole of western Europe, the point is not a trivial one.

The distribution of Anglo-Norman literature within the British Isles no more tells us about the extent to which the language was generally and genuinely used, or where, or by whom, than we can really learn anything about the structures of the everyday language from the intricately crafted verse of a twelfth-century author. Texts can rarely be localized with any great precision from either external evidence or internal linguistic details. These last exhibit a remarkable consistency across literary texts of a given period: it is clear that, in imaginative literature, there existed from an early date a semi-standardized form of written Anglo-Norman which was thought appropriate for compositions of this type. In many respects, it is simply a lightly dialectalized version of literary Old French: a few lexical items betray its geographical provenance (typically, Anglo-Saxon words), there are some phonological divergences, and occasional differences in (for example) verb morphology, but it cannot be described as a language separate from that of the Continent. The earlier literary texts, to which, pending the emergence of Ruth Dean's revision of it, Vising's very dated handbook (Vising 1923) remains the main guide, are typically associated either with major urban centres or with noble houses or religious foundations. Geographically, their origin is predominantly England, with isolated examples from Ireland and from Wales. Socially, it would appear that the bulk of this literature was written for and in many cases at the immediate behest of Anglo-Norman nobles. In this respect, it is thus closely similar to what was being produced in France, and it is no accident that the subject-matter, even if it intermittently displays an Anglo-Norman flavour (conspicuously, in the so-called 'ancestral romances' with their glorification of insular genealogy), differs but little from that encountered in France.

It may well be the relative homogeneity of the linguistic evidence of the earlier literary documents which led earlier scholars mistakenly to posit the existence of an 'Anglo-Norman language' (indeed, of '*the* Anglo-Norman language'), a unified linguistic variety imported into England in 1066. We have, of course, no evidence whatever to support the suggestion that a spoken dialect displaying remotely comparable consistency ever existed: what we do know about William the Conqueror's army, drawn from all across Normandy and western France, runs immediately and directly counter to any such suggestion. Those who came with and after William were from dialectally different areas; there must, too, have been some degree of social stratification in their speech. It is entirely wrong to allow ourselves to be led by the smoothly uniform veneer of literary texts to the conclusion that the same uniformity prevailed in the spoken language.

Few serious scholars would now subscribe to the once prevalent and indeed predominant belief that the whole of Anglo-Norman England was bilingual for the better part of 200 years after 1066. The literary evidence suggests that a small, elite percentage of the population demanded and sustained a similarly elite type of literary entertainment. Just as that literature is unlikely to have been accessible to the vast majority of the population in terms of subject-matter and style, so it remains hard to imagine how the very language in which it was written could have been other than a foreign, imported language to the overwhelming majority of the population of England, and *a fortiori* of the remainder of the British Isles. In purely numerical terms, the demographic impact of the Conquest cannot have been sufficient for generalized bilingualism to ensue. The most plausible pattern of language distribution and use is that elaborated by sociolinguists under the increasingly flexible label of diglossia (or in this case, triglossia). According to this model, one language (in our case two) assumes the functions of the 'high' variety or varieties, being used for official, state, educational, religious and written purposes. Another language (or another variety of the main language not granted high status) will fulfil the role of 'low' variety, being used exclusively in speech, and in informal circumstances. In the case of medieval England, Latin (at a greater or lesser distance from Classical Latin according to the expertise of the writer) remained the supraregional, indeed international variety, of the highest possible status and incontrovertibly so right through the Middle Ages and beyond. Anglo-Norman, spoken by only a tiny minority of the population of England, also enjoyed high status and was used in writing, as well as, though decreasingly, in speech. This is in itself an unusual medieval pattern: in France, for example, Latin and French existed in a state of diglossia, with the added complication of dialectal varieties of French whose exact status it is often hard to determine, but England is unique in that there also existed a true vernacular which, whilst it had enjoyed sufficient status to be used in writing before the Norman Conquest, was subsequently down-graded so that it became for some time after 1066 a uniquely spoken, 'low', language.[2] This model accounts both for the survival of written records from different periods and in different languages from medieval England, and (so far as we can discern it) for the development of the individual languages within this complex and shifting arrangement. Broadly speaking, with additional complications in the form of additional (Celtic) languages, the model may also be transferred to Wales, Ireland and Scotland. For Wales in particular, the evidence adduced so convincingly by Michael Richter (1979, 2000) from the enquiry into the canonization of Thomas Cantilupe of Hereford in 1307, points firmly towards the existence of a linguistic hierarchy placing Latin at the top, followed by Anglo-Norman, then English, then Welsh. The picture which emerges accords gratifyingly with the sociolinguists' hierarchy of language use in a multilingual society of this type.

If only a minority of the population was Anglo–Norman-speaking even in the immediate aftermath of the Conquest, then we must ascertain how the language achieved the type of dissemination which the later history of English makes abundantly clear that it did. Presumably incoming Norman men will have married Anglo-Saxon women. The characteristic pattern to emerge would be bilingualism within the second generation: in any case, many Anglo-Normans, and for that matter many Anglo-Saxons, would have needed crash courses in the language of the conquered or the conquerors respectively in order for the essential requirements of everyday communication to be met. Certain sections of the population, not numerous, but influential, must have acquired fluency in both languages from 1066 onwards. But, over the years, we must also reckon with the certainty that, if Anglo-Norman was being spread through at least parts of the population, then it was also being diluted as the original Normans intermarried with Anglo-Saxons. Mention has already been made of the necessity for men in certain key positions of a broadly administrative type (law, trade, local officers) to acquire, as the case may have been, either Anglo-Norman or Anglo-Saxon. Elementary arithmetic would suggest that the majority of those impelled to such language acquisition must have been Anglo-Saxons who desired to, or were required to, achieve some level of competence in Anglo-Norman. Thus is initiated the major process by which Anglo-Norman came to be spread in English, and to a lesser extent Welsh, Irish and Scottish, society: by its being learnt as a second, foreign language. Here, again, one should not exaggerate the depth or breadth of what occurred. The bulk of the population will never have needed to become significantly acquainted with, still less to acquire, Anglo-Norman. The evidence that survives in the form of language-teaching manuals, dating from the thirteenth century onwards, tends to suggest that it was the higher social classes, or those aspiring to join those classes, who learnt Anglo-Norman (Kristol 1990). From the late thirteenth century, Anglo-Norman was far more a learnt, second language than a true vernacular, with only a small minority of speakers who had acquired it naturally either as monolinguals or as bilinguals. This development has profound implications for the later history of Anglo-Norman, and for the extent to which it influenced and became merged with Middle English.

The question which, of course, might well be asked is why it was that speakers of Anglo-Saxon learned Anglo-Norman, rather than the other way round. Patently, it indeed must have happened the other way round, and of course it was English which ultimately was to triumph. But the explanation for the importance of Anglo-Norman as a vehicular rather than as a vernacular language, long beyond the point at which it was used as a first or even second language by people who could reasonably be described as native speakers, lies in the relative status accorded to the different languages under consideration. For as long as Anglo-Norman enjoyed prestige as a 'high' language, and as what the historian Michael Clanchy (1993) has so brilliantly analysed as a 'language of record', then its hegemony was assured. In addition, of course, it was the language of a major civilization of western Europe: those who knew it had access to a vast range of literary and scientific material. Although much early medical material seems to be recorded in Anglo-Norman before it is found in Continental French, this is often simply because of what has survived (or what has been studied) and it is quite clear that the apparently 'Anglo-Norman' nature of much of these documents is misleading:

they are simply Anglo-Norman exemplifications of a French phenomenon (Hunt 1994, 1997; Trotter 1998b, 1999). Conversely, Middle English, lacking the status which would have allowed it to be used for the recording in writing of official transactions, necessarily remained in the position of 'mere' vernacular. *Mutatis mutandis*, the same situation obtained in the Celtic countries, where, of course, an added complication was that Middle English was itself one of the languages of the conquerors, instead of an indigenous language spoken by the majority of the population. Anglo-Norman was acquired by those with social aspirations or professional responsibilities which brought them into contact with the burgeoning mass of administrative documentation which began to be generated with the emergence of written records in the twelfth and thirteenth centuries. These records, whether couched in Latin or in Anglo-Norman, no more give a reliable indication as to the language of the speaker or speakers whose actions and words were being recorded than do the literary texts of early Anglo-Norman provide us with a true reflection of contemporary language use. Indeed, documents preserved in these languages of record, demonstrably often reflecting not just a distortion (as might be argued in the case of literary texts) but a completely false image, are often visibly transpositions into one language of events which took place in another. Latin documents, from as early as the mid-twelfth century, frequently contain calques of Anglo-Norman legal terms. In a medieval law court, for example, the report of the case will possibly be in Latin, the lawyers' report of the case itself may well be in Anglo-Norman (in the Yearbooks), yet both internal and external evidence may reveal that much of the courtroom discussion is most unlikely to have taken place in either language (Brand 2000). We are thus faced with serious problems regarding the reliability of, and the need carefully to interpret, the written documents of the Middle Ages.

The move from (to quote Clanchy) 'memory to written record' as an essential component in legal process induced an explosion of administrative documentation which has been threatening to engulf us ever since. Anglo-Norman, as one of the two acceptable high-status languages of the British Isles, and perhaps as a language which was slightly more accessible than medieval Latin, was well placed to be extensively deployed across the whole of this new range of non-literary documents. The evidence is that it was clearly up to the task, and capable of expanding and developing to meet the changing needs of society. In turn, the expansion of the need for written documentation fuelled a growth in the market for scribes and clerks capable of functioning not only in Anglo-Norman, but also in written medieval Latin and in at least spoken English. It is this class of polyglot operatives who are implicated by the notion of multilingualism in the British Isles during the medieval period, just as in the immediate post-Conquest era, the existence of a small, elite group capable of functioning in several languages should emphatically not be taken as evidence for an unsubstantiated and implausible generalized multilingualism throughout the British Isles. We are dealing here with a particular group, of highly trained exceptional professionals (Jefferson and Rothwell 1997), about whose education we are well informed (Richardson 1942). And, as the study of the non-literary documents in later Anglo-Norman amply demonstrates, the degree of their language competence varies enormously. Scholars of an earlier period habitually, indeed ritualistically, denigrated later Anglo-Norman, most conspicuously and most famously in Mildred K. Pope's account (1934), still regarded in modern secondary literature as the authoritative version of events. (The fact that this book was reprinted in 1952 bestows on it a spurious freshness which its content, bibliography, and for that matter its entire methodology and rationale belie.)

Medieval French studies have often failed to notice one quite predictable reality which the documentary evidence on both sides of the Channel illustrates quite clearly and quite unambiguously: that there is, especially within later documents of the fourteenth and fifteenth centuries, a tremendous range of what (in French or in Anglo-Norman) could perhaps be described as register (although this does leave open the question of competence in standard French for dialect-speakers). This type of variation is of course endemic in spoken language, and to a lesser extent in written language; it would be surprising had it not surfaced in Anglo-Norman. In medieval Latin, too, certainly in Britain and probably elsewhere, similar variation exists: medieval Latin is no more of a piece in this regard than were the vernaculars. Irrespective of the postulated competence and linguistic aptitude of individual scribes,[3] the issue is one also of the level of a given document, of the use to which it might be put, and of the status of sender and addressee. Some later Anglo-Norman non-literary documents, destined for royalty or for the Papacy, are indistinguishable from central Continental French material.[4] At the other end of the spectrum, documents intended for purely local consumption, and fairly obviously drafted by scribes whose competence in the language may be open to question, are much more conspicuously 'Anglo-Norman' in vocabulary, morphology, orthography, and so on.

To summarize so far: imported as a far from unified range of northern and western French dialects in 1066, Anglo-Norman remained, briefly, a true vernacular within limited social groups and for a limited period of time. From this era (broadly, from 1066 to 1250) date the principal and the most successful literary texts in Anglo-Norman, the earliest of which antedate corresponding material produced in France. During this period, the incoming Normans intermarried with the Saxons, and also pushed westward and northward into Wales, Ireland and Scotland. Anglo-Norman was a high-status language, not only because it was the language of the conquerors, but because it was able to build on the pre-existing tradition of vernacular writing which can certainly be traced back to Anglo-Saxon times and possibly, in Ireland and Wales, to a much earlier date. As Anglo-Norman ceased to be a vernacular, it developed into a vehicular variety, principally if not exclusively acquired as a second language by those who required it for social or professional purposes. At the same time, documentary evidence (and some surviving literary texts) from Wales and Ireland, and probably also from Scotland, attests to the development of written records in Anglo-Norman in those parts of the remainder of the British Isles which were colonized by the Normans (Trotter 1994; Hickey 1997).

We have seen that this fundamental shift in the nature and role of Anglo-Norman coincided with the development of an administrative documentary culture in which a plethora of documents was generated in Anglo-Norman, and which, in turn, increased substantially the need for competent clerical staff who could function in all the languages with which they would come into contact. From the middle of the fourteenth century onwards, this process of contact relexified Middle English with a vast array of words, not of 'French' provenance as the manuals of the history of English erroneously declare, but directly drawn from the Anglo-Norman language with which the scribes and authors of Middle English were in daily contact. The importance of the emergence of written records can hardly be overstated: it brought into being a complete scribal class habitually accustomed to move between languages, to translate and transpose from one to the other, and to appropriate, misappropriate, or simply to merge vocabulary, structures and orthographic features from one language to the next (Rothwell 1994). This process of hybridization culminates in Middle English, not so much displacing or ousting Anglo-Norman, but simply incorporating it, absorbing it, and enlarging English with it. This process cannot be understood without reference to mechanisms associated with language contact, bilingualism (or better, multilingualism), and associated phenomena such as code-switching, language-mixing, and so forth.[5] The massive relexification which took place, and to which modern English owes such a high percentage of its vocabulary, cannot be accounted for by traditional concepts of 'borrowing' (Rothwell 1980; Trotter 1996, 1998a). It is, indeed, even debatable whether the bulk of medieval authors of the type of non-literary document in which this phenomenon is most marked were necessarily consciously aware that they were moving from one language to another, or that they were doing anything unusual or innovative in drawing on lexical items from 'another' language. If the author (anonymous) of the Exe Bridge Wardens' Accounts for 1349 (for some reason this year alone is written in Anglo-Norman, the others all being in medieval Latin)[6] chooses to use the word *weigge* in the expression *weigge de fer* 'iron wedge', rather than the readily available Anglo-Norman alternative which it is hard to believe he did not have at his disposal, then we should perhaps ask ourselves whether the author would necessarily have been conscious of it as originating in a 'separate' language. There is an abundance of multilingual documentation from the later Middle Ages, typically blending in a (to modern eyes) disconcerting fashion lexical items from several languages within a matrix of Latin, Anglo-Norman, or Middle English, which modern scholarship is only just beginning to disinter, let alone account for (Wright 1996, 2000; Hunt 2000; Schendl 2000). Documents of this type, now increasingly being drawn on by the major dictionaries of English (Weiner 2000), Anglo-Norman, and British medieval Latin, exemplify in a perhaps extreme form the processes of language contact characteristic of the later Middle Ages in the British Isles.

What, then, of the role played by Anglo-Norman in the subsequent development of English? It is here that the lasting legacy of Anglo-Norman is to be found. There are of course place-names and large numbers of personal names, many of which originated in Anglo-Norman surnames (*le taillour*, *le spicer*, etc.) in the Middle Ages (Postles 1995), but it is in the lexis of modern English that Anglo-Norman survives to this day. This is the direct consequence of the language contact processes alluded to above. Normally associated with the period from approximately 1300 onwards, the process must have started much earlier than this. The Middle English *Ancrene Wisse*, composed shortly after 1200, provides interesting evidence not hitherto examined from this point of view (Trotter, forthcoming; Rothwell 2000a). In this text, notorious for its high percentage of 'French' (i.e. Anglo-Norman) lexical items, there survives a surprising number of very early attestations of hybrid Anglo-Norman/Middle English forms, several of which are substantially (up to 150 years) earlier than the first recorded dates of the Anglo-Norman component, whether in Anglo-Norman itself or, for that matter, in Continental French. This suggests two things: firstly, that the process of language-mixing as a direct result of language contact must have taken place earlier than records indicate, in speech before it is attested in writing; and that Anglo-Norman (and indeed French) specialists may need to look in Middle English texts for early evidence of words which Anglo-Norman documents themselves only record at later dates.[7] A second aspect of the influence of Anglo-Norman on the history of English lies entirely outside the sphere of written language, and has nothing to do with the development of standard English. This is the survival, in modern English dialects, of words patently deriving from Anglo-Norman.[8] Whilst we may easily account for the merger of Anglo-Norman and Middle English through the activities of the scribal classes discussed at some length above, it is less easy, if we assume that Anglo-Norman was not in fact widespread amongst all social classes across the whole of the country, to account for this evidence of contact in dialects which have never enjoyed prestige status either locally or supraregionally. Taken together with a third category of evidence, namely the Anglo-Norman origin of many of the swear-words in English (e.g. *bastard*, *bugger*: Rothwell 1996), this points to an influence of Anglo-Norman on English at levels not hitherto suspected, and which needs to be much more extensively explored.

Notes

1   Compare, for example, the range covered by the *AND* (by the end of the first edition) with that dealt with by Pope 1934 or Legge 1963. The second edition of the *AND* will expand still further its coverage.
2   See also Möhren 2000.
3   See Möhren's cautionary remarks (2000).
4   See e.g. Chaplais 1982 and the material in Legge 1941. An interesting point is that a number of the documents in this collection are not Anglo-Norman at all, but emanate from France or elsewhere; yet the language of these documents is indistinguishable from those of the Anglo-Norman texts. This may be just a matter of scribal colouring, but it goes beyond mere orthography so this seems insufficient to explain everything.
5   See Romaine 1995 for a recent survey.
6   Devon Record Office, Exe Bridge Wardens' Account 23 Ed III (1349).
7   A study in preparation by W. Rothwell ('Anglo-French and Middle English vocabulary in "Femina Nova"') presents a further dimension to this problem, albeit at a later date.
8   For example: *foreigner* 'moonlighting worker' and *feu* [?] 'enthusiasm, energy' in Cumbrian both clearly preserve Anglo-Norman words and senses. Yorkshire *faus* 'false', *ginnel* 'alley', *mard(y)* 'dirty, mucky', or forms common to more than one dialect area (*causey* 'causeway' in Yorkshire and Devon; *pace-egg* 'Easter egg produced by boiling eggs with onion skins' in Yorkshire and Cumbria; *fash* 'to become angry' in Yorkshire and Scotland) raise similar questions. Welsh *putain* 'whore' is hard to interpret other than as a direct transposition from Anglo-Norman; courtly sources do not immediately suggest themselves. I am grateful to Professor W. Rothwell for the Yorkshire examples, and to Professor Gareth Alban Davies for the Welsh.

References

AND = Rothwell, W. et al. (eds) 1977–92. *Anglo-Norman Dictionary*. London.
Brand, P. 2000. The languages of the law in later medieval England. In Trotter 2000, 63–76.
Calin, W. 1995. *The French Tradition and the Literature of Medieval England*. Toronto/ Buffalo/London.
Cerquiglini, B. 1993. *La naissance du français*. Paris.

Chaplais, P. 1982. *English Medieval Diplomatic Practice*. London.

Clanchy, M. T. 1993. *From Memory to Written Record: England 1066–1307*, 2nd edn. Oxford.

Crane, S. 1986. *Insular Romance: Politics, Faith, and Culture in Anglo-Norman and Middle English Literature*. Berkeley.

Dean, Ruth J. (forthcoming). Revision of Vising 1923.

Hickey, R. 1997. Assessing the relative status of languages in medieval Ireland. In Fisiak, Jacek and Winter, Werner (eds), *Studies in Middle English Linguistics*, Berlin, 181–205.

Howlett, D. R. 1992. *The English Origins of Old French Literature*. Dublin.

Hunt, Tony 1994. *Anglo-Norman Medicine I: Roger of Frugard's 'Chirurgia' and the 'Practica Brevis' of Platearius*. Cambridge.

——1997. *Anglo-Norman Medicine II: Shorter Treatises*. Cambridge.

——2000. Code-switching in medical texts. In Trotter 2000, 131–47.

Jefferson, Lisa and Rothwell, W. 1997. Society and lexis: a study of the Anglo-French vocabulary in the fifteenth-century accounts of the Merchants Taylors' Company. *Zeitschrift für französische Sprache und Literatur*, 107:273–301.

Kristol, A. 1990. L'enseignement du français en Angleterre (XIIIe–XVe siècles): les sources manuscrites. *Romania*, 111:298–330.

Legge, M. Dominica 1941. *Anglo-Norman Letters and Petitions*. Oxford.

——1961. La précocité de la littérature anglo-normande. *Cahiers de civilisation médiévale*, 8:327–49.

——1963. *Anglo-Norman Literature and its Background*. Oxford.

Möhren, F. 2000. One-fold lexicography for a manifold problem? In Trotter 2000, 157–68.

Nielsen, Hans-Frede and Schøsler, Lene (eds) 1996. *The Origins and Development of Emigrant Languages. Proceedings from the Second Rasmus Rask Colloquium, Odense University, November 1994*. Odense.

Pope, Mildred K. 1934. *From Latin to Modern French*. Manchester.

Postles, D. 1995. Noms de personnes en langue française dans l'Angleterre du moyen âge. *Le Moyen Âge*, 101:7–21.

Richardson, H. G. 1942. Letters of the Oxford Dictatores. *Oxford History Society*, New Series, 5:331–450.

Richter, M. 1979. *Sprache und Gesellschaft im Mittelalter: Untersuchungen zur mündlichen Kommunikation in England von der Mitte des 11. bis zum Beginn des 14. Jahrhunderts*. Stuttgart.

——2000. Collecting miracles along the Anglo-Welsh border in the early fourteenth century. In Trotter 2000, 53–61.

Romaine, S. 1995. *Bilingualism*, 2nd edn. Oxford.

Rothwell, W. 1980. Lexical borrowing in a medieval context. *Bulletin of the John Rylands University Library of Manchester*, 63:18–43.

——1985. *From Latin to Modern French*: fifty years on. *Bulletin of the John Rylands University Library of Manchester*, 68:179–209.

——1993. The 'faus franceis d'Angleterre': later Anglo-Norman. In Short, Ian (ed.), *Anglo-Norman Anniversary Essays*, London, 309–26.

——1994. The trilingual England of Geoffrey Chaucer. *Studies in the Age of Chaucer*, 16:45–67.

——1996. Adding insult to injury: the English who curse in borrowed French. In Nielsen and Schøsler, 41–54.

——2000a. Aspects of lexical and morphosyntactical mixing in the languages of medieval England. In Trotter 2000, 213–32.

——2000b. Two verderers and fractured French. Forthcoming in *French Studies Bulletin*.

Schendl, H. 2000. Linguistic aspects of code-switching in medieval English texts. In Trotter 2000, 77–92.

Trotter, D. A. 1994. L'anglo-français au Pays de Galles: une enquête préliminaire. *Revue de linguistique romane*, 58:461–88.

—— 1996. Language contact and lexicography: the case of Anglo-Norman. In Nielsen and Schøsler, 21–39.

—— 1997. *Mossenhor, fet metre aquesta letra en bon francés*: Anglo-French in Gascony. In Gregory, Stewart and Trotter, D. A. (eds), *De mot en mot: Essays in Honour of William Rothwell*, Cardiff, 199–222.

—— 1998a. Translations and loanwords: some Anglo-Norman evidence. In Ellis, R., Tixier, R. and Weitmeier, B. (eds), *The Medieval Translator 6: Proceedings of the International Conference of Göttingen (22–25 July 1996)*, Louvain-la-Neuve, 20–39.

—— 1998b. Les néologismes de l'anglo-français et le *FEW*. *Le Moyen Français*, 39–41: 577–636.

—— 1999. L'importance lexicographique du *Traitier de Cyrurgie* d'Albucasis en ancien français. *Revue de linguistique romane*, 63:23–53.

—— (ed.) 2000. *Multilingualism in Later Medieval Britain*. Cambridge.

—— forthcoming. The Anglo-French lexis of the *Ancrene Wisse*: a re-evaluation. Forthcoming in Wada, Yoko (ed.), *Ancrene Wisse Essays*, Osaka.

Vising, J. 1923. *Anglo-Norman Language and Literature*. Oxford.

Weiner, E. S. C. 2000. Medieval multilingualism and the revision of the *OED*. In Trotter 2000, 169–74.

Wright, Laura 1996. *Sources of London English: Medieval Thames Vocabulary*. Oxford.

—— 2000. Bills, accounts, inventories: everyday trilingual activities in the business world of later medieval England. In Trotter 2000, 149–56.

18 Romani

Glanville Price

Romani is the language of the Gypsies.[1] Its origins, the stages by which it spread to Europe and elsewhere, and its present situation (in terms both of the extent to which it is spoken and the quality of spoken Romani) are all to some degree obscure. It is beyond dispute, however, that Romani originated in India and that it is a member of the Indo-European family of languages. This family includes most of the languages of Europe (among them, the Germanic, Celtic, Romance and Slav languages and Greek), Persian, Sanskrit and a number (though by no means all) of the present-day languages of the Indian sub-continent known collectively as the Indo-Aryan languages.

Though the Indian origin of Romani is certain, its precise relationship to the other Indo-Aryan languages is not. In many respects it seems closest to central Indo-Aryan languages (the best known of which is Hindi), but it also has some features in common with a north-western group (including Kashmiri and Punjabi). The eminent Sanskrit scholar, Sir Ralph Lilley Turner, concluded (Turner 1927) that there was originally a connection between Romani and the central group, but that, at some early stage, probably before 250 BC, the ancestors of the Gypsies migrated north-westwards and settled, probably in the Western Punjab or in the Peshawar district, among speakers of north-western dialects. There they seem to have stayed for perhaps a thousand years or more, which explains the north-western features still to be found in Romani.

At some indeterminate period, not later than the ninth century AD, the Romanis were on the move again, migrating further and further westwards. They were already in south-eastern Europe by the fourteenth century (if not earlier), and in the course of the fifteenth century they reached virtually every country in western Europe (see Clébert 1963, 29–36).

It is not known precisely how or when the Gypsies (or 'Egyptians' as they were first known – 'Gypsies' is a deformation of the same word) first reached Britain, but there is every reason to suppose that they arrived here too in the course of the fifteenth century. It is more than likely that an Act of the Scottish Parliament of 1449, directed against unspecified 'sorners', 'vagabonds' and the like, was directed against the Gypsies. The first recorded mention of them by name (i.e. 'Egyptians') is also from Scotland, in the accounts of the Lord High Treasurer for Scotland of 22 April 1505, and the earliest known reference to them (again as 'Egyptians') in England is in the *Dyalog of Syr Thomas More, Knyght*, of 1514. There are estimated to have been 10,000 Gypsies in England in the reign of Elizabeth I.

In the course of the thousand years or so since they left India, the Gypsies have come into contact with many other peoples, whose languages have had far-reaching influence on Romani. The dispersion of the Romani community in so many different directions has meant that different groups have different patterns of borrowings, but the pattern in any given case is astonishingly varied. Turner estimated (1959, 463) that the dialect of the Gypsies of Wales, for example, contains words from Persian, Armenian, Greek (the Greek element is particularly important), Romanian, Bulgarian, Serbian, Czech, German, French and English (and, one must add, Welsh). Grammar and pronunciation have also evolved differently in different areas, and there are now many distinct dialects of Romani.

One can divide Gypsy communities, in terms of their use of Romani, into three broad categories. There are those (as, for example, in parts of the Balkans) for whom Romani survives, with its own grammatical forms and structures, as a first language. Then there are those communities who speak 'jargons consisting of a framework of the local language, for example, English, in which a certain portion of the vocabulary is replaced by Gypsy words' (Turner 1959, 463). Finally, there are those who have lost the language almost entirely, and use for all purposes the language of their environment, incorporating in it an occasional word of Romani. As we shall see, British Gypsies now fall mainly into the second category, though until recently some Welsh Gypsies still knew and used enough of the grammatical forms of Romani to warrant inclusion on the fringes of the first category.

English Romani is first attested in 1547, when Andrew Borde included in his *Fyrst Boke of the Introduction of Knowledge* thirteen sentences, beginning:

Good morrow!	Lach ittur ydyues!
How farre is it to the next town?	Cater myla barforas?
You be welcome to the towne.	Maysta ves barforas.
Wyl you drynke some wine?	Mole pis lauena?

Thereafter, there is nothing until William Marsden (1784) included thirty-eight words of English Gypsy in an article in *Archaeologia* and, in the same volume, Jacob Bryant (1784) published a list of some 300 English Gypsy words.

In the course of the next hundred years there were a few, but only a few, minor items devoted to Romani, but the 1870s saw a heightening of serious interest in the Gypsies and their language, with the publication of Leland's *The English Gipsies and their Language* (1873), Borrow's *Romano Lavo-Lil* (subtitled *Word-book of the Romany, or English Gypsy Language*) (1874), and, in particular, Smart and Crofton's *The Dialect of the English Gypsies* (1875), which contained a grammar, an extensive vocabulary, and a wide selection of miscellaneous texts.

By this time, the grammatical structure of the language of the English Gypsies was severely undermined. Leland comments (1873, ix) that 'the grammar has well nigh disappeared', though this had apparently happened only recently since 'within the memory of man the popular Rommany of this country was really grammatical' (ibid., xiii). Borrow expresses a similar view. Having estimated the 'scanty' vocabulary of English Gypsy speech at 'probably not more than fourteen hundred words' (1874, 6), he goes on to comment that 'with respect to Grammar, the English Gypsy is perhaps in a worse condition than with respect to words'.

Smart and Crofton (1875, xi) distinguish between 'the common widespread corrupt dialect [. . .] containing but few inflexions, and mixed to a greater or less extent with

English, and conforming to the English method in the arrangement of the sentences. This is the vulgar tongue in every-day use by ordinary Gypsies', whereas 'the "Deep" or old dialect', which has its own grammar and which contains a minimum admixture of English words, is 'known only to a few aged Gypsies'. 'This last,' he says, 'which will soon cease to exist, is *par excellence* the Gypsy language, of which the first is merely the corruption.'

The following (from Leland 1873, 238) well illustrates that the kind of language that has been described as 'really a register of English rather than a dialect of Romani' (Kenrick 1979, 111–12) was in use over a century ago:

> Mandy sūtto'd I was pirraben lang o' tute, an' I dicked mandy's pen odöi 'pre the choomber. Then I was pirryin' ajaw parl the puvius, an' I welled to the panni paul' the Beng's Choomber, an' adoi I dicked some rānis.
> ('I dreamed I was walking with you, and I saw my sister (a fortune-teller) there upon the hill. Then I (found myself) walking again over the field, and I came to the water near the Devil's Dyke, and there I saw some ladies.')

This 'Anglo-Romani', that is, a speech form in which 'Romani words are fitted, inflected as English words, into sentences with English grammar and additional vocabulary' (Acton 1974, 56), seems to be still in widespread use among English Gypsies. Accounts of its use in different parts of England over half a century ago are given, under the general title 'Anglo-Romani Gleanings', in the *Journal of the Gypsy Lore Society*, Third Series, volumes 3 (1924):110–36 (on London Gypsies), 4 (1925):115–39 (Hampshire), 8 (1929):105–34 (East Anglia), and 27 (1948):83–110 and 28 (1949):50–61 (northern counties). In a foreword to the last of these, however, Archdeacon D. M. M. Bartlett comments (p. 83) that, in the North as in the South, 'the old *Romanes* [. . .] is now moribund, if not actually dead'. Donald Kenrick (1979, 114) is almost equally pessimistic, finding that the everyday language in use among Gypsies in England is English, though, 'in addition, they possess a special lexis of between 100 and 1000 words which they can use to replace the English equivalents when they want or need to'.

On the other hand, Ian Hancock (1969) discovered that some Gypsies of the Lee family whom he met at Epsom Races in June 1968 had an extensive vocabulary. None of the Romani he then heard spoken was inflected but 'it was still far from being English and I think it will be many more years before the language expires in Britain'.

In fact, Anglo-Romani now seems not to be a language functioning as 'natural' languages do. This is indicated first by the fact that it is largely acquired not in early childhood but in adolescence. According to Kenrick (1979, 118–19), before reaching puberty children know only about fifty words at most, but:

> At this point the girls learn the language from the younger women and the boys from the younger men. During the long drives looking for work a boy can learn as many as thirty or forty words in a day, and as he learns them he gets into situations where he needs to use them and is allowed to do so.

Secondly, the language is not used for normal everyday communicative and expressive purposes, but, primarily though not exclusively, for a restricted range of functions (see Kenrick 1971, 11, and 1979, 115–19). Among the more important are its use for identification purposes (a Gypsy may, for example, slip a word of Romani into a conversation to ascertain whether someone else present is also a Gypsy), as a source of specialized vocabulary in certain trades or professions, such as horse-dealing, in songs and oaths, and, above all, as a secret language that could be used by Gypsies to communicate with one another in the presence of strangers, a facility that is highly prized, so much so that 'for many Gypsies it is important that even the *fact* that they have a secret language should be concealed' (Kenrick 1979, 117), and 'the secretness of the language is one reason why it is not taught to young children. If they don't know it, then they can't reveal its secrets' (ibid., 118).

Acton and Davies estimated (1979, 100) that at least 50,000 people in England and Wales then spoke Anglo-Romani, with up to 800 words being fairly commonly known, and a beginning had been made on teaching it in some of the Gypsy caravan schools that had recently come into existence.

It had been widely assumed that inflected Romani was virtually extinct in Britain generally by the late nineteenth century. But then Dr John Sampson (later to become Librarian of the University of Liverpool), made a remarkable discovery:

> In the summer of 1894, while on a caravan tour through North Wales, I chanced upon a Welsh Gypsy harper at Bala, and made the discovery that the ancient Romanī tongue, so long extinct in England and Scotland, had been miraculously preserved by the Gypsies of the Principality. (Sampson 1926, vii)

The harpist in question, Edward Wood, and his family proved to be 'the descendants of an eponymous ancestor Abram Wood, reputed King of the Gypsies, who was born before the close of the seventeenth century, and the dialect so religiously kept intact in the fastenesses of Cambria is thus a survival of the oldest and purest form of British Romanī' (ibid.). Furthermore, he discovered that this Welsh Romani 'was still the mother-tongue of a large tribe, who spoke it habitually among themselves and only used Welsh or English when addressing strangers' (ibid., viii).

Over a period of more than twenty years, Sampson came to know many of the Wood family in many localities in North Wales, and as far south as Newtown and Aberystwyth. Regarded by them as one of themselves from whom there was nothing to conceal, he enjoyed a unique opportunity of studying the people and their language.

In 1907, Sampson published in the *Journal of the Gypsy Lore Society* the first of forty-two folk-tales he had collected, the remainder of which were to appear over the next quarter of a century (see Sampson 1907–33). Of even greater importance is Sampson's volume entitled *The Dialect of the Gypsies of Wales, being the Older Form of British Romani preserved in the Speech of the Clan of Abram Wood* (1926). This monumental work of nearly seven hundred pages includes substantial sections on 'Phonology', 'Word-formation' and 'Inflection and syntax', and a vocabulary of over four hundred pages. The grammatical and lexical sections in particular are abundantly illustrated with examples, including thousands of complete sentences.

Good evidence for the continued existence of 'deep Romani' among members of the Wood family on the eve of the Second World War is provided by sixteen letters dictated by the illiterate Harry Wood in 1935–9 to the postmaster at Druid (near Corwen, Denbighshire), Rowland Humphreys, and later published (Huth 1940). The following extract, in Humphreys' orthography derived mainly from that of English, partly from that of Welsh (e.g. *w* = English *u*; *si* = English *sh*), shows how different this is from the 'Anglo-Romani' discussed above:

> Kamlo Pal, Kam diom te shuna teeree chinimangeri ta shanes mishtol tai Rawni. Mwranes nashadoe siomes may pala twte. Fedader siom Kanaw.
> ('Dear Brother, I liked to hear your letter, and that you were well, also the Lady. I was altogether lost without you. I am better now.')

There are no very clear indications as to how far Romani still remains at the level of richness and purity recorded by Sampson.[2] In 1950, Derek Tipler met a Gypsy family in Caernarfonshire and discovered that the older members spoke 'inflected Romani' (see Tipler 1957). While some of the 136 words or (mainly) phrases he quotes are uncorrupted, others show considerable influence of English or Welsh morphosyntax. What is worse, 'the children, unfortunately, were no credit to their parents as regards the language, speaking a much more debased type of Romani'. That was over half a century ago and it seems unlikely that much if any Romani, other than words and perhaps occasional phrases, still survives even in Wales. But no-one can be quite certain of this and it is perhaps not totally beyond the bounds of possibility that something more of the language still remains to be discovered.

Notes

1   The name is derived from the Romani word *rom* 'husband'.
2   For a recent survey of the Romani language with particular reference to Wales, see the chapter 'The Romani language' (partly written by Donald Kenrick) in Jarman and Jarman 1991, 148–58.

References

Acton, Thomas 1974. *Gypsy Politics and Social Change.* London.
—— and Davies, G. 1979. Educational policy and language use among English Romanies and Irish travellers (tinkers) in England and Wales. *International Journal of the Sociology of Language*, no. 19 ('Romani Sociolinguistics'), 91–109.
Borrow, George 1874. *Romano Lavo-Lil.* London.
Bryant, Jacob 1784. Collections on the Zingara, or Gypsey language. *Archaeologia*, 7:388–94.
Clébert, Jean-Paul 1963. *The Gypsies.* New York. (Originally published as *Les Tziganes*, Paris, 1961.)
Hancock, I. F. 1969. Romanes numerals and innovations. *Journal of the Gypsy Lore Society*, Third Series, 48:19–24.
Huth, F. G. 1940. Letters from a Welsh Gypsy to a Tarno Rai. *Journal of the Gypsy Lore Society*, Third Series, 20:1–15, 150–62.
Jarman, Eldra and Jarman, A. O. H. 1991. *The Welsh Gypsies.* Cardiff.
Kenrick, Donald 1971. Anglo-Romani today. In Acton, T. A. (ed.), *Current Changes among British Gypsies and their Place in International Patterns of Development* (Proceedings of the Research and Policy Conference of the National Gypsy Education Council, Oxford, 26–28 March 1971), 5–14.

——1979. Romani English. *International Journal of the Sociology of Language,* no. 19 ('Romani Sociolinguistics'), 111–20.

Leland, C. G. 1873. *The English Gypsies and their Language.* London.

Marsden, W. 1784. Observations on the language of the people commonly called Gypsies. *Archaeologia,* 7:382–6.

Sampson, John (ed.) 1907–33. Welsh Gypsy folk-tales, Nos. 1–42. *Journal of the Gypsy Lore Society,* Second Series, vols 1 (1907–8)–4 (1910–11), 8 (1914–15); Third Series, vols 1 (1922)–9 (1930), 12 (1933).

——1926. *The Dialect of the Gypsies of Wales, being the Older Form of British Romani preserved in the Speech of the Clan of Abram Wood.* Oxford.

Smart, B. and Crofton, S. T. 1875. *The Dialect of the English Gypsies,* 2nd edn. London.

Tipler, D. 1957. Specimens of modern Welsh Romani. *Journal of the Gypsy Lore Society,* Third Series, 36:9–24.

Turner, Ralph L. 1927. *The Position of Romani in Indo-Aryan.* London. (Gypsy Lore Society, Monograph No. 4.)

——1959. Romany Language. *Encyclopaedia Britannica,* vol. 19, 462–4.

19 Community Languages

Viv Edwards

Britain has always been a multilingual society. The nature and extent of linguistic diversity, however, increased dramatically in the second half of the twentieth century in response to various political and economic factors (Alladina and Edwards 1991). Speakers of Welsh and Gaelic are able to claim territorial rights in their efforts to preserve their languages; speakers of non-Celtic languages, in contrast, are dispersed throughout the UK and therefore place greater emphasis on the 'personality principle' (Baker and Prys-Jones 1998) – the distinctive features and long traditions which mark each language as unique. Thus, although their languages are not indigenous, they belong to identifiable communities which centre on places of worship, schools, shopping areas or recreational facilities. In the UK and Australia, such languages are known as 'community languages' (Horvath and Vaughan 1991); in Canada they are called 'heritage languages' (Cummins and Danesi 1990).

This chapter provides an overview of the current state of community languages in the UK. It will discuss the distribution of minority languages, as well as difficulties in making accurate estimates of numbers of speakers. It will explore the sociolinguistic dimensions of language use in minority communities determined by factors such as status, patterns of migration and whether the languages have a written tradition. It will also examine issues in language maintenance and shift and, in particular, the role of formal teaching in both the community and mainstream schooling in helping to ensure that minority languages are transmitted to the next generation. Finally, it will review research which focuses on community languages spoken in Britain.

Precise numbers of speakers of community languages are very difficult to establish. According to the 1991 UK Census, ethnic minorities make up some 5.5 per cent of the population, and are concentrated mainly in industrial and urban areas, especially in the south-east of England and Greater London. These figures fail to take account, however, of mobile families (cf. Graddol 1998) who come from the European Union or who work for multinational companies. A further problem concerns the fact that the census did not include a question on the language of ethnic minority respondents. It is therefore not possible to extrapolate from census data as to the number or size of the different ethnic groups. Nor is ethnicity an automatic guarantee that a respondent is bilingual.

The two main sources of information on linguistic diversity in the UK both date from the 1980s. The first is the Linguistic Minorities Project (1985) which was set up to study mother tongue teaching and the changing patterns of bilingualism in the UK, drawing on data collected in three main centres – Bradford, Coventry and London. The second is the language censuses conducted by the Research and Statistics Department of the Inner London Education Authority (ILEA 1978, 1981, 1983, 1985, 1987). These censuses were able to demonstrate not only the range of languages spoken but also the changing profiles of the different communities over time. For instance, the number of Bangladeshi pupils trebled between 1981 and 1987, at which time they represented over a quarter of all pupils with a home language other than English and the largest linguistic minority in London.

With the disbanding of ILEA this data collection exercise came to a close. The last census published in 1989, however, gives an interesting indication of the extent of diversity. Over 25 per cent of children reported speaking a language other than or in addition to English; and 180 different languages were identified. Some commentators (e.g. Nicholas 1994) argue that even this very large number represents a significant underestimate. Although all schools are now required to report on the ethnicity of pupils, they are not required to collect data on language. It is therefore impossible to estimate with any degree of confidence the numbers of speakers of community languages.

None the less, it is generally agreed that settlers from the Indian subcontinent – and in particular Panjabi-, Urdu-, Gujarati- and Bengali-speakers – constitute the largest linguistic minority communities. Panjabi-speaking Sikhs are usually held to be the biggest of these south Asian groupings and may number at least 500,000. The most important areas of settlement are London, the West Midlands and the northern cities of Leeds and Bradford. Pakistani Muslims from the Mirpur district of Azad Kashmir also speak a variety which is mutually intelligible with the Panjabi spoken by Sikhs, but identify with Urdu as the language of religion and high culture. They are spread throughout the UK but have important settlements in London and the south, the Midlands and the north of England. Gujarati-speakers form the second largest south Asian community. They are scattered throughout the country with particular concentrations in Greater London and the Midlands. The Bengali community consists of a small, mainly Hindu, community from Indian West Bengal and a much larger Muslim Bangladeshi community which is concentrated in the London boroughs of Tower Hamlets and Camden, though smaller settlements are also to be found in cities such as Coventry and Bradford.

The Chinese form another numerically important group, although they differ from the large south Asian communities in that their patterns of settlement are far more dispersed. Most came to the UK in the 1950s and 1960s to escape high levels of unemployment in Hong Kong following the requisition of land from farmers for development purposes, and an influx of refugees from the People's Republic of China during the Cultural Revolution. About 70 per cent of Hong Kong Chinese speak Cantonese which also serves as a *lingua franca* for speakers of languages such as Hakka and Hokkien. Other ethnic Chinese include a refugee community of approximately 25,000 from Vietnam who also use Cantonese as a *lingua franca*, and a small number of Chinese professionals from Singapore and Malaysia, mainly speakers of Putonghua, who often came originally to the UK as students.

The various African-Caribbean communities can also usefully be mentioned at this point. Although similar in size to the south Asian communities in Britain, they are normally considered ethnic rather than linguistic communities, because English is the official language throughout the former British West Indies. There is evidence, however, that distinctively Black British varieties, heavily influenced by Jamaican and other Caribbean creoles, continue to serve as an important marker of identity in the speech of many British-born young people (Edwards 1986; Sutcliffe 1992; Dalphinis 1991; Sebba 1993; Callender 1997).

Other notable minority communities include Arabic-speakers from many different countries, Greek- and Turkish-speakers from Cyprus and, to a lesser extent, mainland Europe, and speakers of Somali, Yoruba and Vietnamese.

Although linguistic minorities in the UK inevitably share many common experiences, they are not a homogenous group and it is important to challenge common stereotypes. It is often incorrectly assumed, for instance, that the language varieties spoken within ethnic minority communities are the same as the national or official language of the country of origin. Such an assumption is, at best, extremely simplistic. Culture and religious affiliation often influence the way in which speakers report their language. As already mentioned, Muslim families from Pakistan who use a dialect of Panjabi in the home identify themselves as speakers of Urdu, the language of religion and high culture. In a similar vein, minorities from within a country show loyalty to their ethnic group rather than the national language. Kurdish refugees from Turkey consider themselves to be speakers of Kurdi, not Turkish; Algerian Berbers are more likely to use Berber in the home than Arabic.

The existence of a written tradition is another important influence on patterns of language use. Most Bangladeshis in the UK come from the region of Sylhet and speak a highly distinctive variety which, according to some writers, is sufficiently distinct from Bengali to be considered a separate language (see, for instance, Husain 1991). The fact that there is no written tradition thus makes it more difficult to promote Sylheti as the medium of community education in the UK. In a similar vein, St Lucian settlers in the UK come from a diglossic situation in which a French Kwéyòl is often spoken in the home, but English remains the sole medium of education (Nwenmely 1996). The fact that an orthography has been available only in recent years has almost certainly been a factor in the invisibility of Kwéyòl as a distinct community language in Britain.

Length of stay also differentiates the various linguistic minority communities. Economic migrants and political refugees (Rutter 1995) often make the UK their permanent home. Other groups, such as the Japanese, Libyans and Mainland Chinese, seldom spend more than three or four years abroad before returning home. Even within the same language group, patterns of migration can be very different. Some Gujarati-speakers came direct from India while others found their way to the UK via East African countries such as Uganda and Kenya where their families had settled in the early part of the twentieth century. East African Asians are often better educated and enjoy higher socio-economic status than settlers who came direct from India. Distinctions can also be made within the Hong Kong Chinese community. Those who made their homes in the UK in the 1960s came from mainly rural backgrounds and tend to have relatively little formal schooling. In contrast, those who came in the 1990s just prior to the handing over of Hong Kong to China are often wealthier and have enjoyed a much higher level of education. Inevitably, there are highly complex relationships between these various social and economic factors and patterns of language use.

There are also questions of language status: whether a particular variety is considered a language or a dialect is essentially a political rather than a linguistic decision. Thus while Danish, Swedish and Norwegian are best described in linguistic terms as forming one dialect continuum, the perceived integrity of each language reflects political separation. In contrast, the differences between colloquial varieties of Arabic, such as Moroccan and Omani, are arguably greater than those found in the Scandinavian continuum; yet, for cultural and political reasons, we normally refer to Arabic as a single entity. Similarly, we refer to both Cantonese and Putonghua as Chinese. It is important to remember, however, that the Putonghua used as a *lingua franca* by speakers from the People's Republic of China (PRC) in Britain and the Cantonese spoken by most families of Hong Kong descent are not mutually intelligible; conversations between Chinese from the PRC and Hong Kong in the UK often take place in English.

The inevitable consequence of settlement in the UK is a shift from the language of the home to English. The speed and extent of this shift, however, will depend on various factors including individual acts of identity (cf. Le Page and Tabouret-Keller 1985) and the ethnolinguistic vitality of the community in question (Giles, Bourhis and Taylor 1977), which in turn will be determined by factors such as status, size and distribution and level of institutional support.

Responsibility for the transmission of language begins in the home. Families can count upon the support of relatives and friends in the country of origin for this task in the form of letter-writing and visits. The development across the decades of the international telephone network, satellite and videos has served to strengthen this ongoing contact. Where links with the home country have been severed for political reasons, strong links are often cultivated with communities in exile in other parts of the world (Alladina and Edwards 1991). The perceived need or urgency to pass on the home language to the next generation, however, is likely to vary considerably from one group to the next. For longer established groups, the shift to English may be so advanced that mother tongue teaching is an urgent priority (see, for instance, Nwenmely's (1996) discussion of the French-Creole-speaking St Lucian and Dominican communities in London). In contrast, recently arrived immigrants or refugees, especially for those who work in jobs with long, anti-social hours, often accord language maintenance low priority.

For those families who are more concerned with survival than with cultural and linguistic issues, the speed of language shift comes as a shock. There are reports of great anxiety as parents realize that children have gradually drifted away from traditional values, and of breakdowns in communication – especially between grandchildren and grandparents – in cases where children refuse to speak the language of the home (Alladina and Edwards 1991). Such problems are less evident in larger, longer established communities which often offer an impressive range of social, political, religious and cultural activities. By broadening the focus for language maintenance from the family to the wider minority community, children have many different opportunities to hear and use community languages.

The church, mosque, gurudwara or temple fulfils a vital welfare and cultural role in the life of many communities, as well as providing for spiritual needs. There are also extensive secular networks. Sometimes the focus is political, reflecting divisions in the country of origin (Mehmet Ali 1991) or addressing issues such as anti-racism in housing (Husain 1991); on other occasions the emphasis is on culture (Papadaki d'Onofrio and Roussou 1991) or sport (Nwenmely 1991). As communities have become better organized, the governments of the groups concerned have often taken a lead. Community language teaching in Spanish, Italian and Greek, for instance, is supported in varying degrees by the High Commission or Embassy in London.

Among the longer established communities, ethnic economies also serve a range of important functions. For instance, in Bangladeshi areas of East London, Mirpuri

Panjabi areas of Bradford or Gujarati areas of Leicester, it is possible to find restaurants, travel agents and food and clothing shops run by and for the communities in question. This ethnic economy not only provides employment for large numbers of workers; it also creates an environment where it is more natural to use the community language than English.

Various informal activities contribute to the ethnolinguistic vitality of community languages; so, too, do the formal classes organized by religious and other bodies within the minority communities. Community provision of this kind burgeoned from the late 1970s onwards. The Directory of Mother Tongue Teaching (Linguistic Minorities Project 1985), for instance, reports classes in 18 different languages for over 8,500 pupils in just three inner city Local Education Authorities (LEAs). These classes continue to thrive, often in spite of chronic shortages of funds, teaching materials and professional development opportunities for teachers.

Sources of funding for community language teaching are an ongoing concern. As we shall see below, pressure from the European Union and the publication of the 1985 Swann Report resulted in a more sympathetic response on the part of LEAs to requests for help from community organizations. It is important to note, however, that such support has always been minimal. LMP (1985) reports that the majority of classes included in the Directory of Mother Tongue Teaching received no help of any kind. Similarly, Bourne (1989) makes it clear that the main form of support for community classes was free accommodation. Other sources of funding for community language classes include charitable foundations such as the Sir John Cass Foundation, the Trust for London and the National Lotteries Charities Board.

The availability of suitably trained teachers is another recurrent issue. Teachers of community languages come from many different backgrounds. Some are qualified teachers, already working in mainstream schools; some have worked in schools only in the country of origin; the only qualification for many others will be that they themselves speak the community language in question. This diversity of backgrounds raises a range of issues.

Teachers trained abroad or with no formal qualifications may adopt a style of classroom management and an approach to learning and teaching which differ in important respects from those prevalent in British schools. This is not necessarily a problem in itself, since children are quite capable of adjusting to one style of teaching in the mainstream and another in a community context (Edwards 1998). However, it is possible to argue that both mainstream and community school teachers would benefit from a better understanding of *all* the learning experiences of the children with whom they work. Qualified teachers who work in both mainstream and community contexts play an important role in mediating the learning environment in British schools to less experienced colleagues, both by example and by offering in-service training.

National networks of community language teachers offer increasing numbers of opportunities for professional development. The Chinese community is a useful case in point. Two associations currently co-ordinate Chinese classes. The UK Federation of Chinese Schools (UKFCS) was established in 1994; it currently incorporates 89 member schools and reaches over 11,000 pupils. It teaches through the medium of Cantonese and serves the longer standing Hong Kong Chinese community. The much smaller and more recent Chinese Teaching Group of the UK Chinese Students and Scholars Association (CSSA) teaches through the medium of Putonghua. Most pupils are the children of students from the People's Republic of China although, following recent political developments, growing numbers of Hong Kong families are keen for their children to learn Putonghua. Liaison between the two associations is good and both provide a range of support for teachers in the form of conferences and seminars. An Ran (1999), for instance, discusses a seminar organized by the CSSA on teaching methods in which participants concluded that teachers in community classes should aim for a synthesis of Chinese and British teaching methods which speak to the experience of the children.

Various local and national initiatives also offer direct and indirect support for community language teachers. The Resource Unit for Supplementary and Mother Tongue Schools is a new initiative set up in 1997 to bridge the gap between mainstream and voluntary sector schools. In addition to computer and photocopying facilities specifically tailored to the needs of community schools, it offers help on staff development, teaching and learning materials and evaluation and assessment. It is also involved in the production of guidelines for supplementary and mother tongue schools, and a directory of mother tongue schools. The Association for Language Learning is another body which encourages teachers of different languages to come together, for instance, for the purpose of materials production. It also supports the notion of a coherent national strategy for language learning in which community languages form an integral part of mainstream education.

The Centre for Information on Language Teaching and Research (CILT) produces two series of information sheets on community languages: *Community Languages in Britain* is aimed at non-speakers of the languages; *Sources and Resources* lists teaching resources held in the CILT library and key contacts, such as professional associations. It also publishes a twice-yearly *Community Languages Bulletin*, which is a valuable forum for the exchange of information and ideas. The University of Reading AIMER (Access to Information of Multicultural Education Resources) database includes information on resources in Bengali, Chinese, Gujarati, Panjabi, Urdu and several other community languages (http://www.ralic.reading.ac.uk).

It is important to remember that teachers in the UK are often dealing with languages taught widely in many other countries. The Internet is likely to be an increasingly important source of information, ideas and resources. In a review of useful sites, Anderson (1997) draws attention, for instance, to resources for Panjabi, Chinese and Japanese teaching available at the British Columbia Ministry of Education, Skills and Training website (http://www.bced.gov.bc.ca/irp). Materials on Tamil language and culture can be found on the website of Siva Pillai, the director of the Lewisham Academy of Language and Arts based in Lewisham, London (http://www.gold.ac.uk/uk/~siva/), while U-Hoo offers a selection of useful sites for Urdu (http://www.urdustan.com/u-hoo). Information on community teaching more generally can be found at the Goldsmiths College website (http://www.gold.ac.uk/clf).

Although most community language teaching takes place within minority communities, mainstream schools have had varying levels of involvement over the years. There has often been a certain tension between the aspirations of teachers at a grassroots level and official attitudes, which have veered between qualified support and indifference.

The 1976 draft Directive of the Council of the European Community on the Education of the Children of Migrant Workers was an important catalyst for the development of community language teaching within mainstream schooling. For the first time, there was discussion of the need for member states to teach the language and culture of migrants' children as part of the normal curriculum. In the UK, the Directive met with considerable resistance. Teacher organizations objected on the grounds that expansion in this area was unacceptable at a time of educational cutbacks and teacher unemployment, while the government foresaw problems related to costs, the difficulty of providing teachers and the inability of a decentralized education system to implement the Directive.

A revised – and considerably 'dumbed-down' – version of the Directive was published in 1977. It called on member states simply to 'promote' community language teaching and to offer tuition only 'in accordance with their national circumstances and legal systems'. There is little evidence to suggest that the British government was willing or able to achieve even these very modest aims (Bellin 1990). An EC report (European Communities 1984) on the implementation of the Directive confirms this assessment. While 80 per cent of eligible children in the Netherlands were receiving 'mother tongue teaching' at school, only 2 per cent of linguistic minority children in the UK had access to state provision of this kind.

However, the appearance of the Directive at least succeeded in placing community language teaching on the agenda of mainstream educators for the first time. It is certainly the case that Local Education Authorities (LEAs) began to offer material support for community-run classes during this period. Community language teaching became part of the curriculum in small but growing numbers of schools. However, the publication of the Swann Report in 1985 represented a considerable setback. It argued that community languages were ultimately the responsibility of minority communities, and that support from LEAs be limited to the provision of accommodation, grants for books and teaching materials, in-service courses and advice from the advisory service. Bourne (1989) reports that three-quarters of English LEAs responding to her survey were offering some level of support, but that this mainly took the form of free accommodation.

Today community language teaching remains mainly the responsibility of ethnic minority communities themselves. However, three factors – Britain's membership of the European Union, the importance of global trade, and the shifting balance between world languages – give some reason to be optimistic about the future of community languages in mainstream education. Of these, Britain's entry into Europe has possibly had the most obvious impact on attitudes towards other languages. The Maastricht Treaty makes provision for the development of 'the European dimension in education through the teaching and dissemination of the languages of the Member States'; one of the general objectives for education of the white paper on 'Teaching and learning: towards the learning society' (European Union 1995) is to develop proficiency in three Community languages. Plurilingualism is also one of the policy objectives of the Council of Europe (Jones 1998).

Entry into Europe has also had important implications for trade. Whereas the English-speaking nations provided the traditional markets for the UK, 60 per cent of British exports are now destined for the European Union (Anderson 2000); and the most important new markets are likely to be in the Far East and China (Hagen 1998). There has been intermittent pressure on government to diversify language provision in response to the challenge of global markets, including initiatives such as the British Overseas Trade Board's (1979) report on languages and export performance, and Parker's (1986) report on oriental languages. Official policy on this question, however, has been rather contradictory: the Department of Education and Science (1988), for instance, accepted the validity of arguments for diversification of the modern foreign language curriculum and acknowledged the need for speakers of Japanese, Chinese and other Asian languages. However, it was not considered cost-effective to provide teaching in these languages for pupils of compulsory school age. The creation of Language Colleges in England and Wales has been rather more successful in this respect: at the time of writing 58 colleges were teaching 18 languages other than French, German and Spanish. The growing support for diversification is also suggested by the Nuffield Foundation's Inquiry (Moys 1998), endorsed by the prime minister, the head of the CBI and other public figures, into the UK's needs over the next twenty years.

The third factor which supports arguments for diversification in language teaching is the shifting balance between world languages. Native speakers of English will soon be outnumbered by speakers of English as a second language. Graddol (1998) also points to two further possible developments in the next fifty years. The first is that Arabic, Hindi/Urdu and Spanish are likely to have similar numbers of native speakers as English, leading to a 'cartel' of languages rather than the pre-eminence of English; the second is that other regional and national languages are likely to gain rather than lose speakers, leading to an increased awareness of the importance of languages such as Vietnamese and Polish.

An important factor in the debate on diversification in language teaching is the relative status of different languages. Despite their historical legacy of multilingualism, the British often behave as though monolingualism is the norm. English has been used as an instrument of social cohesion and control, both internally and in the colonies. Its current position as the international language of communication helps to reinforce both notions of superiority and the feeling that it is unnecessary to learn other languages.

Yet bilingualism has always been desirable amongst the social elite. The ability to read and write Latin, for instance, was associated with English intellectuals for hundreds of years; and, even today, it is predominantly the middle classes who send their children to French immersion programmes in Canada. The bilingualism of less powerful members of society, in contrast, is often undervalued or overlooked. European languages such as French, German and Spanish tend to be viewed a great deal more favourably than, for example, Indian languages such as Panjabi, Gujarati and Bengali (Edwards and Redfern 1992). This widely reported perception of a linguistic hierarchy is supported by current education legislation. The national curriculum accepts twenty languages as the foundation subject languages. The list is divided into the official languages of the EC and non-EC languages, and students may choose a non-EC language only if they have already been offered the chance to study an official EC language. A recent review of the modern foreign languages in the national curriculum, however, proposes that this restriction on non-EC languages be dropped (Qualifications and Curriculum Authority 1999).

Two developments have had a major impact on the provision of community language teaching in the mainstream. The first was the implementation in 1988 of a national curriculum which required such extensive changes in teaching practice that attention was effectively deflected from issues concerning linguistic and cultural diversity (Edwards 1998). The second was the change in regulations concerning Section 11, the main source of additional funding in schools with significant numbers of children of New

Commonwealth origin. Since its introduction in 1966, Section 11 monies had been used not only to support the teaching of English as a second language but also for anti-racist initiatives and community language teaching. The new rules required an exclusive emphasis on English teaching, leading to an inevitable erosion of community language teaching within the mainstream. At the secondary level, community languages, as documented above, continue to be taught as subjects within the framework of Modern Foreign Languages. At the primary level, a small number of LEAs promote transitional bilingualism (Bourne 1989) and employ bilingual staff to support new entrants in their learning of English. There are many isolated examples of schools which continue to offer community languages as part of their programme of extra-curricular activities or in language awareness activities for all children (Edwards 1998). Overall, however, the ability of mainstream schools to support the bilingual develop-ment of children from linguistic minority communities has been seriously impaired by recent developments.

The refusal to recognize qualifications obtained abroad also has the effect of under-mining efforts to promote community language teaching in the mainstream. The lack of suitably qualified teachers, together with the shortage of professional development opportunities, inevitably leads to a lack of teaching posts. This, in turn, has a negative effect on the status of community language teaching in schools.

Two aspects of community language teaching impact upon teachers and children in both mainstream and community contexts: assessment, and resources. Assessment emerges as a recurrent theme in discussions of community language teaching. The ability to speak, read and write another language is important 'currency' within main-stream education when translated into qualifications such as GCSEs and A-levels. Examination boards have provided syllabuses in a growing number of languages, though recent moves to remove 'uneconomic' languages such as Turkish and Arabic were only abandoned after extensive community lobbying. The fact that many universities do not accept community languages as entry qualifications threatens to compromise the viability of school-based A-level classes in more popular community languages (Sneddon 2000).

Anderson (2000) points out that there is no national database that records the lan-guages which are taught in the supplementary school sector for which no examinations are available. Minority communities have responded to the issue of accreditation in a variety of ways. The London-based Gujarati Academy offers its own examinations (see Dave 1991) which are currently being brought into line with GCSE and A-levels. Some community language students are also making use of the Alternative Syllabus for Contemporary Languages (ASCL) provided by the Institute of Linguists. The thirty languages which have been assessed across all five levels of the syllabus include Thai and Vietnamese.

Another recurring problem for the teaching of community languages is the shortage of suitable teaching materials. Very often books and courses produced in the home country fail to speak to the experience of locally born children and the linguistic level for any given age range is far too advanced. As a result teachers have to spend a great deal of time in lesson preparation and the production of resources, an inefficient process which could be handled more effectively on a centralized level.

Materials development in the UK has tended to take place in a fairly haphazard way. Two initiatives have been targeted at community language teaching in mainstream schools. The Inner London Education Authority, the European Commission and the Schools Council jointly sponsored the Mother Tongue Project (Tansley, Navaz and Roussou 1986; Tansley 1986) which developed resources for teaching Bengali and Greek at the primary level. The Community Languages in the Secondary School Curriculum Project produced materials for the diverse situations encountered in the mainstream by teachers of Urdu, Panjabi and Italian. There has also been a range of local initiatives. Bourne (1989), for instance, describes how one LEA supported teacher secondments and drew on supplementary training funds to produce a course in Urdu. The textbooks which the team developed were made available for sale both within and outside the LEA. More recently, the UKFCS have published a set of eleven Chinese textbooks complete with supplementary teaching materials and teachers' guides designed to take pupils to GCSE level; and Ali and McLagan (1998) provide a suggested curriculum framework for the teaching and learning of a community language as mother tongue for pupils aged 5–11.

There has also been a marked growth of minority language publishing in the UK. Specialist publishers such as Mantra, Magi, Roy Yates and Partnership Publishing have led the way, demonstrating that there is indeed a market for children's books in both single language and dual language (English plus community language) format. Dual language books represent perhaps the most important multilingual resource in many classrooms. For sound economic reasons, these are often adaptations of existing good quality picture books in English. The success of the adaptation is, however, variable (Multilingual Resources for Children Project 1995). The second language has to be fitted into the space available and is sometimes printed over a coloured background; the net effect is that it looks less 'important' than the English, thus defeating one of the main objectives of attempts to make books in community languages available to children. The range and quality of dual language books, however, is constantly improving (Edwards and Routh 1999) and there is evidence of serious efforts to ensure that 'the other languages' are given equal status with English.

In a world where access to electronic communication is becoming increasingly common, it is easy to overlook the fact that, in many schools, the most important producers of multilingual resources for children are teachers, parents and children, and not commercial publishers. Projects like the Multilingual Word-processing Project based at the University of Reading (Chana, Edwards and Walker 1997, 1998) have charted the potential of the new technologies for involving parents and others in the production of stories and other learning materials in a range of languages.

One of the recurring issues in any discussion of community languages in the UK is the piecemeal nature of provision. For many years, the ILEA provided highly effective leadership in the areas of both policy and provision for multilingualism. After the disbanding by the Conservative government of the Greater London Council (GLC) in late 1980s, however, the new decentralized boroughs found it impossible to provide the same level of service. In subsequent years, the City of Sheffield has assumed the mantle of the GLC, developing an impressive city-wide approach. A conference on 'Sheffield, the Multilingual City' was organized in 1994 by the LEA and the Association of Sheffield Community Language Schools (ASCLS) with the support of various city Council Departments, educational institutions and the local Chamber of Commerce and Industry. The aim was that within ten years every young person in the city should be fluent in English and another language, 'whether European, Creole, Asian or African' (City of Sheffield n.d., 3). Objectives include the following:

- developing a coherent city-wide approach to the teaching of languages
- gathering information about language courses and carrying out language research
- encouraging the teaching of other languages in primary schools
- encouraging school leavers and adults to use their languages to earn a living
- developing language projects with local business and industry
- promoting languages for leisure, travel, cultural development and pleasure
- supporting voluntary sector language schools and translation services (City of Sheffield n.d., 5)

Annual conferences are used as an opportunity to review progress to date and to identify new priorities. The report of the 1998 conference identified support for existing bilingualism via ASCLS in the form, for instance, of monitoring the grant aid process, the delivery of services to community schools, management training and staff development. Development work had been undertaken on a Somali language pack and on training for the production of multimedia, multilingual resources. Multilingual City also works with a range of agencies 'to strengthen the use of additional languages within communities, creating community networks and pathways for study and work' (ibid., 6).

Support for bilingualism in the wider community is offered through research and training at the Sheffield Universities and Sheffield College; the South Yorkshire/ Pakistan project, involving study trips, teacher exchanges and training in basic Urdu; ongoing work with various embassies; and European events and projects. The Single Regeneration Budget, which supports a range of educational and social projects in urban areas, has been used to fund parent and child language workshops in three Under Fives' centres.

What is notable about the Multilingual City initiative is its inclusive approach. It involves not only educators but politicians, the business sector and many other agencies. European and non-European languages are integrated into the same overarching framework. Support is offered throughout the education system, within the world of work and in the voluntary sector.

Research on community languages has tended to focus on three main areas: sociolinguistic descriptions; community language teaching; and multilingual literacy practices. The data for sociolinguistic descriptions have been collected in a variety of settings.

Oral literature provides the focus for Edwards (1988) in a description of the social functions of the wedding songs of Gujarati women. Several writers explore the interaction of different language systems in the creation of new identities. Edwards (1986) describes the patterns of language use among Black adolescents of Jamaican heritage in the West Midlands in a variety of situations. Sutcliffe (1992), using the same data as Edwards, focuses on code-switching behaviours and the extensive African influences on the structures which they use. Hewitt's work in a youth club serving a mixed community highlights the influence of Black language on the speech of White youths (Hewitt 1986). Rampton (1995) examines the ways in which multiracial friendship groups use each other's ethnic languages.

Other writers are concerned with the very different ways in which speech communities organize discourse and the implications of this diversity. Ogilvy et al. (1992) show how teachers assumed a more controlling style with young children of South Asian origin than with their White peers. In a similar vein, Biggs and Edwards (1992) describe how teachers initiated significantly fewer interactions, had fewer extended exchanges and spent less time discussing the particular task which had been set with five- and six-year-old Black pupils than with their White peers. Roberts, Davies and Jupp (1992), in contrast, focus on the workplace, demonstrating the linguistic dimension of racial discrimination, based on work carried out by the Industrial Language Training Service.

Given the dearth of funding for community language teaching in the voluntary sector, it is not surprising that there have been few attempts to either document or evaluate what takes place. Notable exceptions, however, are descriptions by Wong (1992) and An Ran (1999) of various aspects of language and literacy teaching in the Chinese community; Rashid and Gregory's (1997) account of Arabic and Bengali classes attended by Bangladeshi children; and Sneddon's (2000) description of Urdu teaching in a Muslim Gujarati community in north-east London. Community language teaching in the mainstream has attracted only marginally more attention. Most notable are two European-funded projects – the Mother Tongue and Culture in Bedfordshire Project (Simons 1979; Tosi 1984) which examined the teaching of Panjabi and Italian, and the Schools Council Mother Tongue Project (Tansley et al. 1986) mentioned above which developed resources for Bengali and Greek teaching. The Mother Tongue and English Teaching Project, funded by the Department of Education and Science, demonstrated that five-year-olds taught through Panjabi and English achieved the same level in English as children taught exclusively through English but outperformed the English-only group in Panjabi (Fitzpatrick 1997).

Some progress has been made in recent years in documenting literacy practices in other languages in home and community. The work of American researchers and, in particular, Heath (1983), who have drawn attention to the ways in which literacy has different meanings for members of different groups, has acted as an important catalyst for research in many countries, including the UK. The growing recognition that the uses of literacy in minority communities may differ in important ways from those of the school has drawn attention to the need for teachers to learn more about what happens in home and community.

Baynham (1993) describes the communicative practices of the Moroccan community in London, though his findings may well be generalizable to many other multilingual settings characterized by immigrant bilingualism. His analysis is based on two main strategies: the enlisting of an interpreter for a communicative purpose and the use of mediators of literacy to accomplish literacy tasks. He demonstrates the oral dimension of literacy events in multilingual settings: shifting or switching between the languages available to the speakers helps to avoid misunderstanding when participants have only limited access to the dominant language.

Several writers have documented literacy practices in Panjabi speech communities. Saxena (1994) focuses on the Panjabi community in Southall where Panjabi literacy is used for a wide range of community and commercial functions and the choice of script – Gurmukhi, Devanagari or Perso-Arabic – is determined by cultural and religious factors. Hartley (1994) examines how literacy practices in English and Urdu are negotiated among family members in a community of Panjabi-speakers in East Lancashire. Chana (1999) documents the support for language and literacy learning in three Panjabi Sikh families in Southall. Extended families which include grandparents and have strong community involvement are able to offer high levels of support. Personal identity and individual choice, however, also play an important role, with the family where neither parent was literate in Panjabi offering moral and financial support for their children's participation in daily classes before school.

The Gujarati community has also received some attention. Bhatt, Barton and Martin-Jones (1994) document the ways in which Gujarati literacy skills are put to use in a wide range of religious and community settings in Leicester and the changes which have taken place as people moved from East Africa. Kenner (1997) offers a case study of a four-year-old Gujarati girl who shows the influence of home literacy practices when playing in the home corner in her nursery school, and the influence of nursery when playing school with her older sister at home. Sneddon (2000) investigates the language use and literacy practices of children from Gujarati- and Urdu-speaking families in north-east London.

Several writers explore language and literacy in Chinese communities. Gregory (1996), for instance, draws attention to the tensions created by the very different practices to which a child from a Hong Kong family was exposed at home and in school. An Ran (1999) offers detailed analysis of three mainland Chinese mother–child pairs reading together at home in Chinese, drawing attention to the similarities and differences both between the families included in the study and between home and school. Li Wei (1994) examines the role of social networks in the transmission of Chinese across three generations of the same family.

Rashid and Gregory (1997) and Gregory (1998) offer invaluable insights into literacy practices of Bangladeshi families in East London. They draw attention to the role of older children who are familiar with the traditions of both school and community in the teaching of reading to younger siblings. An analysis of paired reading sessions in the home shows how the older children draw on their knowledge of learning to read in both community and mainstream school settings to provide finely tuned scaffolding which is closely adjusted to the reading ability of the individual child. Analysis of the strategies used by the children's mainstream teachers shows varying sensitivity to community practices. The inevitable conclusion, however, is that teachers who are aware of the full range of children's experiences will be better able to respond to their needs.

After a slow start, attempts to document both sociolinguistic and pedagogical aspects of community languages in the UK have gained considerable momentum. As the more recently arrived linguistic minorities have become established and have developed more political power, they have begun to articulate both the central role of language in their individual and collective identities and the kind of support which is necessary to transmit these languages from one generation to the next. The response from both the wider community and official quarters has tended to be highly variable. The overarching view would seem to be one of tolerance without commitment, and responsibility for language maintenance has been placed very firmly on the communities themselves. However, recent developments – and particularly Britain's membership of the European Community and the Sheffield Multilingual Project – give reason to hope that there has been a softening of the traditionally conservative attitudes to languages other than English.

In the field of education, many community languages clearly do not enjoy the same status as French, German and Spanish, the languages which have traditionally been studied in secondary schools. However, pressure from minority communities has resulted in a much wider range of opportunities for accreditation in lesser used languages and a growing acknowledgement of the value of bilingualism for both individuals and the wider community. Bilinguals have the potential to make a very important contribution, both within a multilingual Europe and in an increasingly global economy.

References

Ali, Ayub and McLagan, Patricia (eds) 1998. *Curriculum Framework for Mother Tongue Teaching to Bengali for Pupils 5–11 years.* London.

Alladina, Safder and Edwards, Viv (eds) 1991. *Multilingualism in the British Isles*, 2 vols. London.

An Ran 1999. Learning in two languages and cultures: the experiences of mainland Chinese families in Britain. Unpublished PhD thesis, University of Reading.

Anderson, J. 1997. Keeping in touch through the Internet. *The Community Language Bulletin*, 1:8–9.

——2000. Which language? An embarrassment of choice (forthcoming in Field, Kit (ed.), *Issues in Modern Foreign Languages Teaching*. London).

Baker, Colin and Prys-Jones, Sylvia 1998. *Encyclopedia of Bilingualism and Bilingual Education.* Clevedon.

Baynham, M. 1993. Code-switching and mode switching: community interpreters and mediators of literacy. In Street, Brian (ed.), *Cross-cultural Approaches to Literacy*, Cambridge, 294–314.

Bellin, W. 1990. The EEC Directive on the Education of the Children of Migrant Workers: a comparison of the Commission's proposed directive and the Council directive together with a parallel text. *Polyglot*, 2, fiche 3.

Bhatt, Arvind, Barton, David and Martin-Jones, Marilyn 1994. *Gujarati Literacies in East Africa and Leicester: Changes in Social Identities and Multilingual Practices.* Working Paper 56, Centre for Language in Social Life, University of Lancaster.

Biggs, A. P. and Edwards, V. 1992. 'I treat them all the same': teacher–pupil talk in multi-ethnic classrooms. *Language and Education*, 5 (3):161–76.

Bourne, Jill 1989. *Moving into the Mainstream: LEA Provision for Bilingual Pupils.* Windsor.

——1997. 'The grown-ups know best': Language policy-making in Britain in the 1990s. In Eggington, W. and Wren, H. (eds), *Language Policy: Dominant English, Pluralist Challenges*, Canberra, 50–65.

British Overseas Trade Board 1979. *Foreign Languages for Overseas Trade: Report of the Study Group.* London.

Callender, Christine 1997. *Education for Empowerment: The Practice and Philosophies of Black Teachers.* Stoke-on-Trent.

Chana, Urmi 1999. Developing literacy in Panjabi: case studies from the Panjabi Sikh community. Discussion paper, Reading and Language Information Centre, University of Reading.

——Edwards, V. and Walker, S. 1997. Hidden resources: multilingual wordprocessing in the primary school. *Race, Ethnicity and Education*, 1 (1):49–61.

——1998. In their own write: wordprocessing in Urdu. In Goodwin, Prue (ed.), *The Literate Classroom*, London, 99–105.

City of Sheffield n.d. *The Multilingual City*, 5. Sheffield.

Cummins, Jim and Danesi, Marcel 1990. *Heritage Languages: The Development and Denial of Canada's Linguistic Resources.* Toronto.

Dalphinis, M. 1991. The Afro-English speech community. In Alladina and Edwards, 33–41.

Dave, J. 1991. The Gujarati speech community. In Alladina and Edwards, 88–102.

Department of Education and Science 1988. *Modern Languages and the School Curriculum: A Statement of Policy.* London.

Edwards, Viv 1986. *Language in a Black Community.* Clevedon.

——1988. The wedding songs of British Gujarati women. In Coates, Jennifer and Cameron, Deborah (eds), *Women in Their Speech Communities,* London, 158–172.

——1998. *The Power of Babel: Teaching and Learning in Multilingual Classrooms.* Stoke-on-Trent.

——and Redfern, Angela 1992. *The World in a Classroom: Language and Education in Britain and Canada.* Clevedon.

Edwards, Viv and Routh, C. 1999. Recent multilingual resources for children. In Elkin, Judith (ed.), *A Guide to Multicultural Children's Literature 0–13.* London and Reading.

European Communities (EC) 1984. *Report on the Implementation of Directive 77/486/EEC on the Education of Children of Migrant Workers.* Brussels.

European Union 1995. *Teaching and Learning: Towards the Learning Society.* Brussels.

Fitzpatrick, Barré 1997. *The Open Door: The Bradford Bilingual Project.* Clevedon.

Giles, H., Bourhis, T. and Taylor, D. 1977. Towards a theory of language in ethnic group relations. In Giles, Howard (ed.), *Language, Ethnicity and Intergroup Relations,* London, 307–48.

Graddol, D. 1998. Will English be enough? In Moys, 24–33.

Gregory, Eve 1996. Sweet and sour: learning to read in a British and Chinese school. *English in Education,* 27 (3):53–9.

——(ed.) 1997. *One Child, Many Worlds: Early Learning in Multicultural Communities.* London.

——1998. Siblings as mediators of literacy in linguistic minority communities. *Language and Education,* 12 (1):33–54.

Hagen, S. 1998. What does global trade mean for UK languages? In Moys, 14–23.

Hamilton, Mary, Barton, David and Ivanic, Roz (eds) 1994. *Worlds of Literacy.* Clevedon.

Hartley, T. 1994. Generations of literacy among women in a bilingual community. In Hamilton, Barton and Ivanic, 29–40.

Heath, Shirley Brice 1983. *Ways with Words.* Cambridge.

Hewitt, Roger 1986. *White Talk, Black Talk: Inter-racial Friendship and Communication among Adolescents.* Cambridge.

Horvath, Barbara and Vaughan, P. 1991. *Community Languages: A Handbook.* Clevedon.

Husain, J. 1991. The Bengali speech community. In Alladina and Edwards, 75–87.

Inner London Education Authority (ILEA) 1978, 1981, 1983, 1985, 1987. *Language Census.* London.

Jones, S. 1998. How does Europe promote languages? In Moys, 6–13.

Kenner, C. 1997. A child writes from her everyday world: using home texts to develop literacy in school. In Gregory, 75–86.

Le Page, R. B. and Tabouret-Keller, A. 1985. *Acts of Identity.* Cambridge.

Li Wei 1994. *Three Generations, Two Languages, One Family: Language Choice and Language Shift in a Chinese Community in Britain.* Clevedon.

Linguistic Minorities Project (LMP) 1985. *The Other Languages of England.* London.

Mehmet Ali, A. 1991. The Turkish speech community. In Alladina and Edwards, 202–13.

Moys, Alan (ed.) 1998. *Where Are We Going with Languages?* London.

Multilingual Resources for Children Project (MRC) 1995. *Building Bridges: Multilingual Resources for Children.* Clevedon.

Nicholas, Joe 1994. *Language Diversity Surveys as Agents of Change.* Clevedon.

Nwenmely, Hubisi 1991. The Kwéyòl speech community. In Alladina and Edwards, 57–73.

——1996. *Language Reclamation: French Creole Teaching in the UK and the Caribbean*. Clevedon.

Ogilvy, C., Boath, E., Cheyne, W., Jahoda, G. and Schaffer, H. 1992. Staff attitudes and perception in multicultural nursery schools. *Early Childhood Development and Care*, 64:1–13.

Papadaki d'Onofrio, E. and Roussou, M. 1991. The Greek speech community. In Alladina and Edwards, 189–201.

Parker, Sir Peter 1986. *Speaking for the Future: A Review of the Requirements of Diplomacy and Commerce for Asian and African Languages and Area Studies*. London.

Qualifications and Curriculum Authority (QCA) 1999. *The Review of the National Curriculum in England: The Consultation Materials*. London.

Rampton, Ben 1995. *Crossing: Language and Ethnicity among Adolescents*. Harlow.

Rashid, N. and Gregory, E. 1997. Learning to read, reading to learn: the importance of siblings in the language development of young bilingual children. In Gregory, 107–21.

Roberts, Celia, Davies, Evelyn and Jupp, Tom 1992. *Language and Discrimination: A Study of Communication in Multi-Ethnic Workplaces*. London.

Rutter, Jill 1995. *Refugee Children in the Classroom*. Stoke-on-Trent.

Saxena, M. 1994. Literacies among the Panjabis in Southall. In Hamilton, Barton and Ivanic, 195–214.

Sebba, Mark 1993. *London Jamaican: Language Systems in Interaction*. London.

Simons, H. 1979. *Mother Tongue and Culture in Bedfordshire: First External Evaluation Report*. Cambridge.

Sneddon, Raymonde 2000. Language and literacy in the multilingual family. Unpublished PhD thesis, University of London.

Sutcliffe, David 1992. *System in Black Language*. Clevedon.

Swann, Lord 1985. *Education for All*. London.

Tansley, Paula 1986. *Community Languages in Primary Education*. Windsor.

——Navaz, H. and Roussou, Maria 1986. *A Handbook for Community Language Teachers*. London.

Tosi, Arturo 1984. *Immigration and Bilingual Education*. Oxford.

Wong, Lornita 1992. *Education of Chinese Children in Britain and the USA*. Clevedon.

Name Index

Subject Index

Anglicization
   Channel Islands 190–2
   Cornwall 109–10
   Ireland 7–9, 10, 12, 27–9, 30–1
   Man 65, 67
   Scotland 44–5, 50
   Wales 79–80, 83, 90, 93–6
Anglo-Norman loan-words, *see* French loan-words
attitudes
   to Channel Islands French 190
   to Cornish 110, 113–15
   to Irish 9–10, 11, 12, 22
   to Manx 67
   to Scottish Gaelic 49, 55

Bible
   English 148–9, 150
   Manx 65–6
   Scots 165, 168
   Welsh 80, 82
bilingualism
   Anglo-Norman England 199–200
   ethnic minorities 213, 220, 223
   Ireland 7–9, 24–5, 28–9, 30–1
   Man 67
   Northern Isles 182
   post-Roman Britain 37, 41
   Roman Britain 136–7
   Scotland 48, 49, 54
   Wales 84, 88, 89–91, 97, 104, 105
Book of Common Prayer
   Irish 24
   Manx 64, 65, 66, 68
   Welsh 80
Brittonic (Brythonic) 4, 13, 23, 58–9, 70, 109, 128–9, 133
broadcasting media
   Ireland 32–3
   Scotland 49–50, 53, 54

Wales 91, 92, 101–4
Brythonic, *see* Brittonic

Celts, early 4
censuses (linguistic), official
   Channel Islands 192
   ethnic minorities 213
   Ireland 7, 9–11
   Man 67, 68
   Scotland 45–9
   Wales 89–91, 93–6
censuses (linguistic), unofficial
   Channel Islands 192
   linguistic minorities 213–15
   Man 67
   Wales 83–4

decline
   Cornish 110, 113–15
   Irish 7–11
   Manx 67
   Norn 182
   Romani 209–11
   Scottish Gaelic 45–9
   Welsh 89–91, 93–5
dialects
   Channel Islands French 188
   community languages 215–16
   English 143–4, 146–9, 153–6
   Irish 21–2; *see also* Gaeltacht
   Scots 160–2
   Welsh 79
dictionaries and glossaries
   Anglo-Norman 204
   Channel Islands French 189–90
   English dialects 155–6
   Irish 20–1, 22–3, 32
   Manx 66–7
   Norn 181
   Romani 210